TAKE THE MONEY AND RUN

Sovereign Wealth Funds and the Demise of American Prosperity

Eric C. Anderson

PRAEGER SECURITY INTERNATIONAL
Westport, Connecticut • London

Library of Congress Cataloging-in-Publication Data

Anderson, Eric, 1962-

Take the money and run : sovereign wealth funds and the demise of American prosperity / by Eric C. Anderson.

p. cm.

Includes bibliographical references and index.

ISBN 978-0-313-36613-0 (alk. paper)

1. Investments, Foreign—United States. 2. Debts, External—United States. 3. National security—United States. I. Title.

HG4910.A713 2009

336.3'4350973—dc22   2008047530

British Library Cataloguing in Publication Data is available.

Library of Congress Catalog Card Number: 2008047530
ISBN: 978-0-313-36613-0

First published in 2009

Praeger Security International, 88 Post Road West, Westport, CT 06881
An imprint of Greenwood Publishing Group, Inc.
www.praeger.com

Printed in the United States of America

The paper used in this book complies with the Permanent Paper Standard issued by the National Information Standards Organization (Z39.48–1984).

10 9 8 7 6 5 4 3 2 1

For Melanie, who made this all possible

Contents

Acknowledgments

I first started wrestling with sovereign wealth funds and their implications for policymakers in the United States as the result of a conversation at a J. P. Morgan Conference during October 2007. This initial dialogue was primarily a sequence of questions, followed by extended pregnant pauses. Suffice it to say, much has changed in the following ten months. In any case, I owe a number of people a special thanks for launching this project—and then ensuring I was able to finish on time.

First, I would like to thank Joyce Chang and Michael Marrese, whose intellectual curiosity suggested the entire endeavor. Equally important was a grant from the New Ideas Fund. Without their generosity, this project would not have been possible. Finally, this list of "acknowledge up front" would not be complete without Tim Furnish, who suffered through multiple conversations concerning what the publisher was going to ask for next. Tim, many thanks for your patience and sense of humor.

I would be remiss in not thanking my colleagues at this point. Cortez Cooper—my counterpart "in crime" at the East Asia Studies Center—had to deal with my endless rambling on sovereign wealth funds. Jeff Engstrom, who joined our team to focus on China, found himself engaged in research and discussions that seemed to cover every topic but Beijing. Cindy Hargett kept us all in line—and paid (no small accomplishment in the world of national security consultants). I wish I were half as efficient.

And then there are the people who made the whole project possible. I would like to thank my parents for suffering though early drafts and offering insights from the "left coast." My good friend Don Pruefer was always willing to spend a few more minutes ironing out an idea I could not adequately express; I owe him more than words here can do justice. That said, the one person who held this whole show together was my wife, Melanie Sloan. Melanie survived the piles of newspaper clippings, late-night musings, and pleas for proofreading, with a sense of humor and long-suffering patience. She offered words of encouragement when I was off-track—and a sharp intellectual wit when I was clearly full of myself. I could not ask for more in this life, or the next. Thank you, Dear! Finally, I have to thank Cheyenne—who was always happy to go for a walk when I could read, write, or think no more.

—Eric C. Anderson, 1 September 2008

SOVEREIGN WEALTH FUNDS: THE PERIL AND POTENTIAL FOR AMERICA

I suspect that most of the negative response to sovereign wealth funds is protectionism. That is extraordinarily counterproductive because the United States has probably gained as much from globalization.

—*Alan Greenspan, 25 February 2008*[1]

Americans used to live in a debtor's paradise. This is not to say money was easy to beg, borrow, or steal in the United States, but rather that Americans appeared to have few second thoughts about spending more than we can earn as individuals, corporations, and a nation. Credit cards behind? Establish a new line of cash from another lender. Can't find the capital for an acquisition or merger? No worries, Wall Street can put together a finance package. Need to pay for ongoing wars in Afghanistan and Iraq while simultaneously maintaining a social safety net? Fear not, someone from Asia, Europe, or the Middle East is sure to purchase the newly minted U.S. Treasury notes. At some basic level it all seems so simple: we in the United States live beyond our means by promising to repay the money sometime in the future, and we like it that way.

Perhaps it would be more appropriate to say it all *used* to seem so simple. The subprime crisis of 2007 has put a lid on personal and corporate spending, and foreign governments appear increasingly less interested in purchasing securities printed in Washington. Although this personal and corporate credit pinch is certainly disquieting, there are signs the Federal Reserve and politicians desire a means of substantively addressing the problem. The real concern, however, is what to do about the lagging interest in our national debt? What happens if foreigners stop buying U.S. Treasury notes in favor of more lucrative options elsewhere?

This quandary is the very real peril and potential America is presented by the emergence of sovereign wealth funds. Peril, as our access to cheap money—particularly as individuals and as an independent nation—may be coming to an abrupt halt. Potential, in that the emergence of sovereign wealth funds may point to a means of ultimately addressing the growing global trade imbalance and resolving Washington's longstanding concerns about the future of Social Security and other government-run social welfare programs. But in order to understand how we proceed in the face of this new challenge, one must understand what stands before us.

International finance is on the cusp of a fundamental change—with potentially profound implications for the United States government and American consumers. With remarkably little fanfare, the premises underpinning financial structures put into effect after World War II are quite literally being placed on their head. The assumption that money would always flow from the developed to the developing world—specifically from the United States to Asia and the Middle East—has been essentially reversed. Profligate American spending on consumer goods and a continued worldwide demand for petroleum has resulted in a situation in which the United States is now compelled to approach nations in Asia and the Middle East with hat in hand—hoping for a stream of private and public investments necessary to subsidize our apparently insatiable ability to spend tomorrow's earnings today.

Although some economists and the occasional politician have warned that this situation cannot continue indefinitely, the truth of the matter is that, until very recently, it largely appeared these warnings were little more than sophisticated versions of Chicken Little's dire prediction. Cries of "The sky is falling!" were rebuffed by pointing to ledgers showing low interest rates and by highlighting a foreign demand for U.S. Treasury notes that has underwritten federal deficit spending to the tune of $2 trillion. Despite trade imbalances totaling almost $800 billion a year and recurring annual government deficits approaching $300 billion, the average American consumer could purchase a home with a 30-year mortgage of approximately 6% and drive a new car at even lower interest rates. All of this was largely made possible by the fact that government investors outside the United States—primarily central bankers in Tokyo, London, and Beijing—were purchasing our national bonds at a rate that allowed Washington to avoid competing with American consumers for access to money.[2]

This outside willingness to purchase U.S. debt can be explained by guidelines widely accepted within the world's central banking community. In layman's terms, the "rules" worked like this: once a nation accrued foreign exchange earnings, it was the central banker's job to invest that money in a safe place where it could be quickly accessed. As any good banker is taught, this meant finding a relatively risk-free investment where regulatory conditions ensured the rules would not suddenly be changed in favor of the debtor. As one might guess, there were really only one or two places on the planet where this was true—the United States and a few countries in Europe. Before the formal establishment of the European Union, however, it is fair to say there really was only *one* place for these national investments—the United States.

Furthermore, central bankers learned, occasionally through brutal experience, that it paid to keep a substantial amount of money in these foreign exchange accounts. Failure to have sufficient cash on hand—or at least available in readily accessible accounts—could result in fiscal crises that caused collapse of currency values, national economic emergencies, and even changes in government. The result: not only were central bankers fiscally prudent, their political bosses demanded this practice be observed in nearly every circumstance. This was particularly true in Asia, where the financial crisis of 1997–98 stimulated government accumulation of foreign exchange reserves at rates probably unanticipated by architects of the existing international financial system.

The caveat "probably unanticipated" has to be employed at this point because, one discovers, there is no definitive requirement as to the amount of money any one nation should maintain in foreign exchange reserves. The most widely recognized "recommendation" concerning the size of these accounts suggests holdings equivalent to the total cost of three months of imports.[3] That is, a nation's fiscal reserves should be sufficient to pay for the foreign goods necessary to maintain factory production and operate the domestic economy without other sources of income for 90 days.[4]

At present, only a few nations with foreign exchange reserves acquired primarily through trade are potentially capable of meeting this requirement. For instance, Japan, with an estimated $1 trillion in foreign reserves, is thought to be able to purchase up to 20 months of necessary imports.[5] China, with more than $1.5 trillion in foreign exchange reserves is also thought to have met the mark—but is nowhere near the standard set in Tokyo. Chinese central bankers are said to believe that foreign exchange reserves totaling over $1.1 trillion are necessary to keep the three months of foreign goods flowing into the country.[6] A similar situation potentially exists in Singapore, South Korea, and Taiwan.

Note, the focus above is on foreign exchange reserves acquired through trade—or more specifically, favorable trade imbalances. Nations specializing in the export of petroleum face a significantly different situation. Oil price increases over the last four years have generated foreign exchange reserves for these countries previously deemed unfathomable. Although Kuwait, Saudi Arabia, or the United Arab Emirates must literally import almost everything, the favorable balance of payments associated with oil priced at $100 or more a barrel essentially renders moot the potential problem of sufficient foreign exchange reserves. As a consequence, some members of the Organization of Petroleum Exporting Countries (OPEC) are in the process of establishing foreign exchange reserves with holdings beyond the uppermost quartile of any existing savings requirement model.

In any case, the accumulation of foreign exchange reserves above the recommended "prudent" minimum creates an interesting problem for central bankers who share a classical education in economics—what to do with the excess? Economists are prone to talk about opportunity costs, as in, "What is the opportunity cost of continuing to place these growing reserves in traditional investments—U.S. Treasury notes—versus exploring options elsewhere?" As it turns out, the lost opportunities are considerable, particularly when one is speaking in terms of billions, nay hundreds of billions, of dollars.

The simplest solution is for the banks to put these "excess" holdings into circulation by printing more money. The problem is that such a move risks stimulating inflation and devaluing a nation's currency. The inflationary concerns, in fact, appear to be one of the primary reasons Beijing has been so cautious about turning China's favorable trade imbalance into increased income for the average citizen. By holding down the supply of money in circulation, Beijing restrains inflation and thereby maintains lower labor costs—essentially setting the conditions for continued international demand for cheap Chinese goods. One can argue that this is unduly punitive for the average Chinese citizen, but with 1.3 billion people to feed, clothe, and house, Beijing appears willing to suffer international criticism of this tight monetary policy almost indefinitely. Chinese leaders, it seems, favor the argument that it is better to have underpaid labor than massive unemployment.

So simply placing the excess foreign earnings into circulation is out. Then what? Here is where the classically trained central banker and would-be venture capitalist part ways. The classically trained central banker would simply go in search of safe investments for the growing foreign exchange reserves. Historically this meant purchasing U.S. Treasury notes, resulting in a typical return of between 2 and 5% (before inflation).

Now consider the following scenario: you are a Chinese central banker who has been charged with investing "excess" foreign exchange holdings, and you have a penchant for capitalist practices—not an unheard-of situation. You, as the central banker/capitalist, realize that these funds can be placed in more risky investments because the money in question is, ipso facto, not required for safe operation of the national economy. You also know that it is possible to earn more than a 2 to 5% return simply by opening a savings account in China. How? First, a typical Chinese passbook account earns approximately 4% annual interest. Second, if you invest it at home, the money will annually appreciate against the dollar anywhere from 4 to 8% depending on Beijing's willingness to adjust yuan values on the international currency market. So simply by investing in a savings account at home, the would-be central banker/capitalist would earn between 6 and 7% more than a more conservative counterpart who purchases U.S. Treasury notes.

This discovery presents an interesting dilemma for central bankers. Charged with serving the public good—maintaining an economy and protecting national treasure—he or she has now come to the realization that historic means of accomplishing this task are actually of marginal value. That is, the traditional central bank investment in U.S. Treasury notes is costing taxpayers, in the form of a lost opportunity to earn greater returns elsewhere. But the central banker also has a fiduciary responsibility to ensure that funds are available to meet short-term requirements—to provide the monies necessary for currency stabilization and other economic contingencies. What to do?

The answer to this dilemma is the establishment of a government-operated investment fund that controls a pool of cash separate from the monies reserved for currency and liquidity management. The first such funds appeared in the 1950s as a means of banking earnings from exhaustible natural resources. Initially called "future generations" or "revenue equalization reserve" funds, these accounts were intended to move a percentage of profit from natural resource exploitation efforts into savings that would continue to pay dividends after the "goose that laid the golden egg" was dead. These savings accounts are now commonly referred to as "sovereign wealth funds." More specifically, sovereign wealth funds can be distinguished from foreign exchange reserves by classifying the former as "a by-product of national budget surpluses, accumulated over the years due to favorable macroeconomic, trade and fiscal positions, coupled with long-term budget planning and spending restraint."[7]

Although scholars have yet to agree on a standard definition for "sovereign wealth funds," this text will employ the criterion currently favored at the U.S. Treasury Department. According to the U.S. Treasury, a sovereign wealth fund is "a government investment vehicle which is funded by foreign reserve assets, and which manages those assets separately from the official reserves of the monetary authorities (the central bank and reserve-related functions of a finance ministry or national treasury office)."[8] Efforts to refine this definition have included highlighting key traits associated with a sovereign wealth fund such as the investment vehicles' high foreign currency exposure, lack of explicit liabilities, high risk tolerances, and long investment horizons.[9] The bottom line: A sovereign wealth fund is a pool of public money that is under governmental supervision and can be invested in a manner more commonly associated with privately held capital. (Note: I do not rule out the possibility that a sovereign wealth fund ultimately has liabilities such as bondholders in the case of the China Investment Corporation, or future pensioners, as with Norway's Government Pension Fund.)

If sovereign wealth funds—or their semantic equivalents—have been in existence for more than 50 years, why the "sudden" interest in them?[10] First, the number of nations seeking to establish and employ this form of investment—with sizable funding—has dramatically increased in the last 15 years. During a study of the existing 20 largest sovereign wealth funds, analysts at Oxford Analytica discovered only seven were in existence before 1990, six more were established in the following ten years, and seven more have opened their doors since 2001.[11] Furthermore, international interest in these investment vehicles continues to grow as rumors of an impending Saudi, Japanese, and/or Indian fund appear regularly in finance-focused journals, newspapers, and Web sites.

The amount of money available to these government investment vehicles is the second reason sovereign wealth funds have become the topic *du jour*. The International Monetary Fund (IMF) estimates these funds accounted for no more than $500 billion in 1990.[12] When the article coining the phrase "sovereign wealth funds" was published in May 2005, the author argued that the "aggregate total of this asset pool globally" was approximately $895 billion.[13] In 2007, that figure had expanded to $3.3 trillion[14] and was estimated to be growing at an annual rate of over $1 trillion—suggesting sovereign wealth funds could control over $12 trillion by 2015.[15]

Although insurance company holdings, mutual funds, and central bank–controlled foreign exchange reserves do, and probably will, continue to dwarf these government investment vehicles,[16] two factors unique to sovereign wealth funds and their associated money appear to cause the greatest concern. The first is the fact this cash pool is controlled by national entities and not private investors. The second is the relatively small number of governing entities involved—roughly 20 major players. (To help frame the conversation, consider the fact that hedge funds currently manage approximately $1.5 trillion but do so through over 7,000 separate firms.) Quite simply, sovereign wealth funds are coming to be feared as potential practitioners of "soft power"[17]—richly endowed government offices that might be more interested in international politics than profit. This specter has given rise to questions about the potential for "state capitalism"—strategic acquisition in the pursuit of national objectives—in countries where these investment vehicles are seeking to purchase assets.

Finally, sovereign wealth funds have become a growing source of concern for national policymakers as a result of the perceived lack of transparency associated with the operation of these official investment vehicles. In the United States, this perceived lack of transparency has generated multiple congressional hearings and resulted in at least two different means of defining and measuring desirable operating procedures. In Europe, sovereign wealth fund activity has raised political hackles in France and Germany, and even resulted in calls for increased transparency in normally foreign-investment friendly Great Britain. While much of Asia has yet to publicly join in this protectionist fervor, similar sentiments have emerged in Japan, and there are voices expressing concern in Australia and New Zealand. In short, the apparently secretive manner in which these funds are perceived to govern has resulted in an international effort to monitor and modify their behavior—an effort embodied in an ongoing IMF drive to establish and publish a set of "best practices" for sovereign wealth funds.[18]

Interestingly, an area that has drawn little attention is the potential long-term impact of sovereign wealth fund investments on debtor nations—particularly nations that depend on a constant flow of funds to sustain economic growth. Here we return to the peril these funds may present to the United States. A quick glance at comments from former and current government officials suggests that Washington is not sure how to proceed. For instance, in a speech to members of the finance community in January 2008, former Fed Chairman Alan Greenspan declared, "I must admit I am a little uncomfortable with [sovereign wealth funds] . . . but I must admit there is very little evidence they are being used inappropriately. On balance, I think they are desirable."[19]

Similar mixed messages came from members of the Bush administration. Although these officials warned about potential political problems associated with sovereign wealth fund investments in the United States, they also emphasized that America remains open to foreign capital. As Treasury Secretary Paulson told reporters in January 2008, "Money is naturally going to gravitate toward dollar-based assets because of the strength of our economy. I'd like nothing more than to get more of that money. But I understand that there's a natural fear they're going to buy up America."[20]

Christopher Cox, chairman of the Securities and Exchange Commission (SEC), offered comparable remarks in December 2007 but was much blunter about the concerns associated with government-controlled investments. According to Cox, "the fundamental question presented by state-owned public companies and sovereign wealth funds does not so much concern the advisability of foreign ownership, but rather of government ownership."[21] How to read Greenspan, Paulson, and Cox? I would contend they are arguing the U.S. and other nations like foreign direct investment but worry about the implications of foreign government direct investment.

What these officials do not appear to be worrying about, however, is the consequence of investors turning away from U.S. Treasury notes in favor of options that provide greater returns. In fact, during off-the-record discussions with top-ranking U.S. Treasury and Commerce officials, I discovered an attitude best characterized as remarkably dismissive of this concern. The prevailing sentiment seems to be that "foreigners will always want to purchase official U.S. securities."

Research on sovereign wealth fund managers' evolving investment patterns suggests this dismissive attitude may be dangerously misplaced. Although the bulk of foreign direct investment is still headed into Western nations, beneficiaries of the global trade imbalance and oil price spike are exhibiting a growing tendency to keep their money closer to home. For instance, over the last two years, Singapore's Temasek Holdings has gone from placing 34% of its investments in other Asian nations to 40% in 2007.[22] The head of Kuwait's sovereign wealth fund explained the logic behind this transition when he told reporters in August 2007, "Why invest in 2% growth economies, when you can invest in 8% growth economies?"[23] More troubling, however, was the U.S. Treasury's own discovery that Beijing is seemingly becoming less interested in serving as America's piggy bank. In 2004 China bought 20% of all the U.S. Treasury securities issued. In 2005 that figure was 30%. In 2006 it was 36%. In 2007 Beijing reversed course and became a net seller of U.S. government notes.[24]

Furthermore, there is evidence that this move away from U.S. Treasury notes and government debt is growing. Between June 2006 and May 2007, private foreign investment in long-term U.S. securities reached $1 trillion. In the following 12 months, June 2007 to May 2008, that figure dropped to $600 billion.[25] As it turns out, private investors were not the only ones detected in headlong flight from the U.S. dollar. In mid-July 2008, the *Financial Times* reported that at least one unnamed Middle East sovereign wealth fund between June 2007 and June 2008 had slashed its dollar-denominated holdings from 80% of its total investment to less than 60%. In addition, the *Financial Times* wrote that China's State Administration of Foreign Exchange (SAFE) has been observed seeking to strike deals with private equity firms in Europe as a means of reducing its dollar holdings.[26] According to the *Times*, "SAFE has been holding talks with Europe-based private equity firms . . . precisely because these funds are not dollar-denominated."[27] Interestingly, Abu Dhabi Investment Authority (ADIA), the world's largest sovereign wealth fund, has remained committed to the dollar—at least for the moment. As the *Financial Times* story made clear, this "loyalty" is not likely to last. One ADIA staffer reportedly told the *Times* that the fund's commitment to the dollar was causing no small amount of "suffering." As the staffer put it, "we are importing inflation for no reason."[28]

Concerns about a weak dollar are only one reason that foreign governments are seeking to invest outside the United States. Balance sheet bottom lines are another reason. As the Congressional Research Service (CRS) reported in January 2008, Beijing's purchase of American debt in 2007 was not a profitable investment. According to the CRS analysts, the yield on U.S. ten-year Treasury notes varied, hovering between 4.5 and 5% in 2007. During the same time period, the Chinese yuan appreciated 6% against the U.S. dollar. This currency appreciation resulted in a negative rate of return on U.S. Treasury notes for Chinese investors—strongly suggesting it made sense to place Beijing's foreign exchange reserves elsewhere.[29]

If the money is not being used to purchase U.S. Treasury notes, where is it going? There are two responses to this question. The short answer is diversification, a word widely bandied about in the world of financial advisors. The long answer requires an examination of what it means to diversify when investing billions of dollars. Take the case of Norway. In an effort to earn a greater return, the managers of Norway's Government Pension Fund adopted a macro-level investment formula that calls for placing 60% of Oslo's portfolio in indexed equities and the remaining 40% in fixed income instruments.[30] The head of the Kuwait Investment Authority contends he seeks to follow a model employed at the Harvard and Yale endowment funds—a mix of stocks, private equity funds, and real estate.[31] The manager of Russia's stabilization fund reports he is required to pursue an even broader mix of investments ranging from foreign currencies to shares in investment funds.[32]

Unfortunately, this turn to private equity does not mean simply shifting the monies from Washington to New York. As investors at Harvard and Yale have discovered, a long-term commitment to indexed funds listed on Wall Street is not as profitable as many Americans would like to believe. Increasingly, diversification in the sovereign wealth fund world means placing the money in assets outside the United States. All of this suggests that the big losers here are not just the U.S. Treasury; corporate America is also poised to begin paying more for the privilege of borrowing money.

In any case, for sovereign wealth fund managers, the goal appears the same: earn a maximum return on what may be best characterized as a public investment. How important is this bottom line? Lou Jiwei, chairman of the China Investment Corporation—Beijing's newly minted sovereign wealth fund—likes to remind audiences that he is solely in the business of making money. Charged with managing a start-up fund of $200 billion, Mr. Lou has repeatedly declared his number one priority is financial performance, and that he is under "big pressures" to generate profits. According to Lou Jiwei, the China Investment Corporation needs to earn about $40 million *a day* to offset the cost of the 5% annual interest it is paying on the bonds used to finance the fund.[33]

In fact, an examination of statements on earnings issued by some of the sovereign wealth funds suggests that profit—not politics—is the most prevalent determinant of these entities' investment behavior. The Kuwait Investment Authority claims it returned 11% on investments in 2005, 15.8% in 2006, and 13.3% in 2007.[34] Singapore's Temasek Holdings reports earned profit margins of 13.9% in 2005, 18.7% in 2006, and 18.2% in 2007.[35] In the same vein, Dubai International Capital's $1 billion stake in DaimlerChrysler purchased in 2005 is said to have paid off handsomely when the fund sold out a year later, doubling its money.[36] More recent acquisitions in the ailing international financial sector also appear—at least for the moment—to have been carefully considered business choices. Abu Dhabi Investment Authority's infusion of $7.5 billion in Citigroup for a three-year 11% return on the money appears a smart move, particularly as Citigroup's dividend yield on common shares was 7.4% at the time of the deal and companies rated as "junk" pay only 9% interest rates.[37]

This focus on the bottom line—earning the greatest return possible by minimizing opportunity costs—is the potential that sovereign wealth funds offer the United States. I come to this conclusion for two reasons. First, as "capitalists entrusted with wisely investing public funds," these government investment vehicles offer a potential model for the long-suffering U.S. Social Security system. Perhaps Washington's endless worries about bankrupting the fund by 2041 can be resolved through wise investment of monies flowing into the government coffers. This is an approach already in play for members of the California Public Employees' Retirement System (CalPERS). Why not do the same thing at a national level?

Second, sovereign wealth funds could serve in a stabilizing role on Wall Street and throughout the international financial markets that government officials have been heretofore poorly equipped to provide. Rather than continually struggling with the evolution of regulatory codes required to match pace with innovation on Wall Street and other "masters of the universe," governments could use sovereign wealth funds to help diminish the market swings that contribute to investor malaise and potential recessionary cycles. Targeted government investment in temporarily ailing industries is arguably in the long-term good for the economy and could pay significant dividends. Some financial analysts are already arguing this case[38]—it remains to be seen if Washington will be willing to accept their argument.[39]

This is a big "if." Even with this potential for serving the greater public good, critics and skeptics are issuing calls for caution—particularly in the United States. In testimony provided to the United States–China Economic and Security Review Commission in February 2008, Senator James Webb (D-VA) declared, "The difference between sovereign wealth funds and other foreign investment is 'the political element' and the desire of the funds to play a more prominent global role. Undoubtedly some funds are interested solely in their financial return and will invest like a commercial investor, but we should not presume all funds will act in this manner."[40] Speaking before the same commission, Representative Marcy Kaptur (D-OH) argued, "Instead of rescuing our economy, these investments only deepen American insecurity, forcing the U.S. further into debt to foreign interests. More often than not, these deals are presented as purely financial when they are, in fact, political and strategic."[41]

These statements from members of the U.S. Congress reflect an apparently widespread American skepticism about the motivations behind sovereign wealth fund acquisitions. In a poll conducted in mid-February 2008, 49% of the respondents said foreign government investments harmed the U.S. economy, and 55% said these investments hurt U.S. national security. Furthermore, over 60% of the Americans questioned opposed investments in the U.S. by official entities operated out of Abu Dhabi, China, Russia, or Saudi Arabia. Over 50% expressed similar feelings about investments originating with government-controlled funds based in Hong Kong or Kuwait. Only money coming from Norway, Japan, or Australia succeeded in eliciting greater support than opposition from poll respondents. All this angst, despite the fact that only 6% of the survey participants said they had "seen or heard anything recently" about sovereign wealth funds.[42]

Before moving on, I should note that not all Americans—specifically, analysts on Wall Street—are so suspicious of sovereign wealth funds. The over $40 billion that these government investment vehicles have provided the ailing U.S. financial sector has been welcomed as a stabilizing factor that helped ward off even larger fiscal problems. *The Wall Street Journal* went so far as to run stories crediting sovereign wealth fund investments as having "mitigated the damage to equity markets after the summer's (2007) subprime problems."[43] A senior analyst with a major Wall Street firm was quoted arguing, "I would not be surprised if the sovereign wealth funds played a meaningful role in September [2007], facilitating recovery in emerging markets equities and equities in general." The analyst went on to note, "sovereign wealth funds could have a much longer investment horizon and a higher tolerance for swings in profits and losses. . . . Having such a different temperament from private funds, sovereign wealth funds should reduce the risk of herd behavior."[44]

So there is room to argue that Americans need to learn to separate the wheat from the chaff, or at least learn how to steer these funds in a manner that allows the United States to benefit from their seemingly bottomless pools of cash. Some in the U.S. policy community contend that the means for accomplishing this task are already in place. Over the course of the last 30-plus years, rising investment in America by OPEC members and other "suspicious entities" has spurred establishment of the Committee on Foreign Investment in the United States (CFIUS), the 1977 passage of the International Emergency Economic Powers Act, the 1988 Exon-Florio Amendment to the Defense Production Act, the 1993 Byrd Amendment to the National Defense Authorization Act, and, most recently, the 2007 Foreign Investment and National Security Act. And yet critics remain adamant that Washington has not done enough, leading to yet another round of calls for revising the statutes and regulatory bodies charged with overseeing foreign investment in the United States.[45]

But does this perceived regulatory shortfall really exist? Legal scholars offer a variety of opinions. Some U.S. students of the issue contend existing American regulations "compel passivity from sovereign wealth funds, and thus minimize the threat that equity investments will be used as political tools." However, they also warn that "aggressive" use of these regulations may frighten away the foreign investment required for continued U.S. economic growth.[46] European legal scholars are more circumspect. Although they agree international law allows a state "effective sovereignty over its internal affairs," there is no single global organization or set of agreements that deals with cross-border investment.[47] These scholars note that international legal guidance for this activity would have to be derived from regional and bilateral trade agreements and other conventions. Furthermore, they argue the Organization for Economic Cooperation and Development (OECD) Code of Liberalization of Capital Movements does not apply to China and the Middle East, as these countries were not parties to the code.[48]

More to the point, the European Union also appears to be struggling with how to address concerns associated with sovereign wealth fund investment. Although the free movement of capital is one of the "four freedoms" enshrined in the European Union Treaty,[49] the issue is legally considered one of "best efforts," as the European Union Council is allowed to adopt measures restricting or affecting the flow of capital into real estate, financial services, and the listing of securities.[50] That said, European Union member states may only effectuate such regulations in very restrictive manners with objective justifications. Furthermore, according to the treaty, these measures must not constitute "a means of arbitrary discrimination or a disguised restriction on the movement of capital."[51] I suspect that governments in Asia and the Middle East have made note of this provision and will be ready to argue its merits in a future legal case involving U.S. restrictions on their investment activity. One only needs to consider the vehement popular reaction to the possibility of investments from these countries noted in the poll of Americans discussed previously to see how "discrimination" would be a convincing legal argument.

What does this mean for the United States? First, Washington can certainly control transactions occurring within U.S. borders. Second, although there is no clear "right to invest" under international law, treaties and agreements among nations may effectively lead to such a conclusion. Third, as a result of these treaties and agreements, specific attempts to regulate sovereign wealth fund investments could be regarded as unlawful. In short, there is no globally recognized legal provision outright permitting or restricting the ability of governments to invest—however defined—in another nation. While arguments over "national security" may temporarily impede some investment efforts, the real issue boils down to economic considerations and a desire to facilitate the flow of capital required for domestic prosperity—a precarious act of balancing the peril and potential associated with sovereign wealth fund investment.

The real debate, then, is to what degree sovereign wealth funds may engage in such activity—and by doing so potentially benefit the public welfare they were purportedly established to serve. Should foreign governments be granted the right to outright ownership of U.S. property, modes of production, and/or financial institutions? Should this investment be allowed to take on a political tenor—the exercise of voting rights in board sessions, participation in deliberations concerning campaign donations and candidate endorsement, and/or a say in product development that may help or hinder national security considerations? And should Washington be engaging in similar activity—essentially providing the United States an equal opportunity to participate in the domestic economic affairs of other nations?

These are the issues that frame the discussion to follow. While I cannot claim to offer definitive answers to every question, my research on the concerns raised by the emergence of sovereign wealth funds should serve to facilitate future policy discussions of these matters and leave the reader better equipped to engage in this dialogue. My hope is to leave the debate participants better off than John James Roberts Manner would have requested. In an age of increasing globalization, we can no longer afford to "let wealth and commerce, laws and learning die, but leave us our old nobility."[52] We must accept the peril with the potential.

CHAPTER 1

THE SOVEREIGN WEALTH FUNDS OF NATIONS

The profusion with which the affairs of a prince are always managed, renders it almost impossible that they should [succeed at business]. The agents of a prince regard the wealth of their masters as inexhaustible; are careless at which price they buy; are careless at what price they sell; are careless at what expense they transport his goods from one place to another.[1]

—*Adam Smith*, The Wealth of Nations

National governments have historically generated revenue through taxation and conservative investments in state-backed Treasury notes. The traditionally educated central banker heeds Adam Smith's warning against dabbling in business affairs, particularly speculation in risky ventures that chanced a "squandering" of the public treasury. Admittedly there have been the aberrant few—primarily governments blessed with natural resources that tipped the balance of payments in favor of the existing regime—but as a whole, central bankers were largely restricted to managing the domestic monetary supply and a limited pool of foreign reserves. This historic norm is on the cusp of a tectonic shift, and very few people seem to understand the potential consequences. Why? First, the issue is relatively new and in largely uncharted waters for the policy community. Second, the consequences are—for the moment—largely restricted to the arcane world of finance. And, third, the potential security ramifications for the United States appear under control.

Now consider the following: rising oil prices and trade imbalances have enriched a few governments to the degree that they are now free to shed restrictive national bankers' vestments and step boldly into the world of venture capitalism. Having acquired balance sheets worthy of the shrewdest entrepreneur, these bureaucrats—the keepers of sovereign wealth funds—are beginning to make investments heretofore limited to risk-savvy hedge-fund managers and cash-laden venture capitalists. Working with a pool of secured money requiring no fixed asset as collateral, these sovereign wealth fund managers are poised to become a new tool of national power, an economic dynamo capable of acquiring, investing, and selling in a manner that could alter a competitor's domestic and foreign policies with seeming impunity. More troubling for U.S. policy makers, this fiscal activity appears to be assuming a vector with potentially significant negative implications for the American economy.

What Is a Sovereign Wealth Fund?

Sovereign wealth funds are best understood as national investment vehicles[2] created with monies considered in excess of, and managed separately from, a country's foreign reserves.[3] As "excess cash on hand," sovereign wealth funds become expendable in ways that are largely never considered by the managers of foreign reserves.[4] Why? Foreign reserves typically serve to provide short-term currency stabilization and liquidity management.[5] Historically these functions dictated the preferred size of a nation's foreign exchange reserve, with the favored solution being maintenance of an account with the funds necessary to cover approximately three months of imports,[6] or equal to the foreign liabilities coming due within one year.[7] Furthermore, in order to ensure ready availability in time of crisis or market fluctuation, foreign reserves have normally been invested in short-term "safe" markets.

Using either of the reserve adequacy measures cited above as a guide, it is safe to conclude that a select handful of states are currently sitting on foreign exchange holdings well in excess of these supposedly prudent requirements. In addition to the piles of cash being accumulated by oil-producing states, there is a small number of noncommodity exporters who are gathering a fortune based on seemingly endless trade imbalances with the West. For instance, China's reserve assets in 2006 were 12.5 times the size of Beijing's short-term foreign debt. During the same time period, Japan and Korea had roughly twice the reserves required to defend against a repeat of the 1997–98 Asian financial crisis.[8]

Monetary holdings in excess of the suggested foreign reserve requirement are considered "surplus" that can be used to increase currency in circulation, support consumption, and/or be invested to meet future needs. When these excess holdings are building more rapidly than they can be incorporated into an economy without risking currency devaluation, inflation, or both, they can be managed as a sovereign wealth fund—a means of engaging in investments that do not have to immediately turn a profit or could even lose money over a short period. This makes the sovereign wealth fund a pool of money that can be put back into international circulation through corporate acquisitions, stock purchases, and even real-estate speculation. In short, sovereign wealth funds

Table 1.1 Top 10 Sovereign Wealth Funds in 2007[9]

Country	Fund	Established	Assets $bn	Origin
UAE	Abu Dhabi Investment Authority	1976	$875	Oil
Singapore	Government of Singapore Investment Corporation	1981	$330	Noncommodity
Norway	Government Pension Fund	1990	$300	Oil
China	China Investment Corporation	2007	$200	Noncommodity
Russia	Stabilization Fund	2003	$100	Oil
Singapore	Temasek Holdings	1974	$100	Noncommodity
Kuwait	Kuwait Investment Authority	1953	$70	Oil
Australia	Australia Future Fund	2004	$40	Noncommodity
United States	Alaska Permanent Fund	1976	$37	Oil
Brunei	Brunei Investment Authority	1983	$30	Oil

provide cash—internationally recognized as resident in a national treasury—that can be used for risky investments without having to secure outside audit, partners, or tangible collateral. While this option is already available to the extremely wealthy and a few corporations, we are now talking about sums unheard of even in those circles—in at least one case, well over $850 billion. (See Table 1.1 for a quick summary of the ten largest sovereign wealth funds.)

Although the sheer size of a handful of these sovereign wealth funds is a relatively new phenomenon, the idea of using "excess" national income for long-term investments is over 50 years old. One of the first government investment vehicles was the Kiribati Revenue Equalization Reserve Fund. Established in 1956 during the British administration of the Micronesian Gilbert Islands, the Kiribati fund was capitalized using revenue from mining bird guano that was used for fertilizer due to its high phosphate content. The Kiribati fund was intended to ensure Gilbert Islanders would continue to benefit from the mining of this exhaustible resource. (The last of the bird manure was mined in 1979.) Today the Kiribati fund is worth an estimated $520 million, a pittance in comparison to its new counterparts on the sovereign wealth fund list, but sufficient to boost the meager Kiribati per capita annual income.[10]

Similar reserve-based investment models were established in the Middle East, with Kuwait and the United Arab Emirates being early practitioners. In each case, the underlying premise was the same—invest the earnings from an exhaustible natural resource in a manner that would benefit future generations and/or potentially secure an existing regime, and do so in a manner that provides a higher return than is historically offered by national Treasury notes and sovereign bonds.

The first break from this commodity-based model came with establishment of the Singapore Global Investment Corporation (GIC) in 1981. Although Singapore had previously sought to invest national earnings by claiming a stake in a variety of domestic corporations and then placing these shares with the Ministry of Finance—the basis of Singapore's Temasek Holdings fund—GIC is primarily focused on earning a greater return from the nation's favorable international trade imbalance.[11] Based on GIC's success, Seoul established a similar fund in 2006—the Korea Investment Corporation—and Beijing has now initiated the China Investment Corporation (CIC). Similar noncommodity-based sovereign wealth funds are being considered in New Delhi and Tokyo.[12]

Why the Sudden Focus on Sovereign Wealth Funds?

Given the fact sovereign wealth funds have been in existence for over 50 years—and that some of these reserve-based portfolios have been handling hundreds of billions of dollars for over a decade—it is only fair to ask why the "sudden" attention to a seemingly benign means of handling excess national earnings? Quite simply, the answer is growth, and thereby potential political impact. The total size of sovereign wealth funds has dramatically increased since 1990. According to the International Monetary Fund, in 1990 sovereign wealth funds probably accounted for no more than $500 billion.[13] The current total is estimated at $3.3 trillion,[14] and Morgan Stanley assesses that these funds could account for up to $12 trillion by 2015.[15] (In contrast, hedge funds are currently estimated to account for a mere $1.6 trillion in invested capital and could just be reaching $4 trillion in 2015.[16]) At this pace, sovereign wealth funds could surpass the size of total national foreign reserves—currently estimated at slightly more than $5 trillion—by 2011.[17] In any case, Western financial analysts now argue sovereign wealth funds are the most rapidly growing institutional investor—outpacing hedge funds, insurance companies, and mutual funds.[18]

These are large figures, but without some basis of comparison, they are hard to comprehend. As a means of offering some perspective, the U.S. gross domestic product (GDP) in 2007 reached approximately $12 trillion, the total value of traded securities denominated in U.S. dollars is thought to be about $50 trillion, and the global value of traded securities is roughly $165 trillion.[19] Turning to national account ledgers, the world's official reserves in 2007 totaled over

$5 trillion and are estimated to be growing at $75 to 80 billion a month—with China accounting for 30% of the increase. Oil exporters and major Asian exporters (China, Japan, Korea, and Singapore) are expected to end the year with aggregate earnings surpluses each totaling $400 billion, with high oil prices and continued trade imbalances promising even larger returns in the future.[20]

China's decision to follow in the path blazed by Singapore and Korea suggests that up to $500 billion a year may now be made available to the managers of the world's largest noncommodity-based sovereign wealth funds—a sum that places managers of these accounts on approximately equal footing with their counterparts charged with investing petrodollars. The result: up to $1 trillion a year in secure "new money" flowing into the coffers of less than ten nationally managed sovereign wealth funds. By way of contrast, the total number of international hedge funds is somewhere in the neighborhood of 7,000 individual businesses.

At this point I've buried you in numbers and still not offered an impact statement. Allow me to address this shortfall. Total global equities—all the publicly listed stocks available through various exchanges—tally in at about $33 trillion. Estimated global government bonds are worth about $21 trillion. Private sector bonds offered across the planet total about $24 trillion.[21] Given the current and projected income available to sovereign wealth funds, State Street financial advisors estimate, "if [the funds] were to collectively allocate 60% of this capital to the FTSE Global All Cap index, they would own about 5.2% of each of the 8,009 companies in the index."[22] That's right—5% of every major corporation on the planet. And that's just the beginning of the story.

But Should We Worry?

Somewhat surprisingly, a majority of initial U.S.-based press commentary on the growth of sovereign wealth funds largely dismissed this new asset pool as much ado about nothing. According to Kenneth Rogoff, a Harvard University professor and former chief economist for the International Monetary Fund, sovereign wealth funds will be "managed inefficiently" and perhaps only garner an annual return of 8%.[23] Anders Aslund, a senior fellow at the Peterson Institute for International Economics in Washington, argues that "such funds are nothing for Americans or Europeans to fear." Like Rogoff, Aslund concludes the average sovereign wealth fund manager can be counted on to behave in a "pernicious" manner that has made these funds a "lousy bargain for the countries that have them."[24] James Suowiecki of *The New Yorker* appears to have come to the same conclusion. In a *New Yorker* financial page commentary, Suowiecki contends, "The rise of sovereign wealth funds will create plenty of strange situations, like having a foreign government own your local supermarket[25] . . . But it's not as radical a shift from the current state of things as one might think."[26] Really?

To fully comprehend the potential impact of this recent transition to placing excess foreign exchange earnings in sovereign wealth funds, one must consider how these monies have historically been spent. In the past, these earnings had generally been handled in the following manner: oil exporters placed the excess in investment funds, whereas the Asian export giants tended to hold the balance in official reserves. As a whole, the petrodollar-based funds appear to have focused on investments that are equity and equitylike—and typically outside the United States.[27] The story for Asian government investors is much different. According to McKinsey Global Institute, in 2006 Asian central banks held approximately $3.1 trillion in foreign reserves—64% of the global total.[28] Of greater concern here, these banks had invested somewhere in the vicinity of 65 to 70% of their reserves in dollar-denominated assets, specifically U.S. Treasury notes.

The consequence of this historic investment focus? A huge net gain for the U.S. consumer. Total foreign purchases of U.S. Treasury bonds since 2002 are estimated to have lowered long-term interest rates in the United States in 2006 by up to 130 basis points[29]—approximately 20 of these basis points can be attributed directly to petrodollar investments, while another 55 appear to have been contributed through Asian central bank investments.[30] Without this influx of foreign capital, interest rates in the United States would be at least 1.3% greater than they are today—thereby pushing down consumer purchases of autos, homes, and other large-ticket items that serve to bolster the state of the overall economy.[31] Quite simply, profligate American petroleum consumption and our purchase of cheaper Asian-made products has been a "self-licking ice cream cone" because the beneficiary foreign governments reinvested the funds in a manner that offset Washington's deficit spending through purchases of U.S. government paper.

Now what happens if these same foreign governments go looking for a more profitable return on their investments? This scenario is not as far-fetched as one might think. U.S. Federal Reserve efforts to stimulate domestic spending by lowering interest rates may have negative long-term consequences for the American economy—the lower return on U.S. bonds and securities could cause customers to look for more lucrative options. This is particularly true of those who can afford more risky investments—like Beijing, Seoul, Singapore, Taipei, and Tokyo—customers whose foreign reserve holdings have now dramatically exceeded even the most conservative definition of a prudent foreign reserve account.

How likely are these traditionally risk-averse money managers to go looking for more lucrative investment opportunities? Well, despite Mr. Rogoff's assurances, there is no reason to believe that even the most "inefficient" Chinese bureaucrat is unlikely to realize he or she can do twice as well simply by leaving his country's money at home. Do the math with me. Following the latest interest rate reduction, U.S. bonds and securities were selling with guaranteed returns of between 3 and 4%. In 2008 the Chinese yuan is expected to appreciate at least 5% against the U.S. dollar, and the average bank account in Beijing offers an annual return of 4%—so just by investing at home Chinese bureaucrats can do twice as well as they could have by purchasing U.S. Treasury notes.

Not coincidentally, there is ample evidence sovereign wealth fund managers throughout the world are capable of making just such market-savvy decisions. The Kuwait Investment Authority claims it returned 11% on investments in 2005, 15.8% in 2006, and 13.3% in 2007.[32] Singapore's Temasek Holdings reports earned profit margins of 13.9% in 2005, 18.7% in 2006, and 18.2% in 2007.[33] In the same vein, Dubai International Capital's $1 billion stake in DaimlerChrysler purchased in 2005 is said to have paid off handsomely when the fund sold out a year later, doubling its money.[34] More recent acquisitions in the ailing international financial sector also appear—at least for the moment—to have been wise business choices. Abu Dhabi Investment Authority's infusion of $7.5 billion in Citigroup for a three-year 11% return on the money appears a smart move, particularly as Citigroup's dividend yield on common shares was 7.4% at the time of the deal and companies rated as "junk" only pay 9% interest rates.[35]

This is not to say all the news for sovereign wealth fund managers has been stellar. Norway's Government Pension Fund managers in the Norges Bank 2006 Annual Report admit that the average nominal returns on equity and fixed income portfolios from 1998–2006 have been 5.37% and 7.02% respectively.[36] Since 1997, the real return on Norway's Pension Fund investments—the nominal return adjusted for inflation—has been 4.58%. According to the Norges Bank Investment Management team, their performance could best be attributed to two events: (1) the fund's move to place more than 40% of its investments in the equity market since 1998, and (2) the "worst decline in global equities markets since the 1930s," which began in 2000.[37] Needless to say, this performance has garnered significant criticism at home, with at least one critic claiming the fund's investment managers only "make Norway more poor."[38] (The Norges Bank team actually did not do as poorly as one might first suspect. A review of stock performance using a buy-and-hold model for the same time period (1998–2006) reveals that the following rates of return could have been expected by purchasing only "name brand" shares: Dow Jones Industrials 6.11%, Standard & Poor's 500 Index 4.94%, Vanguard 500 Index Fund 7.37%, and NASDAQ Composite Index 5.88%.)

China's new sovereign wealth fund managers have also suffered setbacks in their efforts to wisely invest the approximately $200 billion[39] Beijing has placed in their hands.[40] The China Investment Corporation (CIC) purchased a 9.3% share of the Blackstone Group private equity firm for $3 billion prior to the firm's initial public offering (IPO) in June 2007. The deal apparently came as a surprise to many observers and sparked criticism at home after Blackstone's share prices fell by more than 30% following the IPO. International finance reporters noted that domestic criticism of the CIC move was particularly sharp because Chinese officials are used to seeing huge gains in the early months of a newly listed company.[41]

Given Norway and China's experiences, the risk-acceptant sovereign wealth fund manager may be tempted to look elsewhere when investing his or her nation's monies—like U.S. real estate. This is the second area in which the emer-gence of sovereign wealth funds presents a problem for the average American con-sumer. The Economist Intelligence Unit reports that real estate values in developed countries since 2000 have increased by $30 trillion—reaching $70 trillion by 2005—far outpacing GDP growth during the same period.[42] Accord-ing to analysts at McKinsey Global Institute, this rise in developed nations'—particularly U.S.—real estate prices primarily reflects two factors: petrodollar investors putting money into the global property market; and low interest rates on mortgage and home equity loans that made the housing market more attrac-tive to the average American consumer.[43]

Now, increase factor one—foreign consumers interested in safe real estate investments—while diminishing or removing the second—low interest rates in the United States. The result is an escalation in property values—and taxes—in some desirable locales[44]—but fewer Americans able to afford homes. This is exactly what could happen if sovereign wealth fund managers in Asia go looking for more lucrative returns than those offered by the U.S. Treasury. Bottom line, further Federal Reserve reductions in the interest rates are a vicious catch-22 that may pay off in the short run but then cost dearly down the road.

In Fact, The Time to Worry Is Upon Us

The worst-case scenario suggested above appears to be coming to fruition—at least in the sense that foreign investors are clearly looking for new markets. As the London *Times* noted in late October 2007, the imbalance in world trade during 2006 placed over $1.2 trillion dollars in non-Western hands. But the United States, the European Union, and Britain—the main issuers of safe offi-cial securities—only printed approximately $460 billion in government bonds during the same time period.[45] Even if the beneficiaries of this $1.2 trillion net income flow had purchased all these Treasury notes—an unlikely occurrence, as we shall see—there would still be some $720 billion left for discretionary spend-ing. So where is the money going? In a large number of cases, it is staying close to home.

Singapore's Temasek Holdings 2007 Corporate Report provides a snapshot of evolving Asian-based sovereign wealth fund investment strategies. According to Temasek, between 31 March 2006 and 31 March 2007, the Singapore-based fund transitioned from placing 34% of its investments in other Asian nations to 40%.[46] Much of this transition came in the form of reduced investments at home, but the overall figure is illustrative of an expanding pattern of behavior.

The primary beneficiary of this transition in investment patterns? China. In fact, this shift between 2006 and 2007 is the continuation of a trend for Temasek. According to the fund's officers, during 2005 Temasek investment in Singapore accounted for 49% of the firm's monies. In 2006 that figure was 44%, and in 2007 it was 38%. During the same time frame, Temasek's investments in North-east Asia (China, South Korea, and Taiwan) grew from 8% in 2005, to 19% in

2006, and 24% in 2007.[47] Developments at the end of 2007 suggest this trend is going to continue. Temasek announced in early December 2007 that it will be providing half of the funding for a new $2 billion China-focused private equity venture being set up by a Goldman Sachs Group partner. This fund is reportedly geared toward purchasing stakes in state-owned Chinese companies.[48]

A similar trend is developing at sovereign wealth funds charged with investing petrodollars. In an August 2007 interview with *The Wall Street Journal*, Badar Al-Sa'ad, managing director of the Kuwait Investment Authority, stated he is cutting his organization's investment in the United States and Europe from 90% of its holdings to less than 70%. In what could be read as an expression of sentiments found throughout the Middle East, Al-Sa'ad rhetorically asked *The Wall Street Journal* reporter, "Why invest in 2% growth economies when you can invest in 8% growth economies?"[49] The Kuwait Investment Authority's real estate acquisition strategy may also be indicative of a costly change for the United States as Al-Sa'ad claims he is focused on selling in markets regarded as too expensive (i.e., New York City) and looking to buy where growth potential is higher—specifically, smaller Chinese metropolitan areas.

Given the statements above, concerns about the petrodollar-based sovereign wealth fund managers seeking opportunities outside the United States should not be downplayed. The McKinsey Global Institute estimates as of January 2007 that investors from oil-exporting nations collectively owned foreign financial assets worth between $3.4 and $3.8 trillion.[50] As total petrodollar foreign assets are about 41% privately owned and 58% government property, one needs to be cautious in assigning a value to the amounts managed by Middle Eastern sovereign wealth funds. Nonetheless, an overall pattern of behavior—potentially disconcerting for the average American consumer—can be derived from examining macro investment trends in the Middle East.

First, petrodollar-based sovereign wealth funds—like their counterparts elsewhere in the world—have no urgent need to immediately show a return. As such, they can take a long-term approach to investing and safely assume higher levels of risk. What does this mean? In the case of the Abu Dhabi Investment Authority, analysts at the fund assess that at least a third of global growth will come from emerging markets and therefore now allocate 14% of the fund's portfolio to equities in this area.[51] This figure, as the Temasek Holdings investment pattern suggests, is likely to grow.

Second, McKinsey Global Institute estimates that the flow of capital between the Middle East and Asia is likely to only grow larger in the coming years. More specifically, McKinsey analysts predict—if the 22% growth rate detected from 2001–2005 for such activity persists—the annual cross-border flow of cash from the Middle East to Asia will climb from the approximately $15 billion reported in 2006 to as much as $300 billion by 2020.[52]

Finally, in addition to seeking markets abroad, it now appears the Middle Eastern sovereign wealth funds—like their Asian counterparts—are also increasingly looking to invest, and stimulate investment, nearer to home.

Perhaps the most significant development on this front is the ongoing effort to establish an internationally recognized stock exchange in the Middle East.[53] Evidence of this effort is provided by the apparent bidding war Qatar and Dubai are waging over the purchase of off-shore stock exchange shares.

In September 2007, the Qatar Investment Authority—Qatar's sovereign wealth fund—announced spending $1.36 billion for the purchase of a 20% share in the London Stock Exchange and $470 million for a nearly 10% share of the Nordic bourse operator OMX AB.[54] This deal came at the same time that Bourse Dubai—the government-controlled exchange—arranged for a $4.9 billion deal that resulted in a 19.9% stake in the New York-based NASDAQ, a 28% stake in the London exchange, and NASDAQ control of OMX.[55] The ultimate purpose of the purchases was acquisition of the know-how and reputation required to set up and operate a world-class stock exchange in the Middle East. Such a stock exchange, not coincidentally, would also serve to keep Middle Eastern investors focused on options closer to home. If recent trends are any indication of investment patterns to follow, Dubai and Qatar have reason to be optimistic about the prospects of this Middle East stock exchange. In 2002, private investors in the Middle East placed over 85% of their funds in offshore assets; by 2006, that figure had declined to 75%.[56]

Finally, the ongoing U.S.-led global war on terrorism has abetted a growth in Islamic fundamentalism that directly impacts how many Middle Eastern corporations and private investors do business. This development has dovetailed with the surge in oil prices, creating a rapid expansion in the nascent Islamic finance market—investment that complies with *Shariah* laws.[57] In fact, McKinsey Global Institute reports that the Islamic bond—"*sukuk*"—market is one of the most prominent new financial sectors to emerge in the wake of the U.S. invasion of Iraq. More specifically, McKinsey analysts note that at the end of 2006 total Islamic markets were worth approximately $500 billion—of which $70 billion were in *sukuks*, the remainder was in *Shariah*-compliant bank accounts. Although this figure is relatively insignificant given the sums discussed above, the trends are not. McKinsey states that *sukuk* issuance has tripled in the last four years and assesses that petrodollar investors with up to $430 billion in foreign assets likely have at least a moderate interest in these Islamic bonds.[58] Similarly, Standard & Poor's Rating Services now estimates the potential market for Islamic financial services could be as large as $4 trillion and that *sukuk* holdings could grow to $170 billion by 2010.[59]

But the News Is Not All Bad . . . at Least for Now

Not all the news on sovereign wealth funds is grim for the U.S. economy. In fact, some analysts argue that the reinvestment of monies generated by petrodollar and Asian export-focused countries perpetuates global financial growth. Speaking with reporters at *Time*, Alex Patelis, the head of international economics at Merrill Lynch, declared investors ought to "rejoice at the impetus sovereign wealth funds will provide to continued growth in global asset markets."[60] Michael Pettis, a professor of finance at Peking University and director at New York–based Galileo Global Horizons hedge fund, contends that the economic boom American consumers have enjoyed over the last decade can be directly attributed to the "recycling of the massive U.S. trade deficit." Pettis argues, "Excess U.S. consumption is being converted into global excess savings"[61]—which banks and governments then reinvest to the apparent benefit of almost everyone in the developed world.

This rosy macroeconomic perspective—that reinvestment of profligate U.S. consumer spending serves to drive global financial growth—appears to have won favor with analysts examining the recent spate of government entity and sovereign wealth fund purchases in the international financial sector. In the latter half of 2007, foreign governments went on what can best be described as a "shopping spree," acquiring significant shares in banks and investment houses based in the United States and Europe. To be fair, some of this began before the subprime mortgage crisis broke—and can be explained, particularly in Dubai's case, as efforts to spur development of a Middle East financial center. Many of these purchases, however, occurred during the write-downs associated with the subprime crisis—strongly suggesting that foreign government investment vehicles perceived an opportunity to purchase large swaths of the major international financial houses at fire-sale, smoke-damaged prices.[62] These investments were certainly welcomed by the ailing recipients but beg the question of how these shares may ultimately be used to guide the beneficiaries' decisions in the future.

In any case, *The Wall Street Journal* went so far as to run stories crediting sovereign wealth fund investments in the ailing international financial sector as having "mitigated the damage to equity markets after the summer's subprime problems."[63] In early November 2007, *The Wall Street Journal* also provided comments from Stephen Jen, the head of global currency research at Morgan Stanley, who declared, "I would not be surprised if the sovereign wealth funds played a meaningful role in September, facilitating recovery in emerging markets equities and equities in general." Jen continued by noting, "Sovereign wealth funds could have a much longer investment horizon and a higher tolerance for swings in profits and losses . . . Having such a different temperament from private funds," he concluded, "sovereign wealth funds should reduce the risk of herd behavior."[64]

A similar positive spin on sovereign wealth fund fiscal sector acquisitions appeared in *The Wall Street Journal* reporting on the Abu Dhabi Investment Authority $7.5 billion purchase of 4.9% interest in Citigroup during November 2007. While the Abu Dhabi Investment Authority drew plaudits for getting a "3.4% premium for stepping up when everyone else was fleeing," Citigroup drew equal praise for managing "to raise tax-deductible, tier-one capital . . . [and] locking in a long-term investor who has promised not to meddle *much* in its daily affairs"[65] (italics added). The $10 billion GIC purchase of 9% interest in UBS during December 2007 drew comparable spin. In a press statement announcing the deal, UBS chairman Marcel Ospel declared, "our losses in the U.S. mortgage securities market are substantial but could have been absorbed by our earnings and capital base. Nevertheless, it is important to always maintain a notably strong capital position to support the continued growth of our wealth management business, which is the largest generator of value to UBS shareholders."[66] For his part, Government Investment Corporation Deputy Chairman Tony Tan contended GIC's investment in UBS is a long-term venture, and that the Singapore sovereign wealth fund was not looking for management control of the Swiss bank.[67]

Before moving on, a comment on foreign government investment patterns—at least in the U.S. financial sector—is in order. As of mid-March 2008, it appears there is a limit on even sovereign wealth fund interest in ailing U.S. financial firms. Sovereign wealth fund managers were remarkably absent from the last-minute efforts to rescue Bear Stearns—which left J.P. Morgan to "scoop up the bargain" at approximately $2 a share.[68] This reluctance to participate in the "fire sale" likely comes in the wake of losses that the government investment vehicles suffered purchasing shares in Citigroup (down 38% since the buy) and Morgan Stanley (down 25% since the deal).[69]

Leading to Questions about What It All Means . . .

Clearly there are two sides to this story. Bankers, sovereign wealth fund managers, and some financial reporters would have us believe foreign government acquisition of significant shares in the U.S. and European financial sector is nothing to worry about. Furthermore, as noted at the outset, some U.S. observers are quick to dismiss the sovereign wealth funds as inept giants. These sentiments, as might be expected, are not shared in all quarters. In addition to cautioning about the perils of a shift away from purchases of U.S. Treasury notes, some sovereign wealth fund students point to the risks inherent in the establishment and growth of government investment vehicles whose lack of transparency could cause market instability, whose apparent penchant for iconic properties could abet xenophobic tendencies, and whose purchases could ultimately be used to facilitate political agendas.

Perhaps the earliest words of caution concerning the potential behavior of sovereign wealth funds were issued in a May 2005 article published by the *Central Banking Journal*.[70] Written in the aftermath of South Korea's announcement concerning intentions to establish a sovereign wealth fund, this article warned there were at least three reasons that the growth of these government investment vehicles warranted attention:

> First of all, as this asset pool continues to grow in size and importance, so will its potential impact on various asset markets. Secondly, sovereign wealth funds—while not nearly as homogeneous as central banks or public pension funds—do have a

number of interesting and unique characteristics in common, which, in our opinion, make them a distinct and potentially valuable tool for achieving certain public policy and macroeconomic goals. The third reason to look more closely at sovereign wealth funds is to answer the following question: are central bank reserve managers—at least those among them who have accumulated massive foreign exchange reserves in recent years—starting to act more like sovereign wealth managers?[71]

Interestingly, the author avoids focusing on the potential negatives, choosing instead to close with an upbeat observation that these expanding investment vehicles could "provide new and sophisticated tools to economic and monetary policymakers."[72]

More specific concerns were issued almost two years later—as the growth in sovereign wealth funds began to draw greater attention from American politicians. In June 2007, U.S. Treasury Acting Undersecretary for International Affairs Clay Lowery warned an audience in San Francisco that sovereign wealth funds presented four potential risks:

- Little is known about sovereign wealth fund investment policies, resulting in the potential for minor comments or rumors to cause market volatility as other investors react to what they perceive to be government actions on the acquisitions, mergers, and/or sales fronts.
- Sovereign wealth fund investment policies and/or operating methods could fuel financial protectionism. This is particularly true in the case of exercising voting rights inherent in purchased equity shares. Similarly, if sovereign wealth funds obtain operational control of companies in which they invest, the fact that they are government entities may invite additional scrutiny.
- With so much money invested across a wide range of asset classes, sovereign wealth funds will require strong fiduciary controls and good checks and balances to prevent corruption.
- Once a bureaucracy is created, shutting it down becomes difficult. Given this situation, sovereign wealth funds could impede examination of the policies which abetted their creation and may become self-perpetuating long after serving the intended purpose.[73]

These remarks were echoed by analysts at the International Monetary Fund (IMF) in September 2007. Writing for *Finance and Development* magazine, Simon Johnson, economic counselor and director of the IMF Research Department, warned of the "dearth of information" concerning the assets, management, and investment strategies of sovereign wealth funds. Johnson was particularly concerned with the potential of these investment vehicles to generate protectionism, as "recent developments in the world suggest there may be a perception that certain foreign governments shouldn't be allowed to own what are regarded as an economy's 'commanding heights.'"[74]

In a publication titled "The New Power Brokers: How Oil, Asia, Hedge Funds, and Private Equity are Shaping Global Capital Markets," McKinsey Global

Institute offered a slightly more nuanced version of these warnings. Using what might be best described as politically neutral "market analyst" English, the McKinsey analysts concluded that wealth accumulating in government invest-ment vehicles offered "new risks for the global financial system."[75] Specifically, these risks are:

- "The new liquidity brought by petrodollars and Asian central banks may be inflating some asset prices and enabling excessive lending."
- "The government connections of Asian central banks and petrodollar sov-ereign wealth funds may introduce an element of political considerations in their investments. This could lower economic value creation in host economies and, moreover, distort the market signals that allow the financial markets to function efficiently."[76]

On 14 November 2007, the Senate Committee on Banking, Housing, and Urban Affairs held a day of testimony on sovereign wealth funds and foreign investment in the United States. In prepared remarks read to members of the committee, U.S. Treasury Undersecretary for International Affairs David H. McCormick declared that sovereign wealth funds presented three "potential" concerns. First, and "primary among them, is a risk that sovereign wealth funds could provoke a new wave of investment protectionism, which would be very harmful to the global economy." "Second, transactions involving investment by sovereign wealth funds, as with other types of foreign investment, may raise legitimate national security concerns." And, third, "sovereign wealth funds may raise concerns related to financial stability. Sovereign wealth funds can repre-sent large, concentrated, and often nontransparent positions in certain markets and asset classes. Actual shifts in their asset allocations could cause market volatility. In fact, even perceived shifts or rumors can cause volatility as the market reacts to what it perceives sovereign wealth funds to be doing."[77]

Undersecretary McCormick's remarks appear to represent the Bush adminis-tration's overarching policy concerns vis-à-vis the emerging purchasing power of sovereign wealth funds. Indeed, the primary points offered in McCormick's presentation were echoed in early December 2007 by Christopher Cox, Chairman of the Securities and Exchange Commission (SEC). During his speech at the American Enterprise Institute's annual Gauer Lecture, Cox argued U.S. policies concerning sovereign wealth funds needed to "address the underlying issues of transparency, independent regulation, de-politicization of investment decisions, and conflicts of interest."[78]

So where does this leave us? As of March 2008, this "what does it mean" discussion was focused on three major concerns associated with the behavior of sovereign wealth funds. First is transparency—as embodied in the potential for market instability generated by rumors of government buying or selling. Second is the possibility of protectionism spurred by "the specter of undemocratic governments buying up whole U.S. companies, or stakes large enough to have a big influence."[79] And third is national security. As Christopher Cox put it, "the fundamental question presented by state-owned public companies and sovereign wealth funds does not so much concern the advisability of foreign ownership, but rather of government ownership."[80] Translated: the United States and other nations like foreign direct investment but worry about the implications of foreign government direct investment—specifically, how this investment can be used as an instrument of national power.

So What Are We Doing to Answer These Concerns?

Given these concerns about transparency, protectionism, and national security implications, it would seem logical to conclude that U.S. policy makers are actively seeking to address the issues associated with the growth of sovereign wealth funds. Unfortunately, aside from much hand-wringing and the application of a large political "band-aid," Washington has done little to prepare for this emerging challenge to the domestic and foreign policy-making communities.[81] Some of this inaction may be pinned on philosophical differences, but one suspects that much of the perceived acquiescence to these funds' investments is simply attributable to failed understanding of just how poorly existing legislation serves U.S. national interests.[82]

Addressing transparency: There is universal agreement that with few exceptions—specifically New Zealand and Norway—sovereign wealth funds are notoriously opaque. The degree to which this becomes a problem for the U.S. policy-making community was made clear—no pun intended—during the 14 November 2007 Senate Committee on Banking, Housing, and Urban Affairs hearing. Speaking to the Committee, Edwin Truman, senior fellow at the Peterson Institute for International Economics, presented a chart scoring the sovereign wealth funds using four criteria: structure, governance, accountability, and behavior.[83] Truman and his team found the highest scores in New Zealand and Norway with 24 and 23 points, respectively, on a scale ranging from 0 to 25.[84] The bottom end of the scale—this should be disquieting for anyone who recalls the previous table on financial sector acquisitions in 2007—United Arab Emirates' (UAE) Abu Dhabi Investment Authority (0.50 points), Qatar Investment Authority (2.00 points), Government of Singapore Investment Corporation (2.25 points), Brunei Investment Agency (2.50 points), and UAE's Mubadala Development Company (3.50 points).[85]

Overall, Truman reported the average score was 10.27 points, with six of the world's ten largest sovereign wealth funds scoring at or below this international mean.[86] U.S. politicians are aware of concerns associated with this lack of transparency but to date have done little to address the problem. In his 21 June 2007 remarks, Clay Lowery stated, "I believe the IMF and World Bank could take a very useful first step by developing best practices for sovereign wealth funds, perhaps through a joint task force." This was not a throwaway line, as Lowery noted, "the IMF has the requisite expertise on wider systemic and macroeconomic policies . . . the World Bank is knowledgeable about country governance and accounting and fiduciary issues, including the fiduciary duty these funds have to their citizens as investors."[87]

During his 14 November 2007 testimony before the Senate Committee on Banking, Housing, and Urban Affairs, Lowery's replacement, David McCormick, stated U.S. concerns about sovereign wealth fund transparency were being addressed through two U.S. Treasury initiatives. First, "we have proposed that the international community collaborate on a multilateral framework for best practices." Second, "we have proposed the Organization for Economic Cooperation and Development (OECD) . . . identify best practices for countries that receive foreign government–controlled investment . . . These should focus on proportionality, predictability, and accountability." McCormick's statement was of note as this was the first time a U.S. official had publicly emphasized focusing on both sides of the investment equation."[88]

SEC Chairman Cox also acknowledged the transparency problem during his 5 December 2007 remarks but suggested a different approach to the problem. According to Cox, "from the SEC's standpoint, working to ensure the transparency of sovereign business and investment will be of paramount importance." He then went on to imply the SEC plans to take an active role in ensuring this transparency by stating, "we will continue to pursue a cooperative and collaborative dialogue with our regulatory counterparts in other nations, and [will] engage them regarding the best way to apply our regulatory approaches in light of the growing presence of government-owned businesses and investment funds in our markets."[89]

In short, the Bush administration appears to have no ready response to this transparency problem. Nor, however, did most of the U.S. presidential candidates. For instance, the Clinton campaign provided an official statement on sovereign wealth funds and their lack of transparency in a 19 November 2007 Web posting. The statement largely mimics the Bush administration by declaring, "the funds don't have to disclose their holdings, investment objectives, investment returns, or management structures. Consequently we do not know whether they are introducing unnecessary risks into markets or whether they are being used for non-commercial ends." The solution, according to the Clinton campaign, is for "multinational financial institutions like the World Bank and the IMF to craft transparency guidelines for sovereign wealth funds."[90]

The Obama campaign offered little more insight. Speaking to reporters on 7 February 2008, Barack Obama declared, "I am concerned if these . . . sovereign wealth funds are motivated by more than just market considerations, and that's obviously a possibility." The candidate went on to note, "if they are buying big chunks of financial institutions and their board(s) of directors influences how credit flows in this country and they may be swayed by political considerations or foreign policy considerations, I think that is a concern." That said, Obama then stated he did not have a problem with foreign investment in the United States.[91]

Interestingly, as suggested by the Clinton and Obama campaign statements, there is a debate as to the actual level of volatility that the sovereign wealth funds' lack of transparency introduces into the market. *The Wall Street Journal* and the Bush administration appear to disagree on this issue. Echoing sentiments Stephen Jen expressed during November, in early December 2007 the *Journal* reported, "because most sovereign wealth funds buy long-term investments, the funds could have a stabilizing influence on world markets, particularly during periods of high volatility and tight credit." Nevertheless, the newspaper then went on to note that the lack of transparency associated with most sovereign wealth funds' limited ability to raise risk tolerance in financial markets—because so little "is known about many of the funds' investment strategies, structures, or holdings."[92]

Not surprisingly, the fund managers are aware of this concern. The China Investment Corporation, for instance, has made a concerted effort to assure international observers that Beijing seeks to make the government investment vehicle's operations largely transparent. This CIC campaign began in earnest in early August 2007, when Chinese authorities publicly announced the names of the fund's core management team.[93] By early September, members of this management team were reassuring reporters and foreign observers that CIC will be "a passive investor . . . most of our money will be [invested] through outsourcing to fund managers instead of . . . direct investment."[94] Staying on message, in mid-November, the new CIC chairman told an international audience in Beijing his organization would act "as a force to stabilize markets as needed." He also declared CIC's main priority is financial performance, as the management team is under "big pressures" to generate profits.[95]

By mid-December 2007, CIC efforts to assure outside observers had been honed even further. Speaking at a public forum in Beijing, China Investment Corporation President Gao Xiqing—a Duke-trained lawyer with Wall Street experience—announced "our main consideration is economic factors, and we'll run the fund based on business principles." CIC, he continued, will "play by international rules."[96] In an apparent effort to demonstrate a commitment to this pledge, CIC also announced it would seek to hire external money managers to invest in global equity markets. In an online posting, spokespersons for the Chinese sovereign wealth fund said they would seek professionals to actively manage four investment categories: global stocks, emerging markets, Asia—excluding Japan—and other developed markets outside the United States.[97]

Battling protectionism: Despite repeated official assurances since 1983 that "the United States believes foreign investors should be able to make the same kind of investment, under the same conditions, as nationals of the host country," businesses from around the world have discovered setting up shop in America can be a political nightmare.[98] This situation has only grown worse since 9/11. In 2000 foreign investors spent an estimated $321 billion in the United States. By 2003 that figure had dropped to $67 billion, and had only climbed back to $180 billion in 2006.[99] The tumult surrounding the 2006 Dubai Ports World attempt to acquire operating rights for U.S. ports in Baltimore, Miami, New Jersey, New Orleans, New York, and Philadelphia[100] is a classic example of the political difficulties a foreign investor can confront—and is, unfortunately, not the only such episode in the last six years.[101] Americans are sensitive to foreign ownership and express these concerns in no uncertain manner to their elected representatives.[102]

The problem, as most politicians will attest, is that this sensitivity does not reflect a complete understanding of how the United States is now a witting participant in the global economy. In fact, the full scope of the dilemma confronting American politicians only becomes clear when one learns that foreign direct investment provides millions of U.S. jobs. According to the U.S.-based Organization for International Investment, subsidiaries of foreign firms employ 5.1 million Americans. And, although the total stock of foreign long-term investment in the United States has now reached $1.8 trillion, the American share of global foreign direct investment has dropped from 20% a decade ago to 14% in 2006.[103]

Further cold water for this protectionist mindset is evident in the figures cited during Stuart E. Eizenstat's 24 May 2006 testimony before the House Committee on Homeland Security. Eizenstat (President Carter's Chief White House Domestic Policy Adviser; President Clinton's U.S. ambassador to the European Union; Undersecretary of Commerce for International Trade; Undersecretary of State for Economic, Business, and Agricultural Affairs; and Deputy Secretary of the Treasury) told the gathered audience:

> We need to be clear-eyed about our vital national interests. Little direct foreign investment comes from the Middle East: 94% of foreign assets in America are owned by companies from the 25 industrialized, democratic OECD member countries, and 73% of all foreign investments in the U.S. are made by European companies. Our traditionally open investment climate has greatly benefited the American people. At a time when concerns are raised about the "outsourcing" of jobs abroad, foreign investment represents "in-sourcing," a vote of confidence by foreign firms and investors in the openness, flexibility and strength of the U.S. economy.[104]

Eizenstat is hardly alone in suggesting U.S. fears of foreign investment—particularly from Middle Eastern countries—are overstated. As the Council on Foreign Relations notes, the "country with the most holdings in the United States is the United Kingdom, followed by Japan, Germany, the Netherlands, and France."[105]

Even this data fails to reassure the skeptics, rendering policy decisions on sovereign wealth fund investments difficult at best. During the same 21 June 2007 speech in which he warned of the risks inherent in the growth of sovereign wealth funds, Clay Lowery also declared the U.S. government's role in monitoring this development was to "make our investment regime as open and consistent as possible for welcoming sovereign wealth fund investment."[106] On

13 November 2007, Commerce Secretary Carlos Gutierrez took a like approach by stating, "Let me make it clear: as a matter of policy the American government welcomes and encourages foreign investment." His solution for combating against protectionist sentiments: "a public education campaign on the benefits of foreign direct investment."[107]

A day later, U.S. Treasury Undersecretary for International Affairs David McCormick took a similar tack while addressing the Senate Committee on Banking, Housing, and Urban Affairs. Arguing that the U.S. "remains committed to open investment," McCormick contended the Treasury Department is working to combat protectionist sentiments by pressing for greater transparency from the sovereign wealth funds and emphasized the role the new Foreign Investment and National Security Act plays in requiring "heightened scrutiny of foreign government–controlled investments."[108] This line of reasoning also appeared in Christopher Cox's 5 December 2007 presentation. Cox told his audience that, rather than "betraying our commitment to open markets," Washington should "address the underlying issues of transparency, independent regulation, de-politicization of investment decisions, and conflicts of interest."[109]

As of March 2008 a few of the U.S. presidential candidates offered similar comments—albeit with less detail. A sampling of the campaign Web sites reveals the following illustrative examples. The Clinton campaign held, "We welcome foreign investment in America. But we must be especially vigilant when the foreign investor is actually a government."[110] On the Republican side, Mike Huckabee offered the following: "I believe that globalization, done right, done fairly, can be a blessing for our society."[111]

The Bush administration and these campaign statements have done little to cool concerns about potential negative consequences. In fact, one might argue that official hearings in Washington have actually fueled protectionist sentiments. A 7 February 2008 session of the U.S.-China Economic and Security Review Commission is a case in point. During testimony offered by elected officials and academics, the commission members were informed, "the U.S. government must stand up for the American people in the face of this opaque and increasingly-powerful threat to our sovereignty,"[112] and that "in considering America's policy options, it is critical to note that sovereign wealth funds invariably represent the fruit of the poisoned free market tree."[113] Given these statements, it is hardly surprising to learn that U.S. public opinion concerning sovereign wealth fund investment is overwhelmingly negative. A mid-February 2008 survey by Public Strategies, a political consulting firm, found 49% of Americans questioned thought foreign government investment harmed the U.S. economy, and 55% felt the purchases were a threat to national security. Of note, these responses came despite the fact only 6% of the respondents had "seen or heard anything recently" about sovereign wealth funds.[114]

It is only fair to note protectionism is not a uniquely American phenomenon. Some of the United States's largest trading partners are equally suspect about the concept of foreign direct investment—particularly government-controlled foreign direct investment. In a mid-July 2007 speech, Sir John Gieve, deputy governor of the Bank of England, warned that "the switch of reserve-rich countries from lenders to owners of financial or real assets is . . . likely to lead to political tensions and calls for protectionism."[115] Angela Merkel, the German chancellor, was blunter, expressing concern at the way these government-controlled investment vehicles have acquired assets inside the European Union. Merkel went so far as to declare that sovereign wealth funds were frequently driven by "political and other motivations." She also argued, "This is a new phenomenon which we must tackle with some urgency."[116]

Tokyo is also wary of the motivations underlying sovereign wealth fund investments. According to *The Wall Street Journal*, over the last two years the Japanese government has introduced guidelines on implementing "poison pill" takeover defenses and a plan limiting outside firms' employment of shares in purchases of domestic firms. Although some critics claim this legislative activity was Tokyo's effort to establish barriers to investment by foreign private equity firms and other well-capitalized funds, the Japanese argue the moves were driven by national security concerns.[117] Similar sentiments are heard in Taiwan. In a 22 October 2007 editorial, the *Taipei Times* argued concerns about Beijing's new sovereign wealth fund were driven by "a fear that 'political' rather than 'commercial' purposes might be behind the [China Investment Corporation's] investments." While the *Taipei Times* essentially warned against undue protectionism, the newspaper also declared that "the government has the power to block would-be investments if they pose a threat to the nation's financial market and to national security. No one should compromise on issues such as risk management, transparency and accountability associated with the [sovereign wealth] funds."[118]

Is this protectionist sentiment justified? Sovereign wealth fund managers are certainly seeking to assuage this political sensitivity through carefully crafted publicity campaigns and by avoiding thresholds that would automatically trip official investigations of their behavior.[119] Each of the recent financial sector acquisitions has been accompanied by a declared intention to stay out of the front office[120]—and a reaching out to potential congressional critics long before the acquisitions became front-page news.[121] This public relations and political campaign comes only after the investors have carefully avoided federal "trip wires." It is no accident that the financial sector acquisitions remained below 10% for investment firms and 5% for banking interests. Reaching either of these respective thresholds would have almost automatically triggered action at the Committee on Foreign Investment in the United States or the Federal Reserve. In short, sovereign wealth fund managers are well aware of the protectionist dilemma confronting American politicians and are doing their best to avoid the problem.

Providing for national security: The art of balancing protectionist political sentiments with a desire to promote free and open markets comes to the fore in addressing concerns about preserving America's national security. The United

States has a long history of attempting to accomplish this feat—with decidedly mixed results. While Washington's legislative efforts to address the national security risks associated with foreign direct investment arguably may be traced to World War I, more recent official activities in this venue began in the mid-1970s following the oil crisis of 1973–74 and the subsequent oil crisis of 1979. Rising investment in America by members of the Organization of Petroleum Exporting Countries (OPEC) drove establishment of the Committee on Foreign Investment in the United States (CFIUS) in 1975 and the passage of the International Emergency Economic Powers Act (IEEPA) in 1977.[122]

While one can argue the creation of CFIUS and the passage of IEEPA marked the pinnacle of recent efforts to address American concerns about the threat that foreign direct investment presents our national security, the peak of this campaign was not reached until 1988, when Congress passed the Exon-Florio Amendment to the Defense Production Act. Coming at the height of public concerns about Japanese mergers and acquisitions in the United States,[123] the Exon-Florio Amendment gave the president broad powers to block foreign purchases or takeover of an American company if that transaction might "threaten to impair" U.S. national security.[124] As a means of accomplishing this mission, when Exon-Florio became law the president delegated his initial review and decision-making authority, as well as his investigative responsibility, to CFIUS—placing the committee at the heart of Washington's efforts to deal with the potential threat posed by sovereign wealth funds.

A cursory review of CFIUS responsibilities—including authority to review a transaction upon voluntary filing by either party or upon an agency notice filed by one of the committee's members—would suggest that Exon-Florio was sufficient to meet all but the worst critics' fears. Staffed by the most senior members of 12 executive branch offices[125]—or their appointed representatives—and chaired by the Treasury Department, CFIUS provides a 90-day review, investigation, and presidential decision window that seems tailored for Wall Street's tight timelines,[126] yet thorough enough to avoid transactions that endanger U.S. national security. Close observers of the process, however, have not been impressed.[127]

Among the problems that almost immediately came to the fore was the Exon-Florio Act's failure to restrict CFIUS discretion: the committee was not time-limited, nor was there a statute of limitations. Critics also noted the statute did not define "national security"; there was considerable breadth in the term "foreign control;" and CFIUS never specified what constitutes "credible evidence"—the criterion for causing the president to block a proposed transaction.[128] Perhaps the most serious of these problems was the failure to define "national security." Not surprisingly, the Exon-Florio authors had anticipated this criticism, noting in the preamble to the regulations, "The Committee rejected [all of the recommended definitions] because they could improperly curtail the president's broad authority to protect national security."[129] Furthermore, they sought to prevent undue ambiguity by identifying a number of criteria the president should consider in evaluating a potential threat. These criteria included:

- Domestic production needed for projected national defense requirements
- The capability and capacity of domestic industries to meet national defense requirements—including availability of human resources, products, technology, materials, and other supplies and services
- The control of domestic industries and commercial activity by foreign citizens as it affects U.S. capability and capacity to meet national defense requirements
- The potential effects of the transaction on the sales of military goods, equipment, or technology to a state that supports terrorism or proliferates missile technology or chemical and biological weapons
- The potential effects of the transaction on U.S. technological leadership in areas affecting American national security[130]

At first blush, this would appear a fairly all-inclusive list. Unimpressed by the criteria, however, congressional critics of the Exon-Florio Amendment sought to further define when investigations of a potential transaction should be mandated. In 1993 the Byrd Amendment to the National Defense Authorization Act revised the Exon-Florio legislation such that an investigation must be undertaken "in any instances in which an entity controlled by or acting on behalf of a foreign government seeks to engage in any merger, acquisition, or takeover of a U.S. entity that could affect the national security of the United States."[131] As the Dubai Ports World controversy ultimately revealed, this amendment also failed to meet the mark. Why? CFIUS did not extend its review into the 45-day investigation period despite the fact Dubai Ports World was clearly owned by an entity answering to the government of the United Arab Emirates.

In many ways the Dubai Ports World controversy was simply good political cover for revisiting a legislative area that many lawmakers had already found wanting. To understand congressional criticism of the CFIUS process as it existed in 2006, we need to examine two sets of data—merger and acquisition activity in the United States from 1996 to 2006, and CFIUS investigations instituted during the same time period.

Now compare these figures to reporting on CFIUS investigations during the same time period. There certainly appears to be little official impediment to foreign direct investment in the United States, nor would it appear that CFIUS was working overtime to protect the nation's security.[132]

Given the marked difference in the number of reported non-U.S. firms acquiring or merging with American companies from 1996 to 2006 (9,995) and the relatively paltry number of CFIUS investigations during the same time period (32), the legislative initiatives following the Dubai Ports World controversy should have been no surprise. What is surprising, however, is how little this new legislation may have actually changed the CFIUS process. The Foreign Investment and National Security Act signed into law on 26 July 2007 in many ways:

Table 1.2 Merger and Acquisitions (M&A) in the United States, 1996–2006[133]

Year	Total M&A	U.S. Firms Acquiring U.S. Firms	Non-U.S. Firms Acquiring U.S. Firms	U.S. Firms Acquiring Non-U.S. Firms
1996	7,347	5,585	628	1,134
1997	8,479	6,317	775	1,387
1998	10,193	7,575	971	1,647
1999	9,173	6,449	1,148	1,576
2000	8,853	6,032	1,264	1,557
2001	6,296	4,269	923	1,104
2002	5,497	3,989	700	808
2003	5,959	4,357	722	880
2004	7,031	5,084	813	1,134
2005	7,600	5,463	977	1,160
2006	8,203	5,853	1,074	1,276

(1) simply codified the existing CFIUS process; (2) only potentially increased the presidential investigative requirements by adding yet another undefined area—critical infrastructure—to the list of criteria warranting executive review of business transactions; and (3) appears to have only marginally improved congressional oversight.[134]

Table 1.3 CFIUS Notification and Investigation—1996–2006[135]

Year	Notifications	Investigations	Notices Withdrawn	Presidential Decision
1996	55	0	0	0
1997	62	0	0	0
1998	65	2	2	0
1999	79	0	0	0
2000	72	1	0	1
2001	55	1	1	1
2002	43	0	0	0
2003	41	2	1	1
2004	53	2	2	0
2005	65	2	2	0
2006	113	7	5	2

Little substantive change to the CFIUS process. The 2007 Foreign Investment and National Security Act largely retains the existing CFIUS process and structure. On the procedural side, there was no change to the 90-day notification, investigation, and decision timeline. Although critics of the existing process have succeeded in adding a provision mandating investigations of acquisitions by state-owned companies, this step may be eliminated if the Secretary of the Treasury and the secretary of the lead agency charged with a specific case determine the transaction will not impair U.S. national security. In response to critics' charges the CFIUS process had been delegated to "flunkies" with no authority, the committee must now be staffed with department secretaries or their deputies.[136] Additionally, the Director of National Intelligence is now a nonvoting and *ex officio* member of the committee—formalizing a role that the intelligence community was long thought to already be tasked with filling.

This is not to say all the 2007 changes to the CFIUS process were completely toothless. For instance, the withdrawal procedure is now much more stringent. Originally CFIUS regulations stated written requests to withdraw a transaction notification "will ordinarily be granted." The 2007 Foreign Investment and National Security Act removes this proviso and declares withdrawals must be "approved by the Committee." Similarly, the CFIUS "evergreen" authority—the right to reopen reviews and possibly undo a transaction even after original approval has been granted—has now been formally established. Follow-up review is permitted if: (1) a party submitted false or misleading material information in, or omitted material information from a CFIUS notice; or (2) the entity subject to a mitigation agreement intentionally and materially breaches the agreement, and the committee determines that there is no other means of addressing this breach.[137]

Further muddying the criteria for executive branch review. Like Exon-Florio, the 2007 Foreign Investment and National Security Act fails to provide a definition for "national security." In fact, this act further complicates the requirements for executive review by adding the need to protect "critical infrastructure" to the criteria list. According to the 2007 act, "critical infrastructure" is "systems and assets, whether physical or virtual, so vital to the United States that the incapacity or destruction of such systems or assets would have a debilitating impact on national security." Critics have suggested the definition could be used to encompass up to 75% of the American economy. This is a stinging rebuke that may not be far off the mark given the fact the 2007 National Strategy for Homeland Security identifies "critical infrastructure sectors" as agriculture, banking and finance, chemical industry, defense industrial base, emergency services, energy, food, government, information and telecommunications, postal and shipping, public health, transportation, and water.[138]

The 2007 law attempts to prevent such an interpretation by providing additional criteria potentially warranting a CFIUS review of a business transaction. These new criteria include:

- Potential national security-related effects on U.S. critical infrastructure, including energy assets
- Potential national security-related effects on U.S. critical technologies (also not further defined)
- If the transaction in question is controlled by a foreign government
- Potential impact on projected U.S. energy and critical resource requirements
- Other factors the president or the committee may deem appropriate

Despite this bid for clarity, the 2007 Foreign Investment and National Security Act potentially places every business transaction involving a foreign entity on the table for CFIUS review and does little to clarify the ambiguities in key terms that allow cases like the Dubai Ports World deal to slip through the cracks.

Increased congressional oversight. Likely in response to business concerns that leaked transactions could spoil a deal or adversely impact a company's market value, authors of the 1988 Exon-Florio provision codified confidentiality requirements in their legislation. The 1988 legislation stipulated that any information or document filed during the CFIUS process may not be made public "except as may be relevant to any administrative or judicial action or proceeding." Cognizant of the fact, however, the executive branch could use this proviso to preclude congressional oversight; the 1988 statute also declares this confidentiality provision "shall not be construed to prevent disclosure to either House of Congress or to any duly authorized committee or subcommittee of the Congress." Furthermore, Exon-Florio required the president to provide a written report to the Secretary of the Senate and the Clerk of the House detailing decisions and actions relevant to any transaction that was subject to a 45-day CFIUS investigation. Finally the executive branch was required to provide quadrennial reports to the Congress, indicating whether there is evidence of (1) a coordinated strategy by one or more countries to acquire U.S. firms involved in research, development, and production of critical technologies, or (2) industrial espionage activities by foreign governments against private U.S. companies engaged in the acquisition, development, or manufacture of critical technologies.[139]

Outraged by the perceived White House failure to act appropriately in response to the proposed Dubai Ports World deal, members of Congress sought to toughen these reporting requirements in the 2007 Foreign Investment and National Security Act. Under the new statute, CFIUS is required to notify Congress and certain congressional committees, either at the end of a 30-day review that does not result in a 45-day investigation, or after a 45-day investigation that does not result in sending the matter to the president. According to attorneys familiar with the notification process, as a means of avoiding a repeat of the Dubai Ports World incident, CFIUS must include in these reports descriptions of the "transaction at issue and the determinative factors" that resulted in the committee's decision. The reports must also "certify there are no unresolved national security concerns with the transaction."[140] To avoid White House pleas of ignorance, Congress requires the reports be signed by the CFIUS chair—the Treasury Secretary—and the head of the lead investigative agency. Furthermore, the 2007 act stipulates this authority cannot be delegated below the level of officials appointed by the president with the advice and consent of the Senate.

Under the 2007 act, Congress may also require a briefing on any transaction either during or after the CFIUS process. This presentation is to cover compliance with national security mitigation agreements. Finally, as a catch-all, CFIUS must submit annual reports to Congress by 31 July every year on transactions covered during the previous 12 months. Of note, even with all these new reporting guidelines, the confidentiality requirements drafted in 1988 remain in effect. The question, of course, is: Does this new process work?

The initial answer would appear to be no. First, the American and international legal communities are acutely aware the U.S. national security review process for business transactions has "dramatically" increased over the last two years.[141] Second, businesses are even more cognizant of this enhanced CFIUS oversight—particularly the resulting public and political scrutiny. In response, attorneys are warning businesses to be wary of transactions that are quick to draw CFIUS attention—specifically, U.S. companies with export-controlled technologies, classified contracts, or technologies critical to national defense, and/or instances when "CFIUS member agencies have . . . 'derogative intelligence' about a foreign purchaser."[142] The business community, on the other hand, has sought to disarm critics through quiet information campaigns—for instance, notifying potential congressional critics and downplaying the perceived danger to U.S. national security.[143] Finally, there appear to be efforts afoot to place the entire CFIUS process back behind closed doors and out of the press spotlight. While the executive branch has apparently always sought to keep CFIUS activities out of the news, members of Congress are now joining the effort. On 11 December 2007, Representatives Barney Frank (D-MA) and Carolyn Maloney (D-NY) sent a letter to the White House expressing their concerns with "recent leaks of confidential and classified information related to the Committee on Foreign Investment in the United States." The two members of Congress state that "selective leaking . . . while a [CFIUS] review is ongoing damages the integrity of the national security assessment and undermines the ability of the United States to continue to attract foreign investment."[144]

What Is the Next Step?

First, we must recognize that sovereign wealth funds—even in a few emerging market economies—are here to stay. This is true regardless of how much the current situation seems to run against the grain. As Lawrence Summers, former Secretary of the Treasury, notes, sovereign wealth funds—particularly those maintained by emerging-market economies—seem a complete contradiction of how the international finance community was intended to operate. As Summers perceives the current situation:

> The international financial architecture was designed under the presumption that the flow of money would be from the core to the periphery, from richer economies to the poorer economies, from more slowly growing mature economies to rising emerging markets . . . The point is that, not only has the pattern of aggregate capital flows across international borders changed significantly, but also that we are in a very different world from the one that the current international architecture was intended to serve.[145]

How different? Quite frankly, a complete reverse of what the financial community initially expected—money now flows from the "periphery" to the "core," and central bankers are looking to make more than a 1% return on their national savings. As Summers argues, it is no longer fiscally responsible for central bankers to place accumulated foreign reserves in short-term liquid securities offered by industrial countries. These funds should instead be invested in a manner intended to maximize returns and minimize opportunity costs.[146]

Summers' advice should come as a blunt warning for those charged with forging the United States' future fiscal policies. Foreign central bankers are preparing to search for greener pastures—to sink their funds in a manner that will no longer subsidize interest rates for U.S. consumers. In Summers' words:

> . . . the typical central bank portfolio (consisting of 0–3 years dollar-denominated Treasuries) would have earned about 1% in real terms, over the last 60 years. In contrast, a diversified portfolio of stocks and bonds, similar to a typical pension portfolio (60% stocks/40% bonds) would have earned a real return of approximately 6% and a portfolio invested entirely in stocks has earned in excess of 7%.[147]

Given this insight, it is time to rethink those dismissive statements about government bureaucrats being capable of "only" managing to earn returns of 8%. Few investors I know would exchange this return for the 1% apparently to be won from more "careful" investment in U.S. Treasury notes. In fact, Beijing seems to have already learned this lesson. In 2004 China bought 20% of all U.S. Treasury securities issued; in 2005 that figure rose to 30%; and in 2006 it was 36%. In 2007 Beijing reversed course and has become a net seller of Treasury securities.[148]

What does this mean for U.S. fiscal policy? The most immediate problem will be continuing to make official U.S. securities attractive to profit-seeking government bankers. We must keep in mind that these are officials who already maintain the prescribed "safety margin" in foreign reserves. They are now looking for a maximum return on excess national earnings using potentially risky investments. As such, U.S. Federal Reserve interest cuts are not likely to draw much favorable attention or foreign buyers for Treasury notes. There are simply too many other options in today's global economy for central bankers to simply continue investing in the historic low-return old favorite.

Second, if we are going to guard national security against the potential risk presented by sovereign wealth funds, we are going to have to do better than ambiguous definitions and relatively blind "trip wires." Ambiguous legislation in a litigious society like the United States only serves to enrich the attorneys; it does nothing for an entrepreneur's bottom line. Terms such as "national security," "critical infrastructure," or even "foreign control" need to be clearly defined. How might this be accomplished without unduly restricting executive branch flexibility? Consider the case of Japan. Elected officials charged with protecting the world's second largest economy maintain a list of 137 specific items that the government considers sensitive from a national security standpoint. This list includes: specialty steel, carbon fiber, machine tools, and other products deemed strategically important because they could be diverted to military use, such as the production of nuclear weapons or missiles.[149] The United States should consider a similar option—not only would this reduce legal ambiguities that serve to drive up attorneys' fees, it might also help draw foreign investors back to our shores as businesses would no longer have to fret about the potential of being drawn into a political and public fray because American lawmakers could not agree on what constitutes a threat. Furthermore, this specificity would help reduce CFIUS processing times—and allow the committee to be used for more fruitful ventures, like helping predict future risks and updating the proposed list of critical industries.

As for "trip wires," the 5 and 10% rules currently dictating mandatory reporting for firms pursuing mergers and acquisitions in the United States is clearly out of date and of little value. When the expenditure of $7.5 billion to buy a 4.9% share of a major U.S bank or $5 billion to purchase 9.9 % of an internationally renowned investment firm does not automatically dictate executive branch review, it's time to rewrite the rules. A rapid scan of major U.S. corporations—for instance, General Electric or General Motors—reveals that the largest shareholders only own 8% of the business. How can foreign purchase of even larger stakes be allowed to pass unchallenged simply because existing trip wires don't demand action? Furthermore, are these government-owned funds really going to "pass" on management decisions after investing this much money? Perhaps it's time to get these non-interference pledges in writing—or demand that shares be placed in a blind trust where they cannot be used to influence board decisions.

Finally, the United States needs to help the international community draw up a list of standards or best practices for sovereign wealth funds—and then ensure that nations adhere to these guidelines. This is a task of no mean importance; failure to accomplish this mission places markets at risk and suggests these funds could indeed be used as a coercive element of national power. These proposed guidelines should include the measures incorporated in Edwin Truman's evaluative listing—structure, governance, transparency, and behavior[150]—but they also must account for the fact that these are *investment vehicles*, organizations intended to provide a reasonable return on national funds. One concrete suggestion in seeking to accomplish this task is to start with the rule book employed by the Norwegian Government Pension Fund.

The Norwegians know transparency is the key concern, and act accordingly. As Norway's finance minister told *The Wall Street Journal* in November 2007, "transparency is the main issue."[151] One means of ensuring that this dictate reaches Oslo's fund managers—they cannot purchase more than a 5% stake in any one company. They also must adhere to ethics guidelines that prohibit acquiring stock in firms with human rights and other ethical concerns. Are these guidelines met? Decide for yourself. The Norwegian government requires the pension fund managers to publish their annual report—and the results of an independent audit—online every year.[152] Perhaps most tellingly—students typically ask the hardest and most embarrassing questions—Norway is willing to share its lessons and guidelines with others, an offer most recently considered in Chile and Russia.[153]

In short, we should be worried about sovereign wealth funds—because Adam Smith was wrong; the agents of a prince are not always careless about how they spend the regime's funds. For the U.S. taxpayer these decisions would have significant domestic and foreign implications—from how much it takes to purchase a home, to understanding who really controls the international supply of money. The continued enrichment of these funds also speaks to a potential transition of power in the international community. While the use of armed might remains an option for only a few select nations, manipulation of whole economies through careful investment of sovereign wealth appears a growing option for many more regimes. These are not issues that will cause us—or our presidential candidates—to lose sleep today; but tomorrow, or next week, or perhaps next year, one can predict long nights of tossing and turning.

CHAPTER 2

BIRTH OF A SOVEREIGN WEALTH FUND: THE CHINA INVESTMENT CORPORATION

China's sovereign wealth funds threaten a loss of American sovereignty. This danger lies in . . . China's ability to use its vast foreign reserves to destabilize the international financial system in times of conflict—and thereby bully American politicians into submission. In this sense, if China's central bank represents the atomic bomb in China's "financial nuclear option," its rapidly growing sovereign wealth fund will eventually represent a much higher megaton-yielding hydrogen bomb.

—Peter Navarro, Testimony to the U.S.-China Economic and
Security Review Commission, 7 February 2008

While the number of potential candidates that could be used as an object lesson on sovereign wealth fund birthing pains has swelled in recent years, Beijing's China Investment Corporation offers the best—and most controversial—example of how these official government investment vehicles are perceived as a peril and potential for America. China's emergence as a global economic competitor, so long awaited on Wall Street, seems to have caught the U.S. policy community asleep at the switch. Like the proverbial rail yard employee, American politicians appear to have missed a chance to send the roaring China Economic Express down the right track. Or did they? Eager to reap the economic benefits associated with access to China's cheap labor markets, American manufacturers—and presumably the politicians representing their interests in Washington—watched with avarice and wariness as Beijing racked up trade figures perceived to be unmatched anywhere else on the planet.[1]

The data speaks for itself. In 2007, China's global trade surplus surged 48% to a new record of $262.2 billion. Chinese exports in 2007 were up 25.7% for a total of $1.22 trillion, while Beijing's imports expanded 20.8% to $955.8 billion.[2]

Not surprisingly, this mounting trade surplus did wonders for China's foreign exchange reserves—now estimated to be over $1.53 trillion.[3] As a means of placing China's economic performance in context, consider that in 2006 China's foreign reserves were approximately $1.07 trillion, and in 1992 that figure was only $19.4 billion. More astoundingly, China's foreign exchange reserves only surpassed the $100 billion mark in 1996. It took another five years for Beijing's foreign exchange holdings to reach $200 billion, and it was not until 2004 that China amassed over $500 billion in this account.

The rapid growth of China's foreign exchange reserves can be directly attributed to economic globalization and Beijing's monetary policy.[4] This policy both holds down labor costs—thereby making Chinese-manufactured goods the option of choice for many consumers—and centralizes the accumulation of foreign capital. As a means of keeping the yuan valued against the dollar at a level perceived sufficient to stimulate export growth,[5] China "sterilizes" incoming dollars by compelling domestic recipients to convert their earnings into Renminbi (literally, the "people's currency") at a carefully maintained exchange rate. The foreign currency is then shuttled through the finance system to the People's Bank of China (the central bank), and finally to the State Administration for Foreign Exchange, where it was reinvested—usually in the United States—to stimulate further consumption.[6] Although this process costs the national government money at the time of transaction, the net result is a long-term gain for China via increased exports and an associated growth in gross domestic product. Quite simply, Beijing decided the increased earnings from exports and associated domestic job creation outweigh the opportunity cost of forging a more laissez-faire monetary policy.[7]

Needless to say, this policy has generated significant political heat in Washington—where elected representatives like to complain that Beijing's fiscal management addresses China's employment concerns at the cost of American jobs.[8] In the associated sound and fury, U.S. politicians have largely neglected to highlight the benefit of Beijing's monetary policy: China's wholesale purchase of U.S. Treasury notes. In fact, it is possible to draw a direct correlation between Beijing's efforts to promote exports through lower yuan values and China's accumulation of American government securities. Since 2001, the Chinese central bank has invested a lion's share of its trade imbalance earnings in U.S. government debt.[9] As previously mentioned, this trend is evidenced by China's purchase of 20% of all U.S. Treasury securities issued in 2004. In 2005 that figure was 30%. In 2006 it was 36%. However, in 2007 Beijing appeared to reverse course and became a net seller of U.S. government notes.[10]

What happened? As the trade figures above testify, it was not because Chinese foreign exchange earnings diminished in 2007—quite the contrary. Nor can it be argued that the Chinese were compelled to slow investment in U.S. Treasury notes as a result of American political pressure. Although one could suggest that the yuan's appreciation in 2007 was prompted by Washington's ceaseless complaints about currency manipulation, similar pressure was not being brought to bear on China's purchase of U.S. government securities. Quite frankly, Bush administration officials seem to have welcomed Beijing's investment with open arms[11]—and appear to be taking a similar approach to acquisitions by China's new sovereign wealth fund.[12] It is hard to fault the White House for proceeding down this path. Confronted with growing budget deficits, a slowing economy, the subprime crisis, and continuing wars in Afghanistan and Iraq, the Bush administration had little choice but to welcome the Chinese acquisition of U.S. Treasury notes.[13]

While we are on the topic of political motivations, it is important to note there is no reason to believe that China's decision to begin selling U.S. Treasury notes marked the commencement of Beijing's long-suspected financial "nuclear option." According to Chinese authorities, this "nuclear option" would be executed through a rapid sell-off of U.S. government securities.[14] The associated consequences—a dramatic decline in the value of the dollar, collapse of the Treasury bond market, and a potential U.S. economic recession—are considered to be so anathema to Washington that American politicians are thought to be more willing to accept Beijing's demands than to risk the "fallout."[15] (Some analysts contend this "nuclear option" is little more than old-fashioned blackmail. In any case, the problem remains the same: the U.S. is now so indebted to Beijing that Washington cannot afford to aggravate our Chinese creditors.) As might be expected, there is considerable debate about China's willingness to execute this strategy, particularly in light of Beijing's substantial U.S. Treasury note holdings and the damage a rapid sell-off would inflict on the Chinese economy. Chinese officials, in fact, have gone to great lengths to downplay any discussion of the financial "nuclear option." For instance, in August 2007 the People's Bank of China tried to refute rumors of such a plan by releasing a statement declaring Beijing is "a responsible investor in international financial markets" and that "U.S. dollar assets, including American government bonds, are an important component of China's foreign exchange reserves."[16]

Given the apparent absence of external political explanations for Beijing's diminished interest in U.S. Treasury notes, it becomes necessary to investigate other potential causes. There are two likely internal drivers for this decision: political leadership and domestic political pressure. Although direct evidence of an internal political debate concerning disappointment with the returns offered by U.S. Treasury notes is unlikely to be found, circumstantial reporting suggests just such a discussion was underway in Beijing. For instance, in May 2007 Gao Xiping, vice chairman of the National Council for the Social Security Fund, took $3 billion from his agency's coffers to acquire a 9.9% share in the Blackstone Group—a move now considered China's first sovereign wealth fund investment. In July 2007, an academic from Shanghai's Fudan University published a newspaper article arguing that "from a rate of return standpoint . . . buying U.S. Treasury bonds is not very profitable." As such, the scholar continued, China should take its money elsewhere in an effort to "accelerate" the country's rise.[17] In short, there is little doubt Beijing was aware of the official investment vehicles being run from Abu Dhabi, Kuwait, or Singapore. Furthermore, we have little reason to doubt Chinese leaders were aware of the fact they could earn a better return on their investment than that offered by U.S. Treasury notes. (Even if the top leadership was not aware of this situation, one can assume their economic advisors were suitably informed.) All of which suggests high-level discussions driving the formation of a Chinese sovereign wealth fund were underway long before Western press sources became aware of the debate.

The second internal political dynamic behind Beijing's establishment of a sovereign wealth fund is to be found with the nation's citizens. Western scholars are increasingly aware of the fact that Chinese politicians are susceptible to the winds of change generated by popular opinion. Absent a strong ideological underpinning, and increasingly cognizant of the argument its legitimacy hinges on meeting economic expectations, the Chinese Communist Party seeks to address citizen concerns passed through a growing number of intermediaries—including the press and Internet.[18] These citizen concerns appear to have been one of the elements that led to formation of the Chinese sovereign wealth fund.

Rumors of public pressure to more productively employ Beijing's growing foreign exchange reserves began to appear in early 2007. Writing for the *International Herald Tribune*, a reporter working from Hong Kong observed, "in postings on domestic Internet message boards and in conversations among educated urban Chinese, critics are suggesting the central bank should earn higher profits from its vast hoard."[19] One Chinese blogger is said to have rhetorically asked, "China has huge amounts of foreign reserves, why doesn't the government put more of it into education?"[20]

Long-term China watchers have offered a number of possible responses to this query. First, Chinese authorities appear to still be struggling with the question of reserve sufficiency. Unlike their Japanese counterparts, China's central bankers may believe they have yet to amass reserve holdings that could unequivocally be declared sufficient for any liquidity crisis. Second, Beijing remains intent on eliminating official graft—and circumstances that abet this widespread abuse of public trust. In fact, President Hu Jintao has identified corruption as one of the largest challenges confronting the Chinese Communist Party.[21] Given this situation, creating an agency to handle literally billions of dollars in investments of foreign currency must seem a significant risk. Finally, there is the issue of China's entrenched bureaucracies and their vested interests. The Chinese population and political leadership may desire more productive use of the foreign exchange reserves, but until the bureaucrats are on board, little is likely to happen on this front.

The degree to which bureaucratic politics can serve to derail or delay policy is clearly evident in Beijing's efforts to establish a sovereign wealth fund. The battle over who would manage the more aggressive employment of China's foreign exchange reserves initially appears to have created just such a conflict between the Ministry of Finance and officials at the People's Bank of China. Historically, the People's Bank of China (the central bank) managed foreign exchange issues through the State Administration of Foreign Exchange (SAFE)—a secretive office subordinate to the bank. SAFE's functions further evolved in 2003, when Central Huijin Investments was established as a means of using China's foreign exchange reserves to address the country's nonperforming loan problem. This specialization of functions—particularly with the rise of Central Huijin Investments—suggested the most likely candidate to operate the Chinese sovereign wealth fund would be the central bank.

Political leaders in Beijing clearly had thoughts to the contrary. Western press sources report that while SAFE officials were busy declaring their experience was an obvious must for the soon-to-be-announced Chinese sovereign wealth fund,[22] Chinese Communist Party leaders gave the nod to the Ministry of Finance. The result? Arguments over implementation of monetary policy and back-channel challenges to the very organization established for governance of the Chinese sovereign wealth fund.

Evidence of this bureaucratic battle—and its potentially negative implications for Beijing—first appeared in August 2007. According to the *South China Morning Post* (an independent English-language newspaper published in Hong Kong), China suffered a potentially inflationary spike in broad monetary supply (M2)[23] in August 2007 due to an unplanned increase in consumer-available currency. This spike was reportedly caused by officials at the People's Bank of China, who sterilized less money than usual because, they argued, bonds being issued to establish the sovereign wealth fund would serve to accomplish the same mission. According to an unnamed investment banker, the money supply rose as a direct result of the power struggle between the People's Bank and the Finance Ministry.[24]

The second bureaucratic challenge to the China Investment Corporation's (CIC) establishment appears to remain underway. In December 2007, SAFE officials went shopping for shares in Australian banks. Although the actual purchase—approximately $600 million—was modest in a world of billion-dollar deals, the implied message was not. SAFE seemed to be quite literally challenging CIC for the right to invest China's foreign exchange reserves.[25] This bureaucratic back-alley squabble was not lost on Western analysts, one of whom observed, "this shows characteristics of a Chinese bureaucratic rivalry. It might be that, having been forced to surrender control of [foreign exchange reserve expenditures] to CIC, SAFE and the central bankers are now lobbying for the authority to make alternative investments on their own account."[26]

The extent of the central bank's and SAFE's discontent became even clearer in January 2008, when a well-placed source informed the *Financial Times* that the State Administration of Foreign Exchange maintains outposts in Hong Kong, London, New York, and Singapore in an effort to more efficiently manage

China's foreign reserves. The Hong Kong outpost—publically referred to as the "Safe Investment Office"—was set up one month prior to the island's return to China in 1997 and had established a reputation as one of the largest customers for local Treasury bond trading desks.[27] According to the source, SAFE's Hong Kong office continued to have about $20 billion under its direct management despite the fact that CIC is now in operation and responsible for handling investment of China's "excess" foreign exchange reserves.[28]

What SAFE plans to do with these funds, or how the Chinese government will ultimately resolve this apparent bureaucratic battle remains to be seen. Developments in the spring of 2008 suggest that Beijing may employ SAFE as a second sovereign wealth fund—a move that would point to more aggressive investment of an even larger share of China's foreign exchange reserves. In February and March 2008, SAFE officials reportedly spent almost $2.8 billion to acquire a 1.9% share in Total, a French energy company.[29] In mid-April 2008, the *South China Morning Post* published an article indicating that SAFE had gone one step further and was also seeking to invest in BP—a London-based energy firm. According to the *South China Morning Post*, this development suggested "Beijing has deliberately set SAFE and the China Investment Corporation . . . in competition to help boost investment returns."[30] Western financial analysts argued this latest development was a further sign that "the central bank wanted to keep [the ability to invest foreign exchange reserves] separate from CIC and lost the battle. Now they've gone out and are playing ball on their own."[31] A second analyst offered a similar assessment, stating, "the [central bank] doesn't particularly want to manage a growing foreign portfolio, but if China's foreign portfolio is going to grow, it would rather have SAFE manage the funds than outsource management to CIC."[32]

As of mid-June 2008, the Chinese central bank does not appear prepared to back down. According to unnamed sources, SAFE has agreed to invest approximately $2.5 billion with TPG, a U.S.-based private equity company.[33] According to sources familiar with the deal, the money is to be invested with TPG's latest fund—a pool of cash said to total between $15 and 20 billion. Financial industry executives contend this may be the largest-ever governmental investment with a private equity firm. (The previous record had belonged to the Oregon and Washington state pension funds, which are said to have invested between $1 and 1.5 billion with Kholberg Kravis Roberts.)[34] Regardless of the amounts involved, this commitment of capital demonstrated SAFE's continued activity as a sovereign wealth fund and offered further indication Beijing may, in fact, be operating at least two government investment offices.

The employment of SAFE as a second sovereign wealth fund manager should not come as a surprise. Beijing is well aware Singapore currently operates two such entities—Temasek Holdings and the Government of Singapore Investment Corporation—and could be seeking to copy this model. Financial analysts in Singapore certainly believe that this is a logical course of action for Chinese leaders.[35]

In any case, SAFE's continued offshore investments suggest at least three possible developments worthy of continued monitoring:

1. The People's Bank of China via SAFE is directly contesting CIC's ability to wisely invest Beijing's money and is seeking to demonstrate in-house expertise through direct competition with the new kid on the block.
2. SAFE remains in the business of investing Chinese foreign exchange reserves and is branching out to earn greater returns on the bulk of China's holdings—an estimated $1.3 trillion in the wake of CIC's establishment.
3. Both the first and second options are in play, and Chinese authorities are simply allowing the game to continue until the most able contender clearly emerges.

I personally do not subscribe to the third option. Such a move portends disaster for no small number of vested parties. I am similarly skeptical about the first option; even the Chinese bureaucracy can be brought to heel. This leaves the second option: the Chinese are seeking more productive ways to invest an even larger share of Beijing's foreign exchange reserves. This option falls in line with continuing debates over how large a foreign exchange reserve really needs to be, and meets Chinese leadership and public pressure to more lucratively employ these funds.

Structure of the China Investment Corporation

Enough of these tales of bureaucratic infighting and speculation over China's ultimate intentions for the country's foreign exchange reserves; let us return to the issue at hand—the China Investment Corporation. Having made the decision to establish a sovereign wealth fund, Chinese authorities were then confronted with the challenge of fitting the organization into the government structure and selecting a board of directors.

The China Investment Corporation, originally called the State Investment Company, was officially declared in operation as a limited liability company[36] on 29 September 2007.[37] While granted status as a ministerial-level entity answering to the State Council, the CIC is officially subordinate to the Ministry of Finance. Governance for the fund is provided by a seven-person executive team said to represent all interested parties (the State Council, National Social Security Fund, Ministry of Finance, National Development and Reform Commission—China's top economic planner—and the People's Bank of China) and a staff estimated to eventually include approximately 1,000 employees.

The bulk of this staff is to come from Central Huijin Investment Company (hereafter Central Huijin, the central bank's former investment arm) and China Jianyin Investment—a firm formerly charged with managing domestic assets and disposing of nonperforming loans. (Central Huijin and China Jianyin Investment were incorporated into the CIC structure for reasons that will become evident in a moment.) The end result is an organization with three major departments:

1. Central Huijin, to provide capital to domestic financial institutions
2. China Jianyin, to continue management of domestic assets
3. A new department to manage overseas investments

This third department is the most controversial, as CIC has declared an intention to accomplish most of the associated functions by "outsourcing."[38] These "external" money managers are to handle accounts in four areas: global stocks, emerging markets, Asia excluding Japan, and other developed markets outside the United States.[39]

Beijing's effort to ensure representation across a myriad of interested domestic bureaucracies is clearly evident in the composition of the initial executive team. Lou Jiwei, Chairman of the Board or CEO, is a former Deputy Secretary General of the State Council (China's cabinet). Gao Xiping, General Manager or CIO, was the Vice Chairman of the National Council for the Social Security Fund, where he oversaw its investments.[40] Hu Huaibang, Chairman of the Board of Supervisors (Chief Supervisor), is the Commissioner of Discipline Inspection with the China Banking Regulatory Commission. The executive team is rounded out with four deputy general managers: Zhang Hongli, a former vice finance minister, Xie Ping, the former head of Central Huijin (the People's Bank of China's now-defunct investment office), Yang Qingwei, former head of fixed assets investment at the National Development and Reform Commission, and Wang Jianxi (aka "Jesse" Wang), a former vice board chairman for Central Huijin.[41]

In addition to their bureaucratic power bases, the executive board members arrived with an impressive set of credentials. For instance, Lou Jiwei began his career with the People's Liberation Army Navy and eventually earned the title of Deputy Minister of Finance. Xie Ping (a.k.a. "The Iron Fist") is credited with reorganizing much of the Chinese banking system and is rumored to remain in firm control of the country's financial system. Jesse Wang has a doctorate in accounting. Furthermore, Lou, Xie, and Wang are said to have led the effort to prepare China's three largest banks—the Industrial and Commercial Bank of China, the Construction Bank of China, and the Bank of China—for listing on the Hong Kong stock market.

Before proceeding to a discussion of how the CIC was financed, it is important to note a key player was left off the executive board—the Assets Supervision and Administration Commission. This government office holds titles to over 100 of China's largest state-owned enterprises. According to outside observers, the decision to exclude the Assets Supervision and Administration Commission was a victory for Chinese leaders who did not want the CIC used as a state banker for national business interests but rather as a commercial investor without political influence.[42] As we shall see, this assessment may have been a bit of a hasty call. The Chinese Investment Corporation opened its doors as a major investor in the country's largest publicly listed banks.

As for finances, the China Investment Corporation executive board began operations with a fund totaling approximately $200 billion. This money was provided through a Ministry of Finance sale of special bonds used to replace foreign exchange reserves taken from the central bank's balance sheets.[43] In a paperwork shuffle best described as Byzantine, the Ministry of Finance first sold the notes to the Agricultural Bank of China, which then transferred the paper to the People's Bank of China in return for the equivalent sum in foreign exchange assets.[44] These bonds were issued in three tranches. The first set of bonds, worth approximately $67 billion, went on sale 28 August 2007 as ten-year notes with a promised 4.3% interest rate.[45] The second tranche, again approximately $67 billion, was released via the same convoluted route in early December 2007 as 15-year notes with coupon rates of 4.45%.[46] The third installment, covering the balance of the $200 billion, was sold 10 December 2007 as 15-year notes with a return of 4.5%.[47]

Despite the complex funding arrangement, CIC's financial future appears secure. There are reports Beijing plans to entrust the new investment vehicle with up to $425 billion over the coming three years. In a report released in April 2008, Z-Ben Advisers, a financial consulting firm, contends more than $300 billion of that money will be used for purchases in foreign securities.[48] Where will the cash come from? Further special bond issues intended to pull money out of what is expected to be continued growth of Beijing's foreign exchange holdings.

Spending the Money at Home . . .

Now, back to our previous discussion of the CIC's intended purpose. Western observers were aware of a debate over the China Investment Corporation's mandate before the institution even opened its doors for business. In an article published in September 2007, *The Wall Street Journal* reported, the "fund's mandate has been the subject of contention among Chinese officials." According to the *Journal*, "many involved in the [CIC] planning favor passive investments, by turning money over to professional money managers, with the single goal of improving returns on China's $1.53 trillion foreign exchange reserves . . . Other officials are viewing [the CIC] as a more strategic vehicle, such as to back Chinese state-owned companies as they invest overseas."[49] At the moment, the truth seems to lie somewhere between these two extremes.

CIC officials used the first tranche of $67 billion to acquire Central Huijin and thereby win control of the Chinese government's holdings in the largest three recapitalized, publicly listed commercial banks: the Industrial and Commercial Bank of China, the Construction Bank of China, and the Bank of China. Financial analysts contend the price of publicly traded shares in these banks suggest CIC received a good deal. The second tranche was dedicated to recapitalizing two other state-owned banks—the China Development Bank and the Agricultural Bank of China. An estimated $20 billion was passed to the China

Development Bank, with the ailing Agricultural Bank of China receiving the remaining $40–50 billion.[50]

Why proceed down this path? Commercial gain and the nagging issue of nonperforming loans. In 2001, when China won accession to the World Trade Organization, one of the stipulations for Beijing's admittance was opening the country's financial industry to foreign competition. Given the apparently sad state of affairs resident on the balance sheets of China's banks, Beijing was granted a five-year grace period, which stalled outside access to the nation's financial industry until 11 December 2006.[51] This delay can be primarily attributed to the fact that China's banks had long served as a lifeline for struggling state-owned enterprises. Unwilling to allow these unprofitable businesses to fail, and thereby suffer the political consequences of massive unemployment, Chinese authorities had used the banking industry (more specifically, the population's unparalleled savings rate, an estimated 50% of household earnings) to maintain liquidity within the unprofitable enterprises. The result was predictable, a staggering number of nonperforming loans.

The magnitude of the problem is evident in statistics compiled by scholars who have examined Chinese banks. In 2000, more than 30% of the loans outstanding at the largest four state-owned Chinese banks—the Agricultural Bank of China, Bank of China, Construction Bank of China, and Industrial and Commercial Bank of China[52]—were considered to be nonperforming.[53] (Nonperforming loans are commercial debts more than 90 days overdue and consumer loans more than 180 days past due.) The size of China's problem becomes clearer when one considers that U.S. banks in 2000 reported only 1% of their loans could be considered nonperforming.[54] The estimated cleanup cost for the "big four" banks in 2000 was approximately $190 billion.[55] This is a significant sum by any standard, but probably is an understatement of the actual problem.

The marked absence of independent auditor reports on Chinese bank performance has resulted in considerable debate over the exact size of Beijing's nonperforming loan problem. Published figures on the aggregate total of the nonperforming loans range from $150 billion to over $900 billion. The high end of this estimate appeared in May 2006, when Ernst and Young released a study claiming the Chinese banking sector had nonperforming loans totaling more than $911 billion, with the nation's "big four" accounting for an estimated $385 billion of that figure. Interestingly, the global accounting firm subsequently retracted the report, declaring "upon further research, Ernst and Young Global finds that this number cannot be supported, and believes it to be factually erroneous." The decision to retract the report came after the People's Bank of China posted a statement on its Web site contending that the Ernst and Young findings were seriously distorted. Needless to say, some critics claimed Ernst and Young had acted in response to Chinese pressure.[56]

Regardless of the exact figure, Beijing has been engaged in an extensive effort to address, and at least nominally resolve, the nonperforming loan problem. The first step was to follow a procedure used during the 1997–98 Asian financial crisis and transfer some of the nonperforming loans to asset management companies. In 1999, Beijing established four asset management companies that were paired with the "big four" banks.[57] Financial analysts believe that the asset management firms initially "purchased" between $170 and $200 billion in nonperforming loans at book value.[58] This move did not eliminate the debt, but instead served to remove the offending data from the beneficiary banks' balance sheets. According to a Chinese central bank governor, this scheme reduced the nonperforming loan ratio at the nation's leading financial institutions to 25% of the total loan portfolio by the end of 2000.[59]

The second step occurred in 2003, when the Chinese government established Central Huijin—an investment office within the State Administration of Foreign Exchange. In late 2003, Central Huijin "invested" $45 billion from China's foreign exchange reserves in two banks: the Bank of China and the China Construction Bank. (A week after announcing this move, the Finance Ministry quietly decided to write off a $41 billion stake in the two banks in an additional effort to help alleviate their nonperforming loan problem.[60]) This fiscal transfer resulted in Central Huijin owning 100% of the Bank of China and 85% of the shares issued by the China Construction Bank. As it turns out, this purchase gave Central Huijin almost exclusive claim to returns realized from the initial public offering of these banks in 2005—a tidy profit according to some Western analysts. In any case, Central Huijin's realized return on its investments at the end of 2004 was estimated to be almost $6 billion—not bad for a firm that had been open for little more than a year.[61]

The third step in Beijing's war on nonperforming loans took place on the regulatory front. In 2003, Beijing sought to resolve the problem of poor business practices associated with the nonperforming loans by standing up the China Banking Regulatory Commission to supervise and control the country's financial institutions. Despite apparent best intentions, this regulatory body has been criticized for lackluster efforts in resolving the ultimate cause of China's nonperforming loans: politics. A senior associate at the Carnegie Endowment for International Peace concisely outlined the problem confronting Chinese regulators by arguing "as long as the Communist Party relies on state-owned banks to maintain an unreformed core of a command economy, Chinese banks will make more bad loans."[62] The Washington-based senior China-watcher went on to note:

> Systemic economic waste, bank lending practices, political patronage and the survival of a one-party state are inseparably intertwined in China. The party can no longer secure the loyalty of its 70 million members through ideological indoctrination; instead, it uses material perks and careers in government and state-owned enterprises. That is why, after nearly 30 years of economic reform, the state still owns 56% of fixed capital stock. The unreformed core of the economy is the base of political patronage.[63]

Unable to close this political loophole, in 2004 Chinese authorities resumed their efforts to resolve the nonperforming loan problem through further transfers to the asset management companies. Accordingly, these firms purchased another $34 billion in nonperforming loans from the Bank of China and the Construction Bank of China, this time at 50% of book value.[64]

What did all this do for the nonperforming loan problem? By 2006, the "big four" were reportedly confronted with a nonperforming loan ratio of 9.3%.[65] Dollar figures associated with this statistic remain in dispute. Ernst and Young Global issued a revised report in May 2006 claiming the "big four" were then confronted with approximately $133 billion in remaining nonperforming loans.[66] The China Banking Regulatory Commission offered a more nuanced report, declaring that the nonperforming loan ratio for all state-owned banks was 9.5%, but that the same figure for joint-stock banks—specifically the Bank of China, Construction Bank of China, and Industrial and Commercial Bank of China—was actually 3.1%. The official Chinese banking regulatory authority also stated that overall nonperforming loans had declined in value to a total of $160 billion. Western accounting firms immediately dismissed this figure by issuing reports stating that the number was likely closer to $475 billion.[67]

One more set of figures is required before we return to a focus on the China Investment Corporation's purchase of assets within the country's financial sector: nonperforming loan percentages by bank for the "big four." Although Chinese authorities may never completely resolve the country's nonperforming loan problem, they certainly appear to understand targeted bailouts. At the end of 2006, the Chinese "big four" financial institutions reported the following nonperforming loan ratios:

> Bank of China: 4.04%
> Construction Bank of China: 3.39%
> Industrial and Commercial Bank of China: 3.79%
> Agricultural Bank of China: 26.17%[68]

The Agricultural Bank of China's problem—an estimated $114 billion in bad loans—has not gone unnoticed, both in and outside China.[69] In fact, there are rumors that the Agricultural Bank of China is preparing to join the other "big four" with a public stock listing in 2010,[70] and the CIC is reportedly slated to participate in the official effort to address the Bank's nonperforming loan problem.[71]

Given this background on China's nonperforming loan problem, and specifically how that issue was addressed within the "big four" financial institutions, we are now ready for a return to an evaluation of CIC's initial purchases. As stated above, the CIC executive board was apparently caught between those who argued the sovereign wealth fund be strictly used for profit motives and those who felt the money should be used to assist Chinese firms as they venture into the global market. The Chinese Investment Corporation, as any good Chinese bureaucracy will do, sought a middle ground, a decision that probably earned a unanimous vote from the board members.

The first evidence of this effort to find a middle ground came in the form of CIC's acquisition of Central Huijin for an estimated $67 billion.[72] A key participant in Beijing's efforts to prepare China's financial institutions for foreign competition, Central Huijin had become a clearing house for funds headed to the country's ailing banks. The task, though seemingly unproductive, had been lucrative for Central Huijin as the central bank's investment arm was said to own controlling shares in at least three of the "big four"[73] and had engaged in deals that gave the firm significant interest in a number of smaller banks.[74] Thus a decision to use CIC funds to acquire Central Huijin would turn these profitable holdings over to the Chinese Investment Corporation—a potentially lucrative move—and further bolster the "big four's" move into the commercial realm by providing monies that could be used to eliminate remaining nonperforming loans.

Of note, Central Huijin also had served as a CIC role model—and therefore could provide what the new investment office sorely lacked: experienced staff. Central Huijin in many ways was a ready-built model for the Chinese Investment Corporation. First, Central Huijin had been established as a means of diminishing government intervention in the financial sector. In fact, Central Huijin's CEO, Xie Ping, who now serves on the CIC executive board, once declared "the banks in this country have long been under the sway of various 'leadership groups,' which report false information, act without internal constraints, use funds for various exchanges, which result in many (corruption) cases and a high nonperforming loan ratio."[75] Second, Central Huijin officials, like their CIC counterparts, were nominally not government employees and thus could be remunerated in a manner intended to stimulate profit generation.[76] Finally, as noted earlier, Central Huijin could provide staff with Western investment experience, a relatively rare skill in the Chinese bureaucracy.

The employment of CIC's second $67 billion tranche also played to the political middle ground. The transfer of funds to the Agricultural Bank of China and China Development Bank helped ready these financial institutions for market listings and provided the CIC with shares that would almost certainly increase in value after the two banks proceed with initial public offerings.[77] In short, the first two-thirds of the CIC's funding were used to meet its potentially competing missions: assist Chinese firms in their efforts to compete internationally and generate capital over the long run using "excess" foreign exchange reserves. As such, an American observer could not be faulted for concluding the Chinese sovereign wealth fund's expenditure of almost $140 billion had generated little peril or potential for Washington. But what of the remaining $70 billion?

. . . And Spending the Money Abroad

The first foreign investment ascribed to the China Investment Corporation came almost six months before the organization was declared officially open for business. In May 2007, China purchased a 9.3% share of the Blackstone Group private equity firm for a reported $3 billion.[78] According to Chinese authorities, the Blackstone investment came with no voice in corporate affairs and was said to have been negotiated with a 4.5% discount on the $31-a-share price listed at the initial public offering on 22 June 2007.[79] Unfortunately for the CIC investors, what had seemed like a good deal soon went astray. By 1 August 2007, Blackstone share prices had declined to the point the Chinese investors were looking at a $500 million loss.[80] By 1 March 2008, Blackstone share prices had declined to the point CIC was facing a loss of almost half of the initial $3 billion investment, and the U.S. subprime crisis appeared to suggest there was no relief to be found in the foreseeable future.[81]

In November 2007, the China Investment Corporation announced its second international investment—$100 million in shares acquired during the China Railway Group's initial public offering. The announcement came as the China Railway Group, a state-owned construction company, prepared for a listing on the Hong Kong Stock exchange.[82] Western analysts declared the purchase was a "cornerstone" investment that appeared to indicate the CIC was continuing with an acquisition strategy focused on Chinese firms preparing for competition in the global market place. (Cornerstone investments are typically made only by large institutional investors, who commit to share purchases during an initial public offering in exchange for a larger allocation.) It is too early to determine if similar off-shore acquisition of shares in Chinese firms will occur, but one suspects that CIC's involvement in the Hong Kong stock exchange—and further cornerstone investment in domestic firms preparing to list there—is going to increase over time.

The CIC's next major overseas purchase came on 19 December 2007, when the Chinese acquired a 9.9% share of Morgan Stanley for a reported $5 billion. Coming on the heels of Morgan Stanley's first-ever reported quarterly loss, the CIC purchase was heralded as a much-needed cash infusion for the U.S. firm and a welcome indication of China's intention to participate in global markets as a stabilizing force. Morgan Stanley officials buttressed this assessment by telling the press CIC had agreed to serve as a passive investor—albeit one they were going to have to pay a fixed annual rate of 9% on a quarterly basis for the next three years.[83] Chinese Investment Corporation officials refused to publicly comment on the deal. The silence, perhaps prompted by CIC's Blackstone experience, appears to have been wise. By 1 March 2008, the 9.9% share in Morgan Stanley had declined in value to $4.91 billion.[84] Of note, this loss did not go unnoticed in Beijing. When asked to explain CIC's investment in Morgan Stanley, Lou Jiwei told a World Bank audience "if we see a big rabbit, we will shoot at it." But, he continued, "some people may say we were shot by Morgan Stanley."[85]

China's dalliance with Western financial institutions continued in February 2008, when word of a potential CIC deal to place $4 billion in a private equity fund operated by JC Flowers was leaked to the press.[86] The little-known, U.S.-based JC Flowers is run by former Goldman Sachs banker Chris Flowers and is said to focus on investments in distressed financial institutions—a skill CIC may find handy given its shares in the American and Chinese banking industries.

According to news reports, JC Flowers would be responsible for operation of the fund, and CIC would not be involved in day-to-day management issues.[87]

CIC's fourth major acquisition occurred in March and April of 2008. In an apparent effort to avoid the publicity and political controversy associated with previous deals outside China, Beijing's official investment vehicle quietly purchased a 1% share in BP, a London-based corporation now thought to be the world's third largest energy company. News of CIC's approximately $2 billion stake in BP was welcomed by corporate officials, who released a statement declaring "we welcome all shareholders."[88] (The markets also apparently welcomed the news—BP share prices rose almost 2% following release of information concerning the Chinese purchase.) The British government offered no comment on the Chinese move, but press stories were quick to include the fact that Chancellor of the Exchequer Alistair Darling had previously warned sovereign wealth funds would not be allowed to use their power unchecked. "When a company is not acting in a commercial way or we have reason to believe it is going to make an investment where there is an issue of national security, then we have powers to take action."[89]

Chinese Political Sensitivities

Beijing is well aware of British—and other international concerns—about the China Investment Corporation's ultimate intentions. During a September 2007 Federal Reserve Bank of San Francisco seminar, Jesse Wang told his audience "we tried to send a message to the markets and to the regulators that we have no desire to participate in Blackstone's management or have control. But we got feedback that people still worried about our motive."[90] Given this grim welcome, it is fair to contend China subsequently expended considerable effort trying to reassure a skeptical audience—often to little avail. One can also argue this "benign intentions" campaign began the day CIC formally opened for business. Lou Jiwei's 29 September 2007 promises to focus on the bottom line are best read as serving two purposes: assuring a domestic audience he is well aware of the seriousness of his task and convincing an international audience that the CIC will seek to realize economic—not political—goals.

Lou and his masters in the Ministry of Finance appear to have rapidly come to the conclusion that opening day remarks were not going to suffice. The China Investment Corporation's "benign intentions" campaign was going to require elucidation and repetition. The clarification element of this process appears to have begun in earnest during November 2007. In an 8 November 2007 presentation for the International Finance Forum, Chinese Vice Minister of Finance Li Yong told his audience "the CIC will make things more transparent, and learn best practices from other sovereign wealth funds."[91]

Despite this apparently carefully crafted public relations campaign, the China Investment Corporation ran headlong into international opposition. On 14 November 2007, the U.S. Senate Committee on Banking, Housing, and

Urban Affairs convened for a hearing on "Sovereign Wealth Fund Acquisitions and Other Foreign Government Investments in the U.S.: Assessing the Economic and National Security Implications." Speakers told the assembled senators that though sovereign wealth funds were "here to stay," particular attention should be focused on the motivations underlying these investment vehicles' purchases. Furthermore, while the Bush administration made pains to reassert Washington's support for foreign investment,[92] all of the speakers raised, but did not specify, concerns about Beijing's intentions.[93]

These sentiments echoed comments that had been made in Europe over the summer of 2007. France and Germany had led the charge, with German Chancellor Angela Merkel telling audiences "one cannot simply react as if these are completely normal funds of privately pooled capital."[94] The French sentiment was even blunter. Speaking to reporters, Jean-Pierre Jouyet, the French European Affairs Minister, declared "I find that our German friends are totally right to do this, we have to be better organized on the European level to defend our interests."[95]

Nonetheless, in late November 2007 Lou Jiwei resumed delivery of his "bottom line" message, telling an audience in Beijing that CIC's main priority is financial performance and that he was under "big pressures" to generate profits. According to Lou, the China Investment Corporation needed to earn approximately $40 million a day to offset the cost of the special bonds used to capitalize the fund. "Therefore," he continued, "we must have a certain level of income from our investments and [they] must have a certain liquidity."[96] How to accomplish this objective? Lou contended his fund would seek to primarily invest in financial instruments like indexed listings. Lou, however, seems to have slipped on the "benign intent" message, as he told the assembled financial analysts that CIC hoped to help improve corporate governance at firms receiving Chinese funding.[97] So much for the promise of passive investment.

In the meantime, U.S. and international demands for Chinese investment transparency had come under attack. In a publication issued by the Jamestown Foundation—a nonpartisan think tank with the self-declared mission of informing and educating policy makers—Wenran Jiang, acting director of the China Institute at the University of Alberta, wrote:

> If Washington is comfortable having Beijing buy up $400 billion of its treasury bonds to subsidize President Bush's deficit spending economic policy, it needs to answer the question of why it should be so alarmed about Chinese investments in the form of sovereign wealth funds—both are in the nature to seek returns for the money.[98]

A comparable message was issued by the Heritage Foundation. In a paper titled "Sovereign Wealth Funds No Cause for Panic," the conservative Washington-based think tank argued "there is no question that America must ensure that the laws and procedures governing foreign investment are robust, up-to-date, and

functioning effectively . . . But the knee-jerk equation of 'foreign' with 'threatening' . . . is a different sort of reaction, one unworthy of a country like the U.S."[99]
This pubic questioning of sovereign wealth fund critics seemed to embolden the
China Investment Corporation's spokesmen. The next round of CIC's "benign
investment" campaign was delivered with a much sharper tone.

Speaking at a dinner hosted by the Lord Mayor of London, Lou Jiwei told an
audience on 9 December 2007 the China Investment Corporation would not be
held hostage by protectionism or outlandish demands for transparency. Arguing
"national security should not be an excuse for protectionism," Lou declared "if a
[country] will use national security as criteria for entry of sovereign wealth
funds, we will be reluctant to tap the market because you are not sure what will
happen."[100] Lou then went on to note demands for transparency must come with
logical limits—the CIC would not sacrifice competitiveness in the face of
demands for political niceties. As Lou put it, "we will increase transparency
without harming the commercial interests of CIC . . . Transparency is a really
tough issue. If we are transparent on everything, the wolves will eat us."[101]

In Beijing, Gao Xiping offered a similar set of remarks. Speaking to a financial forum convened in the Chinese capital, the CIC general manager declared
"our main consideration is economic factors, and we'll run the fund based on
business principles." According to Gao, other considerations—political, historic,
geographic, or cultural—would not be decisive. Gao went on to state the China
Investment Corporation would "play by international rules."[102]

Interestingly, the next voice in China's "benign investment" campaign came
from the State Administration of Foreign Exchange. In a statement submitted
to the *China Business News* on 6 January 2008, Wei Benhua, SAFE's deputy head,
contended "there should be no discrimination in the treatment of sovereign
wealth funds; the funds of developing and developed countries should be treated
the same way. International society should clearly oppose investment protectionism and financial protectionism in any form." Although Wei agreed that
sovereign wealth funds should "maintain a high level of information disclosure,"
he also noted this transparency would have to reflect restrictions associated with
capitalist competitiveness.[103] The comments from a SAFE official drew no
special attention when they were issued, but it now appears the organization
may have been engaged in lobbying efforts on its own behalf, with CIC's
concerns a secondary consideration.

This steady drumbeat in support of China's right to invest the nation's treasure without fear of undue foreign restriction continued in late January, when
Lou Jiwei traveled to Washington. Speaking to an audience gathered at the
World Bank, Lou reiterated that his offices acted solely on a commercial basis.
Taking aim at the IMF efforts to draft a code of "best practices," Lou said the
effort was going badly because "nobody wants to agree that anyone is better
than themselves" when it comes to the issue of transparency. That said, Lou then
declared the CIC would not seek opportunities in which it was not "welcome."
Taking direct aim at growing protectionist sentiments in the European Union,

Lou stipulated the China Investment Corporation would avoid doing business on the continent as he felt "extremely unwelcome" there.[104]

In late February 2008, the China Investment Corporation took the logical next step in its efforts to assuage potential offshore investment targets by telling European trade Commissioner Peter Mandelson the CIC was drafting a charter of principles based on commercial lines. Following talks with Lou Jiwei on 25 February 2008, Mandelson told reporters the CIC Chairman assured him the Chinese investment vehicle was "already developing its own principles on the basis of which they would make their own decisions without government interference; that they would seek long-term returns to their investments with no political aims; and that they would increase their transparency without harming their commercial interests." Mandelson went on to state "I think that's reasonable. I welcome the fact they intend to publish a charter describing these principles."[105]

This Chinese offer of a "carrot" in the form of a charter of principles was quickly followed by a "stick" aimed at deterring international efforts to establish a code of conduct for sovereign wealth funds. In a set of comments released to foreign reporters, Jesse Wang, the CIC chief risk officer, argued "the claim that sovereign wealth funds are causing threats to state security and economic security is groundless." Wang then declared "we don't need outsiders to come tell us how we should act." This expression of pique with international "meddlers" came on the heels of an announcement that the Group of Seven (G7)[106] would join the IMF in crafting a voluntary set of "best practices" for the state-run investment vehicles. Wang, in fact, took direct aim at the G7 code-of-conduct proposal, stating it was "unfair" and that it would be "very stupid for a country to use its sovereign wealth fund to realize certain strategies and goals abroad" given the scrutiny and criticism such a move would assuredly draw.[107] It should be noted that Wang's apparent outburst was followed by a more measured response to questions about the CIC's plans as an investor. According to Wang, "all evidence supports the fact that we're a passive financial investor"[108]— a very different message than Lou Jiwei's comments had suggested a scant three months earlier.

Wang continued to employ blunt language in April 2008. Speaking to an investment conference in Hong Kong, Wang contended "sovereign wealth funds are not being treated fairly at this point. The reality is that we are seeing rising protectionism and nationalism." Furthermore, he continued, CIC does not have "any secret or strategic mission at all." Then, sounding more than a bit defensive, Wang went on to note "CIC is one of the most transparent sovereign wealth funds in the world." In an interesting twist, Wang also revealed that the China Investment Corporation executive board appeared to be confronting political pressure at home as well as abroad. Speaking about the financial losses incurred following the Blackstone share purchase, Wang admitted "the Chinese public is eager to count our losses every day. I hope the financial sector in the States could turn around quickly so we will feel better."[109]

Perhaps convinced the "stick" was not accomplishing the desired objective, on 6 April 2008 the China Investment Corporation's ablest spokesman, Gao Xiping, appeared on *60 Minutes*. In a wide-ranging interview with one of American television's most famous news programs, Gao reiterated arguments about a sovereign wealth fund code being "stupid," but he also sought to reassure a nervous U.S. and international audience. According to Gao, CIC did not seek to sit on the board of any of its holdings: "it's not our policy to control anything." Gao also sought to echo Wang's statements on CIC transparency, declaring "that is what we mean to be."[110] In fact, Gao went so far as to contend that CIC would follow Norway's lead in producing annual reports.

As of early June 2008, it was clear Gao intended to maintain this "kinder, gentler" approach in explaining CIC investment intentions. Speaking with a Reuters reporter in Paris on 3 June 2008, Gao declared "we don't have horns growing out of our head. Our intention is just to seek financial return on our investment, not political motives." Turning to the issue of CIC transparency, Gao offered a historical explanation for his organization's opacity. "Our government has never been transparent for about the past 5,000 years and all of a sudden we are told we need to be transparent. We are trying."[111] The bottom line: China Investment Corporation leaders are aware they have a profit and political problem. From Beijing's perspective, it appears the former may be easier to resolve than the latter.

Seeking an Investment Strategy

Given Chinese political sensitivities—and Beijing's concerns about how the world will treat the China Investment Corporation—it only seems fair to ask what the CIC investment strategy is. For Lou Jiwei, China Investment Corporation's executive board chairman, the public response is academic and obvious: "the purpose is to realize a maximization of long-term investment returns within an acceptable risk range."[112] I would note Lou's comments are in line with his contention CIC will have to earn a minimum of $40 million a day to meet the interest on bonds used to finance the fund. This requirement translates into at least $14.6 billion a year in profits, or a return of at least 7.3% on the $200 billion used to establish CIC.[113] Other Western analysts contend a more complicated answer is in order. More than one observer agrees that "now comes the hard part: deploying $200 billion in a way that earns robust returns, satisfies domestic political leaders, and avoids exacerbating anxiety abroad about the [fund's] intentions."[114]

In an apparent effort to defuse international suspicions, the CIC directors initially engaged in an effort to clearly enunciate what they would not purchase. In August 2007, Chinese officials told German Chancellor Angela Merkel they had "no intention of buying strategic stakes in big Western companies."[115] Lou Jiwei has declared the fund would not invest in infrastructure.[116] Chinese Vice Minister of Finance Li Yong in November 2007 told an audience the China

Investment Corporation would not buy into overseas airlines, telecommunications, or oil companies.[117] (A promise, as noted above, apparently quickly sacrificed at the altar of earning maximum returns on one's investments.) Finally, a source at CIC told *The New York Times* the fund would not seek shares in foreign technology companies, arguing "that's political, we don't do that."[118]

So what will the China Investment Corporation purchase? Early investigations of CIC's purchases—condemned as politically motivated by some Western critics of Beijing's sovereign wealth fund—found an executive board apparently operating with little strategic direction. In an interview with a *Financial Times* reporter, a source said to have direct access to Chinese government officials participating in the CIC acquisition decisions declared the fund lacked a clear strategy but would soon focus on the natural resources sector. The source went on to state the CIC would diversify away from the ailing U.S. financial sector and was seeking approval for this new approach from the central government. Why natural resources? According to the unnamed source, China's large U.S. dollar holdings were rapidly depreciating, and Beijing was seeking to address this loss by sinking money in the rapidly appreciating commodity markets.[119]

This push for diversification appears to have won Beijing's approval and was expanded to include more than simply natural resources. As noted previously, Chinese officials have repeatedly promised that much of CIC's offshore activity would be limited to the purchase of index funds[120] and a portfolio approach—making many small purchases of equities, bonds, and other investment options.[121] By February 2008, Lou Jiwei had, on more than one occasion, told Western audiences the China Investment Corporation would focus on "portfolios" rather than target individual firms.[122] In March 2008, Jesse Wang made essentially the same promise, declaring the CIC would pursue "highly diversified assets allocation ... [This] will help spread the risk as much as possible and increase returns."[123]

Even as Beijing sets forth on a path intended to maximize returns while minimizing foreign political sensitivities, there has been no shortage of would-be consultants willing to offer the CIC free advice on the most lucrative path to follow. For instance, a strategist at Nomura Securities suggested the Chinese consider the auto industry and a selection of insurance companies. A Roth Capital Partners vice chairman weighed in with the idea of purchasing passive stakes in industries in which the Chinese had the most to learn—like package delivery, rail transport, or trucking and airlines.[124]

Perhaps the most interesting development on the CIC investment front to date was the potential use of China's sovereign wealth fund as a strategic "blocking" tool. December 2007 rumors of Rio Tinto's efforts to acquire BHP Billiton appear to have unleashed a vehement capitalist spirit within Beijing and the CIC. According to Western reporters, "some members of the Chinese leadership believe[d] blocking a merger of the country's two biggest overseas mineral suppliers [was] an appropriate use of the fund."[125] China appears to have ultimately achieved the desired objective by using funds from the state-owned aluminum producer Chinalco. Chinalco purchased 9% of the Rio group for a reported $14.1 billion[126]—presumably thereby gaining access to the Rio Tinto board of directors and a voice in the decision to twice turn down BHP takeover bids.[127]

By June 2008, CIC officials appeared to be settling on elements of a broader investment strategy. Gao Xiping told reporters CIC intended to step up investment in private equity and would explore options in commodities and distressed debt. He also warned, however, that the Chinese investment vehicle was not prepared to rush into any deals. Citing a shortage of in-house experience, Gao is said to have admitted that CIC's interest in commodities and distressed debt was under careful consideration. According to Gao, "it is too early for us to do just commodities, we need specific people to deal with it and we don't have enough experience." That said, the China Investment Corporation's interest in private equity was proceeding at full steam. Speaking as the CIC chief investment offer, Gao declared "we have done a few [other private equity deals]. We are looking at a lot more." The ultimate goal: "We would like to build up a much more balanced portfolio."[128]

As the comments above should indicate, we—and apparently the Chinese—don't really know what investment strategy will guide CIC's future acquisitions. Although there are certainly signs Chinese officials are seeking to follow a strict "profit motive," the push to employ CIC assets in a blocking strategy suggest political dictates will occasionally rule the day. For the moment, it seems likely the China Investment Corporation will seek to avoid the limelight and the associated international examination and criticism. This translates into an investment strategy heavy on indexed funds and stakes below common automatic foreign government investigation levels—typically 5–10% of a corporation. Does this mean we can rule out the potential for Beijing to use the CIC as an element of national power? No, but as Lou and his contemporaries have so publicly noted, such a move is likely to draw a swift and negative response—exactly what the Chinese government appears intent on avoiding.

CIC: The Peril and Potential for America

Initial assessments of how establishment of the China Investment Corporation fund might impact the United States were a mixed bag. In a 22 January 2008 study, the Congressional Research Service declared, "from a macroeconomic perspective, it is unclear how the CIC will affect global financial markets. From a microeconomic perspective, the critical issue will be the types of investments the CIC makes." The Congressional Research Service, however, did go on to state that "implicit in the creation of the CIC is a shift in China's overseas portfolio away from U.S. Treasury debt into other assets"—a move that could place upward pressure on U.S. interest rates.[129]

Having staked out the potential macro- and microeconomic concerns the CIC's establishment has raised for U.S. policymakers, the Congressional

Research Service sketched out four reasons the Chinese fund might be "of interest" to members of Congress. These issues were as follows:

- Concerns that the CIC's investment activities might have adverse effects on certain financial markets and possibly the U.S. economy
- The possibility CIC's creation might signal China's intention to diversify its foreign exchange holdings away from U.S. Treasury securities
- National security concerns raised by specific CIC acquisitions
- The potential for Beijing to use the CIC as a means of pursuing "geopolitical" objectives[130]

While the jury is still out on all four of these potential policy issues, other American voices have been less academic about the peril the China Investment Corporation presents to U.S. national interests. On 7 February 2008, the U.S.-China Economic and Security Review Commission held a day of hearings focused on "the implications of sovereign wealth fund investments for national security." Chaired by a self-declared conservative with a long track record of publicly questioning Beijing's ultimate intentions, the Commission heard a litany of reasons why Americans should worry about the Chinese sovereign wealth fund.

Speaking during the Commissions opening session, Representative Marcy Kaptur (D-OH) chose to focus her remarks by returning to Lou Jiwei's comment "if there is a big fat rabbit, we will also shoot it." According to Representative Kaptur, Lou should be required to purchase a hunting license before continuing his pursuit of lucrative "wild game." Why? Kaptur told the Commission "instead of rescuing our economy, these investments only deepen America's insecurity, forcing the U.S. further into debt to foreign interests. More often than not, these deals are presented as purely financial when they are, in fact, political." Representative Kaptur's bottom line: the CIC, and all sovereign wealth funds, should be required to provide greater transparency as a means of "reclaiming our national security."[131]

In his testimony before the Commission, Peter Morici—a Professor of Business at the University of Maryland—raised more specific concerns about the China Investment Corporation. Contending some sovereign wealth funds are more troubling than others, Morici argued there are two sets of questions that could be used to identify investments of concern. First, "does the sovereign entity share U.S. values about the role of markets and state intervention in managing its national economy and the global economy?" Second, "does the sovereign entity share U.S. political values or does it see itself in competition with the West?" Given this screening criteria, Morici declared CIC was the tool of an entity that pursued sovereign investments for the purpose of creating a socialist market and was best characterized as an "autocratic state." Given this situation, Morici concluded the China Investment Corporation presented a potential peril and should be closely monitored.[132]

As worrisome as representative Kaptur and Professor Morici found the CIC, they were nearly "China apologists" in comparison to the grim picture offered by Peter Navarro, a business professor at the University of California–Irvine. Declaring Beijing's monetary policy a "mercantilist misuse of foreign reserves," Navarro argued China's sovereign wealth fund presented a "strategic danger" and threat to "American sovereignty." For Navarro, the CIC was a tool Beijing could employ to "gain control of critical sectors of the U.S. economy—from ports and telecommunications to energy and defense." Furthermore, he continued, China could "use its vast foreign reserves to destabilize the international financial system in times of conflict—and thereby bully American politicians into submission." As far as Navarro was concerned, the China Investment Corporation represented "the poisonous fruit of a free market shackled by unfair, mercantilist, beggar thy neighbor policies."[133]

It is only fair to note that the Commission received testimony suggesting there was a good deal of "potential" accompanying the CIC "peril" for U.S. taxpayers. In his testimony, Brad Setser, a fellow at the Council of Foreign Relations, agreed China had made "a strategic decision to encourage outward investment," but as a whole the country was a much larger target for foreign businesses seeking to make a profit. Setser went on to note that the approximately $30 billion in outward direct investment by Chinese firms in 2007 was dwarfed by the $80 billion U.S. firms placed in China during the same period. More startling was the difference in Chinese and foreign portfolio investment. In 2006, Chinese offshore portfolio investment totaled $1.5 billion—foreign purchases of Chinese stock during 2006 totaled $106.5 billion. So why all the noise about CIC's offshore activity? For Setser it boiled down to a "U.S. historic aversion to government ownership of private firms" and the concerns of "self-interested, cash-strapped" American firms that Beijing might use the CIC to invest elsewhere. In essence, Setser appeared to argue CIC is caught in a much larger problem—U.S. deficit spending and American demands for access to cheap money, issues not specifically caused by Beijing or a would-be government investment vehicle.[134]

Somewhat surprisingly, the conservative Heritage Foundation also provided testimony that depicted the China Investment Corporation as less than a direct threat to American national security and sovereignty. In her statement Daniella Markheim, a research analyst at the Heritage Foundation, noted CIC's claim to be a "passive global investor" and then highlighted the painful lessons Beijing had learned with its Blackstone purchase. For Markheim, the CIC decision to avoid further investments in the ailing U.S. financial sector suggested the emergence of a risk-adverse executive board seeking to avoid further domestic criticism for poor asset management. Markheim concluded by noting, "the biggest threat to U.S. economic and national security is not foreign sovereign wealth investment from China or any other country; rather, it is the increasing threat the U.S. will adopt protectionist investment policies." As Markheim put it, "erecting barriers to foreign investment would stifle innovation, reduce productivity, undermine economic growth and cost jobs—all without making America any safer."[135]

What then is the peril and potential the China Investment Corporation presents to America? The peril—for the moment—appears largely confined to short-term reinvigoration of jingoistic sentiments and proposals to revisit protectionist legislation aimed at preserving American national security from an amorphous "threat." Over a longer course of time, however, the CIC peril may be profound. It is not that the Chinese will purchase U.S. sovereignty—quite the contrary. The long term peril is that CIC—and likely SAFE—will go shopping for investments offering a greater return than that provided by U.S. government securities. This move away from subsidizing Washington's debt could dramatically curtail American government spending and result in a raise in interest rates that ultimately slows the entire U.S. economy. This is indeed a peril we need to be considering today, tomorrow, and into the future.

And what of CIC's potential for America? Given Americans demonstrated propensity for consumer debt, government deficit spending, and low individual savings rates, the China Investment Corporation may prove a vital source of capital for corporations seeking access to inexpensive money. Although the Chinese government may lose interest in U.S. Treasury notes, there is little indication that they will lose interest in Wall Street. As long as shares in American corporations prove a lucrative investment, Chinese bureaucrats—or their foreign financial advisors—will seek to purchase equity in publicly listed firms. This flow of capital back into American industries is a potential boon that Wall Street—and thus Washington—can ill afford to lose. Thus the potential CIC offers is largely a mirror of the peril CIC could prove to become. The tipping point? How Americans and their legislators chose to tackle or address the future of foreign direct investment in the United States.

CHAPTER 3

INVESTING LIKE A SOVEREIGN WEALTH FUND

The underlying reality is that there's this wall of money coming from big savings in emerging markets and from oil and gas exploiting countries and they are going to invest in real assets all over the world. This massive wealth transfer is going to reshape the political, as well as the consumption, landscape.

—*Willem Buiter, November 2007[1]*

If we accept the argument that sovereign wealth funds are primarily motivated by fiscal rather than political bottom lines, where these government investment vehicles choose to place their money is of as much interest to individual speculators as it is to politicians. While many sovereign wealth fund managers have declared a penchant for long-term investment strategies, there is considerable reason to believe these public officials are wary of being perceived as global loss leaders. Certainly, these funds will purchase assets that do not immediately show a profit—the approximately $60 billion sovereign wealth funds placed in faltering Western financial institutions in late 2007 and early 2008 are demonstration of just such an investment strategy. But, as even bureaucrats running the China Investment Corporation have learned, continued expenditure of public money on losing propositions can be costly—both for one's reputation and potentially for one's job.[2]

That said, sovereign wealth funds have come into their own over the last seven years. In 2000, the government investment vehicles completed $3 billion in publicly-recorded equity transactions. In 2006, the funds doubled their spending, acquiring more than $60 billion in shares offered by domestic and international firms. In 2007, the sovereign wealth fund transactions totaled $92 billion. And during the first quarter of 2008, sovereign wealth fund investments reached $58 billion, surpassing their total for 2000–2005 of approximately

$50 billion.[3] Driven by oil prices and continuing trade imbalances, this figure is only likely to grow.

Rumors of this potential spending spree have investment bankers rubbing their hands together. As one senior financial advisor in London declared in early January 2008, "sovereign funds are unconstrained by the fundraising cycle that dictates the activities of buy-out firms; they have vast pools of capital and can afford to take a very long-term view. We expect them to become increasingly significant players in the mergers and acquisitions market, an increasingly important sector for banks to target for new business."[4] A rosy scenario indeed, but is it realistic?

In fact, more than one observer has come to the conclusion that sovereign wealth funds may not be the world's best investors. In late January 2008, a journalist working for Reuters ably argued, "sovereign wealth funds have other agendas than pure profit, are often attracted to poor value 'trophy' investments, and may well be subsidizing broken business models at banks. Add to this that they are run by governments—hardly known for ruthless efficiency and laser eyes for profit—and investors could be forgiven for running a mile [in the opposite direction]."[5] But is this really a fair criticism? There is considerable reason to believe sovereign wealth fund managers are not going to follow in the footsteps left by Japanese speculators in the late 1980s.[6] To date there has been no rush on iconoclastic real estate, nor is there any indication of an intent to wholesale purchase "national" industries like Ford, General Electric, or Microsoft.

Evidence of sovereign wealth fund fiscal prudence came to light as early as March 2008, when journalists began reporting on the government investment vehicles' growing reluctance to place more money in ailing financial institutions. Sovereign wealth funds were notably absent in the last-minute efforts to save Bear Sterns,[7] and appear markedly wary of further investment in an industry that was still evaluating the subprime mortgage fallout. This wariness appears warranted. The cash infusions sovereign wealth fund investors provided Citigroup and Morgan Stanley in November 2007 were rewarded with dramatic declines in share prices. Citigroup shares in March 2008 had lost 38% of their value, and Morgan Stanley shares had dropped 25%. This bitter experience caused one analyst to declare "sovereign wealth funds are going to be more hesitant." Based on their experience, he continued, "this would call for some diversification away from the U.S. dollar."[8] This was not a heartwarming prediction for politicians in Washington.[9]

There should have been little surprise at the sovereign wealth fund reluctance to place further cash in Wall Street's hands. Even the *Wall Street Journal*, which had heralded the "world rides to Wall Street's rescue" as front-page news on 16 January 2008,[10] was singing a very different tune a short seven days later. In an article published on page six of the "Money and Investing" section, the *Journal* reported sinking share prices suggested sovereign wealth funds had "snapped up stakes in the world's great multinational banks . . . too soon." In addition to the losses at Citigroup and Morgan Stanley, the *Journal* noted Chinese and Singaporean investments in Barclays had lost 36% of their value, and the Singapore Investment

Corporation's share in the Swiss bank UBS had witnessed a 23% decline in value.[11] Despite these losses, some analysts argued the funds would hang in. The most common argument was that sovereign wealth funds are "long-term" investors who can wait for returns. A second refrain focused on the "know-how" to be gleaned from this vested interest in Western financial institutions. But behind this optimistic buzz was a much grimmer tone: sovereign funds were investing where Warren Buffett would not,[12] a trend unlikely to continue given the funds' focus on maximizing returns on their investments.

A growing sovereign wealth fund hesitancy to invest in dollar-denominated assets has not gone unnoticed in official circles. Speaking to a business conference in late March 2008, World Bank principle investment officer Arjan Berkelaar told his audience sovereign wealth funds can be expected to diversify "away from the U.S. dollar" over the next "three to five years." While Berkelaar argued this move would be a "slow process," he also declared it was a logical development, as "the cost of holding reserves is significant in many countries. To reduce this cost, central banks should invest their reserves more aggressively and for the long term." But where should they invest them? According to Berkelaar, viable alternatives to the dollar included the euro and the pound, but may also expand to capture the Australian and New Zealand currencies.[13] This was certainly not the "buy American" message the U.S. Treasury had been working diligently to circulate.

So if Western financial institutions are out, and dollar-denominated assets are of diminishing interest, how does a sovereign wealth fund invest its holdings? The answer to that question is to be found in an interview Bader Al-Sa'ad, manager of the Kuwait Investment Authority, granted the *Wall Street Journal* in August 2007. When Al-Sa'ad assumed his position in 2003, the Kuwait Investment Authority was suffering fiscal neglect. Despite an embarrassment of riches provided by oil exports, the Kuwait fund reported negative returns in 2001 and 2002, and appeared headed for a similar course in 2003. What was the investment strategy offering this miserable performance? Kuwait had 2.5% of the fund in real estate, 1.5% in private-equity funds, and the bulk of its holdings in U.S. Treasury notes. Al-Sa'ad's solution was to commission a study of the investment practices employed by the endowment funds at Harvard and Yale.[14] The results speak for themselves: in 2005 the Kuwait Investment Authority reported an 11% return on its holdings, in 2006 a 15.8% return, and in 2007, 13.3%.[15]

So How Do They Invest at Harvard and Yale?

The Harvard and Yale endowments could, in and of themselves, qualify as sovereign wealth funds. More accurately, the size of the endowments at Harvard and Yale—over $35 and $23 billion, respectively—would qualify the two institutions of higher learning as middling sovereign wealth funds. Harvard would make number 10 on the list of top 20 sovereign wealth funds, while Yale would have to suffice with the eleventh position. More amazing than their sheer size, however, is the long-term performance of these two funds. Over the last 10 years, Yale has averaged a 17.8% return on its investments, while Harvard has realized earnings averaging 15%.[16] Thus, it should come as no surprise that Kuwait went to Harvard and Yale when seeking a model of investment success.

When asked how they achieve these astounding annual returns, fund managers at both institutions start with broad answers. The now-departed Chief Executive of Harvard Management Company, Jack Meyer, told *BusinessWeek* in 2004, "there's not much plain vanilla in our portfolio."[17] When pressed, he then stated Harvard's core strategy is "diversification writ large." His advice to investors was to follow four key principles: (1) "get diversified"; (2) "keep your fees low"; (3) pay close attention to taxes on investments; and (4) invest for the long term. In 2007, Meyer's replacement, Mohamed El-Erian, offered similar advice. Like Meyer, El-Erain offered a simple rule: "high degree of diversification."[18]

While officials at the Harvard Management Company are understandably tight-lipped about exactly where they are invested, it is possible to assemble a "big-picture" summary of their strategy. In 2006, for instance, Harvard shifted its portfolio so that fixed-income assets (bonds) only constituted 13% of the institution's holdings, U.S. stocks accounted for 12% of the total, emerging-markets received 8%, "absolute return" hedge funds pulled 17%, and the remaining 31% was invested in commodities and real estate. That mix resulted in a return of 16.7% in 2006—not Harvard's best year, but certainly not shabby.[19] In 2007, Harvard Management Company reported a 23% return on its investments. The endowment fund portfolio compositions through 2008 are listed below:

Harvard Management Company Portfolio[20]

	1980	2000	2007	2008
Equities:				
– Domestic Equities	66%	22%	12%	12%
– Developed Foreign Equities		15%	11%	12%
– Emerging Markets Equities		9%	8%	10%
– Private Equities			13%	11%
Fixed Income:				
– Domestic Bonds	27%	10%	7%	5%
– Foreign Bonds	8%	4%	3%	3%
– High-yield Bonds		3%	3%	1%
Real Assets:				
– Commodities		6%	16%	17%
– Real Estate		7%	10%	9%
– Inflation Indexed Bonds		7%	5%	7%
Other:				
– Absolute Return		5%	12%	18%

Several observations—and implications for U.S. policy makers—can be gleaned from a quick review of the Harvard Management Company portfolio. First, Harvard is clearly wary of the U.S. stock market.[21] This caution is not without reason. In March 2008 the *Wall Street Journal* published the results of a study that evaluated U.S. stock market performance over the last 200 years. The findings were grim reading for investors overly committed to Wall Street. According to the *Journal*, "stocks, long touted as the best investment for the long term, have been one of the worst investments over the [last nine years.]" Furthermore, the *Journal* found that diversification—when limited to the U.S. stock market—was no universal panacea. As the newspaper put it, "conventional stock-market wisdom holds that if investors buy a broad range of stocks and hold them, they will do better than they would in other investments. But that rule hasn't held up for stocks bought in the late 1990s or 2000." In an effort to explain these findings, one analyst told the *Journal*, "we have to accept that this is no longer a nation of 4% real economic growth."[22] The unstated implication of this statement is to expect similar flat performance in American markets for the foreseeable future.

The second observation one makes upon reviewing the composition of the Harvard Management Company portfolio is that the team in Boston clearly sees little value in fixed income assets—read: U.S. Treasury notes. As with any good investor, the Harvard Management Company clearly realizes almost any other option offers a better return. Despite this understanding, in 2007 Harvard had over $4.5 billion tied up in fixed income assets. This likely reflects an "insurance clause" in the event of catastrophic failure in one of the portfolio's other investment areas. The other point worth noting here is that Harvard reports earning returns of over 13% on these domestic and foreign bonds over the last 10 years. This earnings rate is over double the performance these assets returned in a "benchmark" comparison.[23] Apparently, even when investing in potentially marginal assets, Harvard does better than the average financial team.

Finally, it is informative to evaluate the change in Harvard Management Company's portfolio over time. The University's diminished investment in the U.S. stock market is startling but not unexpected. The rise of new markets—both developed and emerging—clearly caught the Harvard team's attention early. The annual financial report lists 1991 as a start date for investments in overseas developed markets and 1996 for the emerging markets. Given the performance of some of these markets—over 20% in good years[24]—it only makes sense that the Harvard team would have begun moving monies offshore. The other trend, diminished investment in domestic bonds, is also noteworthy. The investors at Harvard realized they could earn better returns elsewhere. The one place Harvard seems to have lagged was in the commodities markets. The annual report suggests a start date of 1991 for commodities and real estate investment, and then at only 6 and 7% of the total portfolio, respectively. Harvard's double-digit interest in commodities did not begin until 2007, making one wonder if the team in Boston came to this asset class late in the game.[25]

Enough about Harvard; let's turn to Yale's endowment fund. While the competition between the two schools for academic performance and sculling excellence is legendry—and often disputed—when it comes to investing Yale is undeniably the top dog. In 2007, Yale reported earning a 28% return on its investments, a full five percentage points ahead of its long-time rival. Over the last 10 years, Yale has consistently outperformed Harvard, earning a record 41% return in 2000. The closest competitor is Princeton, which claims a 16.2% earnings average over the last 10 years.[26] So how does the team at New Haven do it? In a single word: diversification.

Like Harvard, Yale does not disclose the investment team's specific targets, but does provide an over-all snapshot of the university's portfolio. In 2007, 28% of that portfolio was in real assets—real estate, oil, gas, and timberland. The second largest area in the portfolio was "absolute return investments," primarily cash placed with hedge funds. This asset class comprised 25% of Yale's portfolio in 2007. Private equity holdings made up 18.7% of the portfolio, foreign stocks 14%, domestic stocks 12%, and fixed-income assets 4%.[27] The table below provides similar data for June 2007 and 2008, and a comparison with how other institutions of higher learning balance their portfolios.

Yale University Portfolio[28]

Asset Class	2007	2008	Average % in Each Asset Class at Other Educational Investors
- Absolute Return	23.3%	23.0%	19.5%
- Domestic Equity	11.0%	11.0%	26.3%
- Fixed Income	4.0%	4.0%	12.7%
- Foreign Equity	14.1%	15.0%	22.1%
- Private Equity	18.7%	19.0%	7.0%
- Real Assets	27.1%	28.0%	10.1%
- Cash	1.9%	0.0%	2.3%

According to Yale, the school's portfolio is "structured using a combination of academic theory and informed market judgment." Unlike Harvard, Yale also provides a breakout of the asset classes and their associated earning and risk expectations. According to the Yale Endowment annual report, "absolute return" assets are "investments [intended] to generate high long-term real returns by exploiting market inefficiencies." The asset class is divided into two sections: "event-driven strategies," which rely on corporate-specific events like mergers, spin-off, or bankruptcy, and "value-driven strategies." This latter category is based on hedged positions in assets or securities that "diverge from underlying economic value." The Yale team contends that "absolute return" strategies are expected to generate real returns of 6%, with risk levels of 10% for "event-driven strategies" and 15% for "value-driven strategies."[29]

The "domestic equity" asset class, according to Yale, represents investment opportunities in a "large, liquid, and heavily researched market." Interestingly, Yale appears to downplay indexed options within the "domestic equity" area. "Despite recognizing that the U.S. equity market is highly efficient, Yale elects to pursue active management strategies, aspiring to outperform the market index by a few percentage points annually." To accomplish this mission, the Yale endowment fund claims it "favors managers with exceptional bottom-up fundamental research capabilities." Yale contends the "domestic equity" portfolio has an expected annual return of 6%, with a standard deviation of 20%.[30]

Yale's "fixed income" portfolio is introduced as generating "stable flows of income" that provide "greater certainty of nominal cash flow than any other Endowment asset class." The Yale Endowment's bond holdings are said to "exhibit low covariance with other asset classes and serve as a hedge against financial accidents or periods of unanticipated deflation." The university goes on to note, "Yale is not particularly attracted to fixed income assets, as they have the lowest historical and expected returns of the six asset classes that make up the Endowment." Yale exhibits a bit of academic snobbery when it comes to Treasury securities, arguing "the government bond market is arguably the most efficiently priced asset class, offering few opportunities to add significant value through active management." According to Yale, bonds have an expected return of 2%, with a 10% risk.[31]

The "foreign equity" asset class in Yale's portfolio is intended to "give the Endowment exposure to the global economy, providing substantial diversification along with opportunities to earn above-market returns through active management." The fund team also contends, "emerging markets, with their rapidly growing economies, are particularly intriguing." Although these emerging markets offer unique earnings opportunities, Yale is quite cognizant of the fact this comes with significant risk. As such, the Endowment argues it can expect real returns of up to 8% from this asset class, but with an associated risk level of 25%. Foreign developed markets—Australia, Europe, and Japan—come with less risk (20%) but also offer diminished earnings, of an expected rate of 6%. As with domestic equity markets, Yale seeks to make the most of the situation by hiring managers with "bottom-up fundamental research capabilities" but also by allocating funds to these managers based on confidence in the individual and "the appropriate size for a particular strategy."[32] This is tailored investing at its best.

Yale's "private equity" asset class is marketed as "extremely attractive long-term risk-adjusted return." This asset class is said to include participation with venture capitalists and "leveraged buy-out partnerships." Given this build-up, it's not surprising to find that the Endowment believes this asset class can be expected to generate real returns of 11.2%, but with a high risk of 27.7%. Nonetheless, Yale is clearly proud of its track record in private equity, reporting that since inception this area of the portfolio has provided a 31.4% annualized return.[33]

The last asset class, "real assets," is described as providing "attractive return prospects, excellent portfolio diversification, and a hedge against unanticipated inflation." According to the Yale team, real estate, oil, gas, and timberland share three desirable characteristics: (1) sensitivity to inflationary forces; (2) high and visible cash flow; and (3) an opportunity to exploit inefficiencies. Given this promise, Yale has placed a large number of its eggs in this basket (28% of the portfolio), whereas the average for educational institutions as a whole is 10.1%. Surprisingly, this emphasis on "real assets" does not appear supported by expected return and risk. Yale holds that this asset class can be expected to generate 6% returns, with a risk of 13.6%.[34]

So how does the Yale team do in comparison to a set of active and passive benchmarks? According to the 2007 annual report, the Yale Endowment "trounces" the benchmarks for domestic equity, foreign equity, private equity, and real assets. They largely seem to fall on par with the benchmarks when it comes to the portfolio's absolute return and fixed income asset classes. The latter finding supports what sovereign wealth fund managers have already discovered: bonds simply don't pay.[35]

As with Harvard, there are lessons to be learned from a quick glance at Yale's portfolio composition—particularly when compared with other education-based investors. First, Yale provides a case for those who argue the U.S. stock market is not the best place to make money. Yale only places 11% of its portfolio in this category; the education investment average is more than double that. Second, Yale is certainly not bullish on fixed income assets—4% of its portfolio is in this class, three times less than the average reported by other educational institutions. The lesson is that if you want to make money, look beyond bonds. Third, Yale seems to be willing to bet on corporate acumen and commodity markets. This focus of almost 50% of the portfolio suggests there is significant money to be made if you are a smart, well-researched investor. One has to wonder why other education endowment funds have not followed suit.

A final note is in order before returning to actual sovereign wealth fund investments. In November 2006, Seeking Alpha, an investment advice Web site known for in-depth and insightful research, posted a study titled "Learning from the Harvard and Yale Endowments." The analysts at Seeking Alpha examined the percentages Harvard and Yale reported for five major asset classes—domestic stocks, foreign stocks, bonds, real estate, and commodities—and averaged the two schools' focus in each area across time. The results were a bit surprising given the data reported above. According to Seeking Alpha, the cross-temporal average for each of the five asset classes was about equal over time. More specifically, Harvard and Yale were found to have historically placed about 22.44% of their portfolios in domestic and foreign stocks, 21.19% of their investments across time were in bonds, 17.03% were in real estate, and 18.9% of the money was in commodities.[36] In other words, the study found that over time the two schools placed a near equal investment share in each of the five assets classes, suggesting that diversification writ large was a greater trend than specialized focus on an individual asset class. The bottom line: when it comes to investment even the best seek to spread the risk.

What Have the Sovereign Wealth Fund Managers Learned?

Knowing Harvard's and Yale's investment strategies—and the fact some sovereign wealth fund managers have explicitly expressed interest in same—assists in predicting where this pool of money is headed, but only to a limited degree. As the Seeking Alpha study reveals, even the best investors tend toward an even breadth of diversified assets over time. Is the same true for sovereign wealth funds? The dearth of information concerning sovereign wealth fund investment strategies—and these organizations' efforts to participate in commercial markets without revealing potentially profitable insights—makes an evaluation of their spending habits a difficult proposition. That said, a few well-placed financial analysts have set about accomplishing just this task. This research, coupled with the popular media's coverage of a perceived "breaking story," makes it possible to at least discern sovereign wealth fund investment trends.

One of the earliest efforts on this front came from Dr. Gerald Lyons, Chief Economist at England's Standard Chartered Bank. Lead author of an early definitive study on sovereign wealth funds, Dr. Lyons testified before the U.S. Senate subcommittee on Security and International Trade and Finance in mid-November 2007.[37] Lyons again appeared before a U.S. audience focused on sovereign wealth funds in early December 2007 when the Brookings Institution held a panel discussion featuring analysts from private industry and the U.S. "think tank" community.[38]

In his presentation at the Brookings Institution panel, Lyons argued sovereign wealth funds could be expected to have a significant impact in four areas. The first was "emerging markets." The second investment area Lyons mentioned was "alternative investments"—specifically hedge funds and/or private equity. The third option was employment of the money to reinforce strategic aspirations; here he cited the case of Chinese investments in Africa. And finally, Lyons contended, sovereign wealth funds could be expected to place more money in "sensitive sectors."[39] His definition of sensitive sectors was "Buying assets in energy, assets in the financial sector, assets in the media, assets in telecoms, or basically anything that gives you greater access to intellectual property."[40]

Emerging Markets: Like financial analysts in the Western world, sovereign wealth fund managers are predicting growing returns in emerging markets. Not surprisingly, the target of choice is China. As noted previously, Singapore's Temasek Holdings is a case in point. Between 31 March 2006 and 31 March 2007, the Singapore-based fund transitioned from placing 34% of its investments in other Asian nations, to 40%.[41] The primary beneficiary of this transition in investment patterns was China. During 2005, Temasek's investment in Singapore accounted for 49% of the firm's monies. In 2006 that figure was 44%, and in 2007 it was 38%. During the same timeframe, Temasek's investments in Northeast Asia (China, South Korea, and Taiwan), grew from 8% in 2005 to 19% in 2006 and 24% in 2007.[42] Developments at the end of 2007 suggest this trend is going to continue. Temasek announced in early December 2007 it will be providing half of the funding for a new, $2 billion, China-focused, private equity venture being set up by a Goldman Sachs Group partner. This fund is reportedly geared toward purchasing stakes in state-owned Chinese companies.[43]

A similar trend is developing at sovereign wealth funds charged with investing petrodollars. In an August 2007 interview with the *Wall Street Journal*, Badar Al-Sa'ad, Managing Director of the Kuwait Investment Authority, stated he is cutting his organization's investment in the U.S. and Europe from 90% of holdings to less than 70%. In what could be read as an expression of sentiments found throughout the Middle East, Al-Sa'ad rhetorically asked the *Wall Street Journal* reporter, "why invest in 2% growth economies when you can invest in 8% growth economies?"[44] As for potential targets of interest in China, Hong Kong bankers claim the sovereign wealth funds have been investigating natural resources and the financial sector.[45]

Interestingly, this focus on China may be waning—at least for Mr. Al Sa'ad and the Kuwait Investment Authority. In a story published in the *Financial Times* on 1 January 2008, the Kuwait sovereign wealth fund manager offered words of caution concerning China's stock markets: "Asset prices in the China equity market are inflated because in China so much money is chasing so few opportunities. This is a situation of demand and supply." That said, Al Sa'ad did not claim to be preparing to flee investments in China; rather, he was seeking opportunities outside the Chinese stock markets. According to Al Sa'ad, he was now considering real estate in China, but in the secondary cities rather than Beijing or Shanghai.[46] Perhaps more worrying for Chinese officials, Al Sa'ad also claimed to be "bullish" on Vietnam. As Al Sa'ad put it, "The government [of Vietnam] has a will to change the economy; there is a huge jump in direct foreign investment year over year. They are learning from the Chinese experience and it is easier to enter Vietnam than other emerging economies."[47]

Western financial analysts have echoed Al Sa'ad's comments. Speaking with reporters in April 2007, Steven Jen, Morgan Stanley's head of global foreign exchange strategy, noted, "it's possible we are over-estimating [sovereign wealth funds'] intentions to come to the West. In fact, they do have a bias in favor of emerging markets."[48] Simon Derrick, head of currency strategy at the bank of New York Mellon, declared, "why were sovereign wealth funds set up in the first place? It's to diversify their reserves. The U.S. isn't necessarily the place to go into, given how exposed they are to the U.S. already. If you believe in the long-term vibrancy of local regional economies, there is more argument in putting money in Vietnam, Malaysia or Thailand."[49] Rahul Shah, manager of the official institutions group at State Street Global Advisors, was even more directive about emerging market opportunities. For Shah, fiscal long-term returns remain to be made in supporting emerging market infrastructure development—such as airports in China and hydroelectric power in Vietnam.[50]

Concerns about equities performance in the West do appear to be driving even the most conservative funds into emerging markets. In early July 2008, the Norwegian Foreign Ministry announced its sovereign wealth fund, the $400 billion Government Pension Fund-Global, would be increasing its exposure to emerging markets and Asia. Speaking at a sovereign wealth fund conference in Singapore Martin Skancke, the director-general of Norway's Ministry of Finance, announced the Government Pension Fund-Global would be investing up to 5% of its equities portfolio in secondary emerging markets—up from zero exposure in 2007.[51] As Skancke put it, "even though growth in the U.S. probably will be affected by the [market] adjustment, there seems to be healthy growth in some other parts of the world."[52] Skancke went on to note that a Norwegian fund had previously invested 50% of its equities portfolio in Europe, 35% in the United States, and over 10% in Asia.

This sovereign wealth fund interest in emerging markets may not simply be reflective of a desire to earn greater returns on an investment. In mid-January 2008, the Chief Executive Officer of Dubai's Istithmar investment agency declared a renewed interest in China and other new markets as a result of perceived adverse political conditions in the United States. "Everyone is aware of the backlash Dubai Ports World faced in the U.S., and as a result sovereign wealth fund are looking toward non-developed markets to avoid such a backlash. Countries such as China, where we recently opened an office, are very welcoming to sovereign wealth funds, so more are looking to invest there." In an ominous note for Western nations seeking outside investment, the Istithmar Chairman went on to state, "there is a lack of trust in sovereign wealth funds and better initiatives are needed to curb such suspicions. Countries such as the U.S., the U.K. and Germany are very reluctant to allow sovereign wealth funds in."[53]

A final note on emerging markets is in order. Despite an apparent desire to earn maximum returns and avoid the publicity associated with political entanglements in the West, it is important to note there has been no evidence of a mad-dash sovereign wealth fund rush to emerging markets. In a report published in late April 2008, Global Insight stated 93% of sovereign wealth fund equity investment had targeted the Western financial sector. This focus had accounted for approximately $80 billion in sovereign wealth investments in 2007, and Global Insight assessed it would likely consume even more of this capital pool in 2008.[54] What remains to be seen is how this investment breakout will shift in the coming five years, as sovereign wealth funds approach an estimated $10 trillion in total holdings.

Alternative Investments—Hedge Funds and Private Equity: In mid-February 2008, the *Financial Times* published an article declaring, "sovereign wealth funds are beginning to use a new template—investing in private equity funds, apparently as a means to defend themselves from a public backlash against their growing direct investment in banks and industrial companies in the West." The *Financial Times* cited two cases as support for this statement: China Investment Corporation's $4 billion stake in JC Flowers, and the Government of Singapore Investment Corporation's (GIC) move to become a dominant player in TPG Capital—formerly Texas Pacific Group.[55] The little-known JC Flowers is said to focus on investments in distressed financial institutions, while TPG has been a key player in Merrill Lynch's recent efforts to acquire capital infusion. (TPG reportedly asked for a board seat in the deal—GIC is said to have "explicitly renounced" the request, "sort of."[56])

These two cases were certainly not the only examples the *Financial Times* could have offered its readership. Sovereign wealth fund buy-ins with private equity firms can readily be traced back to at least June 2006, when the Abu Dhabi Investment Authority spent $600 million to acquire a 40% stake in U.S.-based Apollo Management,[57] or the China Investment Corporation's $3 billion purchase of Blackstone shares in May 2007. The newspaper could also have cited the $1.35 billion Abu Dhabi spent to acquire a 7.5% share in the Washington DC–based Carlyle Group.

In any of the cases listed above the motive appears to be the same: employment of complicated financial instruments to avoid attracting public attention. This tactic is particularly well-served by investments in private equity funds, as the firms' relationships are exempt from many reporting and disclosure requirements. How much money have the sovereign wealth funds placed in these firms? According to financial industry estimates, we are talking about commitments ranging from $120 to $150 billion, or about 10% of all capital available to this sector.[58]

This lash up between sovereign wealth funds and private investment firms becomes more problematic when one considers Wall Street's growing employment of alternative trading systems—particularly "dark pools." Established as a means of shielding large stock trades from potential competitors, "dark pools" allow brokerages to match orders for large-scale buyers and sellers without having to first route the deal through an exchange or market where the transaction could be publicly monitored. While this procedure—facilitated by software—has reduced processing time and cost, the result is enhanced investor anonymity and further concealment of potentially profitable information.[59]

Furthermore, there is evidence this alternative trading system is growing in popularity. As of October 2007, more than 20% of all trades in the New York Stock Exchange-listed shares were funneled through these "dark pools"—the Exchange reports that figure was closer to 3–5% in 2005.[60] Some analysts warn an increasingly "dark" equities market will call into question the actual meaning of public price quotes and diminish competition in the trading industry.[61] Regulators have sought to restrict the use of alternative trading systems by lowering the ceiling on average daily volume of any given stock handled in this manner from 20% to 5% before being required to disclose the information to the public, but the fact remains, a significant set of deals could be accomplished for any

wealthy customer hours or days ahead of full disclosure. In short, the employment of "dark pools" could serve to at least temporarily mask sovereign wealth
fund transactions and even further diminish the transparency many U.S. politicians would like to impose on these government investors.

It is only fair to note that not all sovereign wealth fund interaction with
private equity is motivated by a desire to obfuscate investment strategies. There
is considerable reason to argue the subprime credit crisis and rise in oil prices
created a "perfect storm" in the lending world. Unable to obtain capital from
traditional sources—specifically, banks—some borrowers went seeking alternative sources, a search that lead head-long into the offices of cash-saturated
sovereign wealth fund managers. This is particularly the case in the Middle
East, where oil-producing states are now estimated to hold 40% of all sovereign
wealth fund capital.[62] As one analyst put it, "the sovereign wealth funds of the
Arabian Gulf are now a crucial source of capital and liquidity, as much of the world
copes with slower economic growth."[63] However, the best summary of the situation at hand came from Aamir Rehman, author of *Dubai and Company: Global
Strategies for Doing Business in the Gulf States.* According to Rehman, "in today's
environment, sovereign wealth funds can insist on a genuine partnership with
private equity firms by which they are more than merely providers of debt. At
the same time, private equity firms can benefit from sovereigns' increased
investment savvy and their ability to help portfolio companies grow."[64]

The potential benefits—both privacy and profit—of this relationship between
sovereign wealth funds and private equity is quickly becoming apparent in real
estate markets. Dubai has been particularly active in this asset class. For instance,
in December 2007 Dubai Istithmar signed on as an equity partner in a $3 billion
real estate project in Los Angeles. The reported $100 million commitment rep-
resented a 40% stake in one of the venture's key properties. In February 2008,
Casino operator MGM Mirage received a $2.96 billion investment from Dubai
for a 50% stake in a 76-acre Las Vegas hotel, condominium, and retail center.[65]
Finally, in July 2008 Abu Dhabi announced its sovereign wealth fund would be
purchasing the Chrysler building for approximately $800 million.[66] Why this
move to real estate? First, for the investment returns, and second, because developers were having a hard time finding cash in the post-subprime lending market.
According to one developer, "sovereign wealth funds are perfect candidates for
solutions to the problems we're encountering."[67]

Perhaps the most noteworthy of these potential real estate deals involves Harry
Macklowe, the struggling New York property tycoon. In late May 2008, press
sources learned sovereign wealth fund managers in Kuwait and Qatar were interested in purchasing up to five of Macklowe's skyscrapers—including the GM
building.[68] (Caught in the subprime credit crisis, Macklowe was seeking to sell the
properties as a means of paying off lenders.) Listed at $2.8 billion, the GM build-
ing would be the highest price paid for a single structure in the United States.

Given this "perfect storm," sovereign wealth fund interest in real estate
appears to be growing. Jan Randolf, head of sovereign risk for London-based

Global Insight Incorporated, in late April 2008 noted that while sovereign wealth funds appear to have "taken a pause" from financial investments, the government offices were demonstrating a "growing interest in real estate and commodities."[69] More specifically, the funds are said to be office-focused—with Boston, Chicago, Los Angeles, New York, San Francisco, and Washington DC high on the list of desirable locales. Why office space? According to John Alvarado, managing director of the capital markets group for Jones Lang LaSalle, the office sector is an easier area to place large amounts of capital with one transaction. He also claimed it is a sector that draws relatively little attention. As Alvarado put it, the sovereign wealth fund's "motivation is primarily the investment performance, not the bragging rights."[70]

This interest in real estate is not limited to properties in the United States. In May 2008, the Qatar Investment Authority told reporters, "we are focusing on prime cities in India, China, Singapore, Korea, Vietnam and Malaysia, cities around the world where there is strong GDP growth and fundamental unmet demand for high quality real estate." More specifically, the Qatar Investment Authority's head of real estate continued, "about 40% of our real-estate investments will be in Asia."[71] This is not to say the Qatar fund was about to completely abandon real estate in the U.S., but rather to "anticipate several opportunities in the U.S. for mezzanine financing, and individual distressed assets."[72]

It is only appropriate to note that this sovereign wealth fund "dabbling" in private equity markets has not gone unnoticed, particularly in the international financial community. There is, in fact, a growing concern the sovereign wealth fund managers could become a direct competitor for traditional financial institutions. The sovereign wealth funds' ability to continue loaning money in a tight credit market has caused some observers to even note these government offices may be poised to "ride off with investment banking fees." As one reporter put it, "banks do not concern themselves with economic protectionism. [But] they are worried that sovereign wealth funds will become an alternative source of funding to public markets, one that companies need no intermediaries to tap."[73]

Furthermore, this sovereign wealth fund interest in serving as an alternative lending source appears to be growing. Craig Coben, the managing director in European, Middle Eastern, and African equities at Merrill Lynch, is reported as claiming, "I've seen sovereign wealth funds act as an important source of capital on several deals and I'd expect them to facilitate more transactions in the future. Sovereign wealth funds are sometimes a key constituency on equity offerings although it depends on the deal. They pursue a range of investment approaches and are just as selective as other institutional investors."[74] What really remains to be seen, according to Western financial analysts, is if the sovereign wealth funds ultimately emerge as true competitors for the banking industry on a long-term basis.

Strategic Aspirations: Evidence of sovereign wealth funds seeking to earn a profit and bolster national political agendas through strategic investments in other regions is hard to find. For instance, while China has been actively engaged in efforts to secure oil and gas rights through business deals with outside producers, there is no indication the China Investment Corporation has been used in this campaign.[75] Nonetheless, there are rumors of sovereign wealth funds seeking investment opportunities in Africa, specifically in infrastructure development.[76]

The problem with pursuing such a strategy is twofold: first, the potential international blow-back if a sovereign wealth fund is detected to be in pursuit of a blatantly political agenda; and second, the mechanics of earning a decent return on an investment in many poor countries, particularly in Africa. As Gerald Lyons puts it, "companies that have invested across Africa have experienced high returns, but despite this Africa has not received large amounts of foreign direct investment. Thus, sovereign wealth funds are seen as a force for good there, if they invest for the longer-term."[77] The problem, according to financial analysts, is that many African economies lack the size to absorb the large pool of money sovereign wealth funds have to invest.[78] This has not stopped international organizations from insisting such a strategy would be appropriate for the government investment vehicles.

In April 2008, World Bank President Robert Zoellick told an audience in Washington,

> We are devising a "One Percent Solution" for equity investment in Africa . . . Where some see sovereign funds as a source of concern, we see opportunity . . . If the World Bank Group can create the equity investment platforms and benchmarks to attract these investors, the allocation of even one percent of their assets would draw $30 billion to African growth, development and opportunity . . . Sovereign funds are already serving as a brace for the recapitalization of financial institutions; I expect in coming months that they will continue to sustain globalization—and broaden its inclusiveness—through further equity investments as the deleveraging of the financial system runs its course and better information clarifies the best buys.[79]

One cannot fault Zoellick and the World Bank for making this suggestion, but the two concerns listed above remain in effect: How does the international community guarantee such sovereign wealth fund investments are not politically motivated? And how do the fund managers know they are going to actually see a return on their investments?

An indirect response to these questions may be possible—if we broaden the targets to options that serve domestic strategic agendas. As previously noted, one of China's strategic aspirations is maintenance of the nation's economic growth.[80] This focus is driven by the Chinese Communist Party's pragmatic understanding that its claim to legitimacy today largely hinges on continuing to improve the economic welfare of 1.3 billion citizens. No mean feat—and Chinese leaders have pulled out all the stops in an effort to accomplish this mission. This, as we noted previously, includes developing an investment strategy for the

China Investment Corporation (CIC) that serves to bolster the international competitiveness of Chinese corporations, from banks to construction firms. In addition, there is reason to believe Beijing used the CIC as a means of blocking acquisitions and mergers that could have driven up commodity prices.

This latter move—using a sovereign wealth fund to shape markets and thus world commodity prices—may have more practitioners than just the Chinese. In March 2008, financial analysts began circulating stories about the possibility petroleum-exporting nations were using their sovereign wealth funds to help drive up the price of oil. Proving this allegation is harder than one might suspect. First, the dollar's decline on international currency markets had already contributed to the rising price of oil but was not sufficient to completely explain the higher costs. (As one analyst ably noted, between January 2007 and March 2008 the dollar had fallen by 18%, but over the same time period the price of oil had increased by 120%.[81]) Second, growing demand for oil—particularly in emerging markets like China and India—was certainly contributing to the price increases. But analysts were also reporting crude stockpiles were continuing to grow, suggesting this new demand was not stressing suppliers and thus driving up prices.

In short, what appeared to be causing the dramatic increase in oil prices was speculation by investors fleeing struggling stock markets in the United States and across the globe.[82] More troubling, however, was the very real possibility of government complicity in this run on oil futures. In a 16 March 2008 wire story, the Associated Press (AP) reported, "government-run investment funds from oil-rich nations may be adding speculative fuel to an already red-hot market." The AP admitted there was a dearth of evidence to support this claim, but noted, "energy analysts say it is likely [that sovereign wealth funds are] making financial wagers on oil—and other commodities—for the same reasons as other institutional investors: to take advantage of rising global demand and to cushion them from the falling dollar." Financial analysts told the AP this speculation could be occurring in two manners. First, sovereign wealth funds—like all profit-seeking investors—had fled to the commodities market as a means of generating returns during the equities' market down-turn. Second, "sovereign wealth funds may also have been betting on oil prices indirectly, by providing capital to hedge funds." In either case, these government investors stood to profit. As Kevin Brook, a senior energy analyst at Friedman, Billings, Ramsey and Company, told the AP, "while Persian Gulf sovereign funds would be taking a risk since oil prices could drop, it isn't the worst investment idea you could have—[particularly] if you control the supply."[83]

In addition to this potential participation in the commodity markets, it now appears sovereign wealth funds are interested in acquiring a stake in emerging oil producers. In mid-May 2008, Canadian sources reported sovereign wealth fund managers were "circling" the country's oil industry and might be willing to bankroll expansion of oil-sands extraction efforts. On 13 May 2008, UTS Energy Corporation told the *Financial Post* that two sovereign wealth funds had approached the firm.[84] Pengrowth Energy Trust, one of Canada's largest petroleum developers, claims it too has had contacts with the government investment vehicles, including funds based in the Middle East, concerning joint-venture opportunities. When asked to comment on this interest, one Western financial analyst simply noted, "at $125 [a barrel for] oil, anything is possible. An oil-sands operation become[s] that much more attractive."[85]

As it turns out, using a sovereign wealth fund to engage in self-serving speculation is not limited to bolstering domestic industries or participating in the commodities market, a similar strategy is under consideration for the international currency exchange. In an interview with the *Financial Times* in December 2007, Brazil's finance minister, Guido Mantega, claimed his country was planning to establish a sovereign wealth fund so as to facilitate intervention in foreign exchange markets. According to Mr. Mantega, Brazil's sovereign wealth fund would "have the function of reducing the offer of dollars in the market and helping the real to appreciate less."[86] (The *real*'s appreciation against the dollar—between January 2007 and May 2008 the Brazilian currency had climbed in value against the dollar by almost 30%—worried the nation's political leaders. They feared *real* appreciation would drive down demand for Brazilian products.)

Brazil's Finance Minister renewed his call for a sovereign wealth fund to be used for stemming a rally in the country's currency in May 2008. While Mr. Mantega claimed the fund would also be used to assist Brazilian firms competing in international markets and as a "rainy day" reserve, his continued focus on currency speculation drew immediate criticism. Speaking with reporters, Claudio Loser, former director of the Western Hemisphere department at the International Monetary Fund, declared, "this goes against the whole philosophy of sovereign wealth funds that seek to diversify risk. It sounds more like a hidden subsidy to Brazilian business."[87] I would hasten to note this angst over Brazil's plans is a bit premature. Mantega's proposed sovereign wealth fund remains in the planning stage,[88] and the amount of money available to Brazil would have a negligible impact on global foreign exchange markets.[89] Nonetheless, Mantega's comments suggest yet another way that sovereign wealth funds could be used to support a government's strategic aspirations.

Sensitive Sectors and Intellectual Property: Gerald Lyons' focus on "sensitive sectors" and "intellectual property" certainly seemed to be on the mark, given the sovereign wealth fund focus on financial institutions in 2007 and Spring 2008. Dubai's purchase of a 2.2% share in Deutsche Bank in May 2007 appeared to be a first visible step in this direction. While the governor of the Dubai International Financial Sector proclaimed the acquisition a "strategic investment" in an institution with a "solid, sustainable growth strategy and the right management team," the international press was more forthright. In a 16 May 2007 news story, the *International Herald Tribune* observed that the purchase appeared to be an element of Dubai's effort to cause investment banks and their ilk to establish businesses within the country's 110-acre nascent financial center.[90] This campaign is certainly warranted, as Dubai is seeking to compensate for a lack of petroleum exports by luring monies into the country from the Middle East's growing pool of would-be investors. To this end, the government aims at establishing two of the globe's ten largest financial institutions by 2015. The potential fiscal know-how that could come with the Deutsche Bank investment is a logical move in that direction.

Dubai's interest in financial institutions was not limited to banks. In late September 2007, Dubai acquired a 19.9% share in the NASDAQ,[91] a 28% stake in the London Stock Exchange, and an apparent controlling role at OMX,[92] a stock-market operator based in Stockholm. At the same time, Dubai picked up a 7.5% stake in the Washington DC–based Carlye Group for a reported $1.35 billion. Bourse Dubai chairman Essa Kazim was very blunt about why his organization was intent on closing this deal. "Our primary objective is to build a world-class, growth-oriented exchange out of Dubai and to become the center for capital markets activities in the merging markets."[93]

Dubai was not alone in its efforts to purchase interest in "sensitive sectors" in September 2007. At the same time the Dubai Bourse was working to close the deal on the London Stock Exchange, NASDAQ, and OMX, Qatar was engaged in an apparent bidding war over the same assets. In a matter of a few hours, Qatar had spent $1.36 billion to purchase a 20% share in the London Stock Exchange and $470 million to acquire 10% of OMX. Unlike Dubai, which seems intent on building know-how and a domestic industry, Qatar may actually have been engaged in the activity as a means of reaping a profit. Officials representing the Gulf state said the country was seeking "long-term investments in a variety of industries."[94] While the statement is disputable, the facts suggest Qatar Investment Authority is indeed more profit-oriented than Dubai. For instance, Qatar's sovereign wealth fund was also involved in a failed $21 billion effort to purchase British supermarket chain J. Sainsbury at about the same time the London Stock Exchange deal went down.

Dubai and Qatar were not the only government investors purchasing stakes in western financial institutions. As the table below illustrates, this bid for shares in what was perceived as a "fire sale" market drew participants from the Middle and Far East. (On 11 December 2007, the *Wall Street Journal* reported that some financial institution stock values had dropped by as much as 25% in 2007.)[95]

Before leaping to the conclusion these purchases were solely or largely unilateral efforts to acquire banking technology and know-how, it is important to note many of the ailing financial institutions went seeking sovereign wealth investors as a means of alleviating a growing liquidity crisis. Speaking with the *Washington Post*, Kuwait's sovereign wealth manager noted, "they called us . . . We receive calls on most transactions."[96] This declaration of innocence appeared to be valid. In early May 2008, Seattle-based Washington Mutual admitted it had contacted eight sovereign wealth funds in its search for a $2.75 billion cash infusion,[97] and in mid-June 2008 Barclays declared it had plans to sell up to $7.8 billion in new shares as a means of lining up further sovereign wealth fund investment.[98] Furthermore, the funds appear to be curtailing spending in the financial sector as a result of political and shareholder opposition. According to Gary Parr, deputy Chairman of Lazard Limited, "because so much money moved so quickly, we saw a quick reaction by governments that began to have a chilling effect. Notably in the U.S., but even in some of the countries in Europe, there began to be pushback by governments and inquiries by governments about what are the motivations of the sovereign wealth funds." He went on to state, "part of it is [also] backlash by the shareholders—their desire to buy these securities rather than see them placed with someone else."[99]

Political problems were not the only reason sovereign wealth funds turned away from the financial industry. Speaking at a meeting in Washington DC in early May 2008, David Rubenstein, Chairman of the Carlyle Group, predicted U.S. banks and financial institutions have "enormous losses" from bad loans that have yet to be recognized and that "the sovereign wealth funds are not likely to jump into the fray again to bail out these institutions." Part of this reluctance, according to Rubenstein, is likely attributable to the fact "many financial institutions aren't going to be able to survive as independent institutions."[100] (As of May 2008, financial institutions in Europe and the U.S. had reported credit losses and write-downs totaling $344 billion. The firms had only managed to raise $263 billion in capital during 2007, leaving $116 billion in losses.[101]) This grim prediction, of course, sets the stage for the sovereign wealth funds to seek better returns elsewhere.

This stream of bad news has not stopped the financial industry from seeking additional business with the sovereign wealth funds. In the spring of 2008, a sequence of news reports highlighted the financial industry's efforts to win business—and likely further cash infusions—from the government investment vehicles. On 1 May 2008, Financial News, an online information service, reported that Goldman Sachs in February 2008 transferred a senior official to Dubai in pursuit of financing business. At approximately the same time, Credit Suisse moved one of its best-connected Middle East investment bankers from his position as the European chief executive to a new role as chairman of the firm's Middle East operation.

In April 2008, Lehman Brothers appointed one of its "star players" to a new position as global head of sovereign wealth coverage, and Morgan Stanley assigned three senior officials to cover Middle East sovereign wealth funds.[102] In an effort to avoid missing this perceived gravy train, in early May 2008 Citigroup announced one of its two senior global investment bankers would be moving from London to Dubai.[103] The official was slated to join Citigroup's growing team of investment bankers already in Dubai. Not to be outdone, in late June 2008, JP Morgan issued a press release declaring it had appointed Bear Sterns former Asia Chief Executive Officer to run the firm's sovereign wealth group.[104] All of this activity begs the question: to what degree are the sovereign wealth funds having to purchase financial know-how, versus simply having it thrown at them?

Table 3.1 Financial Sector Purchases[105]

Date	Purchase	Purchaser	Price/Share
1 June 2006	Apollo Management	Abu Dhabi Invest Authority	$600m/40%
2 May 2007	British bank HSBC	Dubai International Capital	Undisclosed
16 May 2007	Deutsche Bank	Dubai Inter Financial Center	$1.83b/2.2%
20 May 2007	U.S.-based Blackstone	China Investment Corp	$3b/10%
13 July 2007	Indian bank ICICI	Dubai International Capital	$750m/2.87%
23 July 2007	British bank Barclay's	Chinese state agency	$3b/3.1%
23 July 2007	British bank Barclay's	Temasek Holdings	$2b/1.77%
20 Sept 2007	U.S.-based Carlyle Group	Abu Dhabi Mubadala Dev Co	$1.35b/7.5%
22 Oct 2007	U.S.-based Bear Sterns	China's Citic Securities	$1b/unkn
29 Oct 2007	U.S.-based Och-Ziff	Dubai International Capital	$1.1b/9.9%
7 Nov 2007	China Everbright Bank	CIC-Central Huijin	$2.7b/71%
26 Nov 2007	Citigroup Inc	Abu Dhabi Invest Authority	$7.5b/4.9%
10 Dec 2007	British bank UBS	GIC-Singapore	$9.75b/9%
10 Dec 2007	British bank UBS	Undisclosed (Middle East)	$1.77b/unkn
19 Dec 2007	Morgan Stanley	China Investment Corp	$5.0b/9.9%
24 Dec 2007	Merrill Lynch	Temasek Holdings	$5.0b/9.9%
31 Dec 2007	China Development Bank	CIC	$20b
15 Jan 2008	Citigroup Inc.	GIC, Kuwait, Saudi Arabia	$14.5b/7.8%
15 Jan 2008	Merrill Lynch	Kuwait, Korea Invest Corp	$6.6b/unkn
15 Feb 2008	U.S.-based J. C. Flowers	CIC	$4b/unkn
19 Feb 2008	Credit Suisse	Qatar Invest Authority	$500m/1–2%

The financial industry's continuing woes are prompting some sovereign wealth fund managers to stray slightly farther afield—specifically, into the U.S. insurance sector. In mid-May 2008, Bahrain's sovereign wealth fund chief executive officer declared he remains interested in deals to be found in the U.S.—in "the insurance space."[106] With insurance company share prices in a slump following the subprime crisis, some analysts consider the stocks "cheap" in comparison to historic levels. Furthermore, consolidation within the U.S. insurance industry is thought to be on the verge of boosting market values, all of which would make the sector a smart buy for a profit-motivated sovereign wealth fund manager.[107]

A final comment before departing Lyons' hypothesis: The apparent sovereign wealth spending spree on sensitive sector assets was not limited to banks and investment houses. In mid-November 2006, Mubadala Development Company, an official Abu Dhabi investment agency, purchased an 8% share in Advanced Micro Devices for $622 million.[108] Based in Sunnyvale, California, Advanced Micro Devices is the world's second largest supplier of microprocessors and the international community's third-largest manufacturer of graphics processing units. The firm went hunting for capital after it spent $5.4 billion to acquire ATI Technologies in July 2006. This is but one example. Similar purchases have occurred or been proposed, and there is a growing concern some of this activity has been buried in the sovereign wealth funds' latch-up with private equity and hedge funds. In a report released in April 2008, the Services Employees International Union cited three cases where the Carlyle Group apparently acquired shares in sensitive sector industries for Abu Dhabi's Mubadala Development Company. These purchases included a stake in Kinder Morgan, a key player in the U.S. energy sector, ARNIC, a leading provider of communications and integration systems used by airports and international governments, and Allison Transmission, a designer and manufacturer of automatic transmissions used in the medium- and heavy-duty commercial vehicle markets.[109]

Suspicion Has Not Stemmed Desire for Sovereign Wealth Fund Investment

Regardless of the motivations driving sovereign wealth fund investments, there is a growing recognition these government agencies offer access to capital vital for economic growth. As such, initial suspicion of the funds has rapidly evolved into an essentially "open door" policy in some nations. Japan offers a case in point. In early April 2008, two of Japan's top brokerages announced the establishment of special teams dedicated to attracting foreign government investment in domestic industries. The Japanese brokerages are said to be appealing to the sovereign wealth funds by suggesting the Nikkei is riddled with bargains[110] and access to Japan's internationally acclaimed manufacturing know-how.

While sovereign wealth fund investments in Japanese blue-chip companies are currently estimated at an index-linked total of between 3% and 4%, analysts in Tokyo suspect they can draw more foreign government interest. As the managing director at one of Japan's top brokerages put it, "a lot of people now realize the competitive edge in technology, research and development capabilities, and human resources" Japanese companies offer. Furthermore, he continued, sovereign wealth funds now appear interested in Japanese solar energy firms, real estate, and the country's health care industry.[111] This observation is not simply informed speculation. Since 2006, sovereign wealth funds have exhibited a growing penchant for Japanese assets. In August 2006, Singapore's Temasek Holdings spent $197 million to acquire a stake in Mitsui Life Insurance. In September 2007, an Abu Dhabi–based fund spent an estimated $850 million to acquire a 20% share in Cosmo Oil. In November 2007, Sony announced a "significant investment" from Dubai. And, in February 2008, the Government of Singapore Investment Corporation purchased the Westin Tokyo for approximately $750 million.[112] Given Japan's continuing economic woes, one can only conclude that these deals are going to continue as sovereign wealth funds seek to diversify their holdings and acquire assets with potential knowledge and technology transfer options.

It is only fair to note Japan is not the only nation seeking to lure sovereign wealth fund investors. In April 2008, Andrew Cain, chief executive of United Kingdom (U.K.) Trade and Investment, announced his organization would be seeking foreign government capital. According to Cain, "the increased profile of sovereign wealth funds in the international finance system has generated enormous opportunities for inward investment into the U.K." What are the potential draws for this investment? Cain pointed to London's reputation as a leading financial center, and a competitive regulatory environment.[113]

All of which brings us back to the United States. Given the potential access to capital sovereign wealth funds offer, and the possibility of reviving lagging domestic industries through outside investment, how is the United States approaching these government investment funds? "Tentatively" appears to be the best answer one can offer. In testimony before the Senate Banking Committee in late April 2008, a senior Federal Reserve official declared the U.S. banking system is being challenged by current market conditions. As such, the ability to raise capital from both domestic and international investors "under stress conditions" will help "buttress the financial strength of U.S. financial institutions and better position these institutions to weather the current financial turmoil." The response from senators attending the hearing? According to Christopher Dodd (D-CT), "it's one thing to welcome sovereign wealth funds; it's another thing to beg for them." Senator Dodd's colleague, Robert Menendez (D-NJ) was even blunter, putting words to a large number of security fears associated with sovereign wealth investment in the United States: "I find it hard to believe that a foreign government is willing to invest billions and have no say."[114]

Sovereign Wealth Investment: The Peril and Potential for America

On 13 February 2008, the House and Senate Joint Economic Committee convened for an afternoon of testimony on the peril and potential sovereign wealth funds present the United States. In his opening statement, Senator Charles Schumer (D-NY) declared, "the question of the day is whether these huge pools of investment dollars, known as sovereign wealth funds, make the U.S. economy stronger or pose serious national security risks. I'm not sure that we will answer that question to anyone's satisfaction today, but at the very least, this Committee and the federal government needs to spend a great deal of time thinking about it."[115]

The experts who were asked to testify before the Joint Economic Committee on that cold day in February included U.S. Treasury Undersecretary for International Affairs, David McCormick, and former U.S. Ambassador to the European Union, Stuart Eizenstat.[116] Speaking for the Bush administration, Undersecretary McCormick presented the party line on the peril that sovereign wealth funds present to the United States. This litany, well-recited at this point in the game, covered three areas:

1. The primary risk is that sovereign wealth funds could provoke a new wave of protectionism, which could be very harmful to the U.S. and global economies.
2. Transactions involving investment by sovereign wealth funds, as with other types of foreign investment, may raise legitimate national security concerns.
3. Sovereign wealth funds may raise concerns related to financial stability. Sovereign wealth funds can represent large, concentrated, and often non-transparent positions in certain markets and asset classes. Actual shifts in their asset allocations can cause market volatility. In fact, even perceived shifts or rumors can cause volatility as the market reacts to what it perceives sovereign wealth funds to be doing[117]

This list of concerns replicated remarks McCormick had made before the Senate Committee on Banking, Housing, and Urban Affairs in mid-November 2007. Intent on preventing the passage of legislation that might drive away foreign investment, the Bush administration was continuing to focus attention on the evils of "protectionism." Not surprisingly, McCormick's second two points, the potential danger to national security and the possibility of sovereign wealth funds causing market volatility, came with little further illustration. On the issue of national security McCormick chose to highlight the role that the Committee on Foreign Investment in the United States (CFIUS) plays in monitoring potentially threatening transactions. As for sovereign wealth funds and market volatility, McCormick had nothing to say on alternative trading systems (a.k.a. "dark pools") or the hedge funds and private equity options that could serve to abet this problem.

And what of the potential that sovereign wealth funds offered to the United States? On this front McCormick proved a wealth of facts.

> International investment in the United States fuels U.S. economic prosperity by cre-
> ating well-paid jobs, importing new technology and business methods, helping to
> finance U.S. priorities, and providing healthy competition that fosters innovation,
> productivity gains, lower prices, and greater variety for consumers. Over 5 million
> Americans—4.6% of the U.S. private sector—are employed by foreign-owned firms'
> U.S. operations. Over 39% of these 5 million jobs at foreign-owned firms are in man-
> ufacturing, a sector that accounts for 13% of U.S. private sector jobs. These 5 million
> jobs pay 25% higher compensation on average than jobs at other U.S. firms. Addi-
> tionally, foreign-owned firms contributed almost 6% of U.S. output and 14% of U.S.
> research and development spending in 2006. Foreign-owned firms re-invested over
> half of their U.S. income—$71 billion—back into the U.S. economy in 2006. A dis-
> proportionate 13% of U.S. tax payments and 19% of U.S. exports are made by
> foreign-owned firms. Without international investment, Americans would be faced
> with painful choices regarding taxes, spending on government programs, and their
> level of savings and consumption.[118]

McCormick's data, in fact, largely mirrored information that the U.S.-based Organization for International Investment has been providing for years and largely reflected remarks Carlos Gutierrez, the Secretary of Commerce, had made in November 2007. None of this is to take away from McCormick's main point; foreign investment—from private pockets or government coffers—is a major source of jobs in the United States. And he might continue, it would be sorely missed regardless of the party sitting in the White House.

Ambassador Eizenstat offered a less ominous, but equally well-vetted list of possible perils sovereign wealth funds present the United States. According to Eizenstat, "if there has been an underlying theme for most of the concerns ver-balized about sovereign wealth funds it is the assertion that these funds, as a whole, are nontransparent, and consequently policymakers cannot be sure what drives the funds' investments, divestments, and other behaviors." Furthermore, he noted that sovereign wealth funds present the peril of subsidized private business deals in a manner that "would create an unfair advantage over U.S. or foreign corporations who must rely on the private credit markets for competing for the same acquisitions." Finally, Eizenstat declared, "sovereign wealth funds may be political or intelligence-gathering tools out to harm the United States, rather than profit maximizers."[119]

Like Undersecretary McCormick, Ambassador Eizenstat was relatively effu-sive about the potential that sovereign wealth funds could offer the United States. As with McCormick, Eizenstat reminded the Joint Economic Committee about how such investment "support[s] economic growth and job creation . . . help[s] keep industry competitive . . . grease[s] the wheels of the international economy by helping to right financial imbalances . . . [and] can be a ready source of assistance to distressed [business] sectors." As Eizenstat put it, "I strongly believe sovereign wealth funds do bolster the U.S. economy and that on balance they are a significant net plus for the U.S. economy. If we take off the 'welcome sign,' they will invest their growing wealth elsewhere in the world." In short, while Eizenstat was willing to acknowledge the possibility that sovereign wealth funds could threaten U.S. national interests, as a whole he argued their investments were vital to America's continued economic well-being.[120]

At this juncture one has to ask, how can we be sure McCormick and Eizenstat, despite their political differences, are not simply over-enthusiastic cheerleaders for sovereign wealth funds? To answer that question, we need to fast-forward two months, to testimony before the U.S. Senate Banking Committee on 24 April 2008. Chaired by Senator Christopher Dodd (D-CT), the Senate banking Committee spent the 24th of April in hearings titled, "Turmoil in U.S. Credit Markets: Examining the U.S. Regulatory Framework for Assessing Sovereign Investments." Witnesses appearing before the committee included: Scott Alvarez, General Counsel for the Board of Governors of the Federal Reserve System; Jeanne Archibald, Director of the International Trade Practice at Hogan and Hartson LLP; and, Ethiopis Tafara, Director of the Office of International Affairs at the Security and Exchange Commission.

In his testimony, Scott Alvarez assumed responsibility for outlining how the U.S. financial industry was protected from a hostile takeover by sovereign wealth fund investors. Alvarez opened by noting, "as a general matter, the same statutory and regulatory thresholds for review by the federal banking agencies apply to investments by sovereign wealth funds as apply to investments by other domestic and foreign investors." More specifically, Alvarez continued, two federal statutes broadly cover investments in the U.S. banking industry: the Bank Holding Company Act and the Change in Bank Control Act. He then made it quite clear that the Board of Governors at the Federal Reserve "has drawn a distinction between foreign governments themselves, which are not treated as 'companies' subject to the Bank Holding Company Act, and government-owned entities such as sovereign wealth funds, which are treated as companies and are subject to the Bank Holding Company Act."[121]

The decision to treat sovereign wealth funds as companies established a set of legal wickets that Alvarez appeared to believe were sufficient for protecting the American banking industry from a hostile takeover by a foreign government. He came to this conclusion, as the Banking Holding Company Act requires:

1. A company must obtain approval from the Federal Reserve before making a direct or indirect investment in a U.S. bank or bank holding company
2. A review when a potential purchaser acquires:
   a. Ownership or control of 25% or more of any class of voting securities of the bank or bank holding company
   b. Control of the election of a majority of the board of directors of the bank or bank holding company

c. The ability to exercise a controlling influence over the management or policies of the bank or bank holding company[122]

Alvarez then went on to explain how the Board of Governors reaches a formal determination that a company exercises a controlling influence over a board of directors. According to Alvarez, this process requires the Board of Governors to consider the following:

1. The size of the investment
2. The involvement of the investor in the management of the bank or bank holding company
3. Any business relationships between the investor and the bank or bank holding company
4. Any other relevant factors indicating an intent to significantly influence the management or operations of the bank or bank holding company[123]

As might be expected, there is a "cut-line" that helps guide the Board of Governors in deciding what transactions to review. Under the Bank Holding Company Act a presumption is made that an investor who controls less than 5% of the voting shares does not have a controlling influence over the bank or bank holding company. Furthermore, Alvarez stated, the Board of Governors has not found a controlling influence exists if the investment represents less than 10% of the bank or bank holding company's shares.[124] Now all of the sovereign wealth fund investments resulting in a 9.9% stake in a particular financial institute makes sense; they are avoiding U.S. banking regulations.

Apparently aware this very issue would crop up during the Committee hearing, Alvarez then took pains to note, "investments by sovereign wealth funds that do not trigger the requirements of the Bank Holding Company Act may nonetheless require approval from a federal banking agency under the Change in Bank Control Act." According to Alvarez, the Change in Bank Control Act requires the Federal Reserve to grant "prior approval" for any acquisition of 10% or more of any class of voting securities issued by a bank or bank holding company. In addition, the Change in Bank Control Act requires the reviewing federal banking agency to consider specific factors before granting approval. These factors include competitive and informational standards, and whether the transaction would jeopardize the bank's financial stability, prejudice the interests of the depositors, or result in an adverse effect on the Deposit Insurance Fund.[125]

Finally, Alvarez sought to assure his audience that even after a sovereign wealth fund has cleared these legal hurdles, there are stipulations preventing the government investor from using the bank for untoward purposes. These stipulations include the following:

• Section 23A of the Federal Reserve Act, which limits a bank's ability to lend to affiliates. (According to the Federal Reserve Act, a bank may not lend

more than 10% of its capital to any one affiliate or more than 20% of its capital to all affiliates. Section 23A also prohibits the purchase of low-quality assets from a bank's affiliate.)
- Section 23B of the Federal Reserve Act requires that all transactions between a bank and its affiliates be conducted only on "an arms-length" basis[126]

As Alvarez put it, "a U.S. bank controlled by a sovereign wealth fund would not be permitted to fund substantially the operations of other companies controlled by the sovereign wealth fund . . . or provide any uncollateralized loans to such companies, or purchase low-quality assets from those companies."[127]

This testimony from Scott Alvarez suggests the U.S. financial industry is in no immediate danger from sovereign wealth investors, but what about other commercial sectors? In her testimony Jeanne Archibald, a former General Counsel of the U.S. Treasury Department, sought to alleviate at least a few of the assembled senators' fears on this broader concern. Archibald opened by praising recent legislative efforts to address the problem of foreign investors, specifically the Foreign Investment and National Security Act (FINSA) of 2007. She also declared the CFIUS process was alive and well, with compliance remaining at high levels. Archibald argued most companies comply with CFIUS reporting requirements for five reasons:

1. In the absence of a CFIUS "clearance" the foreign acquirer's investment is at risk from a later order of divestment
2. Filing with CFIUS demonstrates a desire to be viewed as a "good corporate citizen"
3. Where a financial institution is funding an acquisition, the institution is virtually certain to require that all applicable regulatory approvals be obtained as a condition for providing the financing
4. In instances in which a foreign investor is taking a minority stake in a U.S. company, the remaining U.S. owners often insist on a CFIUS filing to eliminate the risk from the disruption and possible financial loss that could follow from a future divestment order
5. When CFIUS becomes aware of a proposed transaction, it calls the parties to ask whether they intend to file[128]

In short, Archibald at least found the CFIUS paperwork drill to be reassuring.

Archibald then went on to note that CFIUS "is by no means the only regulatory tool available to the U.S. government to protect against national security risks associated with foreign direct investments." In a sweeping review of existing regulator regimes, Archibald highlighted statutes that serve to protect sensitive industries. These regulations include the following:

- The Communications Act of 1934, which prohibits any foreign government or its representative from holding broadcast or common carrier radio licenses. (The Act also imposes a strict limit of 20% on direct investment in broadcast or common carrier radio licenses by any foreign entity, but does allow for a waiveable limit of 25% on indirect investment by a foreign entity.)

- The National Industrial Security Program, which covers foreign investment in companies that hold classified government contracts
- Nuclear Regulatory Commission requirements for approval of the transfer of existing licenses, a process that considers whether a foreign investor owns or has beneficial ownership in 5% or more of the license holder's voting securities
- The International Traffic in Arms Regulation Act, which requires registrants to provide 60 days' advance notice on an intended sale or transfer of ownership to a foreign person. (Ownership under this regulation is defined as 50% of outstanding voting securities.)
- The International Investment and Trade in Services Survey Act, which requires reporting on all foreign investments in U.S. businesses with assets totaling $3 million when the foreign investment totals 10% or more of the voting securities[129]

As far as Archibald was concerned, this list of sample regulations "serves to illustrate the robust nature of U.S. regulation relating to foreign investment in sectors of the economy that are significant from a national security perspective."[130] Her unstated conclusion is that there is no burning need for further legislation, nor does it appear U.S. national security interests are immediately threatened by the rise of sovereign wealth funds.

The final nail in this regulatory coffin came from Ethiopis Tafara, the Director of the U.S. Securities and Exchange Commission's (SEC) Office of International Affairs. Like Jeanne Archibald, Tafara did not seek to provide an exhaustive list of the regulations the Securities and Exchange Commission monitored in an effort to protect American national interests. Instead he highlighted the fact the SEC was drawing outstanding support from foreign counterparts and then outlined some of the SEC statutes that ensure sovereign wealth fund compliance with U.S. laws. On the issue of international cooperation with the SEC, Tafara claimed that in 2007 the SEC sent more than 550 requests for assistance to outside regulators; more than 450 were reportedly returned, apparently in a favorable manner.[131] Tafara also declared a full 34% of insider trading cases the SEC brought in 2007 came with assistance from foreign counterparts.[132]

But what about on the homefront? According to Tafara, the Securities and Exchange Commission serves U.S. national interests by enforcing compliance with a number of statutes. These include the following:

1. The Securities Exchange Act, Section 16(a) requires completion of a Form 3, disclosing ownership interest for an issuer's officers and directors, as well as any beneficial owner holding 10% or more of an issuer's equity securities.
2. The Securities Exchange Act, Section 13(d) requires the filing of Form 13D by the beneficial owners of more than 5% of an issuer's equity within 10 days of the purchase.

3. The Securities Exchange Act, Section 13(d) requires the filing of Form 13F
   by investment managers with over $100 million in U.S. exchange-traded
   securities, which discloses the name of each reportable issuer in the manager's portfolio at of the end of each calendar quarter, as well as the number
   of shares and market value. This form also provides some information on
   the manager's voting authority.[133]

Having thus buried his audience with SEC forms, Tafara sought to reassure
the senators that even sovereign wealth funds could not escape these disclosure
requirements. As Tafara so eloquently summed up the situation: "it is a well-
established principle of American jurisprudence and international law that sovereign immunity does not extend to a state's commercial activities in another
jurisdiction."[134] In other words, sooner or later the SEC was going to know who
owned what—or seek legal action to accomplish this task.

Parting Thoughts

In June 2008, the Monitor Group, a global consulting firm, released a study
arguing, "national governments are not using [sovereign wealth] funds as tools
of foreign policy . . . Rather, these investments appear to be motivated by financial interest in the prospect of gain and/or ensuring the stability of the financial
system."[135] Titled *Assessing the Risks: The Behaviors of Sovereign Wealth Funds in
the Global Economy*, the report's findings were based on an evaluation of 785
publicly reported deals conducted between 2000 and 2008. According to the
Monitor Group, this assessment of the public record revealed the following:

1. Sovereign wealth funds do not appear to be investing for political motives.
2. While a majority of sovereign wealth fund investments by value occur in
   developed markets, the funds also invest heavily in domestic and emerging
   markets.
3. Sovereign wealth funds are willing to take controlling stakes in target companies. Since 2000, sovereign wealth funds have acquired controlling stakes
   in half of their transactions, but most of these deals occurred in emerging
   markets and sectors not generally deemed politically sensitive.
4. Sovereign wealth funds are taking more financial risk with their investments, including illiquid assets such as equities, real estate, and alternative
   instruments.[136]

More specifically, the Monitor Group found that since 2000, "in terms of
value, nearly half of the [sovereign wealth fund] investments involved financial
services, with a further 19% in real estate and 11% in energy and utilities."[137]
When examining a number of deals, the study revealed sovereign wealth funds
since 2000 had placed approximately 25% of their investments in the financial
sector, 18% in real estate, 15% in industrials, 10% in information technology, and
10% in consumer goods.[138] In other words, the study revealed a sovereign wealth

fund tendency to diversify investments and avoid less lucrative traditional targets like U.S. Treasury notes.

Given the Monitor Group's findings and the discussions earlier—from investment strategies to legal codes—I continue to contend the greatest peril sovereign wealth funds present to the United States is a move away from the purchase of Washington's debt. The funds' demonstrated predominate focus on the bottom line suggests Americans are going to have to either accept higher interest rates as a consequence of our deficit spending or find a means of making U.S. Treasury notes a more lucrative investment.

This loss of interest in U.S. government debt should come as no surprise. A Morgan Stanley estimate published in June 2007 largely came to the same conclusion, noting that "asset prices should depend on the willingness of investors to take risks." As such, Morgan Stanley had argued, "the likely growth of sovereign wealth funds—and the substantially higher risk tolerance of those who will be making their asset allocation decisions—is likely to be rapid enough that it will have a material impact on the average degree of risk tolerance of investors across the globe."[139] The ultimate result? "As sovereign wealth funds grow . . . in importance, the overall global degree of risk tolerance in financial markets rises. This reduces somewhat the attractiveness of relatively safe assets— 'bonds'—and increases the attractiveness of riskier, higher-yielding assets— 'equities.'"[140] This is a rosy scenario for share issuers and holders, but bad news for the U.S. Treasury.

Enough about the peril, what about the potential? The mounting sovereign wealth fund interest in equities markets, both at home and abroad, certainly has the potential to be the "rising tide that lifts all boats." The government investments aboard will help bolster domestic firms and improve employment options in emerging markets. Their investments in the U.S. should ultimately result, as Morgan Stanley predicted in June 2007, in rising stock prices and greater access to the capital necessary for corporate research and development. One could argue that a similar benefit might accrue from the sovereign wealth fund interest in U.S. real estate, but on this issue I suspect the benefits are likely limited to a fortunate few; the rest of us can simply look forward to higher housing costs.

I think it is also safe to predict sovereign wealth funds will offer the potential of a stabilizing force on equities markets. As Bader Al-Sa'ad, Kuwait's sovereign wealth fund manager, argues, "Sovereign wealth funds are not speculative. They are stable and disciplined. They are building long-term portfolios. They don't take advantage of short-term mispricing. And, unlike hedge funds, they don't use leverage. They don't short currencies the way some hedge funds do."[141] I hesitate in reading too much into these remarks, but I appreciate the sentiment. It does appear the sovereign wealth funds will be less volatile participants in the international equity exchanges, a welcome relief from day traders and hedge fund futures betting.

So where does this leave us? Are sovereign wealth funds a peril or potential for the United States? The answer, at least according to the experts, is both. The funds are a peril if not properly monitored and subjected to U.S. laws. Despite current evidence to the contrary, there is a very real possibility the fund managers could be tasked with collecting know-how and sensitive technologies, and yes, they may even be playing the markets (particularly, in oil futures) to bolster their own earnings. Nonetheless, Washington cannot afford to pass legislation that will drive away the sovereign wealth fund investors. The capital these funds offer U.S. businesses is crucial for economic growth in this country. Furthermore, the funds' continuing hunt for underpriced stocks suggests further bailouts of ailing industries, like the financial sector, are possible over time. Quite simply, sovereign wealth funds are becoming an entity we cannot live without, regardless of our efforts to the contrary.

CHAPTER 4

EVALUATING SOVEREIGN WEALTH FUNDS

We believe transparency is a key tool in building trust. Domestically it helps build public support and trust in the management of Norway's petroleum wealth. Openness about the fund's management can [also] contribute to stable financial markets and exert a disciplinary pressure on managers . . . However, we see no need for regulations that would restrict the present investment activities of our fund or any regulation imposing restrictions on sovereign wealth funds over and above those applying to non-sovereign wealth fund investors.

—*Kristin Halvorsen, Norwegian Finance Minister, February 2008*[1]

Despite repeated protests they are simply investing public funds in a manner intended to generate maximum returns, sovereign wealth fund managers have become a favored target for conspiracy theorists, isolationists, and national security hawks. These vocal critics appear convinced the government investment vehicles are largely charged with achieving a political agenda, and they tend to ignore the argument sovereign wealth funds are inherently intended to serve a public good. The result is a continuing demand the funds operate in a more "transparent" manner. The unanswered question, however, is how to meet that requirement without sacrificing the discretion required for executing a profitable investment strategy.

International efforts to address these concerns can be directly traced to 19 October 2007, when the G7[2]—acting under "strong pressure" from the United States and France—called on the International Monetary Fund (IMF) and Organization for Economic Co-operation and Development (OECD) to draw up a code of conduct for sovereign wealth funds. French President Nicolas Sarkozy was particularly adamant about the need for this set of standards, arguing, "we've decided not to let ourselves be sold down the river by speculative funds, by unscrupulous attitudes which do not meet the transparency criteria one is entitled to expect in a civilized world. It's unacceptable and we have decided not to accept it."[3] According to the G7, this code would demand greater transparency and adherence to the "best practices" resident in Norway's Government Pension Fund-Global.

This call for establishment of a formal code dictating transparency and "best practices" encountered almost immediate opposition. Although much of this resistance was apparently initially reserved for formal diplomatic exchanges, an international audience was provided full exposure to investor complaints during the January 2008 World Economic Forum in Davos. In a presentation to the Davos forum, Russian Finance Minister Aleksey Kurdin rejected calls for curbing sovereign wealth funds by arguing, "these funds are for the security of future generations. They are long term and not speculative. They play a very positive role in the global market. Any concern about the political underlining of these funds is exaggerated."[4] Bader Al Sa'ad, managing director of the Kuwait Investment Authority (KIA), assumed a similar position, contending, "the KIA has been operating for 55 years and has never made a political decision. We look to the bottom line."[5] Even the Norwegians, the standard bearer of sovereign wealth fund "best practices," expressed umbrage with the prospect of an IMF dictate. Kristin Halvorsen, Norway's Finance Minister, complained about the U.S. and European Union intransigence by declaring, "they don't like us, but they need our money."[6]

By early February 2008, it was clear that the IMF was going to have a difficult time meeting a proposed April delivery date for the code of conduct. In remarkably candid anonymous background interviews, IMF officials told reporters "these [sovereign wealth] funds do not think of themselves as political . . . What we're hearing from them is, 'what are you so upset about?' But the concerns are there, and they need to be taken care of in a code of best practices."[7] Lawrence Summers, the former U.S. Secretary of the Treasury, offered a similar observation by contending the sovereign wealth funds were appropriately worried about Western xenophobia, but needed to alleviate concerns about their ultimate intentions. Summers went on to argue this xenophobia could be addressed through an acceptance of greater transparency and adoption of apolitical investment strategies. Failure to do so, he warned, would generate "a lot more xenophobia."[8]

These warnings apparently drew little sympathy from the fund managers. Speaking to an audience at the World Bank in February 2008, Lou Jiwei, head of the China Investment Corporation, declared the IMF effort was making little progress as "it seems there wasn't any agreement . . . because nobody wants to accept the fact that anybody's better than themselves."[9] Perhaps the most concise summary of this opposition to a sovereign wealth fund code of conduct came from the *New York Times*. In a story published on 9 February 2008, the *Times* noted, "Leaders of funds in Russia, the Middle East, China, and other parts of Asia say that the West's demands for regulations is hypocritical in light of the failure to regulate European and American banks and hedge funds."[10]

It is only fair to note that not all news on the sovereign wealth fund transparency front in early 2008 was bad. On 12 March 2008, the government of Abu Dhabi—operator of the world's largest sovereign wealth fund—sent a letter to Western financial officials spelling out the United Arab Emirates' investment guidelines. According to the letter, "the Abu Dhabi Government has never and will never use its investments as a foreign policy tool." Rather, Abu Dhabi's "investment organizations have always sought solely to maximize risk-adjusted returns."[11] As evidence supporting this claim, Abu Dhabi declared 80% of the Abu Dhabi Investment Authority's (ADIA) funds are managed by "outside firms" who provide access to "international financial expertise."

In addition to these broad statements clearly intended to assuage Western skeptics, the letter outlined nine principles said to guide Abu Dhabi's capital investment organizations. As listed in the letter, these principles are:

- To operate for the public good, generating long-term, attractive returns for the prosperity of the people of Abu Dhabi
- To operate as strictly individual entities, making independent, commercially driven investment decisions
- To follow meticulously all of the laws, regulations, and rules of the countries and exchanges in which investments are made
- To meet all disclosure requirements of relevant government and regulatory bodies in countries in which they invest
- To maximize risk-adjusted returns, relative to well-established market indices
- To recruit and retain world-class financial professionals either as in-house or external managers
- To invest with a long-term perspective
- To invest in a well-diversified portfolio across asset classes, geographies, and sectors
- To maintain appropriate standards of governance and accountability[12]

The letter closed by noting Abu Dhabi realized its investments "are good for the global economy—providing increased liquidity, injecting capital for growth, expanding market access, creating jobs, and encouraging a common interest and commitment to mutual prosperity."[13] Quite clearly, the authors had been reading through U.S. Congressional testimony provided by the advocates of foreign direct investment.

On 21 March 2008, this news from Abu Dhabi was trumped by the release of a joint statement on the "Policy Principles for Sovereign Wealth Funds and Countries Receiving Sovereign Wealth Fund Investment." Signed by Abu Dhabi, Singapore, and the United States, the joint statement was said to be "aimed at contributing to the work of the IMF and OECD in developing voluntary best practices for sovereign wealth funds and . . . countries receiving investments."[14] In the joint statement, the three parties outlined five policy principles for sovereign wealth funds and four policy principles for countries receiving sovereign wealth fund investment. The five policy principles for sovereign wealth funds stated:

1. Sovereign wealth fund investment decisions should be based solely on commercial grounds, rather than to advance, directly or indirectly, the geopolitical goals of the controlling government
2. Greater information disclosure by sovereign wealth funds in areas such as purpose, investment objectives, institutional arrangements, and financial information can help reduce uncertainty in financial markets and build trust in recipient countries
3. Sovereign wealth funds should have in place strong governance structures, internal controls, and operational and risk management systems
4. Sovereign wealth funds and the private sector should compete fairly
5. Sovereign wealth funds should respect host-country rules by complying with all applicable regulatory and disclosure requirements of the countries in which they invest[15]

The four policy principles for recipient countries held:

1. Countries receiving sovereign wealth fund investment should not erect protectionist barriers to portfolio or foreign direct investment
2. Recipient countries should ensure predictable investment frameworks—investment rules should be publicly available, clearly articulated, predictable, and supported by strong and consistent rule of law
3. Recipient countries should not discriminate among investors
4. Recipient countries should respect investor decisions by being as nonintrusive as possible, rather than seeking to direct sovereign wealth fund investment[16]

On 28 March 2008, European Union Trade Commissioner Peter Mandelson took the examples provided by Abu Dhabi and Singapore a step further—and called on all sovereign wealth funds to agree to a global code of conduct. In a speech before the OECD, Mandelson declared, "Our chief focus should be on integrating sovereign wealth funds effectively in the global financial system by working with them on a voluntary international code." The government investment vehicles, Mandelson argued, need to be integrated "in a way that reassures the recipients of investment without casting the [sovereign wealth] funds as potential villains."[17]

Taken as a whole, Abu Dhabi's letter, the joint statement, and Mandelson's speech all suggested the time had come for establishment of a code of conduct for sovereign wealth funds and their intended targets. In an effort to assure both sides of the debate—investors and potential targets—received a fair hearing, the IMF established the International Working Group of Sovereign Wealth Funds.[18] According to the IMF, this new organization was to develop a list of commonly accepted "best practices" for release in October 2008. The 23-member body convened its first session at the IMF headquarters in Washington DC on 30 April to 1 May 2008.[19] Cochairs for the first session were selected by the participating sovereign wealth funds, who named a senior representative of the Abu Dhabi

Investment Authority and the Director of the IMF Monetary and Capital Markets Department. According to a news release published following this first session, the International Working Group is charged with identifying a "common set of voluntary principles for sovereign wealth funds." These principles are to be drawn from existing codes and practices, and are intended to assist in maintaining the free flow of cross-border investment and a stable international financial system.[20]

It should come as no surprise to learn that these first steps toward establishing a common set of principles for sovereign wealth funds were not met with unanimous approval. In mid-May 2008, the Kuwait Investment Authority (KIA) took direct aim at Germany's efforts to regulate sovereign wealth funds by threatening to spend KIA monies elsewhere. In an interview with *Der Spiegel*, a German-language weekly news magazine, Badar Al Sa'ad expressed reservations about Berlin's future intentions regarding sovereign wealth fund investments and then stated Kuwait's plans for dealing with potentially unfavorable legislation. "We are very concerned," Al Sa'ad declared, "we still regard Germany as an economic anchor in Europe and the World . . . But in the future any regulation of sovereign wealth funds could restrict our commitment to your country."[21]

Kuwait was not alone in this battle to derail international efforts aimed at regulating sovereign wealth funds. In a June 2008 presentation before the OECD Forum on "Climate Change, Growth, and Stability," the Norwegian Finance Minister, Kristin Halvorsen, expressed concerns about continuing demands for sovereign wealth fund transparency. While Halvorsen was quick to note Norway maintained one of the most transparent government investment vehicles, she also declared that there were logical limits to what could be expected when it comes to disclosure. As Halvorsen put it, "There is a need to strike a balance . . . between the need for transparency on the one hand, and on the other hand to use business sense and not be put at a disadvantage in the market place." "Furthermore," she continued, "transparency has to run both ways. If recipient countries set up screening processes to address national security concerns, there must be transparency with respect to how such screening decisions are made, by whom and under what criteria."[22]

As for Norway's efforts to reassure target or recipient countries, Halvorsen contended Oslo's Government Pension Fund-Global adhered to five factors that serve to avoid criticism. According to Halvorsen these five factors are:

1. The Government Pension Fund-Global has an *explicit aim to maximize financial returns*
2. The Fund is a *financial investor* with non-strategic holdings
3. There are *clear lines of responsibility* between political authorities and the Fund's operational management
4. There is a *high degree of transparency* in all aspects of the Fund's purpose and operation
5. The Fund's *ethical guidelines are transparent and predictable*, and are based on internationally recognized standards. More specifically, these ethical guidelines recognize the objective of sound financial return, along with the

obligation to respect fundamental rights of those that are affected by the companies in which the Fund invests.[23]

Halvorsen's "responsible actor" sales pitch, however, was the exception to the rule. Other sovereign wealth fund managers adopted Kuwait's "iron fist in a velvet glove" approach to dealing with regulatory campaigns. For example, at a mergers and acquisition conference held in early July 2008, China Investment Corporation president Gao Xiping argued, "If there is too much political pressure and too much unpredictability, you just go away. Fortunately, there are more than 200 countries in the world. And fortunately, there are many countries who are happy with [sovereign wealth funds]."[24]

Given the statements from Kuwait, Norway, and China, it was clear that significant lifting remained to be accomplished as the International Working Group prepared for its second session in July 2008. According to the International Working Group cochairs, the body continues to be "committed to a goal of establishing voluntary principles and practices by October 2008." The ultimate objective is "to promote a clearer understanding of the institutional framework, governance, and investment operations of sovereign wealth funds."[25] In addition to the official statements, financial analysts welcomed the Group's efforts. Speaking with a Reuters reporter, an analyst with Deutsche Bank argued, "It's important to establish some guiding principles. This will help contain the risk of a backlash in the West and also establish some kind of trust."[26]

Participants in the International Working Group's second session indicated the organization might indeed accomplish its intended mission. Speaking with reporters following the Singapore meetings, Hamad Al Hurr Al Suwaidi, one of the two Group cochairs, announced, "The legal and governance issues have been agreed upon."[27] Al Suwaidi went on to state terms of the "Generally Accepted Principles and Practices" would be finalized in October—after the International Working Group completes a third session, slated to occur in September 2008. To that end, an unnamed participant in the discussions told reporters,

> . . . we are asked to be transparent. There is a common feeling among members that sovereign wealth fund holdings in so-called strategic assets are greatly exaggerated. As such, we could disclose holdings in the most sensitive—defense companies, for instance. Or a more general figure to show how much each fund has in the companies of a particular country.[28]

I would highlight the fact this "unnamed" participant was also quick to note, "No final decisions have been made," suggesting we should not expect too much from the final document. This assessment is further buttressed by Al Suwaidi's repeated insistence that the terms of the agreement will be voluntary, and affected parties will not be expected to report to any oversight body.[29]

Progress on Recipient States Policy

Although efforts to establish a commonly-accepted code of conduct for sovereign wealth funds appears an endless uphill battle, the same can not be said of the drive to develop a set of standards for target/recipient countries. On 4 April 2008, the OECD released an Investment Committee report titled "Sovereign Wealth Funds and Recipient Country Policy." In a cover letter for the report, the OECD Secretary-General declared, "Our findings show [sovereign wealth] funds bring benefits to home and host countries and that existing OECD investment instruments are well-suited to develop guidance for countries receiving investments from sovereign wealth funds."[30]

Given this inclusive opening statement, it is not surprising to find the OECD arguing, "sovereign wealth funds represent efforts by owners of these assets to manage them in a more proactive and sophisticated way." As for the differences of opinion between fund managers and their intended targets, the OECD simply states, "As is often the case, when new actors emerge on the international financial scene, the players need to become better acquainted."[31] One can be forgiven at this point for confusing the statement from an international organization with a lecture from a handbook for second-grade teachers, but, yes, the OECD actually argued that the "new kids on the block" just needed to be properly introduced to the existing clique.

This line of reasoning apparently serves to explain the OECD's contention that "existing instruments already contain fundamental principles for recipient country policies . . . transparency, non-discrimination, and liberalism." According to the OECD, these principles "(1) express a common understanding of fair treatment of foreign investors, including sovereign wealth funds; (2) commit adhering governments to build this fair treatment into their investment policies; and (3) provide for 'peer review' of adhering governments' observance of these commitments."[32]

In an effort to clarify this largely philosophical statement, the OECD went on to provide "investment policy guidance." In a tone box prefaced with the remark, "participants have agreed on the following guidance for investment policy measures designed to safeguard national security," the OECD lays out four areas of concern: nondiscrimination, transparency/predictability, regulatory proportionality, and accountability. According to the OECD, these four areas can then be converted to policy guidance using the following criteria:

- *Nondiscrimination*—Governments should rely on measures of general application that treat similarly situated investors in similar fashion
- *Transparency/predictability*—Regulatory objectives and practices should be made as transparent as possible so as to increase the predictability of outcomes
  - *Codification and publication*—Primary and subordinate laws should be codified and made available to the public
  - *Prior notification*—Notify interested parties about plans to change investment policies

- *Consultation*—Seek the views of interested parties when considering a change in investment policies
- *Procedural fairness and predictability*—Strict time limits should be applied to review procedures for foreign investments. Commercially-sensitive information provided by the investor should be protected
- *Disclosure of investment policy actions*—Adequate disclosure is required for accountability
- *Regulatory proportionality*—Restrictions on investment or conditions on transactions should not be greater than needed to protect national security . . . and should be avoided when other existing measures are adequate and appropriate to address a national security concern
  - *Essential security concerns are self-judging*—Based on each state's individual calculus, but the relationship between the investment restrictions and the national security risk should be clear
  - *Narrow focus*—Investment restrictions should be narrowly focused on concerns related to national security
  - *Appropriate expertise*—Security-related investment measures should be designed so that they benefit from adequate expertise as well as expertise necessary to weigh the implications of actions with respect to the benefits of open investment policies and the impact of restrictions
  - *Tailored responses*—Restrictive investment measures should be tailored to the specific risks posed by specific investment proposals
  - *Last resort*—Restrictive investment measures should be used, if at all, as a last resort when other policies cannot be used to eliminate security-related concerns
- *Accountability*—Procedures for parliamentary oversight, judicial review, periodic regulatory impact assessments, and decisions to block an investment should be taken at high government levels to ensure accountability of the implementing authorities[33]

As with the guidance the IMF was preparing for the sovereign wealth funds, this set of policy recommendations for target/recipient nations is voluntary and provides for no oversight body. The OECD apparently believes that the intended audience will act in good faith and in a potentially parsimonious manner. A quick glance at regulations concerning foreign direct investment in Australia, France, Germany, Japan, and the United States, however, indicates that nothing could be further from the truth. Would-be overseas investors are engaging in an activity where the rules change with every border crossing. It seems the best advice one can offer a sovereign wealth fund manager is to hire a good team of lawyers and hope the recipient is unlikely to fundamentally change the rules of the game in midstream.

Evaluating Sovereign Wealth Funds

In the absence of an internationally accepted code of conduct for sovereign wealth funds, how does a potential target/recipient evaluate the risk associated with opening its borders to these government investment vehicles? To date, the best answer appears to be an appeal to one of the four "transparency" or "risk" indexes developed by nongovernmental agencies. All four of these indices were publicly released between June 2007 and May 2008, and the criteria of all four may change with time. At the moment, however, these indices are the "best answer" one can hand a decision-maker tasked with evaluating competing sovereign wealth funds.

Edwin Truman's "Scoreboard for Sovereign Wealth Funds": Edwin Truman's "Scoreboard" is probably the best-known of the sovereign wealth fund transparency indexes. Truman, a senior fellow with the Peterson Institute for International Economics, was Assistant Secretary for International Affairs of the U.S. Treasury from 1998 to 2000, and directed the Division of International Finance on the Board of Governors of the Federal Reserve System from 1977 to 1998. Truman's "Scoreboard" can be traced back to a briefing titled "Nonrenewable Resource Funds" he presented at a workshop sponsored by the U.S. Treasury in May 2008. Criteria used for evaluating sovereign wealth funds included on the "Scoreboard" were further enunciated in a Peterson Institute "Policy Brief" published in August 2007[34]— and the final product has since been used in congressional testimony[35] and widely distributed on the internet.

In developing his sovereign wealth fund "Scoreboard," Truman began with the premise that an international standard on cross-border investments by these government agencies should cover four areas: objectives and investment strategy; governance; transparency; and behavior. According to Truman, a standard for "objectives and investment strategy" should be based on the "presumption that the international investment activities of governments are based on clearly stated policy objectives." More specifically, he argued, these objectives and strategies should be evaluated through access to information concerning how funds are incorporated into the investment mechanism, how earnings and/or principal should be spent, what type of assets are included in portfolios, how the assets are managed, where these management responsibilities reside, what investment and risk-management strategies should be followed, and how these elements can be changed.[36]

The standard for "governance," Truman argues, "should set out clearly the role of government and the managers of the investment mechanism, what entity sets the policies, how these policies are executed, and the accountability arrangements."[37] Transparency, he declares, should include at least annual reports but preferably quarterly updates. In these reports, Truman contends, the sovereign wealth fund should include investment strategies, outcomes, and "the nature and location of actual investments." Not surprisingly, this transparency standard also calls for published independent audits of the investment activities.[38] Truman's proposed standard for "behavior" is more open-ended. As he puts it, "the behavior guidelines might cover the scale and rapidity with which the entity adjusts its portfolio. They might also create the presumption of consultation with the relevant countries with respect to the allocation among assets denominated in different currencies or located in different countries."[39]

Using these proposed standards as a philosophical foundation, Truman then set about developing a numeric scoreboard for sovereign wealth funds. Truman's efforts to quantify these relatively arbitrary qualities is accomplished through the employment of 33 questions phrased in a manner designed to result in a dichotomous (yes or no, 1 or 0) response.[42] His intention is to provide a measure of four broad categories: structure, governance, transparency, and behavior. The questions are as follows:

Table 4.1 Scoreboard for Sovereign Wealth Funds: The Scoring Criteria[41]

– Structure

1. Is the sovereign wealth fund's objective clearly communicated?

   • *Fiscal Treatment*

2. Is the source of the sovereign wealth fund's money clearly specified?

3. Is nature of the subsequent use of the principal and earnings of the fund clearly stated?

4. Are these elements of fiscal treatment integrated with the budget?

5. Are the guidelines for fiscal treatment generally followed without frequent adjustment?

   • *Other Structural Elements*

6. Is the overall investment strategy clearly communicated?

7. Is the procedure for changing the structure of the sovereign wealth fund clear?

8. Is the sovereign wealth fund separate from the country's international reserves?

– Governance

9. Is the role of the government in setting the investment strategy of the sovereign wealth fund clearly established?

10. Is the role of the managers in executing the investment strategy clearly established?

11. Are decisions on specific investments made by the managers?

12. Does the sovereign wealth fund have in place and publicly available guidelines for corporate responsibility that it follows?

13. Does the sovereign wealth fund have ethical guidelines that it follows?

– Transparency and Accountability

   • *Investment Strategy Implementation*

14. Do regular reports on investments by the sovereign wealth fund include information on the categories of investments?

15. Does the strategy use benchmarks?

16. Does the strategy limit investments based on credit ratings?

17. Are the holders of investment mandates identified?

Table 4.1 *(Continued)*

• *Investment Activities*

18. Do regular reports on the investments by the sovereign wealth fund include the size of the fund?

19. Do regular reports on the investments by the sovereign wealth fund include information on its returns?

20. Do regular reports on the investments by the sovereign wealth fund include information on the geographic location of investments?

21. Do regular reports on the investments by the sovereign wealth fund include information on the specific investments?

22. Do regular reports on the investments by the sovereign wealth fund include information on the currency composition of investments?

• *Reports*

23. Does the sovereign wealth fund provide at least an annual report on its activities and results?

24. Does the sovereign wealth fund provide quarterly reports?

• *Audits*

25. Is the sovereign wealth fund subjected to a regular annual audit?

26. Is the audit published promptly?

27. Is the audit independent?

– **Behavior**

28. Does the sovereign wealth fund indicate the nature and speed of adjustment in its portfolio?

29. Does the sovereign wealth fund have limits on the size of its stakes?

30. Does the sovereign wealth fund not take controlling stakes?

31. Does the sovereign wealth fund have a policy on the use of leverage?

32. Does the sovereign wealth fund have a policy on the use of derivatives?

33. Are derivatives used primarily for hedging?

Having thus established the criteria for evaluating sovereign wealth funds, Truman sets about providing a scoreboard for 46 of the government investment vehicles. According to Truman—although he does not provide specific sources—the assigned scores are based on "systematic, regularly available, public information."[42] As such, he contends the scoreboard rates sovereign wealth funds on their current practices and can be updated as required.

Truman's findings can be summarized as follows:

• All sovereign wealth funds are not the same. There is no one cluster of "good" or "bad" funds. Rather the funds fall into three broad groups: 22 with scores above 60, 14 with scores below 30, and 10 in the middle. Overall,

scores for the 46 rated sovereign wealth funds ranged from 9 to 95 out of
100 possible points.

- Sovereign wealth fund liabilities, pension or nonpension, do not serve to
clearly determine where they fall in the ratings. Thus, Truman concludes,
"it is not unreasonable to hold nonpension sovereign wealth funds to the
[same] standard of accountability [as] pension funds."
- There appears to be little, or no, correlation between a sovereign wealth
fund and the economic or political characteristics of the government
responsible for the investment vehicle.[43]

For Truman, these findings offer two lessons for those charged with developing a set of "best practices" for sovereign wealth funds. First, the diversity in
current practices suggests arriving at a common standard is going to be very
"challenging." Second, the diversity of current practices, and their apparent
absence of correlation with any particular economic or political system, suggest
an "opportunity to converge on a common high standard."[44]

I note that Truman's findings are not without controversy. This is particularly true of his contention there appears to be little, or no, correlation between
the transparency/behavior of a sovereign wealth fund and the political characteristics of the government responsible for operating the investment vehicle. As
a political scientist, I would argue there appears to be a clear tie between a sovereign wealth fund's transparency score and its association with a democracy or
authoritarian regime. The more transparent funds are likely to be associated
with democracies, while the least transparent funds are more likely to be found
in an authoritarian state. My observations are supported by work at the U.S.
Council on Foreign Relations. As Jagdish Bhagwati, a professor of economics
and law at Columbia University, highlighted in his 11 June 2008 testimony
before the U.S. Senate Foreign Relations Committee, when it comes to sovereign
wealth fund, "non-transparency and lack of democratic governance tend to go
more or less together."[45]

Linaburg-Maduell Transparency Index: Established in the Spring of 2008,
the Linaburg-Maduell Transparency Index has become a favorite with reporters
in search of a quick evaluative guide for sovereign wealth funds. According to
the developers, Carl Linaburg[46] and Michael Maduell[47], this index provides a
measure of transparency for government investment vehicles. In keeping with
Truman's lead, the Linaburg-Maduell Transparency Index is also based on a
quantitative measure of qualitative criteria. In this case, Linaburg and Maduell
argue they have identified ten "essential principles that depict sovereign wealth
fund transparency to the public."[48] A fund is scored by adding a point for
achieved "essential principle." As such, the minimum score is a 1, but Linaburg
and Maduell recommend a minimum rating of 8 for an organization to claim
"adequate" transparency. Of note, unlike Truman, Linaburg and Maduell do not
reveal the sources of the data used to address these questions, but they do indicate a "current-as-of date," which suggests that the index is subject to periodic
review and updating.

Table 4.2 Scoreboard for Sovereign Wealth Funds (Transparency and Total Score)[49]

Country	Fund Name	Transparency	Total Score
New Zealand	Superannuation Fund	100	95
U.S.-Alaska	Permanent Fund	100	94
Norway	Government Pension Fund-Global	100	92
U.S.-Wyoming	Permanent Mineral Trust Fund	82	91
Ireland	National Pensions Reserve Fund	86	86
Australia	Future Fund	68	80
East Timor	Petroleum Fund	96	80
Azerbaijan	State Oil Fund	89	77
Chile	Social and Economic Stabilization Fund	86	71
Kazakhstan	National Fund	64	64
South Korea	Korea Investment Corporation	45	51
Russia	Reserve Fund	50	51
Kuwait	Kuwait Investment Corporation	41	48
Singapore	Temasek Holdings	61	45
Singapore	Government Investment Corporation	39	41
Malaysia	Khazanah National	46	38
China	China Investment Corporation	14	29
Kiribati	Revenue Equalization Reserve Fund	7	29
Iran	Oil Stabilization Fund	18	23
Venezuela	National Development Fund	27	23
Oman	State General Reserve Fund	18	20
UAE	Mubadala Development Company	7	15
UAE	Istithmar	7	14
Qatar	Qatar Investment Authority	2	9
UAE	Abu Dhabi Investment Authority	4	9

Table 4.3 Principles of the Linaburg-Maduell Transparency Index[50]

Fund provides a history including reason for creation, origins of wealth, and government ownership structure

1. Fund provides updated independently audited annual reports

2. Fund provides percent ownership of company holdings, financial returns, and geographic locations of holdings

3. If applicable, the fund provides size, composition, and return of foreign exchange reserves

4. Fund provides guidelines in reference to ethical standards, investment policies, remuneration polices, and enforcer of guidelines

5. Fund provides clear strategies and objectives

6. If applicable, the fund clearly identifies subsidies and contact information

7. If applicable, the fund identifies external managers

8. Fund manages its own Web site

9. Fund provides main office location address and contact information such as telephone and fax.

Table 4.4 Linaburg-Maduell Sovereign Wealth Fund Rating[51]

Country	Fund Name	Assets in $Billion	Rating
Norway	Government Pension Fund-Global	395	10
New Zealand	Superannuation Fund	14	10
Australia	Future Fund	59	9
U.S.-Alaska	Permanent Fund	40	9
South Korea	Korea Investment Corporation	30	9
U.S.-New Mexico	State Investment Office Trust	16	9
Azerbaijan	State Oil Fund	5	9
Canada	Alberta's Heritage Fund	17	8
U.S.-Wyoming	Permanent Mineral Trust Fund	4	8
Hong Kong	Monetary Authority Investment Portfolio	173	7
Singapore	Temasek Holdings	159	7
Ireland	National Pensions Reserve Fund	31	7
Malaysia	Khazanah National	26	7
East Timor	Petroleum Fund	3	7
Singapore	Government Investment Corporation	330	6
Kuwait	Investment Authority	265	6

Table 4.4 *(Continued)*

Country	Fund Name	Assets in $Billion	Rating
Bahrain	Mumtalakat Holding Company	10	6
UAE–Abu Dhabi	Mudadala Development Company	10	6
Russia	National Welfare Fund	163	5
Trinidad&Tobago	Heritage and Stabilization Fund	1	5
UAE	Investment Corporation of Dubai	unkn	5
Saudi Arabia	SAMA Foreign Holdings	365	4
Vietnam	State Capital Investment Corporation	2	4
UAE–Abu Dhabi	Abu Dhabi Investment Authority	875	3
Kazakhstan	National Fund	22	3
Chile	Social and Economic Stabilization Fund	16	3
Taiwan	National Stabilization Fund	15	3
Botswana	Pula Fund	7	3
UAE	RAK Investment Authority	1	3
China	SAFE Investment Company	312	2
China	China Investment Corporation	200	2
Iran	Oil Stabilization Fund	13	2
Oman	State General Reserve Fund	2	2
Venezuela	FIEM	1	2
Qatar	Investment Authority	60	1
Libya	Libyan Investment Authority	50	1
Algeria	Revenue Regulation Front	47	1
Brunei	Investment Authority	30	1
Nigeria	Excess Crude Account	11	1
Kiribati	Revenue Equalization Reserve Fund	0.4	1
Mauritania	National Fund for Hydrocarbon Reserves	0.3	1
Angola	Reserve Fund for Oil	0.2	1
UAE–Federal	Emirates Investment Authority	unkn	1

As Linaburg and Maduell have selected Norway's Government Pension Fund-Global as their ultimate standard for sovereign wealth transparency, it is not surprising to find Oslo's investment vehicle at the top of this listing. Aside from this clearly declared bias, and the apparently "blunt" nature of their instrument—10 questions in comparison to the "Scoreboard's" 33 data points—I would contend Linaburg and Madeull seem to verify Truman's findings:

- All sovereign wealth funds are not the same: scoring variances range from 1 to 10.
- As with Truman's "Scoreboard," sovereign wealth funds with and without pension liabilities appear to score with equal variance on the Linaburg and Madeull index.
- The size of a sovereign wealth fund's holdings is not a good predictor of its performance on a transparency index.

Beyond these observations there is little to be said of the Linaburg-Maduell Transparency Index. My suspicion is that ease of access and the authors' promise to regularly update their assessments suggest this particular measure of sovereign wealth fund behavior is going to receive a lot of media and, therefore, congressional attention.

Gerald Lyons: Transparency of the Largest Sovereign Wealth Funds: As part of his October 2007 report, "State Capitalism: The Rise of Sovereign Wealth Funds," Gerald Lyons[52] and Oxford Analytica[53] provided an evaluation of the transparency associated with the wealthiest sovereign wealth funds. As a means of determining government investment vehicles suitable for inclusion in this listing, Lyons and company employed four criteria:

- The fund had to be owned by a sovereign national state rather than a regional or local state entity. (Interestingly, this did not eliminate the Alaska fund.)
- The fund could not be a national pension endowment, unless it was directly financed by foreign exchange assets generated by commodity exports. (This immediately included Norway's Government Pension Fund-Global.)
- The fund could not be a direct function of a central bank or authority that performs roles typical of a central bank (e.g., supervision of currency issuance), even if these organizations also manage foreign exchange assets. (This ruled out the Saudi Arabian Monetary Authority.)
- The funds had to be investment-focused and not producers of goods or services. (This excluded energy companies and state-development banks.)[54]

This set of criteria resulted in the identification of 20 sovereign wealth funds that were then evaluated for transparency. Unlike Truman or Linaburg and Maduell, Lyons unfortunately does not provide a quantifiable scale for measuring transparency, nor does he provide a set of definitions that would make it possible to replicate his findings. Instead, we are simply told data used to create the listing were taken from Web sites, media reports, and research concerning sovereign wealth funds "other" financial institutions had provided.[55]

Table 4.5 The Lyons and Oxford Analytica Top 20 Sovereign Wealth Funds[56]

Country	Fund Name	Transparency Rating
Canada-Alberta	Heritage Savings Trust	High—Quarterly and annual reports, and business plans publicly available
Malaysia	Khazanah National	High—Annual reports provide good data
Norway	Global Pension Fund	High—Annual and quarterly reports publicly available
Singapore	Temasek Holdings	High—Audited annual financial reports and periodic updates provided to the Ministry of Finance—while not required, since 2004 annual financial highlights publicly released
U.S.-Alaska	Permanent Reserve Fund	High—Public reports
Kazakhstan	National Fund	Medium—Website provides current data on revenues and expenditure, but specific explanations on how fund's resources are being used is lacking
Singapore	Government Invest Corp	Medium—Information about structure and investments, but no detailed financial reports on website
South Korea	Korean Invest Corp	Medium—Plans to disclose financial statements and accounting standards; also plans to release audit reports
China	Investment Authority	Low—No further comment in Lyons' report
Kuwait	Investment Authority	Low—Public disclosure of any information on fund's work legally prohibited
Qatar	Investment Authority	Low—No reports provided
UAE	Dubai International Capital	Low—No public reports available, but list of selected investments available
UAE	Istithmar	Low—No reports provided, but list of investments available
Brunei	Investment Authority	Very low—No further comment in Lyons' report
Chile	Economic and Social	Very low—Transparency may increase Stabilization Fund once fund is fully functional

Table 4.5 *(Continued)*

Country	Fund Name	Transparency Rating
Oman	State General Reserve Fund	Very low—No further comment in Lyons' report
Taiwan	National Stabilization Fund	Very low—Management and others associated with fund are subject to imprisonment and fines if found guilty of leaking information on investment plans
UAE	Abu Dhabi Invest Authority	Very low—Has never publicly declared value of assets under management
Venezuela	National Development Fund	Very low—No auditing, accountability, or parliamentary oversight of fund
Russia	Stabilization Fund	No rating—Publishes monthly public report on fund accumulation, spending, and balance. Details on investment reported quarterly to parliament

Although Lyons provides no summary statement on this transparency rating, he does include four observations concerning investment patterns that speak to this concern. According to Lyons, "Investment policies vary, [depending on] the sovereign wealth fund's primary aim and purpose."[57] More specifically, Lyons concludes sovereign wealth fund investments in 2007 reveal:

- A number of funds have acquired significant stakes in foreign companies.
- "Future generations" funds with high levels of transparency, such as Norway's Government Pension Fund-Global, have a high level of diversification and hold only small stakes.
- Stabilization funds, such as Russia's, are tasked with delivering stable and low-risk returns, and therefore they are limited to investment in AAA-rated sovereign bonds, with a given currency composition to manage risk.
- Low-transparency funds, such as the Abu Dhabi Investment Authority, usually prefer investing in small stakes to avoid disclosure requirements.[58]

In short, Lyons' transparency rating suggests there is a pattern to sovereign wealth fund investment that might lend itself to establishing a set of "best practices." That is, it would appear direct accountability to future generations, or service as a currency stabilization measure, results in greater disclosure of business practices and assets. Sovereign wealth funds without this direct commitment to the public good appear to be more likely to operate in manners that evoke target/recipient country suspicions.

Breakingviews' Sovereign Wealth Fund Risk Index: The least well-known of the sovereign wealth fund evaluative indices was developed by Breakingviews.com. A self-proclaimed "leading source of agenda-setting financial insight," Breakingviews is said to have 25 correspondents and columnists based in London, Madrid, New York, Paris, and Washington. A primarily web-based organization, Breakingviews states that it has over 15,000 subscribers and reaches a potential audience of over 4.5 million through columns published in some of the world's largest newspapers.

Breakingviews entered the world of sovereign wealth fund evaluative indexing in January 2008. According to Breakingviews, their Sovereign Wealth Fund Risk Index provides a first-ever ranking of "the top 20 prominent funds according to the potential risk they present to Western interests."[59] These rankings were determined using quantified responses to 15 questions covering "transparency," "strategic control," and "political threat."[60] These 15 questions were assigned values ranging from 1 to 5, with 1 being the most favorable score and 5 being the least desired score. The final result is three separate evaluative scales with minimum and maximum scores of one and five. The definitions and scoring values for questions in each of the three categories are listed in Table 4.6.

Unfortunately, Breakingviews does not provide the data sources used in assigning values for the 20 sovereign wealth funds ranked on their index. One presumes much of the information used to arrive at the findings presented in Table 4.7 was taken from Web sites and news stories.

Breakingviews contends a number of observations flow from this ranking system. First, any fund drawing a double-digit total score is "considered a high potential risk to Western investor interests."[61] Second, the "bulk of sovereign wealth funds pose little risk to Western interests."[62] Third, if a sovereign wealth fund is "alarmed" at its ranking and "the risk [that] unscrupulous western politicians might use it as a cover for protectionism, the solution lies in their hands. Most sovereign wealth funds could reduce their score simply by improving their transparency."[63] Finally, Breakingviews, like Linaburg-Maduell, reaches the conclusion that Norway's Government Pension Fund-Global is "the gold standard of sovereign wealth funds." Breakingviews comes to this conclusion because Oslo's fund "offers the highest level of disclosure," "its strategy is uncontroversial," and "it actively avoids taking strategic investments."[64]

What, then, are we to make of these four efforts to evaluate the "transparency" or "risk" associated with a given sovereign wealth fund? I would argue that two broad lessons come to the fore. First, the suggested measures of transparency, particularly as regards specific investment targets, are so demanding that most American firms would have a difficult time scoring at the upper end of these indices. Corporate investors chose to remain tight-lipped about their investment strategies so as to maximize returns. Truman, Linaburg-Maduell, and Breakingviews have all established standards that do not appear to keep

Table 4.6 Breakingviews—Measuring Risk

- Transparency
  1. Clearly identified investment criteria; full disclosure
  2. Clearly identified investment criteria; limited disclosure
  3. Vaguely identifiable investment criteria; limited disclosure
  4. No clearly identified investment criteria; limited disclosure
  5. No clearly identified investment criteria; no disclosure
- Strategic Control
  1. Explicitly limited to small scale investments (less than 10%)
  2. Substantial minority stakes (10%-plus) without board representation in nonstrategic sectors, no evidence
  3. Substantial stakes (10%-plus) plus board representation in semi-strategic sectors such as banks and utilities
  4. Substantial minority stakes (10%-plus) or/plus board representation in strategic sectors
  5. Seeks controlling stakes (30%-plus) in strategic industry (defense-related)
- Political Relationship
  1. Western-style democratic market economy
  2. Nondemocratic, Western-style market economy
  3. Unstable countries, potentially hostile to Western-style market economies
  4. Major nondemocratic countries, potentially hostile to Western-style market economies
  5. Major nondemocratic countries, actively hostile to Western-style market economies[65]

this concern for the bottom line at the forefront. One can only conclude that most sovereign wealth fund managers will come to a similar conclusion and simply choose to ignore the implied "requirement" to provide such detailed information.

Second, there clearly is a tendency for government investment vehicles operating in a democracy to be more forthcoming than similar organizations in authoritarian states. This suggests the primary factor driving transparency is domestic accountability and not demands from target/recipient states. As such, it seems the press for sovereign wealth fund transparency has to begin at home. Citizens need to be made aware these funds are investing taxpayer monies, and therefore they should be more open about how they are serving a greater public good. Promoting domestic demands for such accountability seems a far easier task than attempting to impose such standards from abroad.

Table 4.7 Breakingviews Sovereign Wealth Fund Risk Index[66]

Country	Fund Name	Transparency	Strategic Control	Political Relationship	Total Score
Norway	Pension Fund-Global	1	1	1	3
Canada-Alberta	Heritage Saving Trust	1	1	1	3
U.S.-Alaska	Alaska Permanent Fund	1	1	1	3
Malaysia	Khazanah National	2	1	2	5
Korea	Investment Corporation	2	2	2	6
UAE	Dubai Inter Capital	2	2	2	6
Singapore	Temasek Holdings	2	3	1	6
Singapore	Government Invest Corp	2	3	1	6
UAE	Istithmar	3	2	2	7
Taiwan	National Stab Fund	4	1	2	7
Kuwait	Investment Authority	3	2	2	7
Chile	Economic and Social Stabilization Fund	4	2	2	8
Brunei	Investment Authority	4	2	2	8
Russia	Stabilization Fund	2	2	4	8
Kazakhstan	National Fund	4	2	3	9
Oman	State General Reserve	5	2	2	9
UAE	Abu Dhabi Invest Authority	4	3	2	9
Venezuela	National Development Fund	5	2	3	10
Qatar	Investment Authority	5	3	2	10
China	Investment Corporation	4	3	4	11

The Gold Standard—Norway's Government Pension Fund-Global

The validity of my contention that demands for sovereign wealth fund transparency must begin at home—and is more likely to happen in a democracy than any other form of governance—draws its greatest support from the example of Norway's Government Pension Fund-Global. Originally established in 1990 as the Petroleum Fund, the Norwegian investment vehicle seeks to transform Oslo's current oil export windfall into a source of revenue that continues to serve the public long after the last "black gold" is pumped from the ground. In January 2006, the Petroleum Fund was renamed the Government Pension Fund-Global, but remained committed to a mission of securing capital for Norway's future generations. Internationally acclaimed for its commitment to publicly accountable management, the fund has nonetheless proved to be a source of controversy inside Norway.

Aside from continuing debates about the business savvy of the fund's former and/or current managers,[67] three major domestic concerns have come to the fore:

1. Whether Norway should use more of the oil revenues to address current problems instead of putting money aside for the future and thereby "gambling" the funds by investing in financial instruments.
2. Whether high exposure to private equity markets is financially wise or secure. An argument that often boils down to the question, is the oil worth more in ground?
3. Whether the Government Pension Fund-Global investment policy is ethical.[68]

What's striking about these three concerns, aside from their remarkably philosophical nature, is the marked absence of an expressed fear about how the Government Pension Fund-Global is actually managed on a day-to-day basis. A dredge of Norwegian press reporting does not reveal abiding suspicions about poor government business practices, nor is there a circle of conspiracy theorists suggesting that the fund is being used to line bureaucrats' or politicians' pockets. Given the amount of money involved—approximately $400 billion—this is truly remarkable and begs the question, how does Oslo accomplish this feat?

As a means of answering this question in full, it seems appropriate to start with the basics. As such, stop one is the Government Pension Fund-Global's income sources. According to annual performance reports—publicly available via the World Wide Web—Norway abets fiscal growth in the fund through three sources: (1) cash flow from petroleum activities that is transferred from the central government; (2) net financial transactions associated with petroleum activities; and (3) the return on Fund assets.[69] By law, the Norwegian Ministry of Finance is responsible for the management of these monies; however, the Ministry of Finance has delegated operational management of the Fund to Norges Bank. By regulation, Norges Bank is then charged with seeking "to achieve the highest possible return within the limits set out in the regulation and supplementary guidelines."[70]

This reference to regulations and guidelines serves to indicate Norges Bank is not free to invest the Government Pension Fund-Global monies simply in the most profitable manner possible. Regardless of how deeply engrained their capitalist spirit may be, the Norges Bank Fund managers are explicitly prohibited from speculating on the Norwegian kroner or purchasing securities issued by Norwegian companies. And this is just the beginning of the investment restrictions. According to strictly enforced guidelines, the Fund's monies may only be invested in fixed income instruments (e.g., bonds) that are issued in the currency of a country approved by the Norwegian Ministry of Finance or in equities that are listed on regulated and recognized stock exchanges in countries that are approved by the Ministry of Finance.[71]

But wait; there's more. As a means of measuring how astutely Norges Bank manages the Government Pension Fund-Global's money, the Norwegian Ministry of Finance maintains a benchmark portfolio. This theoretical investment portfolio is supposed to reflect a neutral investment strategy for both fixed income instruments and equities. As further means of ensuring that Norges Bank is meeting investment expectations and avoiding questions of impropriety, this benchmark is composed of the Lehman Global Aggregate[72] fixed income indices in the currencies of 21 countries[73] and the FTSE[74] equity indexes for large- and medium-sized companies in 27 total nations.[75] Each year, in the annual report, Norges Bank must provide specifics on how these benchmark funds performed (the "beta" or "expected return for a given market" in investment parlance) versus the value-add (or "alpha") provided by the Fund managers. In this manner Norway's citizens have a very visible report card on how their fund and, more importantly, its managers have been doing. Furthermore, they have an arguably unbiased standard by which to gauge this performance— all in black in white or on the World Wide Web.

Let's turn for a moment to the contents of this Government Pension Fund-Global Annual Report. Published by Norges Bank Investment Management, the annual report provides explicit statements on the Fund's mandate, return, corporate governance activities, risk, organization, management costs, and overall balance sheet. In addition, the annual report provides a by-name breakout of all holdings and any external managers who might have been employed to more effectively select these assets. For fixed income investments these spreadsheets include the country, a bank or corporate entity name, and the amount of money the Government Pension Fund-Global has committed. For equities holdings, this data includes the country where an entity is located, corporate identity, market value, ownership stake, and total voting rights.[76] Yes, the Norwegian sovereign wealth fund managers track their acquired voting rights, and, as we shall see, they have no qualms about exercising this franchise.

So far, the Government Pension Fund-Global Annual Report appears little more than an overly-forthcoming publication from any publicly-listed corporation or major university. To get a better feeling for why outside observers consider the Norwegian sovereign wealth fund the gold standard for transparency let's consider some illustrative language concerning fiscal management. According to the Norges Bank Investment Management team,

> The return on the Government Pension Fund-Global . . . since 1997, the average annual nominal return has been 6.29% measured in international currency. The return has been positive in nine of those years and negative in two . . . The real return is the nominal return adjusted for inflation. For the Fund as a whole, the annual real return since 1997 has been 4.34%. On average, management costs have amounted to 0.09% of assets under management. The annual real return since 1997 net of management costs has therefore been 4.25%.[77]

As anyone used to reading corporate annual reports will attest, this is remarkably straightforward English. There is no attempt to bury unfavorable statistics in "financial-ese," and charts are provided to illustrate what the printed text cannot clearly convey. And, yes, the fund managers compare their efforts to the Ministry of Finance's benchmarks. According to Norges Bank Investment Management,

> . . . the average annual gross real return [on the benchmark portfolios—fixed income and equities combined] since 1998 has been 3.71%. On average, management costs have amounted to 0.06% of assets under management. The annual net real return since 1998 has therefore been 3.65%.[78]

OK, you say, the Norges Bank team seems to be relatively straightforward about reporting their successes and management fees, but what about poor performance, how is that handled? Again, I quote from the Government Pension Fund-Global Annual Report for 2007.

> The return on the [Fund's] investments . . . in 2007 was 3.4% in measured in international currency . . . The return achieved by the Norwegian Bank Investment Management was 1.12% lower than the return on the benchmark portfolio defined by Norges Bank's Executive Board. There were negative contributions from both fixed income and equity management in 2007.[79]

Well, with the exception of the last line, "negative contributions from both fixed income and equity management," we are again treated to easily understood English text. I would note the Norges Bank team is also highlighting a shortfall here, despite the fact they surpassed the standard set by the Ministry of Finance benchmark portfolio in 2007. According to the Ministry of Finance, the performance standard on fixed income and equity investments combined in 2007 was 3.37%. Therefore, the Norges Bank has reported a performance shortfall revealed by employing a standard more demanding than that provided by the customer—an impressive act of honesty.

These specifics on asset ownership and management performance are not the only reason Norway's Government Pension Fund-Global is known as the gold standard for sovereign wealth fund transparency. Regular public distribution of key documentation and annual independent audits are also essential for securing this reputation. As each annual report makes clear, the Government Pension Fund Act and the regulatory provisions and guidelines associated with it can be viewed on the Norges Bank Web site. Furthermore, the Norges Bank investment team is required by law to provide the government with quarterly and annual reports and also to make these documents available via the World Wide Web. (The annual reports are published in late February or early March. Quarterly reports are published in May, August, and November. The reports are published in conjunction with a press conference, which is also Webcast.)

Finally, the government of Norway requires that an outside, independent auditor examine the management of the Fund and publish an annual report on their findings. The 2006 Annual Performance Evaluation Report, provided by Mercer Investment Consulting, is a case-in-point. According to the 2006 audit, "the purpose . . . is for Mercer to verify Norges Bank's internal performance measurements and to strengthen the Ministry's basis for evaluating the competence and actions of Norges Bank."[80] Mercer Investment Consulting then goes on to state that the outside auditor performed three primary functions:

1. Measured and verified the Government Pension Fund-Global's monthly returns
2. Provided the Norwegian Ministry of Finance monthly performance reports on the total, fixed income, and equity investments
3. In the event of discrepancies in performance calculation between Norges Bank and an outside firm, when measured to two decimal places (e.g., 0.01% difference), conducted further checks and then reported on the same to the Ministry of Finance[81]

This final report, which is also placed online via the Ministry of Finance, listed a single performance discrepancy in 2006. This discrepancy, a variance in the market value calculations provided by Norges Bank and an outside firm, was found to be caused by "different methodologies in the calculation of currency rates." Over the course of a year, however, these variances were no more than 0.01% to 2 decimal places and therefore not considered a significant problem.[82] All of which causes an outside observer to conclude that Oslo and Norwegian taxpayers are well informed on their sovereign wealth fund's performance and management.

A Gold Standard Fraught with Peril and Potential

Although the Norwegians have demonstrated an outstanding willingness to disclose information on the business practices of their sovereign wealth fund, one has to wonder if Oslo's international advocates failed to read an entire Government Pension Fund-Global Annual Report. Suffice it to say Norway is not a passive investor, nor does Oslo enter the equities markets absent of a political agenda. While the Norwegian Ministry of Finance likes to contend Oslo is a "politically friendly" investor who never purchases more than a 5% share in any corporation, the Government Pension Fund-Global's stance on ownership rights should cause more than a momentary pause in Washington DC and boardrooms across America.

In the 2007 Government Pension Fund-Global Annual Report, Norges Bank declares, "The exercise of ownership rights is an integral and ever-growing part of our investment management."[83] Furthermore, Norges Bank notes that the Fund management team is expanding this ability to exercise ownership voting rights by making more employees responsible for overseeing related activities. The annual report goes on to note that in 2006 Norges Bank had six full-time employees focused on ownership rights, and in 2007 that number had grown to ten.

At first blush, Oslo's insistence on exercising ownership rights would seem good common sense. As Norges Bank puts it, "The objective for the exercise of ownership rights is to promote long-term financial returns."[84] As such, the Government Pension Fund-Global management team claims to exercise these rights through assisting regulator authorities, casting ballots, conducting research, cooperating with other investors, and engaging in dialogue with corporate boards. How actively does the Norges Bank management team engage for the Government Pension Fund-Global? According to the 2007 annual report, Fund representatives initiated or continued dialogue with 93 companies. The team is said to have engaged in direct dialogue with approximately 30 companies—normally with the chief executive officer or other member of the board—and exercised its franchise rights with 4,202 companies, voting on 38,962 proposals.[85] To place this in a broader perspective, Government Pension Fund-Global votes were cast in 92% of all occasions where the Fund had ownership in an American firm, 85% of similar events involving Asian-based firms, but only 50% of the time where the corporate entity was based in Europe.

Let's go a step further and examine how the Government Pension Fund-Global representatives cast their ballots. In approximately 90% of the cases, according to the 2007 annual report, Norway's owners voted in support of management proposals. It is the remaining 10% that make an interesting case study. In 41% of the cases where Norway's representatives voted against management the proposal was associated with antitakeover mechanisms. These included casting ballots against bids to give the board unrestricted rights to issue shares ("poison pills") to protect against a takeover, changing articles of association during a takeover bid to depart from the annual re-election of all board members, and proposals to increase the majority required to initiate the process of replacing a director.[86]

Another 25% of the cases where Government Pension Fund-Global representatives voted against board of director proposals were linked to non-salary compensation. As it turns out, Norwegian taxpayers objected to compensation plans that were not performance-based, option repricing, overly generous pension schemes or bonuses, and plans that lacked "adequate information."[87]

Similar concerns about poor business practices explain the 18% of the time Government Pension Fund-Global voted against management capitalization proposals. I am not casting aspersions here. It is easy to understand why the Fund, as a shareholder, would vote against proposals to dilute ownership interests or set the stage for below market-value deals. And, in at least one case, Norway's representatives even voted against a proposal to pay dividends considered too low to be in relation with earnings.[88]

As for the remainder of the Government Pension Fund-Global's votes against management, 11% concerned reorganizations, 7% were director related, and 4% fell into the category of routine/operational. According to the 2007 annual report, votes against routine/operational proposals included rejecting auditors perceived to have strong conflict of interest issues (a problem Norges Bank linked specifically with Japan and South Korea), annual reports lacking sufficient information, and changes to the articles of association because the proposals would transfer more power to the board of directors or lacked the information necessary for an educated decision.[89]

At this point in the conversation, the behavior of the Government Pension Fund-Global representatives would appear to be nothing more than an exercise of good business practices and an example for other sovereign wealth funds to follow. After all, what responsible shareholder does not want a board of directors to remain accountable and maximize corporate profits? The real problem, then, is not Oslo's insistence on good corporate leadership; instead, I contend the real peril of Norway's gold-standard sovereign wealth fund is the ethical guidelines the Norwegian government has imposed on the Norges Bank Investment Management team.

On 19 November 2004, the Norwegian Ministry of Finance published "Ethical Guidelines for the Government Pension Fund-Global." On the same date that these "Ethical Guidelines" were formally established via a government cabinet decision, Oslo stipulated that a Council on Ethics be established to advise the Ministry of Finance. This five-member, government-appointed body is charged with providing the Ministry of Finance an annual report on its activities and, upon request, is supposed to issue recommendations on whether an investment may constitute a violation of Norway's obligations under international law. To accomplish this mission, the Council on Ethics "receives a monthly report regarding companies that are accused of environmental damage, human rights violations, corruption, or other contraventions."[90] According to the Council on Ethics' Annual Report, this information is provided by an unnamed source who conducts daily news searches on all companies in the Government Pension Fund-Global's portfolio.

The ethical guidelines intended to frame this council's work were issued on 22 December 2005. According to these ethical guidelines, the Council is to operate with two fundamental premises in mind:

1. The Government Pension Fund-Global is an instrument for ensuring a reasonable portion of the country's petroleum wealth benefits future

generations. The financial wealth must be managed so as to generate a sound return in the long term, which is contingent on sustainable development in the economic, environmental, and social sense.

2. The Government Pension Fund-Global should not make investments that constitute an unacceptable risk and may contribute to unethical actions or omissions, such as violations of fundamental humanitarian principles, serious violations of human rights, gross corruption, or severe environmental damages.[91]

Clearly these basic premises tread squarely onto contentious political battlefields. Almost immediately one is drawn into debates over what is "sustainable development in the economic, environmental, and social sense," and how to determine "investments that constitute an unacceptable risk . . . such as violations of fundamental humanitarian principles, serious violations of human rights, gross corruption, or severe environmental damages."

As a means of accomplishing this mission and diminishing charges of investment tainted by political favoritism, Oslo identifies three standards of ethical behavior for the Government Pension Fund-Global. These standards of behavior are:

- To exercise ownership rights in a manner intended to promote long-term financial returns based on the United Nation's Global Compact[92] and OECD Guidelines for Corporate Governance and for Multinational Enterprises[93]
- To conduct negative screening of companies from the investment universe that either themselves, or through entities they control, produce weapons that through normal use may violate fundamental humanitarian principles
- Exclude companies from the investment universe where there is considered to be an unacceptable risk of contributing to:
  - Serious or systematic human rights violations, such as murder, torture, deprivation of liberty, forced labor, the worst forms of child labor, and other child exploitation
  - Grave breaches of individual rights in situations of war or conflict
  - Severe environmental damages
  - Gross corruption
  - Other particularly serious violations of fundamental ethical norms[94]

At this point in the conversation skeptics are permitted to sadly shake their heads and conclude that such high-minded standards are "wonderful" but unlikely to ever be practiced or realized. I would have to agree—if we were discussing ethics and the U.S. Congress. The Norwegians, as it turns out, are deadly serious about adhering to these "Ethical Guidelines."

Since 2002, Oslo has identified 27 corporate entities that are excluded from the Government Pension Fund-Global investment. I hasten to add that these corporate entities are not just "flight-by-night" businesses with little potential for offering a return on one's dollar. For ethical reasons, the Norwegians have decided to not invest in corporate powerhouses including Boeing, General Dynamics, Lockheed, and Wal-Mart. Yes, you read correctly, Wal-Mart.

To date, Norway has excluded Government Pension Fund-Global investments from corporations found to violate ethical concerns in five categories: cluster munitions manufacturing, nuclear weapons assembly, anti-personnel landmine construction, human rights, and environmental damages. The affected firms as of 31 December 2007 are listed below by category:

- Cluster Weapons
  - Alliant Techsystems Incorporated
  - General Dynamics Corporation
  - Hanwha Corporation
  - L3 Communications Holdings Incorporated
  - Lockheed Martin Corporation
  - Poongsan Corporation
  - Raytheon Company
  - Thales S.A.
- Nuclear Weapons
  - BAE Systems Public Limited Company
  - Boeing Company
  - EADS Company, including its subsidiary
  - EADS Finance B.V.
  - Finmeccanica Sp. A.
  - GenCorp Incorporated
  - Honeywell International Corporation
  - Northrop Grumman Corporation
  - Safran S.A.
  - Serco Group Public Limited Company
  - United Technologies Corporation
- Anti Personnel Landmines
  - Singapore Technologies Engineering
- Human Rights
  - Wal-Mart Stores Incorporated, including its subsidiary
  - Wal-Mart de Mexico S.A. de CV.
- Environmental Damages
  - Freeport McMoRan Copper & Gold Incorporated
  - DRD Gold Limited
  - Vedanta Resources Limited, including its subsidiaries
  - Sterlite Industries Limited
  - Madras Aluminum Company Limited[95]

Although Norway's decision to exclude investment in businesses associated with the manufacturing of anti-personnel landmines, cluster munitions, and nuclear weapons is arguably a foregone conclusion given Oslo's focus on fundamental humanitarian principles, the Council on Ethics findings concerning human rights and environmental damage have proven much more controversial. In fact, following Oslo's decision to divest from Wal-Mart in June 2006, the U.S. ambassador to Norway declared the Fund uses an "arbitratry" process with "no set standards on how and why it picks a certain company" for ethical screening.[96]

Is this a fair charge? Does the Government Pension Fund-Global have a process for screening corporations on ethical issues? And, if Oslo does have such a process, is it really absent "set standards"? As it turns out, Norway does indeed have a process for screening corporations, and there are indeed a set of standards for even such contentious issues as human rights and environmental damage.

As previously noted, the Government Pension Fund-Global's Council on Ethics employs an "information supplier" who conducts a daily search for news concerning all corporations in the Fund's holdings. This daily cull is compiled into a monthly report that is focused on corruption, environmental damage, human rights, and other contraventions. When a firm is identified as a potential "bad actor" (my term), the Council begins a months-long investigation that includes examination of the evidence, soliciting a response from the corporation in question, drafting of a recommendation, and finally public notification. Of note, as the Council readily admits, "Most of the company assessments . . . do not lead to a recommendation of exclusion—either because the Council does not deem the offenses serious enough, or because it is not probable that the company's unacceptable practice will continue."[97] Once a determination for exclusion has been made, the Ministry of Finance is notified for further action, and the entire case, with bibliographies providing supporting documentation, is included in the Council's annual report.

As for a set of standards in addition to the "Ethical Guidelines," which are under review in 2008 and may be revised accordingly, the Council has established definitions for "severe environmental damage" and clearly identified causes for removing a corporation under humanitarian concerns. According to the Government Pension Fund Global's Council on Ethics, "severe environmental damage" is determined by examining the following criteria:

- The damage is significant
- The damage has considered negative consequences for human life and health
- The damage is the result of violations of national law or international norms
- The company has failed to act in order to prevent damage
- The company has not implemented adequate measures to rectify the damage
- It is probable that the company's unacceptable practice will continue[98]

As indicated in the preceding list, Norway has used these standards to identify five corporate entities Oslo believes should be excluded from Government Pension Fund-Global investment.

The debate over exclusions associated with perceived human rights violations, specifically Wal-Mart, provides an overview of a second list of standards that the Council on Ethics uses for evaluating suspect companies. In their 2006 annual report, the Government Pension Fund-Global Council on Ethics provides a lengthy discussion of the factors that resulted in Wal-Mart's exclusion. Coming after a year of study,[99] the report opens by noting:

The Council takes internationally recognized human rights conventions and labor rights conventions as its point of departure when assessing possible violations of standards on the part of Wal-Mart. Firstly, it must be assessed whether alleged violations of these standards take place and, secondly, whether they are serious or systematic. Furthermore, based on the Ethical Guidelines' preparatory work, the Council [has identified a] list . . . [of] . . . criteria which constitute decisive elements in an overall assessment of whether an unacceptable risk exists of the Fund contributing to human rights violations.[100]

According to the Council on Ethics, these criteria for evaluating potential human rights violations are:

- There must be some kind of linkage between the company's operations and the existing violations of the Ethical Guidelines, which must be visible to the Fund.
- The violations must have been carried out with a view to serving the company's interests or to facilitate conditions for the company.
- The company must have either contributed actively or had knowledge of the violations without seeking to prevent them.
- The violations must be either ongoing or have an unacceptable risk that such violations will occur in the future. Earlier violations might indicate future patterns of conduct.[101]

Now, if we return to the original "Ethical Guidelines," one will recall human rights for the Council are identified as including "murder, torture, deprivation of liberty, forced labor, the worst forms of child labor and other child exploitation." The Council's finding after a year of investigation? Wal-Mart had violated the human rights standards via its supply chain[102] and the corporation's own operations.[103] As such, the "Council on Ethics accordingly considers that there is an unacceptable risk that the Fund, through its investments in Wal-Mart . . . may be complicit in serious or systematic violations of human rights. The Council recommends that Wal-Mart . . . be excluded from the . . . Fund's portfolio."[104] And with that, the Government Pension Fund-Global managers were dispatched to sell off over $400 million in Wal-Mart shares.[105]

Needless to say, the Council on Ethic's Wal-Mart decision drew sharp criticism from Washington. As I noted before, the U.S. ambassador to Norway was quick to offer scathing remarks suggesting the Council lacked both a uniform process and a set of standards for making such recommendations. But Ambassador Benson Whitney then went on to make a number of statements that suggest longer-term problems with Norway's focus on ethics. First, Whitney correctly highlighted the fact that near two-thirds of the companies on Norway's exclusion list are based in America.[106] Second, the ambassador noted that this is likely true because U.S. companies receive more media scrutiny than firms in parts of Asia or the Middle East. This results in situations like Wal-Mart's, the ambassador continued, where "Norway [has] found [an American corporation] unethical for allegedly discouraging unions, but [Oslo's] Government Pension Fund-Global stands silent about firms in its portfolio from countries in which no unions, or only state unions, are allowed."[107]

The Norwegian government has been largely dismissive of such complaints. Oslo likes to contend that Norway has devised a policy comparable to that practiced by major funds found elsewhere in Europe and the United States. This so-called "socially responsible investing," Kristen Halvorsen, Norway's finance minister, told the *New York Times*, "combines professional fund management with an ethical approach. We see them as two sides of the same coin."[108]

Given this attitude, it should not be surprising to discover Oslo is preparing to take on even larger targets. In an 11 October 2007 letter, the Government Pension Fund-Global Council on Ethics responded to a Finance Ministry request the body consider excluding firms conducting business in Burma.[109] Harkening back to the "Ethical Guidelines," the Council prefaced their answer by reminding the Finance Ministry of the two "fundamental prerequisites" for a recommendation of exclusion:

1. There must be a connection between the company's operations and the relevant violations.
2. There must be an unacceptable risk for the company, and thus also for the Fund, of contributing to future violations.[110]

With these two prerequisites firmly in mind, the Council concludes, "The fact that a company has operations in states controlled by repressive regimes does not, in itself, constitute sufficient grounds to exclude a company from the Fund." Furthermore, the Council continued, even though it can be inferred a company's presence in a state controlled by repressive state generates revenue for the government in question, "such a connection between a company and the state's unethical actions should not, in itself, be sufficient to exclude a company from the Fund."[111] That said, the Council left open its investigation of companies with operations in Burma, with the implication that further investigation might warrant excluding a company from Government Pension Fund-Global investment.

At this juncture I want to ensure the reader understands that Norway's list of corporations to be investigated and engaged on issues of ethical/political concern is only going to grow. In the Norges Bank 2007–2010 strategic plan, two priority areas of concern for the Fund's management are identified:

- Children's rights in the value chains of multinational companies, in particular limiting child labor and protecting children's health
- Companies' lobbying of national and supranational authorities on questions related to long-term environmental change[112]

As the Wal-Mart and Burma case demonstrate, the Council of Ethics is willing to use children's rights and labor concerns as a reason for excluding a firm from Government Pension Fund-Global investments. The issue of lobbying on environmental concerns also threatens to place the Fund's managers—as Norway's official representatives—squarely in the political arena.

As first declared in the Government Pension Fund-Global Annual Report for 2006, the Norges Bank Investment Management team "has singled out companies lobbying of national and supranational authorities on questions related to long-term environmental change." This focus, according to the Fund's managers, is derived from their responsibility for generating long-term earnings and therefore, a need to foster "sustainable development." In a none-too-subtle attempt to prevent this discussion from crossing into political territory, the Fund managers argue their concerns are ultimately based on the premise that "the potential costs of serious climate change could lead to substantial costs for the portfolio."[113]

Up to this point, there appears little ground for argument with the Fund managers concerns. Then, we learn about how they intend to go about addressing these fiscal considerations. It appears Oslo's fund managers have mastered the fundamentals of lobbying as it is practiced in Washington DC. As the 2007 annual report so bluntly states,

> To begin with, [the Fund managers] analyzed more than 100 companies in the portfolio to identify the companies which are most active in lobbying on climate issues, and [we have] initiated contact with 24 companies to date. These companies have been chosen because they will be affected by future climate legislation, and because their stance will influence the design of this legislation. [The Government Pension Fund-Global's management] key message to these companies is that their lobbying should naturally reflect broad and long-term investor interest in effective climate legislation. The companies are mainly in the energy and transport sectors.[114]

The ultimate goal, through direct dialogue between the managers of a $400 billion sovereign wealth fund and corporate boards of directors, is to shape national and supranational legislation concerning environmental issues, specifically, global warming. The skeptic in me cries out at the logic of an oil-exporter assuming such a role, but the pragmatist in me is reassured by the fact this function is being performed by the Norwegians and not the Chinese.[115] In any case, the real message here is that the Norwegian sovereign wealth fund is now officially serving as a political activist under the guise of pursing the financial bottom line.

In their defense, the Norwegian Fund managers have publicly declared, "Norges Bank Investment Management is not a political player with its own view of how domestic legislation in the U.S. or other countries should be formulated. However, Norges Bank Investment Management represents a type of investor with a real financial interest in seeing effective climate legislation within a reasonable timeframe."[116] I leave the reader to decide whether these protests of innocence or, at best, of political neutrality are credible. For the record, I would simply like to note the gold standard of sovereign wealth fund transparency may not be the example of apolitical behavior that Washington or any other capital would want to see widely emulated.

Parting Thoughts

Mounting international demands for sovereign wealth fund transparency and implementation of a globally-recognized set of best practices may serve to alleviate short-term concerns about how these investment vehicles operate within equity markets—the results, however, ultimately may generate more controversy than ever envisioned or intended. As Norway's Government Pension Fund-Global illustrates, when it comes to investing hundreds of billions of dollars there is a fine line between good management and pursuit of covert or overt political agendas. Oslo's pursuit of human rights and environmental considerations is admirable, but what happens when there is a disagreement over what constitutes a basic human right or when sufficient effort has been made to address global warming? In a world of tight credit markets, one could reasonably argue that the answer to these questions will ultimately be provided by the lenders. As Washington is clearly not in that category—and Oslo and other sovereign wealth fund managers are well aware of that fact—one begins to wonder who will be authoring the lobbyist's cue cards.

I suspect decision-makers would be well advised to keep in mind Jagdish Bhagwati's warning to the Senate Committee on Foreign Relations:

> . . . even transparency does not ensure sovereign wealth funds will not be used to promote non-commercial, non-economic objectives. Thus, the Norwegian [Government Pension Fund-Global] proudly refuses to invest in sectors and countries which do not satisfy Norway's own menu of social responsibility criteria. Is it alright for Norway then to be influencing other countries social policies while it would not want other countries to influence (in however limited and paltry a fashion) Norwegian politics?[117]

Alas, we have discovered that when it comes to sovereign wealth funds, transparency does not by definition guarantee neutrality or apolitical behavior. Nor should one conclude that one's own transparency suggest openness to policy dictates from afar.

CHAPTER 5

TRUST BUT VERIFY[1]

The expansion of sovereign wealth funds is not an inherently negative development. They have infused helpful liquidity into international financial markets and, in some cases, promoted beneficial local development. Yet sovereign wealth funds are not ordinary investors. Their ties to foreign governments create the potential that they will be used to apply political pressure, manipulate markets, gain access to sensitive technologies, or undermine economic rivals . . . In this context, we must examine whether U.S. agencies have the resources and expertise to effectively respond to the policy complexities inherent in sovereign wealth funds . . . Our government must find the right balance between promoting investment in the United States and safeguarding security interests through regulation.[2]

—*Senator Richard Lugar (R-IN), Opening Statement for*
Hearing on Sovereign Wealth Funds, 11 June 2008

Sovereign wealth funds present a vexing problem for politicians in Washington DC. Members of the executive and legislative branches have made clear that they have no desire to kill the goose that laid the golden egg, but are very much afraid of the "avian flu" that might accompany a gaggle of sovereign wealth funds. That is to say, the United States remains committed to welcoming outside investment but is less certain about this activity when it is directly associated with foreign governments. The full extent of this discomfort becomes evident when one considers that between November 2007 and July 2008, Congress held no less than six hearings on sovereign wealth funds and their potential implications for American foreign policy, markets, and national security.[3] A glance at the titles used for a few of these sessions provides a sense of the trepidation on Capitol Hill: "Hearings on the Implications of Sovereign Wealth Fund Investments for National Security"; "Do Sovereign Wealth Funds Make the U.S.

Economy Stronger or Pose National Security Risks?"; and "Sovereign Wealth Funds: Foreign Policy Consequences in an Era of New Money."

This sense of being confronted with a potential catch-22—a desire to protect American interests while simultaneously leaving the door open to foreign investment—is clearly evident in the hands-off manner in which Barack Obama and John McCain addressed sovereign wealth funds. In February 2008, Barack Obama told an audience in Omaha, Nebraska, "I am concerned if these . . . sovereign wealth funds are motivated by more than just market considerations, and that's obviously a possibility." But then Obama went on to note that he has no problem with foreign investment in the United States and has made no further comments on the matter.[4] On the Republican side of the aisle, John McCain's response to the sovereign wealth fund issue has been characterized as even more "reserved and cautious" than Obama's.[5] An exhaustive search of McCain's press statements revealed no comments on sovereign wealth funds—and his official campaign Web site as of 1 August 2008 was markedly silent on the whole issue.

This sense of caution on the policy front was perhaps best captured by Senator Biden in June 2008. In opening remarks for a Senate Foreign Relations Committee hearing on sovereign wealth funds, Biden argued his goal for the session was to "get a better understanding" of the "the threats, opportunities, and challenges" sovereign wealth funds present to the United States. The senior senator from Delaware then declared there are three issues that must be considered when weighing policy options concerning these government investment vehicles:

1. We need a strategy to identify and to deal with sovereign wealth funds that use their assets to achieve political objectives.
2. We must strike an appropriate balance between protecting against threats and remaining open to political opportunities.
3. As we develop a policy toward sovereign wealth funds, we should be careful not to confuse the symptom with the cause . . . These funds exist and are growing because, in my view, we have no national energy policy, no coherent trade policy.

Biden closed by observing, "Short-sighted restrictions on international investments won't eliminate those underlying problems. We need to be smarter, more strategic, and more long-term in our thinking. And we need to get our house in order, to reduce our economic vulnerability."[6]

Although I find much to applaud in Biden's remarks—particularly his focus on crafting policies intended to address the factors contributing to the rise of sovereign wealth funds—for the moment we will examine his short-term concern, balancing U.S. national security with our need for foreign investment. We will return to Biden's "long-term" thinking in the coming pages, but for the present let's examine exactly what Washington has done to secure our national interests from potentially hostile foreign governments masquerading as entrepreneurial investors.

Foreign Investment and National Security Act of 2007

On 26 July 2007, President Bush signed the Foreign Investment and National Security Act (FINSA) into law. FINSA went into effect on 24 October 2007. Drafted in response to political upheaval that followed the 2006 Dubai Ports World controversy, FINSA is the latest iteration in Washington's decades-long effort to assuage populist protectionist sentiments without resorting to isolationist policies. As previously noted, this modern "tradition"—a seemingly appropriate term given the 30-year track record—can be directly traced to the 1975 establishment of the Committee on Foreign Investment in the United States (CFIUS) and the 1977 International Emergency Economic Powers Act. Revived in 1988 with the Exon-Florio Amendment to the Defense Production Act, political efforts to appease protectionist rabble-rousers again surfaced in 1993, when Senator Robert Byrd (D-WV) sought to stiffen CFIUS requirements by stipulating that the body investigate "any instances" where a foreign government was seeking to acquire a U.S. business associated with American national security.

Given this legislative history, what does FINSA bring to the table? First, the 2007 Act formally establishes CFIUS in statute; previously the Committee had existed only via executive order. FINSA also specifies executive branch members required to participate in the CFIUS process: the Secretary of the Treasury, the Attorney General, and the Secretaries of Commerce, Defense, Energy, Homeland Security, and State. In addition, FINSA names the Director of National Intelligence (DNI) and Secretary of Labor as ex officio[7] CFIUS members. FINSA stipulates that the DNI is to provide an assessment of the national security threats presented by a transaction—but is to have no other policy function.[8] The role of the Secretary of Labor is to be defined by applicable regulations.

The second major development FINSA offers is a formalization of the process by which CFIUS conducts national security reviews of transactions that could result in foreign control of a U.S. entity engaged in interstate commerce. FINSA specifically requires a 30-day CFIUS *review* to determine the impact of a proposed transaction on national security—and to address any perceived threat. FINSA then goes on to require an additional 45-day *investigation* in 4 types of cases:[9]

1. Where the transaction threatens to impair national security, and the threat has not been mitigated prior to, or during, the initial 30-day review.
2. Where the transaction is controlled by a foreign government.
3. Where a transaction would result in foreign control over critical infrastructure in a manner that CFIUS determines could imperil national security if not properly mitigated.
4. Where the agency leading a particular case recommends and CFIUS concurs.

In an effort to avoid a repeat of the Dubai Ports World controversy—in part sparked by concerns that the deal had not been vetted at the highest levels within the executive branch—FINSA seeks to ensure high-level accountability by requiring that CFIUS certification concerning national security concerns be made at the Assistant Secretary-level or above if the decision is made following the initial 30-day *review*. If the CFIUS process moves to the 45-day *investigation*, the certification concerning an absence of a national security threat must be made at the Deputy Secretary-level or above. Finally, FINSA stipulates that if the president concludes action on a transaction, he or she must publicly announce this decision.

While we are on the subject of accountability, sovereign wealth fund managers should note FINSA decrees that certification of a foreign government-controlled transaction following the 30-day initial *review*—that is, a decision waiving the 45-day *investigation*—must be made at the Deputy Secretary-level within the Department of the Treasury and the agency leading the CFIUS case in question. This language is likely included in an effort to capture the intent of the 1993 Byrd Amendment to the Defense Production Act.

What about instances where a transaction is determined to present a threat to national security? This is the third major new development FINSA offers students of foreign investment. In cases where a threat to national security is determined to exist, or potentially exist, FINSA provides statutory authority for CFIUS (or a lead agency acting on behalf of CFIUS) to enter into mitigation agreements with the parties involved in the transaction, or to impose conditions on the transaction intended to address these concerns. The intention here is to provide CFIUS the authority to mitigate a national security risk posed by a transaction. Previously, CFIUS was essentially limited to simply sending the president a recommendation that a particular transaction be prohibited on the grounds that it could imperil U.S. national security.

The fourth significant FINSA contribution? A process for transactions that were initially approved but subsequently prove problematic due to submission of false or misleading materials. Under FINSA, CFIUS may reopen such cases. CFIUS may also reopen a case where a party involved in the transaction intentionally breaches a mitigation agreement or condition. I would note, such instances are limited to incidents where no other remedies are available to address the breach. Again, for accountability purposes, a decision to reopen must be made at the highest levels—here, an Undersecretary or above.

The final major change that FINSA brings to the CFIUS process—again, as a result of the Dubai Ports World controversy—is increased reporting to Congress. Under FINSA, in addition to reporting on certifications concerning absence of a threat to national security—which CFIUS must provide to Congress after concluding action on a proposed transaction—CFIUS also must hand over an annual statement on its work, including a list of transactions the body *reviewed* or *investigated* in the preceding 12 months. This annual report is also to provide analysis related to foreign direct investment in the United States, and a statement concerning foreign direct investment from certain countries.

Does FINSA Meet the Requirement?

This, as the saying goes, is the $64,000 question.[10] As the Government Account-ability Office (GAO) notes in a February 2008 report prepared for Senator Richard Shelby (R-AL), FINSA has certainly expanded the number of factors CFIUS and the president must consider during a *review*, *investigation*, and final determination concerning any transaction subjected to the process. These factors include:

- Potential national security-related effects on critical infrastructure, includ-ing major energy assets
- Potential national security-related effects on U.S. critical technologies
- Whether the transaction is controlled by foreign government
- Where appropriate, a review of current assessments concerning:
  - The acquiring country's adherence to nonproliferation regimes
  - The acquiring country's relations with the U.S.—particularly on cooper-ating with Washington's counterterrorism efforts
  - Potential for transshipment or diversion of technologies with military applications—includes analysis of the acquiring country's national export-control laws and regulations
- Long-term projection of U.S. requirements for energy sources and other critical resources
- Potential effect of the transaction on sales of military goods, equipment, or technology to any country the Secretary of Defense identifies as a potential regional threat to U.S. interests[11]

Furthermore, FINSA was widely praised for clarifying that "national secu-rity" for the United States includes "homeland security" and requires special attention to acquisitions of "critical infrastructure."[12] All told, some legal schol-ars were willing to express satisfaction with the lawmakers' efforts, and contend that FINSA—when coupled with other U.S. statutes and regulations—would serve to protect the country from hostile foreign investors.[13]

Not surprisingly, this sense of satisfaction was far from unanimous. In September 2007, the New America Foundation, a nonpartisan policy think tank based in Washington DC, issued a paper declaring the revised investment statutes were about to be outpaced by the emergence of sovereign wealth funds. According to the New America Foundation,

> CFIUS/FINSA and other U.S. legislation were not crafted as a unified means of addressing the rise of foreign government–owned portfolio and other foreign direct investment on the scale that now confronts us . . . For example, it is unclear whether sovereign wealth fund investments at a level below that which would trigger CFIUS/FINSA review, but is still material enough to exert material influence, is currently considered and addressed.[14]

This drumbeat for further legislation aimed at protecting U.S. national secu-rity from potentially hostile sovereign wealth fund investors appeared to pick up speed over the course of the next several months. Alarmed by the pace at which sovereign wealth funds were purchasing shares in the ailing U.S. financial industry, in January 2008 members of Congress ordered federal investigators to examine the government investment vehicles and whether their activity in the financial sector raised economic or security concerns. The probe, which ultimately appeared as a GAO publication, was also charged with examining what oversight—domestic and international—is being employed to monitor the funds.[15]

At the same time this press for further investigations was making its way through official Washington, U.S. media sources began running stories concerning the extralegal means sovereign wealth funds were employing to avoid America's domestic political minefields. For instance, on 25 January 2008 the *Wall Street Journal* published a front-page article titled "Lobbyists Smoothed the Way for a Spate of Foreign Deals." The story's opening paragraph sets the tone:

> Two years ago, the U.S. Congress pressured the Arab emirate of Dubai to back out of a deal to manage U.S. ports. Today, governments in the Persian Gulf, China, and Singapore have snapped up $37 billion of stakes in Wall Street, the bedrock of the U.S. financial system. Lawmakers and the White House are welcoming the cash, and there is hardly a peep from the public.[16]

Why? According to the *Journal*, "the warm reception reflects the millions of dollars in shrewd lobbying by both overseas governments and their Wall Street targets." The domestic protagonists in this campaign proved to be lobbyists representing both sides of the aisle and the senior senator from New York. The lobbyists for the Democrats: Richard Mintz (a former Hillary Clinton campaign aide) and Joel Johnson (a former Clinton White House communications advisor). On the Republican side: Wayne Berman, a well-known "Grand Old Party" fundraiser and former Commerce Department official.[17] (Of note, Wayne Berman also served as the McCain campaign's deputy finance chairman[18]— providing Berman access to the Republican presidential candidate that may help explain John McCain's lack of comment on sovereign wealth funds.)

The primary political protagonist is Senator Charles "Chuck" Schumer (D-NY). A graduate of Harvard Law School, Schumer is a career politician who reportedly has never held a job in the private sector. Schumer began his career in the New York State Assembly in 1974 and moved up to the U.S. House of Representatives in 1980. As a "son of New York," Schumer advocated a tough stance on terrorism following the events of 11 September 2001. This focus came to the fore in 2006, when Senator Schumer led a bipartisan effort to halt the transfer of control of six United States ports to a corporation owned by the government of the United Arab Emirates[19] (UAE). (Previously discussed here as the Dubai Ports World controversy.) Schumer's tough stance appeared to be based on the 9/11 Commission report, which stated the UAE had strong ties to Osama bin Laden and Al Qaeda prior to the attacks on World Trade Center and the Pentagon.

Schumer's efforts contributed to Dubai Ports World withdrawing its application on 9 March 2006.

Now let's fast-forward 15 months. U.S. financial institutions are confronted with a mounting fiscal crisis associated with the collapsing subprime mortgage industry. Anxious to recruit new capital, the U.S. banking industry—and much of Wall Street—has gone, hat in hand, to the largest source of secured money they can find: sovereign wealth funds. And right behind the ailing financiers? Their friends from Capitol Hill—most prominently, Senator Chuck Schumer. In place of the angry politician who argued that the Dubai Ports World deal had not been properly vetted and shared with Congress,[20] Chuck Schumer has apparently emerged as an advocate for foreign investment from, of all places—you guessed—the UAE.

The ultimate cause for Senator Schumer's change of heart can apparently be traced to two sources: first, his concern for the voters of New York; and second, his campaign coffers. A well-known advocate for Wall Street (and the jobs it provides his constituents), Senator Schumer expressed his support for a $7.5 billion deal linking Citigroup with Abu Dhabi by simply noting the transaction will bolster the bank's competitiveness and "help preserve New York's status as the world's finance center."[21] In a more specific statement intended to justify his expression of support for the deal, Senator Schumer told reporters, "what would the average American say if Citigroup is faced with the choice of 10,000 layoffs or more foreign investment?"[22] This explanation appears to have become Schumer's favorite, as he subsequently was quoted as arguing, "compared with the choice of Citigroup laying off another 20,000 people, I'd rather have the sovereign wealth funds in there. We can't be one of those walled-off medieval-type countries."[23] As for the issue of Schumer's campaign coffers, according to the nonpartisan Center for Responsive Politics, during the 2006 election cycle commercial banks, security firms, and their employees contributed $96.3 million to congressional campaigns—32 times as much as the sea-transport industry.[24] So, as far as votes and money are concerned, Senator Schumer's support for sovereign wealth fund investments in the U.S. financial industry certainly appears to make good common sense.[25]

To be fair, Senator Schumer has not completely rolled over for sovereign wealth funds seeking to invest in the United States. In September 2007, Schumer pressed Treasury Secretary Henry Paulson to thoroughly review Bourse Dubai's proposal to purchase a nearly 20% stake in the NASDAQ Stock Exchange. In a letter to Paulson, Schumer declared, "I believe that the acquisition of such a large stake in a U.S. exchange by a foreign government raises some serious questions." (CFIUS ultimately approved the deal between Bourse Dubai and NASDAQ in December 2007.[26]) In February 2008, the senior senator from New York declared that if the International Monetary Fund (IMF) could not quickly develop a voluntary does of conduct for sovereign wealth funds, Congress would consider legislation intended to ensure that the government investment vehicles operate in a transparent manner.[27] Finally, Schumer has made it known he wants to closely examine FINSA and the CFIUS reforms in an effort to "close any loopholes" the 2007 Act failed to address.[28]

Given Senator Schumer's apparently duplicitous behavior, and the perceived absence of political consensus concerning when the president should deny a business deal due to national security considerations—why allow Citibank to go forward, but not Dubai Ports Worlds?—it's time we return to FINSA and the CFIUS reporting requirements.

Crafting the Regulations for FINSA 2007

On 21 April 2008, the Department of the Treasury posted proposed regulations implementing section 721 of the Defense Production Act, as amended. This posting followed a public meeting on 24 October 2007, during which the Treasury solicited views from businesses and professionals active in international mergers and acquisitions. (The Treasury subsequently held a public meeting on the regulations on 2 May 2008—again, as a means of soliciting feedback. In the interim, the American public and foreign governments were invited to submit their comments, which were then placed on a Treasury Web site.) According to a Treasury press release, "the proposed regulations provide an update to regulations issued in 1991 that govern . . . CFIUS and its process for national security review of certain foreign investments in U.S. businesses. They reflect reforms made to the CFIUS process by FINSA, and the CFIUS executive order issued by President Bush on January 23 of this year."[29]

What hath they wrought? Given the contentious nature of the subject at hand, the proposed regulations appropriately open with a list of definitions. Although most of the terms are familiar and require little explanation, there are a few items in this list that deserve our attention. For openers, what constitutes a "transaction?" I start here, as everything CFIUS does is based on a tacit agreement concerning the subject of the body's review or investigations. According to the Treasury, a "transaction" for FINSA purposes is a "merger, acquisition, or takeover that is proposed or consummated."[30] Significantly, the Treasury explicitly excludes "greenfield investment"[31] and only a very limited type of long-term leases in this definition. As such, CFIUS is to focus almost exclusively on business deals involving a sale or partnership between a foreign entity and an existing U.S. commercial enterprise.

Control. There is no more controversial term in the FINSA or CFIUS worlds than "control." As the proposed regulations note, "FINSA does not define 'control,' but rather requires CFIUS prescribe a definition by regulation."[32] Why the dodge? The definition of "control" provides justification for all CFIUS actions. Congress sought to make this clear in the 1988 Conference Report that accompanied the original Exon-Florio amendment by noting, "the Conferees in no way intend to impose barriers to foreign investment. [The statute] is not intended to authorize investigations on investments [that] could not result in foreign control of persons engaged in interstate commerce."[33] Legalese at its worst.

What the lawmakers were trying to say in 1988 is that CFIUS investigations are not authorized for all foreign investments in the United States—just those cases where the transaction results in control of what heretofore had appeared to be an exclusively American enterprise.

So what is control? Back to the proposed FINSA regulations. According to the Treasury, "control" for CFIUS must be defined in functional terms. As such, the Treasury states, "control" is:

> . . . *the power*, direct or indirect—whether or not exercised—through the ownership of a majority or a dominant minority of the total outstanding voting interest in an entity, board representation, proxy voting, a special share, contractual agreements, formal or informal arrangements to act in concert, or other means, *to determine, direct, take, reach, or cause decisions regarding . . . important matters affecting an entity.*[34]

The Treasury then goes on to stipulate this definition "eschews bright lines"; that is, there is no explicit statement concerning a percentage of ownership that automatically infers control. Accordingly, "control is not defined in terms of a specified percentage of shares or numbers of board seats." Instead, the proposed regulations contend, control is determined by evaluating "all relevant factors . . . together in light of their potential impact on a foreign person's ability to determine, direct, or decide important matters affecting a company."[35]

In case we missed this point on raw percentages of ownership not serving as a "bright line" for CFIUS reviews and investigations, the Treasury offers the following examples. First, "a foreign person does not control an entity if it holds 10% or less of the voting interest in the entity and it holds that interest 'solely of the purpose of investment'." The second example is even more to the point. "A transaction involving a foreign person with an interest of 9% . . . who has bargained for rights to determine, direct, take, reach, or cause decisions regarding important matters affecting that business would be a . . . transaction [open to CFIUS review and/or investigation]." As a means of hammering the point home, the Treasury concludes by declaring, "*the regulations do not provide, and have never provided, an exemption based solely on whether an investment is 10% or less in a U.S. business.*"[36]

How does one escape the "control" clause? In the proposed regulations, the Treasury states, a foreign person is considered to not be in control if a two-pronged test is satisfied:

1. The acquiring entity holds 10% or less of the voting interests in the target business.
2. The acquiring entity holds its interest solely for investment purposes.[37]

This two-pronged evaluation, as one might suspect, is not as simple as it first appears. In order to meet the "investment test," the acquiring entity must essentially waive the "capability and intention to control," and has to act in a manner consistent with an intent to own solely for the purposes of investment. This is no small matter. As we have previously noted, the Norwegian Government Pension Fund-Global would not meet such a test—nor, apparently, would any other sovereign wealth fund that announced an intention to exercise voting rights associated with purchase of shares or any other stake in a corporation.

The third critical definition for CFIUS and our conversation is "foreign person." For the Treasury, a foreign person is "any foreign national, foreign government, or foreign entity, or any entity over which control is exercised or exercisable by a foreign national, foreign government, or foreign entity." Although no explicit mention is made of sovereign wealth funds, one suspects that the Treasury attempted to cover this ground by going on to note, "a foreign government-controlled transaction is one that could result in the control of a U.S. business by a foreign government or person controlled by or acting on behalf of a foreign government."[38] In other words, sovereign wealth fund investments in the United States are subject to CFIUS review and/or investigation, as the fund is acting on the behalf of a foreign government.

Finally, we turn to the definition of a U.S. business. Under the proposed regulations, a U.S. business is defined as "any entity engaged in interstate commerce in the United States." CFIUS is directed to apply this criterion to any entity targeted by a foreign person, including associations, branches, corporations, divisions, estates, groups, partnerships, sub-groups, and trusts.[39]

With these definitions in hand, we are ready to consider the CFIUS process. As we step through the requirements that a potential buyer is supposed to accomplish, keep firmly in mind, "the focus of CFIUS's analysis [is] whether a particular transaction could result in the acquisition of foreign control . . . the ability of a foreign person to determine, direct, or decide important matters affecting a U.S. business." Furthermore, I would note, the American government admits these regulations largely establish a voluntary system—"and historically less than 10% of all foreign acquisitions of U.S. businesses are notified to CFIUS."[40] Why? First, "the average filing requires about 100 hours of preparation time."[41] And, second, of the notices actually filed, only about 10% are actually subject to an investigation or mitigation agreement.[42] In other words, in approximately 99% of all cases where a foreign entity acquires a stake in a U.S. business, CFIUS does nothing. This makes one wonder why any investor would bother to file—particularly if the purchase can be 'buried" in a private equity firm or "lost" in a "dark pools" transaction.[43]

When Should a Foreign Entity Think About Filing a CFIUS Notification?

As the above discussion of "control" should indicate, there is no clear means of avoiding a CFIUS review and/or investigation based simply on claims that one is seeking to acquire a minority stake in a particular U.S. business. The proposed definition of "control" appears to indicate all such activities are potentially subject to a review and/or investigation. Certainly, there has to be a smarter means of proceeding than routinely planning for over 100 hours of paperwork each time acquisition of a U.S. entity is up for consideration. In fact, there is. A careful reading of the proposed regulations suggests that there are obvious cases where a "preemptive" filing is suggested—or even mandatory. For all other cases, consult with a legal professional.[44]

The first of these "must notify" categories are acquisitions involving critical infrastructure. According to the proposed regulations, "critical infrastructure" in the United States are "systems and assets, whether physical or virtual, so vital to the United States that the incapacity or destruction of the particular systems or assets . . . would have a debilitating impact on national security."[45] As I have mentioned previously, the current definition of "critical infrastructure" in the United States encompasses approximately 75% of the American economy. As such, unless one is preparing to acquire a U.S. firm engaged in antique wagon wheel refurbishment, plan on preparing a CFIUS notification.

The second area that appears to generate an automatic CFIUS notification is acquisitions involving critical technologies. What is a "critical technology"? According to the proposed regulations, critical technologies fall in four categories:

1. Defense articles or defense services covered by the United States Munitions List[46]
2. Those items specified on the Commercial Control List[47]
3. Specifically designed and prepared nuclear equipment, parts and components, materials, software, and technology specified in the Assistance to Foreign Energy Activities regulation, and nuclear facilities, equipment, and material specified in the Export and Import of Nuclear Equipment and Materials regulation
4. Select agents and toxins specified in the Export and Import of Selected Agents and Toxins regulations[48]

When coupled with the "critical infrastructure" criterion, this list of "critical technologies" would make it appear as though every proposed foreign acquisition or merger with a U.S. business entity should result in a CFIUS filing. This is particularly true if one considers the fact that globalization has resulted in the "disassembly"[49] of the manufacturing process. In this new "supply chain" manufacturing process, the foreign acquisition or merger with a U.S. software firm or circuit board manufacturer could, potentially, expose our "critical infrastructure," or allow for the export of "critical technologies." Add these "critical" criterion to the much broadened definition of "control," and it now appears that FINSA 2007 is going to result in a sudden rush on the CFIUS process; a cautious, and/or prudent, foreign investor should see no way around the need for filing.

So what does this mean? What kind of data is assembled for review during the 100-plus hours foreign investors are expected to spend on preparing a CFIUS filing? According to the proposed regulations, a voluntary CFIUS filing should describe at the least:[50]

- The transaction in question—to include:
  - Statement of purpose—why are you spending money on this
  - Nature of the transaction—acquisition, consolidation, merger, purchase of voting rights, etc.
  - Name, U.S. address, Web site, nationality, and address of principle place of business for each foreign person involved in the transaction
  - Name, address, Web site, principle place of business for the U.S. business involved in the transaction
    - Name, address, and nationality (for individuals) or place of incorporation or other legal organization (for entities) of: The immediate parent (a person who holds or will hold at least 50% of the outstanding voting interest in an entity; or holds or will hold the right to at least 50% of the profits of an entity; or has or will have the right, in the event of dissolution, of at least 50% of the assets of that entity), the ultimate parent, and each intermediate parent—if any—of the foreign person that is party to the transaction
    - Where the ultimate parent is a private company—the name of the ultimate owner
    - Where the ultimate parent is a public company—the name of any shareholder with an interest of greater than 5% in such parent
  - Name, address, Web site, and nationality or place of incorporation for the person ultimately controlling the U.S. business being acquired
  - Expected date for completion of the transaction, or date completed
  - Price paid in U.S. dollars
  - Name of any and all financial institutions involved in the transaction
- When a transaction is structured as an acquisition of assets—provide a detailed description of the assets of the U.S. business, including approximate value
- With respect to the U.S. business that is the subject of the transaction, and any entity of which that U.S. business is a parent that is also a subject of the transaction—provide:
  - Respective business activities—i.e., product and/or service lines, including U.S. market share and explanation of how that estimate was derived; and a list of direct competitors
  - U.S. address and Web site of each facility that is manufacturing classified or unclassified products under government contract
  - Each contract that is currently in effect, or was in effect within the last five years, with any agency of the U.S. government involving any information, technology, or data that is classified under Executive Order 12958.[51] This information will include estimated final completion date; and name, office, and telephone number of the contracting official
  - Any other contract currently in effect, or that was in effect within the last three years, with any agency of the U.S. government
  - Any products or services that the U.S. business supplies, directly or indirectly, to any agency of the U.S. government

- Any products or services the U.S. business supplies to third parties and that it knows are rebranded or incorporated into the products of another entity
- For the prior three years:
  - The number of priority-rated contracts or orders that the U.S. business has provided under the Defense Priorities and Allocations System regulation
  - The number of such priority-rated contracts or orders that the U.S. business has placed with other entities—and its plan to ensure that any new entity formed at the completion of the notified transaction complies with the Defense Priorities and Allocations System regulation
  - Description and copy of the cyber security plan, if any, that will be used to protect against cyber attacks on the operation, design, and development of the U.S. business's services, networks, systems, data storage, and facilities
- Whether the U.S. business that is being acquired produces or trades in:
  - Items that are subject to Export Administration regulations—if so, describe these items and a list of commodity classifications as outlined in the Commerce Controls List
  - Defense articles, services, and related technical data covered by the United States Munitions List
  - Products and technology that are subject to export authorization administration by the Department of Energy
  - Select agents and toxins
- Whether the U.S. business that is the subject of the transaction:
  - Possesses any licenses, permits, or other authorizations—in addition to those covered above—granted by an agency of the U.S. government
  - Has technology that has military applications
- With respect to the foreign person engaged in the transaction, and potential parents, provide:
  - Description of the foreign person's business(s)
  - Plans of the foreign person for the U.S. business with respect to:
    - Reducing, eliminating, or selling research and development facilities
    - Changing product quality
    - Shutting down or moving outside the U.S.
    - Consolidating or selling product lines or technology
    - Modifying or terminating sensitive contracts described above
    - Eliminating domestic supply by selling products solely to non-domestic audiences
  - Whether the foreign person is controlled by or acting on behalf of a foreign government
  - Whether a foreign government or person controlled by, or acting on behalf of a foreign government:
    - Has or controls ownership interests of the acquiring foreign person or any parent of the acquiring foreign person. If so, the nature and percentage amount of such instruments
    - Has the right or power to appoint any of the principle officers or members of the board of directors of the acquiring foreign entity

- Holds any contingent interest in the foreign acquiring party
- Has any other affirmative or negative rights or powers that could be relevant for CFIUS decision-making
- Description of any formal or informal arrangements among the foreign ownership interest holders of the foreign person
- Biographical information on members of the board of directors, senior management, and ultimate beneficial owner of 5% or more of the following:
  - The foreign person engaged in the transaction
  - The immediate parent of the foreign person engaged in the transaction
  - The ultimate parent of the foreign person engaged in the transaction
- The following "personal identifier information":
  - Full name
  - All other names
  - Business address
  - Country and city of residence
  - Date of birth
  - Place of birth
  - U.S. Social Security number (where applicable)
  - National identity number
  - U.S. and foreign passport number
  - Dates and nature of foreign government and foreign military service
- The following "business identifier information":
  - Business name
  - Business address
  - Business phone number, fax, and email
  - Employer identification number
  - Most recent annual report (in English)
  - Copy of most recent asset or stock purchase agreement
  - An organizational chart
  - Whether any party has been involved in a previous CFIUS mitigation agreement

Given the extensive scrub of products, persons, financial arrangements, contracts, and business processes entailed, one begins to understand why a CFIUS filing has proven a daunting challenge for would-be overseas investors. A requirement to divulge business plans, financial data, and complete personal profiles are frequently disparaged as "odious" at best—and "espionage" at worst. As such, it's not surprising to discover that outside feedback on these filing requirements was less than laudatory.

In a formal response to the proposed regulations, the China Ministry of Commerce declared:

Information required for submission by all parties to the transaction . . . is too complicated. The list of documents itself is several pages long. Some of the information required covers too broadly, and has no direct or tangible impact over the transaction, such as the requests for the directors and senior executives of the foreign person, its immediate acquirer and its ultimate parent to provide dates and nature of foreign government and foreign military service where applicable. Such provisions add a lot of costs to the parties to the transaction. It is suggested that the amount of required information be cut down to facilitate the transactions.[52]

The China Securities Regulatory Commission (CSRC) was even blunter. First, the CSRC noted, a significant translation burden for foreign parties could be eliminated by only requiring "a summary of the relevant documents in English for review purpose . . . Such [a] summary should include essential information adequate for the reviewing authority which will have the discretion to request additional information in English."[53] Having offered this "gracious" criticism, the CSRC took direct aim at the most intrusive filing CFIUS filing requirement. As the Chinese put it, "it is unreasonable and unnecessary for the members of the board or boards of directors and senior executives to disclose "dates and nature of foreign government and foreign military service."

Interestingly, the Chinese were not the only party to chafe at these filing requirements. In their comment on the proposed regulations, the Canada Pension Plan Investment Board argued the stipulated data could "require parties to a transaction to gather and provide information that has no possible relevance to the review of the particular transaction."[54] Similar comments were provided by the Confederation of British Industry—"the voice of British business." As best the Confederation of British Industry could tell, "the proposed regulations will substantially increase the amount of information that companies have to submit as part of their voluntary notification to CFIUS, and we have some concerns about this." More specifically, the Confederation of British Industry continued, "it should be made explicit that if a particular type of information is not relevant to a specific deal notification, a CFIUS submission should allow a return of 'not relevant'." Finally, the Confederation declared, "the amount of personal identifier information requested, and the number of individuals for whom it is requested, is very substantial"—a polite way of suggesting that the Yanks are asking for too much data.[55]

Back to the Pesky Debate over "Control"

While we are on the subject of outside comments and the proposed FINSA regulations, it seems only to appropriate to revisit the subject of "control." Frustration over ambiguity in the definition of "control" has not been limited to would-be offshore investors. In March 2008, three members of the U.S. House of Representatives urged the Treasury Department to more exactly specify what triggers a CFIUS review and/or investigation. In a letter addressed to Secretary of the Treasury Henry Paulson, Representative Barney Frank (D-MA), Carolyn Maloney (D-NY), and Luis Gutierrez (D-IL) explicitly asked whether the 10% ownership threshold remains a "bright line" for CFIUS. The letter went on to state, "we urge you to clarify in the new regulations that this threshold is only one of the indicia of control and does not represent a bright line below which CFIUS has no ability or intent to review a transaction."[56]

I think it is safe to say the Treasury may have succeeded in meeting this requirement beyond all best intentions. If there was a single item in the proposed regulations that appears to have caught the attention of almost every outside observer, it was the definition of "control." In a subtle condemnation of the entire FINSA exercise, the Norwegian Ministry of Finance had this to say about the proposed regulation's definition of control:

> One element that may contribute to the apparent unpredictability of the regulations is the absence of clear thresholds defining the concept of "control" in the legislation. There has been a perception that investment up to 10% will not constitute control. However, it now appears that this is not necessarily the case, and that many factors may determine whether an investment will constitute control. A system where many different factors are considered before making an overall assessment may lead to more targeted investigations and may, perhaps, enhance national security. On the other hand, the result can also be reduced transparency and predictability for foreign investors.[57]

Beijing had equally unkind words to offer on the proposed regulation's arm wrestling with the definition of control. The China Ministry of Commerce wrote:

> This section lists out ten criteria for determining the existence of control, with a fairly broad coverage. The definition of "control" is overly rigorous as "control" is established so long as any one criterion is satisfied. Furthermore, criteria such as "the entry into, termination or non-fulfillment by the entity of significant contracts" and "the policies or procedures of the entity governing the treatment of non-pubic technical, financial or other proprietary information of the entity" are defined in a rather vague manner and therefore difficult to implement in actual practice. We suggest that reasonable explanations and explicit definitions be made to the above-mentioned criteria.[58]

Even the British appeared a bit flummoxed by the proposed definition of control. In their comments on the regulations, the Confederation of British Industry observed,

> In order to maintain CFIUS's status as a flexible mechanism, we respect the decision to avoid "bright line" tests, or statements about what sort of transactions would never be regarded as covered. This in effect creates a functional definition of control applied to the circumstances in each case. Nevertheless, we feel that more could be done to provide companies with guidance and assurance as to whether or not a proposed transaction needs to be notified to CFIUS or not. This is important for two reasons. First, uncertainty in any form always discourages investment, so the more it can be limited, the better. Second, the lack of a bright line test will always mean that the most cautious investors may want to notify their transactions to CFIUS "just in case"—which in turn could mean a significant burden on the Committee's already stretched resources.[59]

What are we to make of this consternation over the definition of "control"? First, semantic ambiguity is clearly doing nothing for investor confidence. While the open-ended definition of control in the proposed regulations certainly answers domestic protectionists' requirement for maximum investigative flexibility—it has also caused would-be foreign investors to openly state that they might be more comfortable taking their money elsewhere. Second, there appears to be come confusion at the Treasury as to what constitutes a "bright line" for "control." The proposed regulations take great efforts to eschew the perceived 10% rule—but then make clear in CFIUS filing requirements that 5% ownership is sufficient to cause consternation in Washington.[60] As foreign "control" over a U.S. business is the very lynchpin of any CFIUS review or investigation, one suspects that more time will need to be spent on answering these concerns.

Lessons from Abroad

U.S. politicians are not alone in the struggle over balancing national security and a desire for foreign investment. Globalization of the manufacturing and service sectors has been accompanied by an international diversification of investments and holdings—tangible and otherwise. Foreign direct investment has expanded to targets across the planet and with it, efforts to regulate how and where potentially hostile outsiders can spend their money. In the pages that follow, we will examine three other nations' efforts to regulate foreign investment—specifically, China, the United Arab Emirates, and the United Kingdom. I have selected these three examples for two reasons: First, China and the UAE are preeminent members of the sovereign wealth club, and how these governments protect their own industries may help explain what they expect from Washington. Second, the UK is internationally renowned as being "user friendly" for foreign investors. As such, London's approach to governing this activity may prove useful for informing Washington's efforts to legislate for sovereign wealth investors.

As previously noted, in February 2008 the U.S. Government Accountability Office released a study of laws and policies regulating foreign investment in ten countries outside the United States.[61] (See Table 5.1 for a list of the top ten targets for foreign direct investment.) Crafted in response to congressional concerns about widespread outside investment in the U.S. financial industry, the report provides a layman's summary of other nations' legislative efforts to protect against potentially hostile investors and the process of implementing those laws and policies.

Before stepping to the three cases I have selected for our discussion, we should touch upon the general observations GAO analysts made after reviewing investment laws and policies outside the United States. First, the GAO discovered many similarities between the foreign investment review processes employed in Washington and elsewhere. For instance, the GAO discovered that eight of the ten countries employed a formal review process—typically

**Table 5.1 Top Ten Targets for
Foreign Direct Investment in 2006**[62]

Country
United States
United Kingdom
Hong Kong
Germany
China
France
Belgium
Netherlands
Spain
Canada

conducted by a government economic office with input from security agencies. Second, national security concerns appear to be the primary factor behind this review process. Third, the GAO found all of the studied nations share concerns about a "core" set of national security issues—specifically, defense industries, energy, and investment by government-controlled funds.[63]

As might be expected, the GAO also discovered significant differences in the approaches various governments employ when seeking to legislate for foreign investment. Perhaps the most significant of these differences concerns the notification process. While U.S. law provides for voluntary notifications, the GAO found most other countries mandate national security reviews if an investment reaches a certain dollar amount or if the purchaser is to acquire a controlling share in the target business. A further break with U.S. procedures appeared in the appeal process. Whereas Washington does not provide for a CFIUS appeal process, five of the countries studied allowed such decisions to be reconsidered in court or through administrative means.[64] Finally, unlike the United States, a few of the countries studied were found to either completely restrict investment in certain sectors or simply limit the extent of ownership in all sectors. In short, the GAO study revealed that broad policy concerns—such as national security—serve to direct legislative efforts, but final laws are more indicative of unique societal and governmental norms than an overarching campaign to dictate foreign investment behavior. This finding helps explain problems the IMF is confronting in its drive to establish a "best practices" policy for sovereign wealth funds. All parties may agree on a need to protect national interests, but defining those interests is an entirely different matter.

China: Having provided an overall context for the conversation, let us now turn to the specific case studies. In 2007, China—absent Hong Kong—was the international community's third largest recipient of total foreign direct investment, drawing $82.7 billion.[65] In attempting to outline how Beijing goes about legislating for this inflow of foreign capital, the GAO discovered "the development of Chinese investment regulations has not kept pace with the development of its markets, and the complexity of the foreign investment review process reflects vestiges of China's past as a planned economy."[66] This is not to say Chinese authorities have ignored the potential problem. In 2006, Beijing began the process of crafting laws and regulations required for establishing a foreign investment review process. The first step in this process was promulgation of an updated "Provisions for Merger and Acquisition of Domestic Enterprises by Foreign Investors." These regulations establish the requirement for government approval of a foreign investment if the transaction is found to:

- Affect national economic security
- Involve a major industry
- Result in transfer of famous trademarks or traditional Chinese brands

According to the Provisions, a foreign investor who fails to apply for governmental approval in a transaction meeting one or more of these criteria faces the possibility of forced divestiture.

Like Washington, Beijing seeks to provide further guidance on what constitutes a potentially sensitive sector through official publications. For the Chinese this document is the "Catalog for the Guidance of Foreign Investment." In the Catalog, foreign investments are divided into three classes: encouraged, restricted, and prohibited. When a proposed transaction does not fall into one of these classes, it is considered "permitted" but may come under further government review.[67] This all seems quite logical, until one considers that the Catalog does not provide a definition of "national security," and fails to specify reasons for why an investment would be prohibited. That said, the Catalog does indentify sensitive industries in which a foreign investor can expect to encounter the infamous Chinese bureaucracy. These sectors include: weapons and ammunition manufacturing; mining and processing of radioactive materials; and construction and operation of power networks. Other prohibited sectors include: film, publishing, and television; processing of special Chinese teas; preparation of traditional Chinese medicines; and production of enamelware and rice paper.[68]

According to the GAO, China's review process for foreign investments is best characterized as "nominal." As the GAO puts it: "the standards that China uses to conduct reviews of foreign investment are opaque, and have resulted in a system that is not fully transparent. However, it is clear that in addition to national security concerns, they also include an assessment of whether a given investment conforms to China's economic plans."[69] The GAO then goes on to highlight five factors that can render Beijing's foreign investment review practice "unpredictable." These factors are:

1. Negative publicity generated by competitor firms that serves to influence evaluating officials
2. Bureaucratic infighting
3. Differences between local and national priorities
4. China's political calendar
5. Regulator ambiguity and lack of procedural transparency[70]

The bottom line: a foreign investor seeking to place money in China faces a review process absent definitive legal codes or a set timeline. Although the GAO contends that a "great majority of transactions are cleared without incident," the potential for intervention by private and public officials remains high.[71] Furthermore, as China races forward with its economic development, the promulgation of new regulations is likely to generate even more uncertainty. The relatively immature Chinese legal system, and a growing awareness of the potential dangers associated with foreign investment, suggest that Beijing is still a long way from promulgating its own version of FINSA 2007.

United Arab Emirates: As home to the world's largest sovereign wealth fund—the Abu Dhabi Investment Authority—and the inadvertent progenitor of FINSA 2007, the UAE appeared a prime target for our examination of overseas foreign investment laws and policies. The GAO reports U.S. State Department officials consider the UAE to be one of the most open economies in the Middle East. When it comes to foreign investment, the UAE has attempted to establish a set of codes in the form of the "Companies Law" and "Agencies Law." The Companies Law states a foreign entity is prohibited from owning more than 49% of a UAE business, while the Agencies Law stipulates foreign importers must operate through an agent to bring goods into the country.[72]

Although the Companies and Agencies Laws may appear unduly restrictive, the UAE has set about removing some of the string through establishment of 32 free trade zones. UAE officials have told the GAO these free trade zones are exempt from all but the country's criminal code—thereby permitting foreigners to own 100% of any enterprise located within such an area. However, a foreign company located in a free trade zone that attempts to invest elsewhere in the country is once again subject to the Companies and Agencies Laws. As a result, the UAE is said to have two separate and distinct economies: the free trade zone economy and the regular UAE economy.[73]

This distinction between what can legally transpire within the free trade zones and elsewhere in UAE has at least one more level of complexity for foreign investors. According to the GAO, many of the legal barriers associated with foreign direct investment do not apply to citizens of countries who belong to the Gulf Cooperation Council.[74] As a result, the UAE is said to have three levels of access for investors: citizens, Gulf Cooperation Council nationals, and everyone else.

The GAO contends the UAE does not have a formal foreign investment review process. Instead, foreign investors are informally notified of potential official sensitivity concerning a proposed transaction—and steered elsewhere. This is not to say the UAE is absent a list of sensitive sectors; rather, it appears that this spread sheet is not widely distributed. GAO officials state they were informed, "some sectors, like military production, contain sensitive technologies, and are clearly, if not explicitly, off limits to foreign investors."[75] Other sectors, such as oil and gas production, are apparently also considered sensitive but, again, do not seem to have warranted the establishment of a formal review process. Why this lack of a formal review process? GOA analysts state they were provided four explanations: (1) the UAE seeks to maintain its reputation as an open business environment; (2) business in the UAE is largely conducted at the personal level, and such notifications are handled the same way; (3) the UAE seeks to direct foreign investors into sectors requiring outside expertise; and (4) the UAE has only existed as a nation since 1971—and has yet to institutional-ize a large number of practices.[76]

The bottom line: the UAE is reportedly in the process of even further relax-ing its investment laws. However, State Department officials indicate that domestic opposition to such a move is alive and well, and will require overcom-ing entrenched opposition. As such, plans to scrap the Companies and Agencies Laws will likely be turned into an incremental process, in which foreign owner-ship is allowed to reach 75 and maybe even 100% over an unspecified number of years. It remains to be seen whether this will be true across all business sectors; the GAO analysts suspect that sensitive industries will be excluded from the lib-eralization process.[77]

United Kingdom: Second only to the United States as a destination for for-eign direct investment, the United Kingdom takes great pride in London's open door policies. In fact, the GAO reports that the United Kingdom "generally makes no policy distinction between domestic and foreign investment"[78]—with one notable exception: transactions affecting national security. That said, the GAO also notes that London has "no legal framework specifically designed to monitor foreign direct investment for national security reasons."

So how do the British defend against potentially hostile foreign investors? Officials in London claim that the legal guidance for such situations is provided by the Enterprise Act of 2002. While the Enterprise Act was primarily intended to serve anti-trust concerns, the law also allows for "special intervention" when the Secretary of State determines a transaction may threaten the public interest. More specifically, the Enterprise Act states the Secretary of State may intervene on the public's behalf if a foreign investment is of potential harm to national secu-rity, the media, or water. (Interestingly, the Enterprise Act of 2002 also allows the Secretary of State to issue an order effectively modifying the Act so as to update legal codes when considerations not previously addressed arise. This open-ended clause essentially allows the Secretary of State to ensure technology does not dangerously outpace the law.) Since the Enterprise Act went into effect in 2003, the Secretary of State has issued six intervention notices. All six cases involved protection of sensitive information associated with military programs. Of note, all six cases were ultimately approved under the condition that appropriate mitigation steps be implemented so as to address the security risk.

In addition to the public interest oversight provided by the Enterprise Act, London may seek to review transactions that exceed $34 million or involve a firm whose market share exceeds 25% of a particular sector. But the real veto clause in London's foreign investment code is provided by the government ownership of a "golden share" in companies that British officials consider important to national security. This "golden share"—established in the affected companies' articles of association—provides the United Kingdom a say in board of directors citizenship requirements, control over percentages of foreign-owned shares, and/or approval requirements for the dissolution or disposal of any strategic assets.[79] Of note, the "golden share" does not give the government control over a firm's routine business activity, investment decisions, or employment appointments.

As one might suspect, would-be foreign investors consider London's "golden share" the ultimate trump card. In fact, the European Court of Justice has sought to limit employment of this option. According to would-be investors, the "golden share" constitutes a violation of the European Union Treaty. The free movement of capital is one of the "four freedoms" enshrined in the European Union Treaty;[80] as such, foreign investors argue London's "golden share" is discriminatory and a violation of the Treaty's principles. London has countered by arguing European Union member states are allowed to effectuate such regulations in very restrictive manners with objective justifications. Furthermore, Britain contends these measures are not "a means of arbitrary discrimination or a disguised restriction on the movement of capital."[81] As such, the GAO reports London continues to use the "golden shares" for national security purposes and "does not intend to dispose of these shares in certain strategic areas."[82]

The GAO goes on to state London's reviews of foreign investment are conducted by the Office of Fair Trade. If the Office of Fair Trade determines that the transaction establishes potential for anticompetitive practices, it refers the case to the Competition Commission. The Competition Commission then may consult with the parties engaged in the transaction—and normally issues decisions in 30 days, but is allowed up to six months to complete the review. Once a transaction is approved, the decision is final. The case cannot be reopened. Why does this seem so straightforward? Well, as the GAO notes, prior to an official review, most companies meet informally with the relevant agency to discuss the proposed transaction. Although there is no official requirement to take this step, the pre-notifications appear to help eliminate potential problems before they result in legal action.

The bottom line here: London seeks to remain open to foreign investment. While the Brits have warned about the potential dangers associated with sovereign wealth fund investments, London has taken no steps to formally alter the nation's legal codes. In fact, Alistair Darling, the British Chancellor of the Exchequer, made the case for London's path of "least resistance" when he used his first speech in office to declare:

> I welcome investment to Britain. It is a sign of our success . . . Of course, all investors, including government backed companies need to operate according to the rules of the market in which they participate, including high standards of governance and appropriate transparency. So I welcome the IMF's work in leading further analysis of this and look forward to the results at the next annual meetings in October . . . But across the world, investment needs to be a two way process. So just as we welcome investment here, there needs to be a level playing field for British investment overseas. Openness should be a commitment by all. Free trade should be just that.[83]

In short, London appears prepared to "stay the course," but is unwilling to surrender rights to play a "golden" trump card should the perceived need arise.

But What about the Rest of Europe?

London's insistence on maintaining an open door for foreign investment has met with less-than-enthusiastic support on the other side of the English Channel. Both Berlin and Paris have publicly expressed mounting dismay with the potential political agenda that sovereign wealth funds bring to the market place. The Germans have been particularly adamant about crafting a national policy intended to protect against hostile foreign investors. As early as July 2007, German Chancellor Angela Merkel was voicing concerns about the manner in which sovereign wealth funds were acquiring assets throughout the European Union. Just a week before Alistair Darling declared Britain's intention to remain open to foreign investors, Merkel was telling reporters that sovereign wealth funds are "a new phenomenon . . . we must tackle with some urgency."[84]

Speaking for Paris, French President Nicolas Sarkozy has been equally adamant about establishing defenses against foreign investors. During his first press conference upon taking office, Sarkozy told reporters, "in the face of the increasing power of speculative funds, which are extremely aggressive, and of sovereign wealth funds, which do not only obey to economic logic, there's no reason for France not to react. France must protect its companies."[85]

Merkel and Sarkozy's vehement response to sovereign wealth funds can largely be attributed to a single nation: Russia. Moscow's emergence as a significant actor on the sovereign wealth front is a direct result of Russia's abundant energy supply—and Europe's need for same. Under President Putin, not only did Russia succeed in paying off the former Soviet Union's debts, Moscow re-emerged as a viable political broker who is willing to use gas supplies and a ready supply of cash to purchase influence and lucrative assets throughout the European Union (EU).[86] While Moscow's stabilization fund and the Russian sovereign wealth fund have largely been kept out of this fray, Putin's cronies—and Russia's questionably "private" oil industry—have not. To date, these "suspicious actors" have acquired Getty Oil filling stations, Nelson Resources, and a 5% share of General Motors.[87]

As Marshall Goldman points out in his book, *Petrostate: Putin, Power and the New Russia*, some Europeans—specifically, the Germans—have become quite wary of this newfound Russian fiscal prowess.[88] As Goldman puts it, the Germans fear that the Russians will use their foreign currency reserves to acquire equity in defense-related industries and other recently privatized sensitive sectors. As one German official told Goldman, "we didn't just go through all our efforts to privatize industries like Deutsche Telekom or the Deutsche Post only so that the Russians can nationalize them."[89]

As noted above, the Germans are not alone in this concern. In the aftermath of Russia's blatant attempt to manipulate political developments through selective cessation of gas supplies, even the EU felt compelled to act. On 19 September 2007, the European Commission of the European Union adopted a resolution stipulating no company from outside the EU be allowed to acquire energy infrastructures (i.e., natural gas pipelines) "in Europe unless there is 'reciprocity with that country'."[90] According to Marshall Goldman, this resolution was intended as a direct shot across Moscow's bow. More specifically, members of the Russian Duma are said to have perceived the resolution as directly intended to curtail Gazprom's[91] further acquisition of natural gas distribution systems—thereby impinging on Moscow's ability to use gas supplies as a political weapon.[92]

In any case, Russia's emergence as a potentially hostile investor has spurred a protectionist backlash in Berlin. In 2006, the German government halted Russian efforts to purchase a share of Deutsche Telekom, and in 2007 Berlin offered very public criticism of Russian plans to acquire shares in German banks and Airbus.[93] Furthermore, the German government set about the task of crafting a law to enable a vetting of non–EU business transactions and expressed interest in establishing a "superfund" that could be used to defend "German crown jewels."[94] The results of this legislative effort? In late January 2008, Berlin announced that it would continue to welcome foreign investment but was preparing legislation that would provide for a review of transactions resulting in acquisition of 25% or more of a company's voting rights.[95]

On 9 April 2008, the German government announced it would be formally introducing controls for investments from sovereign wealth funds. Under the new laws, an automatic review process will be put into effect if a non–EU investor seeks to purchase more than a 25% share in a German firm. In addition, the German Labor Ministry can seek to halt a transaction involving a foreign purchaser if the deal threatens local jobs or involves a strategic sector, such as electrical generation. As a means of ensuring that all such transactions are properly reported, Berlin now has the right to force divestiture in cases where notification is not correctly accomplished.[96]

Not surprisingly, Germany's decision to press ahead with the sovereign wealth fund legislation drew an immediate negative response from would-be investors. (As we have previously noted, the Kuwait Investment Authority offered very public condemnation of the legislation.[97]) In an effort to reassure this wealthy "mob," Berlin launched what can best be described as an international "appeasement" campaign. In the run-up to a May 2008 Middle East trip, German Finance Minister Peer Steinbrueck told reporters, "sovereign wealth funds are welcome in Germany." In fact, Steinbrueck continued, "their commitment contributes to value creation and employment in Germany, and also to stabilization in times of financial market turbulence." Steinbrueck concluded by declaring, "we will not lead the discussion about sovereign wealth funds so as to stimulate protectionist powers in Germany."[98]

Steinbrueck's statements of contrition did not end with the remarks in Berlin. During a stop in Kuwait, the German Finance Minister told his hosts, "nobody wants to build obstacles for investments . . . that would be crazy." Speaking with Kuwaiti businessmen, Steinbrueck argued, "we should have a strong interest to attract sovereign wealth funds." As for Berlin's new legislation, Steinbrueck declared that Berlin was only following in the path blazed by London, Paris, and Washington. As the German official put it, "we just want to prevent the possibility in theory that we open the door to bad guys."[99]

Given Berlin's humbling—and, arguably, readily predictable—negative experience, the European Union's failure to follow in Germany's footprints seems only logical. What do I mean? Let's back up for a minute. During the October 2007 G7 finance ministers' meetings in Washington, it became clear there was no Western consensus on how to handle sovereign wealth fund investments. As a newspaper in Tokyo so ably noted, "some lawmakers in developed nations regard the sovereign wealth funds as a threat because the funds are used to buy companies in their countries . . . others say sovereign wealth funds have contributed to boosting the world economy."[100] Although statements from Berlin and Paris would appear to suggest that Europe was favoring the "threat" factor in this debate, official comments from the EU indicated many other nations were arguing for maintenance of an open door for sovereign wealth fund investors. This push for avoiding seemingly protectionist legislation was made evident in a speech Charlie McCreevy, the European Commissioner for Internal Market Services, made on 4 December 2007. Speaking to a group of European Parliament members, McCreevy declared, "Europe must remain an attractive place for investment. Without continued inward investment our economies will stagnate. We have no interest in erecting barriers to investment." For McCreevy—and apparently for his fellow EU commissioners—the bottom line was quite simple: "openness to investment, avoid protectionism."[101]

McCreevy largely repeated these remarks during a speech in February 2008. Standing before an audience in Washington, McCreevy argued,

. . . sovereign wealth funds play an essential role. They provide necessary support at a time when access to more traditional sources of capital is severely curtailed. I welcome these new sources of liquidity and investment. This might make me unpopular with some elements . . . in Europe, but I mean what I say.[102]

This statement of support for sovereign wealth funds served to foretell the European Commission's response to demands for a formal EU policy concerning the government investment vehicles. On 27 February 2008, the European Commission proposed an EU approach to sovereign wealth funds that sought to avoid new laws in favor of a policy encouraging the government investors to adopt a common code of conduct. The European Commission also rejected a CFIUS-like review process or a "golden shares" approach for contending with the sovereign wealth funds. As the European Commission's policy paper put it, "all these suggestions run the risk of sending a misleading signal—that the EU is stepping back from its commitment to an open investment regime."[103]

What is the substance of the EU's position on sovereign wealth funds? The answer to that question was provided in a forum held on 2 April 2008. Speaking before an audience assembled in Brussels, Joaquin Almunia, the European Commissioner for Economic and Financial Affairs, argued the EU is calling on sovereign wealth funds ". . . to commit to good governance practices, adequate accountability, and a sufficient level of transparency." As such, Almunia reiterated EU support for the Organization for Co-operation and Economic Development and International Monetary Fund efforts to establish "best practices" standards for sovereign wealth funds. However, he then closed by declaring, "the European economy is built on the principles of openness to trade and investment. The EU will, therefore, not take a defensive approach to sovereign wealth funds. They represent a major source of investment for the European economy and we recognize the benefits they bring and will continue to bring to global financial markets."[104] In short, Berlin be damned, the EU is not about to establish laws or policies that serve to drive sovereign wealth fund investors elsewhere.

Policy: The Peril and Potential for the United States

The international struggle to craft laws and policies sufficient to meet the potential threat posed by sovereign wealth funds presents a number of object lessons for policymakers in Washington. First, the absence of consensus on how to proceed, even within the European Union, strongly suggests that widespread support for a comprehensive policy is going to be difficult—if not impossible—to achieve. As we have already seen, politicians in Washington are caught between ardent protectionists and those who believe the United States cannot afford to implement more restrictive laws for foreign investors. This battle is only made more difficult by the emergence of lobbyists seeking to represent the interests of potential clients with very deep pockets.[105]

The second object lesson one can draw from these international efforts—and Washington's own proposed legislation—is the marked absence of agreement on what constitutes "control" or a "bright line" justifying national security reviews. As I noted previously, Washington is clearly reluctant to draw the line for "control" at 10% . . . but appears interested in considering 5% ownership as justification for a CFIUS review. London's employment of "golden shares" to protect domestic interests seems to have focused on 15%, whereas Berlin seems to be willing to draw the line at 25%. This debate is unlikely to be resolved in the near future, but is sure to draw bitter responses from would-be investors regardless of the final decision. Furthermore, as soon as a definition for "control" is achieved, a well-meaning attorney is sure to find an escape clause.

The third object lesson concerns sovereign wealth funds' ability to pick and choose their investment targets. As China and Kuwait have made perfectly clear, any effort to impose "odious" regulations will be countered with a decision to take one's money elsewhere. The EU seems to have taken this lesson on board—hence the multiple public statements declaring Europe open to all sovereign wealth fund investors. Washington, on the other hand, is struggling with the issue. Although high-profile political leaders in the United States have repeatedly enunciated their support for maintaining an open foreign investment environment, other political actors are demanding far more restrictive policies. This latter group includes the Service Employees International Union (SEIU), which has called for stronger federal oversight of sovereign wealth fund deals with private equity firms.[106] As a means of ensuring this call does not go unheeded, SEIU has launched a television, radio, print, and online campaign demanding the federal government answer the union's concerns.

Finally, legislative and policy debates abroad suggest that the best way of regulating sovereign wealth fund activities may be through imposition of a tit-for-tat or mutual reciprocity agreement. This idea is not new. In October 2007, Bob Davis, a reporter with *The Wall Street Journal*, suggested Washington ". . . make the activities of the [sovereign wealth] funds a new issue in global trade and negotiate a bargain between the countries that have funds and the countries where the funds invest." "Violations of the accord," Davis argued, "could be enforced by prohibitions on future investment."[107] The problem, as a Yale University professor told Davis, is that such an approach requires at least the U.S. and EU coordinate their policies; otherwise, "investment funds could play one country against another."[108] A similar argument emerged in March 2008, when media sources highlighted the fact sovereign wealth funds receive a tax break from Washington because U.S. laws exempt foreign state-owned entities from paying taxes on portfolio investments. A Breakingviews analyst writing for *The Wall Street Journal* suggested this tax break might be leveraged to Washington's advantage when considering means of regulating sovereign wealth fund investors. As the analyst put it, "perhaps the best way forward for U.S. politicians is to use the tax exemption as a political lever. Funds could be allowed to keep the exemption so long as they follow some fair rules on transparent investing."[109] This would certainly be a tit-for-tat policy at its best—putting a bite on the sovereign wealth funds where it hurts the most, the bottom line.

As these four lessons from abroad illustrate, there are a number of options Washington could consider while in pursuit of policies and laws governing sovereign wealth fund activities in the United States. I would also note that one does not have to go offshore in search of policy recommendations. A literal barrage of policy suggestions has flowed from American think tanks and would-be power brokers since September 2007.

The New American Foundation appears to be one of the earliest contributors to this policy debate. In a paper titled "Foreign Investment and Sovereign Wealth Funds," the New American Foundation presented five "recommendations" for establishing policies and laws concerning the government investment vehicles:

1. A comprehensive review of existing U.S. legislation to ensure that the rise of sovereign wealth funds does not result in an unforeseen situation in which national interests and those of U.S. investors and companies are somehow compromised
2. Call for increased voluntary transparency and disclosure
3. Support calls for the IMF to establish a code of best practices for sovereign wealth funds
4. Engage in a global "Invest in America" marketing program
5. Consider the possibility of allowing—or even encouraging—the purchase of shares or other securities by foreign-owned funds in public companies, but apply specific restrictions on the exercise of control or voting rights above a to-be-determined threshold[110]

A comment on one of the options listed above is in order. As best I can determine, the New America Foundation was a very early advocate for linking an "invest in America" campaign with the sovereign wealth fund debate. As the Foundation appropriately notes, "rather than fearing global investment, we must be aggressively competing for it."[111] With a net outflow of almost $2 billion a day, the United States cannot afford to behave in any other manner.

A second set of proposed policy options appeared in February 2008, when the Heritage Foundation published a monograph titled "Sovereign Wealth Funds and U.S. National Security." Declaring the "biggest threat to U.S. economic and national security is not foreign sovereign wealth investment . . . rather, it is the increasing threat that the U.S. will adopt protectionist investment policies,"[112] the Heritage Foundation put forth four policy recommendations:

1. Encourage sovereign investors to promote sound macroeconomic policies, financial development, and liberalization in their own economies
2. Support IMF and World Bank efforts to establish a voluntary set of best practices for sovereign wealth funds

3. Promote meaningful debate and research about sovereign wealth funds to better understand their impact on both the U.S. and world markets and on sovereign wealth investors themselves

4. Stand firm against implementing protectionist barriers against foreign investment and ensure that U.S. national security and financial reviews of foreign investments remain nondiscriminatory and fair[113]

The Heritage Foundation recommendations touch on a pair of raw nerves. First, the call for further research on government investment vehicles likely reflects a widespread perception that most participants in this conversation have little to no idea what a sovereign wealth fund is—or how their actions might imperil and/or benefit the United States. Although a poll conducted in mid-February 2008, found that 49% of the U.S. respondents said foreign-government investments harmed the U.S. economy, only 6% of the survey participants said they had "seen or heard anything recently" about sovereign wealth funds.[114] Second, by calling for reviews of foreign investments to remain nondiscriminatory and fair, the Heritage Foundation runs the danger of reopening wounds created by the Dubai Ports World controversy. As more than one wag has observed, the congressional tumult over the Dubai Ports World deal might have been very different if the company had been based in— oh, say, London. As sovereign wealth funds in the Middle East continue to grow, we can ill afford to turn away potential investors simply because of stereotypes engendered by the attacks of 11 September 2001.

Yet a third set of policy recommendations has emerged from Senator Evan Bayh's office. The Democratic Senator from Indiana offered the following two proposals in mid-February 2008:

1. At a minimum the U.S. ought to require passive investment by sovereign wealth funds

2. CFIUS reviews are only triggered when an investment exceeds 10% of total ownership . . . a more realistic standard is required[115]

Allow me to comment on these proposals in reverse order. As we have seen above, proposed regulations for implementing FINSA 2007 do indeed end the perceived 10% ownership "rule." It increasingly appears as though CFIUS is going to be tasked with conducting a review and/or investigation any time a sovereign wealth fund invests in the United States. As for the argument concerning passive investment, the Norwegian Government Pension Fund-Global, for one, has made it quite clear such rules will drive their investments elsewhere. Furthermore, there is a very open debate in the U.S. as to the wisdom of enacting such a policy. Some Bush administration officials have sided with Oslo and argued that a requirement for "passive investment" would drive the sovereign wealth funds to look elsewhere.[116] Other critics of this potential policy have contended passive investor requirements only contribute to poor business practices and reciprocal restraints on U.S. investments abroad.[117] Clearly, this is an option that awaits further investigation.

In April 2008, the Service Employees International Union issued its own set of policy recommendations for dealing with sovereign wealth funds. In a paper labeled "Sovereign Wealth Funds and Private Equity: Increased Access, Decreased Transparency," SEIU highlighted an issue that heretofore had been largely ignored in the sovereign wealth fund debate. As the SEIU document so ably argues:

> Current U.S. regulations, designed to address foreign entities taking a direct ownership interest in domestic assets, miss the peculiar nature of voting covenants and indirect ownership structures that characterize private equity. Because the private equity firm is recognized as a domestic company and the lack of publicly traded shares makes verifying the magnitude of a sovereign wealth fund's ownership interest difficult . . . proposed private equity buyouts of sensitive companies fail to trigger the Committee on Foreign Investment in the United States process for examining the risks and benefits of foreign investment or ownership of American companies.[118]

Given this legal loophole—a shortfall apparently not addressed in the proposed FINSA 2007 regulations, SEIU forwarded four policy recommendations:

1. The beneficial ownership structure of the general partnership/management company and/or limited partnerships controlling [private equity] funds must be disclosed—particularly if their portfolio companies contract for the U.S. government
2. Mandatory CFIUS investigation of proposed deals involving private equity firms and sovereign wealth funds. CFIUS review should not be voluntary in these transactions, nor should it be contingent on self-reported levels of control under the 10% guidelines
3. New Securities and Exchange Commission rules that will eliminate the requirement to name investors should be rescinded
4. All representatives of a sovereign wealth fund, including advisers, fund managers, or others acting on its behalf, must register under the Foreign Agent Registration Act[119]

The SEIU proposals place the labor organization in the midst of an interesting academic debate: What is more transparent, a hedge fund or a sovereign wealth fund? Securities and Exchange Commission Chairman Christopher Cox once declared sovereign wealth funds as "significantly less transparent" than hedge funds,[120] an argument that more than one Wall Street analyst has been publicly willing to defend. In fact, *Seeking Alpha*, a respected online financial analysis news service, posted a story in June 2008 announcing a recent poll had discovered "hedge fund managers report more frequently than managers of other alternative assets."[121] Okay, but this does not resolve the problem with sovereign wealth fund investments in private equity firms. On this issue SEIU appears to have struck a home run; policymakers need to address this shortfall if they are serious about protecting U.S. national security from potentially hostile foreign-government investors.

A final comment on the SEIU proposals. One hopes the labor union is anticipating push-back—because they are certain to encounter a political brick wall on the issue of registering sovereign wealth fund advisors, managers, and other support crew as "Foreign Agents."[122] Given the political stigma associated with such an official designation, one can be certain lobbyists in Washington and financial advisors on Wall Street are going to fight this proposal tooth and nail.

Where does this leave us? I would argue that the United States, as the world's primary recipient of foreign direct investment, also has some of the planet's most stringent policies and legislation concerning this activity. That said, Washington may not be home to some of the best policies and legislation when it comes to foreign investment. We clearly have allowed the lawyers to craft language that will keep many of their fellow attorneys employed for years to come. As Jagdish Bhagwati, a Senior Fellow at the Council on Foreign Relations, told the Senate Foreign Relations Committee in June 2008, it would be in the United States distinct favor to develop a "short list of sensitive sectors where 'enhanced security' is exercised over inflows of funds, whether private or sovereign wealth."[123] This argument for increased specificity comes with many merits— not the least of which is reduced paperwork, fewer legal arguments, and, potentially, a more effective and efficient CFIUS review and/or investigation process.

In the interim, I contend the preceding conversation points to three areas in need of immediate attention. First, Washington must craft a definition of "control" that captures the activities of conventional and unconventional investors—that is, direct participants in commodities, equities, and real estate markets, and those who enter these venues via hedge funds and private equity firms. Furthermore, this definition of "control" should eschew ownership "bright lines," but not be so broad as to include every foreign investment in the United States. Second, CFIUS needs to be provided an experienced, trained staff who can rapidly process what appears to be an impending tidal wave of voluntary notifications. There is no surer way to deter investors than time and potential competitive advantage lost to bureaucratic inefficiencies. Finally, Washington needs to find a way of informing Americans about sovereign wealth funds and the very necessary function they are to play in our financial future. There is little good to come from ignorance that fosters protectionist sentiments.

CHAPTER 6

TAKE THE MONEY AND RUN

If the U.S. does not take policy steps to reduce its need for external financing before it exhausts the world's central banks' willingness to keep adding to their dollar reserves— and if the rest of the world does not take steps to reduce its dependence on an unsustainable expansion in U.S. domestic demand to support [economic] growth—the risk of a hard landing will grow . . . a sharp fall in the value of the U.S. dollar, a rapid increase in U.S. long-term interest rates and a sharp fall in the value of a range of risk assets including equities and housing.[1]

—Nouriel Roubini and Brad Setser, February 2005

The rise of sovereign wealth funds suggest Washington's day of fiscal reckoning is close at hand. The world's central banks appear to be losing interest and/or willingness to further fund our profligate spending. Spurred by official and public demands to earn a greater return on invested taxpayer monies, foreign government bankers are turning away from U.S. Treasury notes and may even be losing interest in Wall Street. Why? The reason is primarily dismay at Washington's inability to put its fiscal house in order. As the *Financial Times* reported in mid-July 2008, "some of the world's largest sovereign wealth funds are seeking to scale back their exposure to the U.S. dollar in a sign of global concern about the currency." According to the *Financial Times*, this scaling back includes an unnamed Persian Gulf fund that reduced its dollar-denominated funds from 80% of total holdings in 2007 to 60% in 2008, and China's State Administration of Foreign Exchange (SAFE), keeper of Beijing's ever-mounting foreign exchange reserves. SAFE, the newspaper claims, is now seeking to diversify its overseas holdings by striking deals with private equity firms in Europe.[2]

But, you argue, these are isolated cases; certainly there are more fish in the financial sea? Yes, and, as we have previously noted, there is an even larger universe of investment opportunities. Let's return to the *Financial Times* story again. It turns out SAFE's move, "is significant because . . . [China] has lagged behind other governments, such as Singapore, in diversifying it currency exposure."[3] Is this move a sign of Chinese willingness to finally employ their fiscal nuclear option? No, according to the *Financial Times*, "by allocating money to Europe-based private equity firms, SAFE could diversify away from the dollar, at least at the margin, without spooking the currency markets and driving the dollar down in a disorderly manner."[4] Nor, I would note, are the Chinese alone in this flight from the dollar. Kuwait has severed its currency link with the dollar, and the United Arab Emirates—home to the world's largest sovereign wealth fund—may not be far behind. An official at the Abu Dhabi Investment Authority had this to say of his nation's monetary peg to the U.S. dollar, "we are importing inflation for no reason."[5]

Other signs of this fiscal flight from U.S. shores? The U.S. Treasury International Capital report for May 2008 revealed that over the preceding 12 months American banks sustained a $422 billion decline in deposits held by private foreign investors.[6] What this means is that private foreign investment in all U.S. securities fell to a total of $600 billion, down from the over $1 trillion mark achieved in the previous year. This loss of private interest in dollar-denominated assets was felt across the board, with one exception: long-term Treasury notes. More specifically, the Treasury report for May 2008 revealed that purchases of corporate bonds over the previous year had declined from $534 billion to $172 billion. Sales of U.S. equities during the same period were down from $174 billion to $65 billion, and movement of U.S. government agency bonds had declined from $154 billion to $126 billion. Treasury security sales, on the other hand, were up: from $182 billion the preceding year to $225 billion between June 2007 and May 2008. Why the spike in Treasury securities sales to private foreign investors? It was a "flight to safety," according to one financial analyst.[7] A second school contends this spike in private purchases of Treasury notes is actually foreign governments working through commercial entities. (This explanation, as we shall see shortly, lends credence to the argument there is an effort afoot to prevent further decline in the dollar's international value. If so, this spike in "private" acquisition of U.S. Treasury securities could end as abruptly as it began, particularly as other nations unpeg their currencies from the dollar and, therefore, are less concerned about propping up the greenback.)

A similar breakout for foreign government transactions on U.S. shores during the June 2007 to May 2008 time period reveals a markedly different story. According to the May 2008 Treasury International Capital report, during the preceding 12 months, total official foreign investment increased by $57 billion. This included a $37 billion spike in the official foreign purchase of corporate bonds, from $2 billion to $25 billion; a $29 billion increase in the acquisition of corporate bonds, from $33 billion to $62 billion; and a $19 billion lift in Treasury note sales, from $60 billion to $79 billion. The one decline was a $29 billion drop in the official foreign purchase of government agency bonds.[8] As with the spike in private investment in U.S. securities, this apparent continued interest in official dollar-denominated assets is likely the result of foreign governments attempting to maintain the value of the greenback on international currency markets.[9] As we shall see shortly, there is little reason to believe this phenomena is going to last.

At this juncture in the conversation, the reader is pardoned for expressing puzzlement. Yes, I opened this discussion by highlighting reports suggesting foreign governments were seeking to divest themselves of dollar-denominated funds. And, yes, I then proceeded to Treasury data showing private foreign investors were indeed departing U.S. shores, but that also indicated official foreign investors appeared to be sinking more money in American securities. So, you ask, what is one to make of this apparently contradictory evidence? Are sovereign wealth funds preparing to take the money and run? Or is this shift in investment patterns simply a case of investors chasing profit-making opportunities? To answer that question we need to change gears and take a moment to discuss the current international monetary "system"—or at least what remains of the 1944 Bretton Woods Agreement.

Back to Bretton Woods

In July 1944, 730 delegates from the 44 allied nations gathered at the Mount Washington Hotel in Bretton Woods, New Hampshire, for the United Nations Monetary and Financial Conference. The three-week conference resulted in the signing of the Bretton Woods Agreement, a system of rules, institutions, and procedures designed to regulate the international monetary system and thereby avoid a repeat of the conflicting national policies that contributed to the Great Depression of the 1930s.[10] The chief features of the Bretton Woods system were an agreement that each nation would adopt a monetary policy that maintained the exchange rate of its currency within a fixed value, and the use of the International Monetary Fund to temporarily bridge payment imbalances.

The devil, as the saying goes, is in the details. While the intention of the original Bretton Woods Agreement was to establish a "pegged-rate" currency regime based on the gold standard, in reality the delegates established a principle "reserve currency"—the U.S. dollar. Under this gentlemen's agreement, Washington promised to link the dollar to gold at the rate of $35 an ounce, and other nations would then "peg" their currencies to the U.S. dollar. As such, the original Bretton Woods Agreement (henceforth "Bretton Woods I") directly lashed the currencies of a re-emerging Europe and Japan to the U.S. dollar. This meant the values of all other currencies were to be based on their dollar conversion rate. (For instance, in 1948 it took 3.33 Deutsche Marks to equal a single U.S. dollar.[11]) This standard was intended to facilitate free trade, avoid nationalist arguments over monetary values, and foster recovery from the Second World War.

Under Bretton Woods I, U.S. dollars became *the* international currency. This preeminent role was based on the promise that every dollar a foreign government held could, on demand, be converted into gold. (Thus the phrase, "as good as gold.") As a whole, Bretton Woods I worked because the U.S. was the world's largest economy and had accumulated a remarkable stockpile of gold as a result of payments made during World War II. (The U.S. reportedly held $26 billion in gold reserves at the end of World War II, 65% of the international total, which was estimated to be approximately $40 billion in 1945.) And, more importantly, it worked because Washington was willing to facilitate development of a trading pattern that enriched the recovering economies in Europe and Japan at the United States' expense.

In any case, Bretton Woods I initially lived up to its promise. While Europe struggled with a balance of payments problem between 1945 and 1950, the Marshall Plan and U.S. efforts elsewhere served to revive the international economy. In 1950, the balance of payments reversed direction, with monies flowing out of the United States and back into central banks throughout Europe. While this could have resulted in a run on Washington's gold stockpile, most nations chose to forgo converting dollars to hard metal. Why? *U.S. trade deficits kept the international economy liquid and promoted further economic development in exporting countries.* Furthermore, with gold set at a fixed price, holding dollars was more lucrative than acquiring a bank vault of bullion. Dollars could be used to earn interest; gold holdings were simply not as easy to convert into a return on one's investment.[12] Keep these observations in mind as we proceed. The lessons learned in London, Paris, and Rome were to be carefully studied and applied in Beijing, Singapore, and Seoul. Furthermore, there is mounting evidence that finance ministries in Kuwait, Saudi Arabia, and the United Arab Emirates have been reading from the same aging crib sheets.

The trade imbalance that spurred Europe's recovery in the 1950s proved to be a dual-edged sword. In 1960, economist Robert Triffin stood before members of the U.S. Congress and laid bare the essential nature of the beast. According to Triffin, the U.S. and the international community were confronted with a fundamental dilemma: if Washington successfully ended its trade imbalance the international monetary system would lose the liquidity necessary for continued economic development. However, if the U.S. allowed this trade imbalance to continue indefinitely the mounting deficits would erode confidence in the dollar and potentially foster international instability.[13]

Triffin's warning did not go unheeded. Fixes included establishment of the "London Gold Pool"[14] and Kennedy administration policies aimed at encouraging exports. Nonetheless, by the late 1960s it was clear Bretton Woods I was no longer a viable means of governing the international currency system. The "official" end to Bretton Woods I came on 15 August 1971, when then-President Nixon "closed the gold window," ending the dollar's direct convertibility to bullion. Nixon's decision, apparently reached without consultation with members of the international monetary system or his own State Department, effectively left the dollar in "free float" on currency exchanges.

Efforts to address this situation resulted in 18 months of negotiation and, finally, the February 1973 Smithsonian Agreement. Under the Smithsonian Agreement, national currencies were all free to float independently. That is, the value of a currency was/is based upon international perceptions of a particular nation's economic strengths and weaknesses. In place of the "gold standard," a currency's place on the monetary exchange market could fluctuate based on economic, military, and political performance, at home and abroad.

This is not to say, however, that the fundamental economic principles underlying Bretton Woods had been buried and forgotten. In 2003, Michael Dooley, David Folkerts-Landau, and Peter Garber released a paper titled, "An Essay on the Revived Bretton Woods System."[15] According to the authors, the international economic and political system existent during Bretton Woods I is best envisioned as consisting of a "core" and a "periphery." The United States served as the core, whereas Europe and Japan constituted an emerging periphery. According to Dooley, Folkerts-Landau, and Garber, "the periphery countries chose a development strategy of undervalued currencies, controls on capital flows, trade reserve accumulation, and the use of the [core] as a financial intermediary that lent credibility to their own financial systems. In turn, the U.S. lent long term to the periphery, generally through foreign direct investment."[16]

As Dooley, Folkerts-Landau, and Garber understood economic history in 2003, the collapse of Bretton Woods I was the result of growing prosperity in Europe and Japan. However, they go on to argue that the subsequent period of free-floating exchange rates was "only a transition during which there was no important [economic] periphery."[17] (As Dooley, Folkerts-Landau, and Garber put it, "the communist countries were irrelevant to the international monetary system.") Europe and Japan, Dooley, Folkerts-Landau, and Garber contend, have now been replaced by an "Asian periphery" that is proceeding down the same path as their predecessors in Berlin, Paris, and Tokyo. That is, "the dynamics of the international monetary system, reserve accumulation, net capital flows, and exchange rate movements, are driven by the developments of these periphery countries," with the U.S. again serving as the "core." The result was the emergence of Bretton Woods II.[18]

Why Washington at the center? According to Dooley, Folkerts-Landau, and Garber:

> Asia's proclivity to hold U.S. assets does not reflect an irrational affinity for the U.S. Asia would export anywhere else if it could and happily finance any resulting imbalances. But the U.S. is open; Europe is not. Europe could not absorb the flood of goods, given its structural problems and in the face of absorbing Eastern Europe as well. So Asia's exports go to the U.S., as does its finance . . .[19]

The bottom line: Dooley, Folkerts-Landau, and Garber would have us believe the economic relationships critical for Bretton Woods I have been revived in

Bretton Woods II, with the periphery using trade imbalances with the U.S. to finance domestic economic development. In turn, the periphery supports American spending by investing in the U.S., purchasing corporate and government debt that American consumers no longer have the cash to acquire. The problem with this picture? We still appear to be ensnared in Triffin's dilemma. At some point, U.S. spending will dramatically slow, thereby causing significant economic woes in the periphery, or Asian bankers and consumers will lose faith in the weakening dollar and thereby foster international instability. In either case, Bretton Woods II should either unravel like its predecessor, and/or the international monetary system will enter another transition period.

But here is where we part company with Triffin and *add* new dimensions to Dooley, Folkerts-Landau, and Garber's argument. When Robert Triffin stood before Congress in 1960, there was no realistic replacement for the United States as a global economic generator. That is certainly not the case today. And when Dooley, Folkerts-Landau, and Garber were crafting their 2003 paper, oil prices had yet to so astoundingly enrich a select set of Middle East nations. These fundamental changes in the international economic and political environment gave rise to a new school of thought; Bretton Woods II was indeed on its way out, and in a manner suggesting that we are not simply in for another "transition" period.

At a February 2005 seminar organized by the Federal Reserve Bank of San Francisco and the University of California-Berkeley, Nouriel Roubini[20] and Brad Setser presented a paper titled "Will the Bretton Woods II Regime Unravel Soon? The Risk of a Hard Landing in 2005–2006." The opening line in Roubini and Setser's paper sets the tone for the argument to follow: "The defining feature of the global economy . . . is the . . . U.S. current account deficit."[21] According to Roubini and Setser, the U.S. current account deficit, estimated to be more than $800 billion in 2008,[22] serves to absorb at least 80% of the international savings not invested at home and has, in recent past, been 90% financed by foreign central banks. These are all grim statistics, but not news. The real showstopper from Roubini and Setser comes on page three of their paper, when the two authors argue "the scale of the financing required to sustain U.S. current account deficits is increasing faster than the willingness of the world's central banks to build up their dollar reserves." The potential consequence? "The risk of a hard landing for the U.S. and global economy will grow."[23]

As Roubini and Setser understand the current international monetary system, Bretton Woods II, foreign central bank investments in the United States have "limited the impact of large deficits on the [sale of Treasury securities] and helped to keep U.S. interest rates low." "Low interest rates," they continue, "increase the value of a wide range of assets—including housing—and thus encourage Americans to borrow against their existing stock of assets, and to otherwise let asset price appreciation substitute for savings." (Keep in mind, this was written 18 months before the subprime market debacle and the collapse in American housing prices; clearly, more than one analyst was predicting problems and telling the Fed.) How evident was this requirement for foreign investment and the lack of U.S. savings in 2005? According to Roubini and Setser, "the stock of [Treasury securities] held by U.S. investors has stayed constant since 2001 even though the overall stock of U.S. debt has increased dramatically." As such, they conclude, "foreign central banks actual holdings of Treasury bonds no doubt exceed their recorded holdings."[24]

Now, what happens if these foreign investors find a more lucrative place to sink their money? What if, as the Treasury reports cited earlier indicate, financial flows back into the U.S. appear to be dramatically slowing? As Roubini and Setser logically argue, there is a very real potential that U.S. interests rates will begin to climb. This increase can be attributed to a number of interrelated factors. For instance, there is no ready replacement for this set of central bank investors—who, since 2000, are thought to have acquired between 80% and 90% of all new Treasury notes. And then there is the problem of central bankers leading a pack of investment sheep. Should the central banks begin to walk away, Roubini and Setser go on to note, there is a high probability other investors will do likewise. This coattails effect of a move away from dollar-denominated assets by central banks suggests the U.S. currency could lose even more value and raises the possibility these investments are no longer as "safe" as they were once considered. In any case, Roubini and Setser come to the conclusion a marked decline in foreign central bank investment in U.S. Treasury notes could result in a 200-basis-point increase in American consumer interest rates. In short, Roubini and Setser join a significant pool of analysts who believe that your interest rates on a car or a home loan could rise by as much as 2% in the event foreign governments turn to investment options outside the United States.[25]

But none of this addresses the issue of the Bretton Woods II demise. Are we really that close to a fundamental change in the way the international monetary system operates? I, for one, would argue yes. Why? First, as Roubini and Setser so ably argue, maintaining Bretton Woods II requires that the key Asian players (China, Japan, Singapore, and South Korea) do more than just hold onto their existing U.S. shares.[26] In order for Bretton Woods II to continue, these Asian central banks, and their counterparts in the Middle East, must continue to substantially add to these U.S. holdings. My suspicion is that the shift of private investment away from America that we discussed earlier is simply an indication of things to come. Private investors, as a rule, are always ahead of their government counterparts. If private foreign investors are pulling away from the U.S., foreign government investors, particularly sovereign wealth funds, can not be far behind.

The second reason I believe Bretton Woods II is on the wane can be directly attributed to greed. As Roubini and Setser so ably argue, "at current interest rates, U.S. dollar assets do not compensate foreign investors fully for the risk of future dollar depreciation . . . Consequently, financing the U.S. is more a burden than an opportunity."[27] I would add one more insight to this conversation. As we previously noted, in 2008 foreign central bankers and sovereign wealth funds are not caught in Triffin's dilemma for the simple reason that there are now numerous other places to sink one's money. Collapse of the U.S. dollar does not *ipso facto* have to equate to a catastrophic loss around the world, nor does it necessarily imply the entire international economic system will be plunged into instability. The "deep pockets" resident in Asia and the Middle East should be capable of sustaining economic development—admittedly at lower levels—with or without significant U.S. participation. In short, the entire international system is not solely dependent on the U.S. to drive economic growth in the periphery through continued trade imbalances and deficit spending. As the emergence of sovereign wealth funds ably demonstrates, there are now other players more than capable of sharing the burden.

A quick note on what a Bretton Woods III international monetary system might look like, before we return to sovereign wealth fund-specific concerns. First, it seems highly unlikely there will ever be a complete decoupling of a developed economic core and the developing periphery. As such, there will always be a need for the core to spend more on periphery-provided goods and services as a means of promoting development in these "newer" economies, to say nothing of the fact good economic sense promotes such spending patterns; a penny-wise capitalist always shops where the best deal is to be found. Furthermore, as many of the periphery nations are unable to domestically incorporate these earnings without abetting runaway inflation, this "core" money is likely to be returned in the form of investment. But here's the rub: the "core" is no longer simply to be found in North America. Under Bretton Woods III this core could include Brazil, China, India, and Russia.[28] In other words, we are moving further away from Triffin's dilemma.

Second, the dollar's central role in the international monetary system will likely diminish to a "partnership" or even a trilateral relationship. As one analyst put it, "the dollar's global monopoly will give way to a duopoly of the dollar and the Euro."[29] Certainly this "duopoly" is one option, but with the Euro apparently poised to decline in value almost as precipitously as the dollar, one can make the case for the addition of a third player. These options could include the Japanese yen or China's renminbi, either of which is backed by large foreign exchange reserves and economies that at least have the potential to rival their Western counterparts.

Finally, there is a potential for a further "regionalization" of the international monetary system under Bretton Woods III. In this scenario, we have the emergence of additional euro counterparts, for instance the long-awaited "Khaleeji"[30] in the Middle East, and a similar development in Asia. Under such conditions the "core" and "periphery" could be divided into three or four subsets. The United States and Brazil might serve as a "core" economy for North and South America, while the European Union and Russia anchor Europe and the Mediterranean states. The Gulf Cooperation Council (GCC) could be the core for the Middle East and Non-Mediterranean states in Africa, while China and India serve a similar role in central and Southeast Asia. Ironically, this regionalization would almost inevitably result in monetary conflicts along the "seams," thereby promoting a revisit of the entire Bretton Woods Agreement.

What all this suggests is that the international movement away from the dollar, signaled by the emergence of sovereign wealth funds, could fundamentally change the international monetary system. I am not suggesting dependence on nations that serve as "economic engines" will disappear. But rather, that we appear poised for the emergence of a more "democratic" international monetary system. In place of Bretton Woods I or II, where periphery economies depended on the U.S to maintain favorable trade imbalances, a Bretton Woods III could witness the rise of several "cores" that support smaller peripheries and resultantly do not generate such large and potentially unsustainable balance of payment imbalances. This vision, of course, comes with a significant political setback for Washington. A "democraticization" of the international monetary system would curtail the United States' ability to dictate rules and open the way for other players to balance what has been, since World War II, Washington's largely unchallenged seat atop the "free market" international economic and political system.

Back to the Present

For the moment (2008) it does not appear as though Washington will have to grapple with the consequences of Bretton Woods III before the November 2008 presidential election. As of early August 2008, oil-exporting countries in the Middle East were still pouring capital from their central banks into the U.S. Treasury.[31] This cash flow appears primarily driven by efforts to maintain the value of the U.S. dollar. Having decided to retain currency pegs to the U.S. dollar, UAE, Saudi Arabia, Qatar, Oman, and Bahrain are confronted with a growing problem. The 33% decline in the dollar's value against the Euro since 2003 has been accompanied by similar currency degeneration in these Middle Eastern states.[32] The result has been a surge to double-digit inflation. With oil ranging between $120 and $150 a barrel, however, these major oil producers have struggled to place a finger in the dike by shifting their windfall into U.S. Treasury securities.

For the record, I want to make it clear this "Band-Aid" is unlikely to last. I come to this conclusion for three reasons. First, with inflation running at 10% in Saudi Arabia and the UAE, and 14% in Qatar, these governments are going to seek solutions to their fiscal nightmare.[33] Second, cash flows generated by high oil prices are estimated to push net GCC foreign asset holdings above $1.6 trillion by January 2009, thereby opening the door to multiple options outside the United States.[34] And, third, the Gulf rulers already have a positive example of what decoupling from the dollar will do for one's economy.

In May 2007, Kuwait announced its decision to drop the dinar's peg to the dollar. According to Kuwait's central bankers, this move to abandon the dollar was a direct result of the U.S. currency's plunging value. As Salem Abdel Aziz al-Sabah, governor of Kuwait's central bank told reporters, "the significant drop in the exchange rate of the American dollar against other major currencies had a negative impact on the Kuwaiti economy over the past two years."[35] The immediate results of this decision are best described as a mixed blessing. Since May 2007, the Kuwaiti dinar has appreciated against the dollar by 7.9%,[36] but as of May 2008 inflation in Kuwait was still running at over 11%.[37] This continued inflation is not completely unexpected. The spike in oil prices has caused significant cost increases in transportation, food stuffs, and almost all other commodities. As such, Kuwait's decision to decouple from the dollar is likely to prove wise in the long run, but not to resolve inflation concerns in the near term.

There are certainly indications other Gulf Cooperation Council members believe Kuwait's decision to end its dollar peg was a step in the right direction. In early July 2008, the central bank of the United Arab Emirates announced the country would end its 30-year-long tie to the U.S. dollar by June 2009. According to UAE central bank governor Sultan Bin Nasser al-Suwaidi, the dirham's peg to the dollar was limiting the Emirates' ability to control inflation in the face of rising wheat, rice, and other product prices. In place of exclusive ties to the dollar, UAE was said to be considering linking the dirham to "a basket of currencies," including the dollar and the Euro. The UAE's final comment on the decision was that "pegging was adopted when oil prices were low and the greenback was still at the height of its strength. Today, the dollar is falling relentlessly, and oil prices are skyrocketing. This new reality calls for a rethink of monetary policies."[38]

The UAE is not alone in coming to this conclusion. For instance, Qatar has reportedly reduced its exposure to the dollar by 60%, distributing the country's reserves between the dollar (40%), Euro (40%), and a basket of other currencies, including Japan's yen and London's pound.[39] Other GCC members are also said to be seriously contemplating a move to break from the dollar. In May 2008, Kuwait's Finance Minister told reporters other Gulf States are considering the option, and then declared, "some countries will do what we are doing."[40] All of this means that the Gulf Cooperation Council efforts to prop up the dollar by dumping money into U.S. Treasuries may be coming to an end sooner rather than later. Like other international investors, the GCC members understand they can earn a greater return on their investment by looking outside the United States—or at least somewhere besides U.S. Treasury notes.

One More Look at the Warnings about "State Capitalism"

At this point it would appear safe to conclude the emergence of sovereign wealth funds appears to signal the end of Washington's preeminent position atop the international monetary system, but should we conclude the government investment vehicles are also indications of further challenge to the United States' place in the international political hierarchy? Recall for a moment

Gerald Lyons' contention that the rise of sovereign wealth funds could mark the emergence of "state capitalism" and "the use of government controlled funds to acquire strategic stakes around the world."[41] In newspaper articles and presentations before U.S. Congressional committees, Lyons warned these official investment vehicles could be used to purchase a stake in strategic industries— energy, the financial sector, or telecommunications—or to secure key commodities and resources (i.e., zinc, rice, and oil).[42] Was Lyons right? Does Washington need to be on the watch for these potential dangers to the United States' national interests and national security?

The jury appears to remain out on this question. In mid-July 2008, the *Wall Street Journal* ran a commentary titled "Don't Pick on Sovereign Wealth Funds," in which the authors suggested Lyons' proposed angst was misplaced. Rather than focusing on sovereign wealth funds, the authors instead contend:

> The broader use of finance as a foreign policy tool is an increasingly important 21st-century phenomenon. Sovereign wealth funds, though, don't necessarily pose the biggest risks in this category. If a country wanted to use financial tools to advance its foreign policy, it would more likely do so through the use (or threat of use) of its generally much greater central bank reserves to affect currency markets. While sovereign wealth funds are believed to control about $3 trillion worth of assets, the IMF estimates that government-owned central bank reserves exceed $7 trillion.[43]

Needless to say, this argument did not meet with unanimous support. In a response published a short week later, Edwin Truman, designer of the sovereign wealth "scoreboard," declared, "sovereign wealth funds are political because they are owned and ultimately controlled by governments. It is naive to think that they can or should be treated as apolitical in general or because particular government owners are currently among friends or allies in which they invest."[44] So who is correct: those who would contend sovereign wealth funds are largely neutral investment vehicles focused on the bottom line, or their critics, who argue sovereign wealth funds are by definition political animals and therefore must be carefully monitored?

As we have previously discussed, there are reasons to believe both sides are correct. While a number of the sovereign wealth fund investments appear to be efforts to duplicate the profits generated at Harvard and Yale, there are also signs the government investment vehicles are indeed being employed in support of state capitalism. Consider for a moment two stories on sovereign wealth fund investment published in mid-August 2008. In an item run on 10 August 2008, the *New York Post* announced that a sovereign wealth fund had "earmarked $29 billion" to purchase foreclosed residential properties in the United States and had hired a West Coast mortgage broker to search for "bargains." The *New York Post* went on to note some foreclosed properties were selling for 60–80 cents on the dollar, suggesting there was certainly money to be made in this asset class.[45]

Now we turn to an article the *Washington Post* ran on 12 August 2008. In a story titled "Sovereign Funds Become Big Speculators," the *Washington Post* declared "sovereign wealth funds . . . are now among the biggest speculators in the trading of oil and other vital goods, like corn and cotton, in the United States." According to the *Washington Post*, the U.S. government agency charged with regulating the market had not picked up on this activity because the sovereign wealth funds were investing through "swap dealers,"[46] who often operate on unregulated markets. Of note, the *Washington Post* went on to state the sovereign wealth funds engaged in the commodity trading were not from oil-producing countries; instead, the bulk of the activity appeared to originate with Asian-based government investment vehicles.[47]

What are we to make of these two stories? The item from the *New York Post* would appear to indicate at least one sovereign wealth fund is looking to profit from the U.S. housing crisis. While we can bemoan the mean-spirited nature of this investment, the properties clearly cannot be removed from the United States and are, therefore, likely to eventually once again land in American hands. My vote is that it is profit-motivated behavior.[48] Now, what about the commodities speculation? This story is a more difficult read. I can understand how some readers would argue this is a case of strategic investment—governments using sovereign wealth funds to purchase future rights to scarce resources. On the flip side of the coin, I also have empathy for readers who conclude the sovereign wealth funds were simply engaging in profit-motivated commodities speculation. In either case, this second story should cause policy makers to consider the viability of our existing foreign investment laws and regulations. Is Washington really unable to monitor the activities of swap dealers? And what are we doing to ensure a foreign government is not engaged in commodities speculation as a means of further burdening U.S. taxpayers with higher prices? Quite simply, the second story lends credence to those who warn about the dangers of state capitalism, as it is abetted by the emergence of sovereign wealth funds.

Where Does This Leave Us?

By now it should be clear not all members of the international community share Washington's concerns about sovereign wealth fund motivations. As we noted earlier, the European Union is doing its best to reach out and welcome these foreign government investors. This includes the Germans, who, while seemingly bent on passing "protectionist" legislation intended to ward off potentially hostile sovereign wealth funds,[49] are working overtime to convince Middle East investors their money remains welcome in Berlin. Even Tokyo, renowned for being relatively unfriendly to foreign funds, has sought to roll out the welcome mat. On 4 August 2008, Japan's new trade minister told reporters, "our basic stance is to welcome these investments by state funds." He went on to state, "some sovereign funds are investing in Japanese enterprises that have accumulated bad loans, other funds target companies that have developed new, cutting-edge technologies. Either way, those investments should lead to Japan's economic growth."[50]

I, for one, would contend the United States should assume a similar position. The 28 July 2008 announcement that the U.S. federal budget deficit will reach $482 billion in fiscal year 2009 is yet another sign of Washington's continued dependence on foreign investors.[51] Nor does it appear a change in presidential administrations is going to diminish this requirement. According to the Tax Policy Center, a joint project sponsored by the Urban Institute and the Brookings Institution, Senator Obama's budget plans would add approximately $3.4 trillion to the national debt by 2018, while Senator McCain's proposal would increase the national debt by almost $5 trillion during the same time period.[52] The bottom line: whether one likes them or not, the United States is going to require investments from sovereign wealth funds if we are to recover from the current economic slump and continue enjoying the lifestyle to which many of us have become accustomed.

It is not only our lifestyles, however, that may be endangered by a press to enact protectionist legislation aimed at warding off potentially hostile foreign investors. The United States' increasingly precarious fiscal situation could significantly curtail Washington's foreign policy options. This is particularly true of U.S. decision-makers' efforts to employ the full spectrum of national power: diplomacy, the military, information, and economics.

What do I mean? Consider the following observations from Jonathan Kirshner's seminal text, *Currency and Coercion: The Political Economy of International Monetary Power*. Published in 1995, Kirshner's book is a poignant history lesson on why it pays to maintain the value of one's currency. According to Kirshner, there are three means of exercising what he calls "international monetary power." These are currency manipulation, the fostering and exploitation of monetary dependence, and the exercise of systemic disruption.[53] Kirshner argues currency manipulation is the "simplest instrument" of monetary power and that it can be used in a positive or negative manner. Positive currency manipulation is an effort to maintain the value of a particular nation's money— think of England and France in the 1960s and, more recent and pertinent to our argument, the apparent GCC member states' campaign to maintain the dollar's position on international currency markets. Negative currency manipulation is an effort to drive a currency away from a preferred value, typically down. Why execute such a campaign? As Kirshner notes, negative currency manipulation "can cause increased inflation, capital flight, difficulty in attracting new foreign investment, real debt burden, and a reduction in . . . living standards."[54] This, quite simply, is the threatened Chinese fiscal nuclear option come to life.

The fostering and exploitation of monetary dependence hinges upon a particular state's vulnerability to economic shifts within another nation. This type of monetary dependence, according to Kirshner, has historically been associated with the establishment of formal or informal currency zones, areas, or "blocs."[55] For instance, prior to the collapse of the Soviet Union there were two prominent currency areas, the U.S.-dominated Bretton Woods I and the Moscow-led

Council for Mutual Economic Assistance (COMECON). The fostering and exploitation of monetary dependence within a bloc was relatively straightforward, as expulsion from one or the other ultimately suggested almost immediate failure for the economy targeted by this move. Furthermore, forced removal from Bretton Woods I or COMECON would likely have also resulted in a change of government for the nation involved. On the flip side of the coin, staying within a currency bloc could certainly be beneficial for one's political career and national economy—think of Castro in Cuba or de Gaulle in France.

Finally, Kirshner argues, monetary power can be exercised through systemic disruption. According to Kirshner, systemic disruption is the "threatened or actual disruption of monetary arrangements to destroy the system or to extract some other benefits."[56] There are two types of states said to be most vulnerable to this type of monetary power: (1) small system members who do not have the wherewithal to fend off threatened changes; and (2) the dominant state, who values the political rewards of leading the system. What are the states most likely to disrupt a system? They are mid-sized nations, who have sufficient power but lack a dominant stake. Kirshner points to France as a classic case of a mid-sized state in such a situation. More specifically, he refers to the role Paris played in unraveling Bretton Woods I. My own suspicion is that a similar role is now open to UAE, Saudi Arabia, or China, states that could use their existing foreign exchange reserves to compel a revision of the existing monetary order.

My point here, however, is not to highlight states that could use their current wealth as an instrument of national power, but rather to point out Washington's apparent inability to follow suit, or even prevent such a move. While the United States' willingness to incur seemingly endless trade deficits served to foster economic development in the periphery and subsequently enrich the oil exporters, it has done very little for our own interests over the last ten years. We were not able to fiscally coerce Europe into joining the 2003 invasion of Iraq, and it does not appear Washington will be able to exercise monetary power as a means of preventing a GCC decoupling from the U.S. dollar. Furthermore, it does not appear Washington will be able to use monetary power as a means of changing Beijing's human rights policies or as a means of deterring Moscow's "imperialistic" behavior in Georgia or the Ukraine. The world has changed, and our fiscal policies have left us poorly equipped for operating in the emerging international economic and political environment. As such, it seems safe to conclude Bretton Woods III will be absent a Washington able to employ monetary power as an element of the United States' international diplomatic "kit bag."

Sovereign Wealth Funds: The Peril and Potential for America

The rise of sovereign wealth funds is a milepost on the road to change. In this case, we are witnessing the emergence of a new international monetary system—a system in which carefully marshaled foreign exchange reserves could become a legacy of the past. Rather than sink hard-earned cash in the United States' "safe" national debt, central bankers of the world appear prepared to assume the title of "entrepreneurial investors." Pressed to garner greater returns than the 2–4% historically offered by U.S. Treasury notes, these bankers are off to seek profits in Brasilia, Moscow, New Delhi, and Shanghai. At first blush, this move should appear promising; such activity is, after all, a complete expression of faith in Adam Smith's marketplace. But on further examination it bodes poorly for Washington. It now appears 50 years of U.S. dependence on the largesse of strangers is about to come to an end. U.S. consumers and politicians are no longer going to be able to depend on access to cheap money as a means of affording a lifestyle significantly beyond our means.

Sovereign wealth funds are, however, more than a sign of change to come, they also represent a potential arrival of the bill collector. As central banks turn increasingly larger slices of a nation's foreign exchange reserve over to aggressive investors, there is apt to be an associated decline in the propensity to sit on nonperforming loans. In this case, I am explicitly referring to low interest U.S. Treasury notes. The subsequent loss of foreign subsidies for our deficit spending means one thing: higher interest rates. This spike in the cost in borrowing will either result from increased competition within the nation (the U.S. government competing with private consumers for access to scarce money) or without—a demand for greater return on capital lent to Americans from abroad. Regardless of where the increased burden originates, the result will be the same: lower demand for high-value goods (i.e., cars and houses) and enhanced attention on how the government uses our hard-won tax dollars.

This focus on Washington's bottom line is not without merit. Consider, for instance, the much-discussed Social Security "fund." After spending the greater part of a year focused on sovereign wealth funds, I can tell you what I think the word "fund" means: a pool of existing money. The U.S. government, or at least our elected representatives, seem to believe "fund" has an entirely different definition. In Washington, a "fund" is a collection of promissory notes that have no fiscal backing other than a threat to tax future income. I am not kidding. Here is what the Clinton Administration had to say about the Social Security Trust Fund in 2000:

> These [trust fund] balances are available to finance future benefit payments and other trust fund expenditures—but only in a bookkeeping sense. These funds are not set up to be pension funds, like the funds of private pension plans. They do not consist of real economic assets that can be drawn down in the future to fund benefits. Instead they are claims on the Treasury that, when redeemed, will have to be financed by raising taxes, borrowing from the public, or reducing benefits or other expenditures.[57]

According to the Congressional Research Service (CRS), this mythical trust fund is nothing to be scoffed at. If the CRS analysts have done their math correctly, at the conclusion of 2007, the Social Security Trust Fund was report-edly worth $2.24 trillion. That's right, $2.24 trillion, and by 2026, the nadir of the Fund's cumulative process, the Social Security Trust Fund is supposed to hold $6.03 trillion.[58] Imagine what could be done with that money if: (1) it were actually existent; and, (2) the cash was invested as wisely as the money available to the teams at Harvard and Yale. Instead of worrying about Social Security going "bankrupt" in 2042,[59] we might instead be back to considering employ-ment of monetary power and paying down the federal deficit. That's what an American sovereign wealth fund could accomplish if we had the money to estab-lish such a beast. At the moment, Washington would have to go abroad and bor-row the money for such a venture. I'm not betting on the number of takers, given our current fiscal management shortfalls.

I would note that California has come to realize the benefit of operating in such a manner. As of August 2008, the California Public Employees' Retirement System (CalPERS) was managing an investment portfolio worth $248.4 billion. Over the last five years, the CalPERS investment team has provided returns ranging from 23.3% in 2003 to 10.2% in 2007. This is no mean feat and is cer-tainly better than the zero percent return offered by the so-called Social Secu-rity Trust Fund. The CalPERS beneficiaries appear to believe so—at least the 1,086,900 active and inactive members and the 455,208 retirees.[60] What CalPERS, and Harvard or Yale, demonstrates is that a sovereign wealth fund in the United States could work to the taxpayers' benefit and be potentially quite lucrative. In the interim, we will simply have to watch from the sidelines as other nations' leaders turn capital stockpiles into a net benefit for their own citizens rather than subsidizing the American way of living.

As Americans look forward to 2010 and the decade that follows, I think it is safe to conclude that the world will be a very different place. The Pax Americana has come and gone, as has our ability to seemingly demand or dic-tate a standard of international behavior beneficial for free trade and the emer-gence of additional democracies. This is not to say Adam Smith's marketplace has become passé—far from it. But rather that our place atop the global eco-nomic, military, and political hierarchy no longer appears secure, or even unchallenged. How did this happen? Theories intended to explain the changes are legion, but perhaps none better fits our current fiscal dilemma than the words offered in *Hamlet* over 500 years ago: "Neither a borrower nor a lender be; for loan oft loses both itself and friend, and borrowing dulls the edge of hus-bandry."[61] Aye, we clearly appear to have lost our edge on husbandry. It only remains to be seen whether the purveyor of a sovereign wealth fund will offer us a chance to improve our future skills.

EPILOGUE

A simple rule dictates my buying: be fearful when others are greedy, and be greedy when others are fearful. And most certainly, fear is now widespread, gripping even seasoned investors. To be sure, investors are right to be wary of highly leveraged entities or businesses in weak competitive positions . . . Today people who hold cash equivalents feel comfortable. They shouldn't. They have opted for a terrible long-term asset, one that pays virtually nothing and is certain to depreciate in value. Indeed, the policies that government will follow in its efforts to alleviate the current crisis will probably prove inflationary and therefore accelerate declines in the real value of cash accounts . . . Equities will almost certainly outperform cash over the next decade, probably by a substantial degree . . . Today my money and my mouth both say equities.[1]

— *Warren Buffett, 17 October 2008*

The events of late September and early October 2008 provide a gloomy setting for my revisit of events on the sovereign wealth front. Over the course of eight trading days, the U.S. stock market dropped 22%—a dismal figure that even surpassed Wall Street's dark performance during the Great Depression. Perhaps even more telling was the tally of losses associated with the markets' plunge from all-time highs achieved in October 2007. According to the *Wall Street Journal*, "investors' paper losses on U.S. stocks now total $8.4 trillion since the market peak."[2] In less than 12 months, commercial equities—literally around the world—had seemingly gone from the investor's asset class of choice to a burden everyone wanted to unload.

This was particularly true of stocks associated with financial institutions in the United States and European Union (EU). Between July 2007 and October 2008, some of the largest financial institutions in the world lost anywhere from

30 to 50% of their market value. This, of course, says nothing of Wall Street's five major investment banks—Bear Sterns, Goldman Sachs, Lehman Brothers, Merrill Lynch, and Morgan Stanley—which effectively ceased to exist in their original form by the first week of October 2008. For American bankers, the bill generated by unprecedented levels of subprime mortgage lending[3] and an unrealistic dependence on escalating housing values[4] had come due—and no one in the private equity world appeared to be willing to pay.

Not that we should have been surprised by this development. Signs of a banking/credit crisis had emerged by midsummer 2007, and in December 2007 Warren Buffett was bluntly warning there were no deals in the U.S. financial sector that "cause me to start salivating."[5] Certainly the sovereign wealth funds understood Buffett's message, as their interest in the U.S. financial industry essentially disappeared by May 2008. Quite aware of the fact their approximately $60 billion investment in American banking was largely vanishing before their eyes, the sovereign wealth fund managers went in search of greener pastures—or simply placed money in the safest place one could find, U.S. Treasury notes. In fact, it now seems these government investors had become as conservative as their counterparts at the central banks.

Needless to say, this sovereign wealth flight from financial equities has not gone unnoticed. In mid-September 2008, the *New York Times* published an article titled, "To Avoid Risk and Diversify, Sovereign Funds Move on from Banks." According to the *Times,* "as the American investment banking industry seems to teeter, many investors are asking why the sovereign wealth funds from the Middle East have not stepped up . . . The explanation is simple, bankers in the region say. Plenty of other, more attractive assets are out there right now."[6] As Badar al-Saad, the Kuwait Investment Authority manager, told Al Arabyia Television, "we are not responsible for saving a bank, an economy, or anyone." He went on to argue, "it is the business of the central banks in these countries. We are long-term investors and we have long-term social and economic obligations to our country."[7] A seemingly reasonable response, but not what Wall Street wanted to hear.

On 6 October 2008, the *Wall Street Journal* ran an article titled, "Caution, Inexperience Limit Extent of Asia's Newfound Clout in Crisis." Although specifically aimed at Asian investment practices during the ongoing credit crisis, it required little reading between the lines to discern the *Journal's* apparent intent—sovereign wealth managers everywhere were holding out on the West because they lacked the courage or investment moxie necessary to tackle the current situation. According to paragraph one of the *Journal's* story, "Asian institutions' caution and relative lack of international experience are limiting the extent of their newfound clout."[8] It is not until paragraph six that we learn the rest of the story. "Sovereign wealth funds . . . have largely stayed on the sidelines in recent months, after big investments last year—some of which performed poorly."[9] How poorly? As the *Journal* eventually admits, for example, "Morgan Stanley shares have fallen 50% since the China Investment Corporation investment in December 2007." This type of performance should fail to impress any investor, not just the cautious and inexperienced.

Of note, an equally pejorative story appeared in the *Washington Post*. Titled "Gulf States Lose Their Swagger Amid Regionwide Sell-Off," the article focused on comments from a U.S.-based analyst who argued, "stock markets in [the Middle East] are still immature, both in terms of regulation and investors' experience." The *Post*—like the *Wall Street Journal*—did not disclose until late in the story that sovereign wealth fund financial losses in the Middle East could be directly attributed to investments in the U.S. and Europe.[10] (A story with similar verbiage had previously appeared in the *Financial Times*. Running under the headline "Sovereign Wealth Funds Appear to Have Lost Their Way," the article declared, "the forward march of the sovereign wealth funds seems in slight disarray these days."[11])

Nor, by the way, does it appear as though the U.S. financial equities market is set to revive any time in the near future. The nationalization of American mortgage giants Fannie Mae and Freddie Mac on 7 September 2008, Lehman Brothers' bankruptcy on 15 September 2008, and the government rescue of American International Group on the same day, have done little to reassure international investors. Furthermore, the U.S. government's efforts to cobble together a bailout package have proven somewhat less than overwhelmingly professional. (Not that Washington should feel "special" on this account. The EU members have also struggled to craft an appropriate response to their financial institutions' problems. The piecemeal declaration of national backing for banks in Ireland, Germany, and elsewhere in Europe is suggestive of a systematic inability to develop an adequate policy for resolving the credit crisis.) In sum, it is hard to blame the sovereign wealth funds—or any investor—for fleeing the equities markets. The question that remains to be addressed is, where did the money go, and what does this mean for the future?

At the macro level, there has clearly been a move to U.S. Treasury notes. The Treasury Department's "Major Foreign Holders of Treasury Securities" report on 16 October 2008 suggests that a shift to this "safe" haven was already underway by January 2008. Consider, for instance, Beijing's U.S. Treasury holdings between December 2007 and August 2008. In December 2007—when analysts were warning of China's apparent intention to begin selling U.S. bonds—Beijing had $477.6 billion invested in Treasury notes. In January 2008 that figure was $492.6 billion; in April 2008, $502.0 billion; in July 2008, $518.7 billion; and, in August 2008, $541.0 billion.[12] A similar pattern is also evident in U.S. Treasury note acquisitions by the "Oil Exporters"—a group of nations including Kuwait, Qatar, Saudi Arabia, and the United Arab Emirates.

While the U.S. Treasury reporting for investments after August 2008 is not available as this book goes to press, news stories suggest bond purchases escalated during September and October 2008. According to the *Wall Street Journal*, central banks increased their stake in U.S. Treasury notes by approximately $100 billion between mid-September and mid-October 2008. The *Journal* then goes on to argue this decision "signals foreigners' confidence, which is critical to the U.S. financial system."[13] Hold on. I would immediately counter that what this investment reveals is central banks fleeing for the safest investment they can find—and purchases by nations who stand to significantly benefit from maintaining the existing international financial order—it is not a an overwhelming statement of confidence in Washington's ability to iron out the current mess or reduce America's ever-mounting national debt.

What causes me to come to this conclusion? Two sets of data. The first is to be found in the 16 October 2008 Treasury Department report on "Major Foreign Holders of Treasury Securities." At the same time China, and the oil exporters with currencies linked to the dollar, were busily purchasing U.S. Treasury notes, nations with options and less direct stakes in the existing international financial order were busy looking elsewhere. Consider, for instance, Norway's record of U.S. Treasury note purchases between December 2007 and August 2008. Despite the fiscal glut Oslo was enjoying as a result of skyrocketing oil prices, Norway's U.S. Treasury note holdings in December 2007 totaled a mere $26.2 billion. In January 2008 that figure had climbed to $33.6 billion; in April 2008, $45.3 billion; but in July 2008 it had dropped to $41.8 billion; and in August 2008, to $41.3 billion.[14] Hardly a rush to purchase "safe" U.S. bonds. Even more striking is Singapore's track record during the same time period. In December 2007, Singapore held $39.8 billion in U.S. Treasury notes. In January 2008 that figure had declined to $38.6 billion; in April 2008, $33.5 billion; in July 2008, $31.4 billion; and in August 2008, $31.0 billion. Clearly, these national investors were not rushing to the dollar—which brings me to the second set of data: sovereign wealth fund purchasing patterns during the run-up to the credit crisis.

Where Are the Sovereign Wealth Fund Investors?

Although Warren Buffett, the"Oracle of Omaha," is hardly offering deep analytical insight with his assessment that equities tend to pay greater dividends than fixed-income holdings,[15] sovereign wealth fund managers appear skeptical of his mid-October 2008 call for a return to the American or European stock markets. In fact, a sovereign wealth fund flight from the U.S. market was already evident in the second quarter (April–June) of 2008, according to a report the Monitor Group released during the first week of October 2008. In an update to its June 2008 publication, "Assessing the Risks: The Behaviors of Sovereign Wealth Funds in the Global Economy," the Monitor Group—a financial consulting firm based in Cambridge, Massachusetts—highlighted four trends that bode ill for U.S. and European markets:

1. During the second quarter of 2008, sovereign wealth fund investment in North America dropped dramatically. In the first quarter of 2008 there were 7 sovereign wealth fund deals in North America, totaling $23 billion;

in the second quarter of 2008 this dropped to 4 deals, totaling less than $1 billion.

2. During the second quarter of 2008, sovereign wealth fund investment shifted away from financial services. In marked contrast with the first quarter of 2008, when sovereign wealth funds signed 13 financial-sector deals, worth over $43 billion, during the second quarter of 2008 this had dropped to 10 deals, totaling an estimated $4 billion.

3. During the second quarter of 2008, sovereign wealth funds continued to actively invest in emerging markets. More than half of the known ventures, including sovereign wealth funds, during the second quarter of 2008 were in emerging markets—a total of 26 deals, worth approximately $15 billion.

4. During the second quarter of 2008, half of the sovereign wealth fund deals—by value—were in real estate. Between April and June 2008, there were 12 of these real estate transactions, worth a grand total of $13.7 billion.[16]

Selective Flight from the Financial Sector: In April 2007, sovereign wealth fund managers essentially ceased their acquisition of shares in Western financial institutions. Examples of this flight from the financial institutions' equities market abound. In August 2008, the Korea Investment Corporation turned down a reported $5 billion deal with Lehman Brothers.[17] In September 2008, the manager of Norway's Government Pension Fund-Global told reporters that Oslo's fund was "cool" on taking part in recapitalization of the U.S. financial sector, for fiscal and political reasons. As Yngve Slyngstad put it:

We are a long-term investor . . . investing with financial interest. Currently the game in the U.S. financial sector looks more short-term, more political and is more momentum driven. And with our approach in investing, these are not necessarily the circumstances that we feel so comfortable with . . . We have had a credit crisis, a liquidity crisis, and now a banking crisis. You don't go through this type of situation without having some sort of [new] regulations.[18]

Similar sentiments—as we noted above—were expressed throughout the Middle East, where sovereign fund managers either were directed to assist ailing domestic markets[19] or were seeking regional opportunities.[20]

This is not to say sovereign wealth funds are completely avoiding investments in Western financial institutions—or that no sovereign wealth fund has profited from these investments. Singapore's Temasek Holdings is a classic case in point. With what can best be described as outstanding business skill, Temasek parlayed its original $2.5 billion investment in Merrill Lynch into a $5.9 billion stake[21]—that may have ultimately yielded $1.5 billion in profit when Bank of America purchased Merrill Lynch for an estimated $50 billion.[22] (I would also note that Temasek ultimately owned a 14% stake in Merrill Lynch—a development that drew no comment from Capitol Hill.[23]) The China Investment Corporation (CIC) could be headed down a similar path. Although CIC's original $3 billion investment in Blackstone has declined in value by almost 70%, on

16 October 2008 the Blackstone Group announced a decision to raise the Chinese sovereign wealth fund's ownership limit in the firm from 9.9% to 12.5%.[24] (A second significant push above the 10% ownership mark that drew no backlash from the politicians in Washington.) According to press reports, CIC will be allowed to purchase the additional shares in Blackstone at market price— approximately $9.50 per stake, a marked improvement over the $29 a share the China Investment Corporation paid in the spring of 2007.[25] Could this deal be as lucrative as the Temasek holdings in Merrill Lynch? Only Blackstone's performance, and time, will tell. Given CIC's insistence that it is in for the long term, Beijing appears willing to wait and see.

The Qatar Investment Authority (QIA) now also appears interested in purchasing shares in financial institutions. On 16 October 2008, Swiss bank Credit Suisse Group announced it had raised $8.75 billion in new capital—primarily from QIA.[26] Armed with an estimated $65 billion war chest, QIA has purchased an approximately 10% interest in Credit Suisse Group. (The Qatar-based sovereign wealth fund had previously owned a little under 2% of the Swiss bank.[27]) Given Zurich's ongoing efforts to shore up Swiss banks,[28] this decision—like Temasek's purchase of Merrill Lynch shares and the China Investment Corporation's increased stake in Blackstone—appears to be a wise move that ultimately could pay significant dividends.

Turning/Returning to Emerging Markets: As the Monitor Group study found, sovereign wealth funds are increasingly turning to emerging markets. At this stage in the global credit crisis, this focus can be explained at two levels. The first is a continuing search for profits; the second is related to many governments' effort to save domestic economies. Let's open with the search for profits. In mid-September 2008, the Government of Singapore Investment Corporation declared an intention to pursue a greater stake in emerging markets. Although this statement was typically short on details, the Singaporean fund did note that its stake in U.S. assets had declined 5% over the last two years, while investments in Asia now account for 23% of the fund's investments.[29] In a further sign of this shift to more lucrative options, the Government of Singapore Investment Corporation also announced its share of fixed-income investments now constituted about 25% of its portfolio—down from about 75% in the early 1980s.[30]

In mid-October, the Kuwait Investment Authority told reporters that it was preparing to further investigate options in the Gulf region and North Africa. According to the Executive Director of Kuwait Investment Authority's General Reserves Fund, "we need to strengthen our investments in the Arab countries during the coming stage . . . Egypt and Morocco are among countries . . . we will focus on for years."[31] Finally, in late October 2008, Norway's Government Pension Fund-Global announced plans to invest $2 billion in India's Bombay Stock Exchange. According to the Deputy Secretary General of the Norwegian Finance Ministry, there is "potential in India, though its financial markets still have to go a long way."[32]

The second explanation for this sovereign wealth fund focus on emerging markets is directly linked to the global credit crisis—and to subsequent official bids to shore up ailing domestic industries and markets.[33] As Stephen Jen—the global head of currency research at Morgan Stanley—so aptly stated, this focus on domestic markets "makes good sense." He went on to note, "by investing at home, [the sovereign wealth funds] do three things, they support their own assets, they keep trophy assets in domestic hands, and when they convert dollar holdings to buy domestic assets, they're intervening and supporting their currencies."[34] There is certainly no shortage of evidence to support Jen's hypothesis. In Beijing, the China Investment Corporation has been employed to shore up the nation's distressed stock market and rally share prices for the Bank of China, the China Construction Bank, and the Industrial and Commercial Bank of China. Kuwait and Russia have taken a similar course of action. In September 2008, the Kuwait Investment Authority placed more than $1.1 billion in the Kuwait bourse as a means of arresting a slide in share prices.[35] On 20 October 2008, Russia's Finance Ministry announced that Moscow's National Wealth Fund would be put to a similar use—declaring an intent to invest $6.9 billion in domestic stocks as part of an effort to halt the flight of foreign investors from that country's equities market.[36]

Shopping for Real Estate: There has been no shortage of press reports concerning the continuing sovereign wealth fund interest in real estate. In an apparent bet on the prospect of an ever-growing global population and thus an equal expansion in the demand for housing, sovereign wealth funds have maintained their interest in international real estate. In early September 2008, the Abu Dhabi Investment Authority acquired a $280 million stake in a new office tower project, overlooking Australia's Sydney Harbor.[37] In mid-September 2008, a report published by the world's largest property consultant—CB Richard Ellis—declared sovereign wealth fund spending on commercial real estate could reach $725 billion by 2015. The firm's chief economist told reporters, "given that the real estate sector's investment characteristics—current income combined with long-term appreciation—closely match sovereign wealth fund requirements, we expect them to increase their weighting of commercial property." Likely targets for these investments: Japan and the United Kingdom.[38] In what appears a logical step in this direction, in late September 2008, the Qatar Investment Authority acquired a 20% stake in Chelsfield, a London property group. QIA is thought to have paid approximately $160 million for its share in Chelsfield.[39]

In early October 2008, a Singapore-based property investment manger declared its intention to raise over $1 billion from Middle Eastern sovereign wealth funds seeking to purchase real estate in Asia. According to the president of Pacific Star, the property management firm in question, "our strategy has always been to focus on prime properties which have been much less affected by the financial turmoil." In this case, the real estate of interest is said to be in Japan, South Korea, and Vietnam.[40] Speculation on sovereign wealth fund interest in real estate is also rampant in Europe. A day after Pacific Star announced its search for sovereign wealth fund investors interested in Asian real estate, financial analysts in Europe declared that German properties were also a "stable option." In this case, sovereign wealth funds were said to be interested in commercial real estate in Berlin, Cologne, and Munich—German cities where revenues from the sales of office, retail, and other business properties were down 75, 82, and 68%, respectively. The German housing market was also offered as "a safe, if unspectacular, bet."[41]

Other Options on the Table: While flight from the U.S. and financial instructions to emerging markets and real estate is the most evident trend in sovereign wealth fund investment, other spending patterns have also come to the fore. According to the U.S. Commodities Futures Trading Commission, as of June 2008 sovereign wealth funds had spent approximately $20 billion on investments in commodities futures. The funds were said to be focused on gold as a hedge against a continued drop in dollar values, and agricultural products.[42] Financial analysts also noted sovereign wealth funds remain interested in energy-related futures and related joint ventures. Evidence of this interest includes Kuwait's stake in British Petroleum (BP), the United Arab Emirate's joint energy ventures with General Electric (GE), and Temasek's acquisition of shares in oil rigs, alternative energy, and Orchard Energy.[43]

In addition to this spending on commodities and energy options, the sovereign wealth funds have joined other major investors in an international effort to hoard cash. In an article published 12 October 2008, the *International Herald Tribune* reported that the Abu Dhabi Investment Authority now has a cash position totaling between 10 and 20% of the fund's approximately $850 billion—or an estimated $100 billion. The Kuwait Investment Authority is also thought to be accumulating cash, but no estimate is available on the amount thought to be stowed in the fund's coffers.[44] On 16 October 2008, the *Economist* took this story a step further, arguing, "sovereign wealth funds have assets of $2 trillion to $3 trillion, much of which is sitting idly in American Treasury bonds."[45] The cause for this cash hoarding? Loss of faith in the international stock markets—particularly during the ongoing credit crisis.[46] A more specific assessment came from Brad Setser, an international finance analyst at the Council of Foreign Relations. As Setser put it, "sovereign wealth funds are piling up cash because there has not been a big reward for putting your money to work."[47]

Progress on the Policy Front

While Western firms and investors were bemoaning the sovereign wealth fund departure from stock markets in the United States and Europe, there were positive developments in the campaign to establish international guidance concerning the governance and conduct of these government investment vehicles. On 1 and 2 September 2008, the International Working Group (IWG) met in Santiago, Chile, in an effort to finalize a set of voluntary principles and practices intended to guide sovereign wealth fund operations. Initial reports from the conference indicated that "significant progress" had been made during the sessions, but the campaign was not wanting for critics.[48] On 3 September 2008 Brazil's Finance Minister, Guido Mantega, told reporters, "if we have to regulate it should be on hedge funds, not so much on wealth funds." According to Mantega, hedge funds were to blame for the ongoing financial turmoil; sovereign wealth funds, he argued, helped to stabilize the global economy.[49]

Mantega's complaints appear to have won few supporters, as the conference attendees ultimately announced they had come to an agreement on the "Generally Accepted Principles and Practices" (GAPP). As the agreement's name suggests, the document is a stellar example of writing by committee. According to the document's authors, the GAPP do not require the funds to reveal their size, investment holdings, what companies they are bidding on, or how they vote on company business once shares in a particular firm have been acquired. Why the secrecy? The director of the Abu Dhabi Investment Authority—a key participant in the IWG process—explained, "a lot of discussion focused on the need to preserve the economic and financial interests of the [funds] so as to not put them at a disadvantage when compared to other types of investors such as hedge funds, insurance companies, and other institutional investors."[50]

Perhaps the full extent of the political sensitivity associated with the GAPP drafting process was revealed in an article published in the *Times* of London:

> The Generally Accepted Principles and Practices, as the agreement is known, was not allowed to be called a code of practices or rules of conduct because the funds did not want to imply that they needed controlling. A source involved in the Santiago discussions said that the funds would not accept anything that implied guilt or bad behavior in the past.[51]

All of which begs the question, what does the GAPP accomplish? According to an IWG press release following the Santiago sessions, "these principles and practices will promote a clearer understanding of the institutional framework, governance, and investment operations of sovereign wealth funds, thereby fostering trust and confidence in the international financial system."[52] Outside observers offered a similar sentiment. Commenting on the document as finally published in October 2008, Oxford Analytica, an independent strategic consulting firm drawing on scholars around the world, declared: "while the GAPP are voluntary . . . they should help alleviate concerns in the West. In fact, they may obviate the need for a national level response."[53] The scholars at Oxford Analytica may have been pleased with the GAPP, but as we shall see in a moment, not all members of the international community were so delighted.

Before proceeding to the GAPP critics, allow me to briefly outline the structure and areas covered in the so-called "Santiago Principles." The GAPP authors contend that the agreement covers practices and principles in three key areas:

(1) legal, (2) institutional, and (3) investment and risk management. This is accomplished through the delineation of 24 principles, which follow below:

- **GAPP 1. Principle:** The legal framework for the sovereign wealth fund should be sound and support its effective operation and the achievement of its stated objective(s)
  - *GAPP 1.1 Subprinciple:* The legal framework for the sovereign wealth fund should ensure the legal soundness of the fund and its transactions
  - *GAPP 1.2 Subprinciple:* The key features of the sovereign wealth fund's legal basis and structure, as well as the legal relationship between the fund and the other state bodies, should be publicly disclosed
- **GAPP 2. Principle:** The policy purpose of the sovereign wealth fund should be clearly defined and publicly disclosed
- **GAPP 3. Principle:** Where the sovereign wealth fund's activities have significant direct domestic macroeconomic implications, those activities should be closely coordinated with the domestic fiscal and monetary authorities, so as to ensure consistency with the overall macroeconomic policies
- **GAPP 4. Principle:** There should be clear and publicly disclosed policies, rules, procedures, or arrangements in relation to the sovereign wealth fund's general approach to funding, withdrawal, and spending operations.
  - *GAPP 4.1 Subprinciple:* The source of sovereign wealth fund capital should be publicly disclosed
  - *GAPP 4.2 Subprinciple:* The general approach to withdrawals from the sovereign wealth fund, and spending on behalf of the government, should be publicly disclosed
- **GAPP 5. Principle:** The relevant statistical data pertaining to the sovereign wealth fund should be reported on a timely basis to the owner, or as otherwise required, for inclusion where appropriate in macroeconomic data sets
- **GAPP 6. Principle:** The governance framework for the sovereign wealth fund should be sound and should establish a clear and effective division of roles and responsibilities in order to facilitate accountability and operational independence in the management of the fund to pursue its objectives
- **GAPP 7. Principle:** The owner should set the objectives of the sovereign wealth fund, appoint the members of its governing body or bodies in accordance with clearly defined procedures, and exercise oversight over the fund's operations
- **GAPP 8. Principle:** The governing body or bodies should act in the best interests of the sovereign wealth fund, and should have a clear mandate and adequate authority and competency to carry out its functions
- **GAPP 9. Principle:** The operational management of the sovereign wealth fund should implement the fund's strategies in an independent manner and in accordance with clearly defined responsibilities
- **GAPP 10. Principle:** The accountability framework for the sovereign wealth fund's operations should be clearly defined in the relevant legislation, charter, other constitutive documents, or management agreement
- **GAPP 11. Principle:** An annual report and accompanying financial statements on the sovereign wealth fund's operations and performance should be

prepared in a timely fashion and in accordance with recognized international or national accounting standards, in a consistent manner

- **GAPP 12. Principle:** The sovereign wealth fund's operations and financial statements should be audited annually, in accordance with recognized international or national auditing standards, in a consistent manner
- **GAPP 13. Principle:** Professional and ethical standards should be clearly defined and made known to the members of the sovereign wealth fund's governing body or bodies, management, and staff
- **GAPP 14. Principle:** Dealing with third parties for the purpose of the sovereign wealth fund's operational management should be based on economic and financial grounds, and should follow clear rules and procedures
- **GAPP 15. Principle:** Sovereign wealth fund operations and activities in host countries should be conducted in compliance with all applicable regulatory and disclosure requirements of the countries in which they operate
- **GAPP 16. Principle:** The governance framework and objectives, as well as the manner in which the sovereign wealth fund's management is operationally independent from the owner, should be publicly disclosed
- **GAPP 17. Principle:** Relevant financial information regarding the sovereign wealth fund should be publicly disclosed to demonstrate its economic and financial orientation, so as to contribute to stability in international financial markets and enhance trust in recipient countries
- **GAPP 18. Principle:** The sovereign wealth fund's investment policy should be clear and consistent with its defined objectives, risk tolerance, and investment strategy, as set by the owner or the governing body or bodies, and should be based on sound portfolio management principles
  - *GAPP 18.1 Subprinciple:* The investment policy should guide the sovereign wealth fund's financial risk exposures and the possible use of leverage
  - *GAPP 18.2 Subprinciple:* The investment policy should address the extent to which internal and/or external investment managers are used, the range of their activities and authority, and the process by which they are selected and their performance monitored
  - *GAPP 18.3 Subprinciple:* A description of the investment policy of the sovereign wealth fund should be publicly disclosed
- **GAPP 19. Principle:** The fund's investment decisions should aim to maximize risk-adjusted financial returns in a manner consistent with its investment policy, and based on economic and financial grounds
  - *GAPP 19.1 Subprinciple:* If investment decisions are subject to other than economic and financial considerations, these should be clearly set out in the investment policy and should be publicly disclosed
  - *GAPP 19.2 Subprinciple:* The management of a sovereign wealth fund's assets should be consistent with what is generally accepted as sound asset management principles
- **GAPP 20. Principle:** The sovereign wealth fund should not seek or take advantage of privileged information or inappropriate influence by the broader government in competing with private entities
- **GAPP 21. Principle:** Sovereign wealth funds view shareholder ownership rights as a fundamental element of their equity investments' value. If a fund chooses to exercise its ownership rights, it should do so in a manner that is

consistent with its investment policy and that protects the financial value of its investments. The sovereign wealth fund should publicly disclose its general approach to voting securities of listed entities, including the key factors guiding its exercise of ownership rights
- **GAPP 22. Principle:** The sovereign wealth fund should have a framework that identifies, assesses, and manages the risks of its operations
  - *GAPP 22.1 Subprinciple:* The risk-management framework should include reliable information and timely reporting systems, which should enable the adequate monitoring and management of relevant risks within acceptable parameters and levels, control and incentive mechanisms, codes of conduct, business continuity planning, and an independent audit function
  - *GAPP 22.2 Subprinciple:* The general approach to the sovereign wealth fund's risk-management framework should be publicly disclosed
- **GAPP 23. Principle:** The assets and investment performance (absolute and relative to benchmarks, if any) of the sovereign wealth fund should be measured and reported to the owner according to clearly defined principles or standards
- **GAPP 24. Principle:** A process of regular review of the implementation of the GAPP should be engaged in by or on behalf of the sovereign wealth fund[54]

Initial expert outside review of the GAPP has been relatively positive. In an online article titled, "Making the World Safe for Sovereign Wealth Funds," Edwin Truman, developer of the sovereign wealth "scoreboard," declared, "the GAPP is a solid piece of work that should help to dispel some of the mystery and suspicion surrounding sovereign wealth funds." As far as Truman is concerned, the GAPP "is quite forthcoming in confronting the issue of political motivation by calling . . . for sovereign wealth funds to declare publicly their use of noneconomic considerations in their investment policies." But, he goes on to note, the document's weakest area is "accountability and transparency." As Truman put it, "disturbingly, many of the principles are silent about disclosure to the general public or only call for disclosure to the fund's owner. That approach does not promote the needed accountability to citizens of the country with the sovereign wealth fund or of other countries."[55] I, for one, agree with Truman, but am less enthusiastic. The GAPP fails specifically because it does not resolve accountability and transparency concerns—nor, I would note, do the agreements provide for anything approaching mandatory compliance. Nations with sovereign wealth funds are free to accept or reject the principles as they see fit. Given the current global credit crisis, and widespread demand for capital, it seems unlikely that anyone—including the United States—is going to seek a means of addressing this critical shortfall.

Why do I suspect the GAPP is toothless and has already been tossed into many a sovereign wealth fund manager's dustbin? On 12 October 2008, the Abu Dhabi Investment Authority—widely considered one of the least transparent sovereign wealth funds—announced it would move swiftly to comply with the voluntary principles. In a pair of statements sure to warm the heart of political spokespeople everywhere, the Abu Dhabi Investment Authority declared: "to underline commitment to full compliance, [we have] established an inter-department committee to oversee compliance with the GAPP."[56] Abu Dhabi Investment Authority goes on to declare that it "is analyzing the feasibility of establishing a mechanism that would provide independent verification of [the fund's] compliance with the GAPP." Anyone want to take bets the study finds this option unachievable?

Clearly, Rome was not impressed by the GAPP announcement or the Abu Dhabi Investment Authority's press statement. In mid-October 2008, the Italian foreign minister announced formal opposition to sovereign wealth funds acquiring more than 5% in his country's domestic industries. In an effort to "promote investments that are useful and prevent those that are dangerous," the Italians have set up a national interests committee to establish rules concerning sovereign wealth fund activity within Italy.[57] Although analysts contend the Italian effort came about as a result of concerns about Chinese and Russian sovereign wealth funds, the Italian prime minister has also expressed trepidation about investments by oil-rich countries.[58]

As it turns out, Rome was not alone in choosing a "realist" interpretation of the "Santiago Principles." On 21 October 2008, French President Nicolas Sarkozy—who was also serving as the rotating EU leader—suggested that governments in Europe take stakes in key industries to prevent takeovers by non-European investors. In a speech before the European Parliament, Sarkozy declared, "I wouldn't want to see European citizens wake up in a few months and discover that a European company is owned by non-European investors who bought at a rock-bottom price."[59] Sarkozy's solution? The French president has recommended purchase of shares in key industries by EU government-run investment funds. Or, as Sarkozy put it: "I would ask that all of us consider how interesting it would be to set up sovereign funds in each of our countries—and maybe these sovereign funds could now and again coordinate to give an industrial response to the crisis."[60]

Sarkozy's idea drew immediate condemnation from Berlin. German Economy Minister Michael Glos told reporters, "the French proposal . . . contradicts all the principles of success that we've had in our economic policies. Germany will remain open for capital from around the world."[61] Although EU member opposition to Sarkozy's sovereign wealth fund proposal was not unexpected, it seems more than a little incongruous coming from the Germans. On 20 August 2008, Berlin formally approved legislation that allowed for official examination of non-European purchases of 25% or more of a German company's voting shares. Under this new law, the German government would only be able to initiate an investigation within three months of a deal, but could impose restrictions—or even block the agreement—if this examination found "a threat to public order or security."[62] The European Commission has asked to review the German law for possible violations of EU Treaty provisions regarding the free movement of capital, but has yet to return a finding.[63]

The Road Ahead

Despite this European tempest in a teapot, there is no end to interest in setting up sovereign wealth funds or in bidding for investment from these state-run venture capitalists. During the first week of October 2008, Taiwan's Council for Economic Planning and Development discussed establishing a sovereign wealth fund as a vehicle for government investment.[64] (At the end of August 2008, Taiwan's foreign exchange reserves totaled approximately $282 billion— suggesting the need for such a move.) On 2 October 2008, Taipei announced that it had rejected such a move for the time being. Interestingly, the Taiwan central bank formally declared that it had not agreed to establish a sovereign wealth fund—a public statement suggestive of the bureaucratic infighting witnessed in other nations contemplating creation of investment offices operating outside the preview of traditional foreign exchange reserve managers.[65] The Japanese government finds itself caught in a similar debate, with the current discussion focused on using a portion of the nation's more than $1 trillion in foreign exchange reserves to establish a sovereign wealth fund focused on encouraging development of alternative energy options.[66]

Continuing debates over the threat posed by sovereign wealth funds have certainly not diminished international interest in luring their investment. In early September 2008, Japanese authorities announced they had begun talks with sovereign wealth funds in the Middle East so as to draw almost $1 billion in foreign investment. According to Japanese officials, the bid for sovereign wealth fund money was driven by a desire to sustain economic growth.[67] Spain has also proceeded down the path of wooing sovereign wealth investors. In late October 2008, Madrid publicly announced an appeal to Middle East sovereign wealth funds, with a specific focus on selling Spain's mounting public debt. As the Spanish Industry Minister put it, "you can only increase liquidity in the system if we attract liquidity from abroad. We are offering these sovereign wealth funds the chance to buy Spanish bonds." This positive spin on a desperate situation was followed by a much more honest admission that sovereign wealth funds were essential if Madrid was going to meet Spain's foreign financing needs given the ongoing credit crisis.[68]

Why this focus on sovereign wealth? In August 2008, Temasek announced that its annual earnings for the just-closed reporting period (April 2007 to April 2008) had increased by 13%, despite the fact measures of international stock exchange performance during a similar period had declined 5.1%.[69] The sovereign wealth fund's gross value was $185 billion as of 1 April 2008, up from $164 billion the previous year. While the Government of Singapore Investment Corporation could not boast of similar earnings, its team has also done well. According to official press releases, Temasek's conservative "older brother" averaged a 7.8% growth rate over a 20-year period. During the same timeframe, international stock markets could only boast of an average 7.0% growth rate.[70] And then there is Harvard. Between 1 October 2007 and 1 October 2008, the Harvard

University Endowment Fund earned an 8.6% return—growing from $34.9 to $36.9 billion. Although well short of the previous year's stellar performance—a 23% return—Harvard is still out-earning investors who placed their money in U.S. Treasury notes.

The Peril and Potential for America

As the events of September and October 2008 unfolded, a number of acquaintances asked whether I would be rewriting my "lessons learned." "No," I replied, but perhaps there is a need to go back and reconsider the "peril and potential" for America these funds now present. I've done that—and there seems little need for a fundamental rewrite. I would note, however, that all previous timelines are certainly off the table. As long as foreign investors believe that their money is safest when stowed in U.S. Treasury notes, there is no danger of our government running out of cash. However, when the markets stabilize, we are likely to find ourselves worse off, not better, as a result of this short-term cash infusion. Washington's decision to tackle the credit crisis by throwing money at banks, consumers, and anyone else who appears willing to stimulate spending, only means that the annual deficit and overall national debt will have grown larger. A prudent international investor will note that the U.S. national debt is likely to reach 100% of our gross domestic product (GDP) in 2009—a marked change from the approximately 65% of GDP we reached in 2006.

Furthermore, as the Warren Buffett quote at the beginning of this chapter implies, the lack of individual and government savings in this country means that all the money Washington has used for bailouts and economic stimulation was printed with little apparent regard for the future. Capitol Hill went in search of a short-term fix (nothing like trying to placate voters right before a national election) with seemingly little thought about what could happen as a result in the coming two, five or ten years. Over the long term, all this new money is likely to drag down the value of the dollar, increase inflation at home, and encourage Middle Eastern nations to renew efforts to decouple their currencies from a weakened greenback. Add to this the Federal Reserve's efforts to prevent or shorten a recession by lowering interest rates, and one has the perfect reason for sovereign wealth funds to seek investment options anywhere but the United States. On second thought, however, sovereign wealth funds will come back to shop in America—but it will be to purchase real estate and increasingly larger shares in corporations that have no were else to turn.

And what about U.S. policy concerning sovereign wealth funds? Given Wall Street's plight since September 2008, and the ailing state of America's largest banks, there now appears to be little interest in pursuing tougher investment laws that could discourage any potential source of capital. Recall that in September 2008 Singapore was allowed to purchase a 14% stake in Merrill Lynch and that in October 2008 China was offered the possibility of acquiring a 12.5% share in Blackstone—all without any comment from Congress or the

White House. (Nor, by the way, did either of the two presidential campaigns offer any statement.) It seems the current search for cash has overwhelmed all previous laments America's national security was on the sales block—not that this is such a bad thing. Although our economic conditions may prove less than appealing for a potential foreign investor, the decline in threats to impose odious restrictions on their behavior could be a compensatory factor working in our favor. (One has to wonder when the Europeans will come to a similar conclusion—particularly in light of comments coming from France, Germany, and Italy.)

Regardless of what Congress and the White House choose to do on the regulatory front, I continue to assert sovereign wealth funds represent the day of reckoning for Washington's history of poor fiscal management. The credit crisis of 2008 may serve to delay that reckoning, but it will not halt the bill collector in his tracks. Unless Americans choose to live within our means, we will remain beholden to investors from abroad. The current woes Wall Street has brought to our—and their—front doors has likely done little to improve our future ability to continue winning the hearts and minds of these potential financial suitors.

The consequence—while not immediately apparent—will be felt on the domestic and foreign policy fronts. Although neither presidential candidate was willing to explain how our current fiscal crisis might serve to curtail their policy options, cutbacks in domestic spending—for defense, education, health, and law enforcement—seem inevitable. Unless the next administration is willing to risk imposing higher borrowing costs on all consumers, federal and state spending is going to have to be reduced. These cuts may be more palatable once the American electorate understands continued government spending can only occur with significant increases in interest rates—but one has to wonder how many times an elected official has to explain that cash is a scarce commodity, and what "basis points" are, before this argument wins the day.

The cost on the foreign policy front is equally formidable. As the Council on Foreign Relations noted in a September 2008 publication:

> The United States shaped global norms—and could use the threat to limit countries' access to the U.S. financial market to try to shape their behavior. Today borrowers from around the world looking to raise funds already are traveling to the Gulf States or to China rather than to New York to explore their options. There is less pressure on other countries to conform to U.S. financial norms—and less scope for the U.S. government to use other countries' desire to raise funds in the United States to shape their policies.[71]

According to the Council on Foreign Relations, the ultimate result of this situation is that "the United States will have less influence, and non-democratic countries will likely have a much larger voice in global economic governance."[72] I would hasten to add, this may already be true about influencing domestic politics abroad. Polls in China and Russia already indicate a preference for authoritarian regimes that maintain economic growth. After all, where would you rather live, Singapore or Thailand? I suspect most Chinese and Russians would choose Singapore.

I would like to close with that thought—and open the door to future scholarship. Over the course of this investigation, I have repeatedly come to the conclusion that sovereign wealth funds are a benchmark of authoritarian capitalism. What that means, for Americans and for international relations, remains to be addressed. Are democracies simply unsuited to conduct good fiscal management? Or is there a means of balancing constituent demands with the Constitution's stipulations on appropriations? I, for one, have yet to reach a definitive answer to that question.

NOTES

Introduction

1. Mirna Sleiman, "U.S. Should Welcome Sovereign Wealth Funds—Greenspan," Dow Jones Newswires, New York, 26 February 2008. Alan Greenspan, the former U.S. Federal Reserve Chairman, made his remarks before an investors' conference in Abu Dhabi. Interestingly, Greenspan had been an early critic of the United States establishing its own sovereign wealth fund in the late 1990s, when U.S. budget surpluses presented the potential for finally eliminating Washington's outstanding national debts. (For more on Greenspan's position see: Alan Greenspan, *The Age of Turbulence: Adventures in a New World*, Penguin Press, New York, 2007, 164–205.)

2. For additional thoughts on this subject, see also: James Jackson, "Foreign Investment in U.S. Securities," CRS Report for Congress, Congressional Research Service, Washington DC, 24 April 2006.

3. J. Onno de Beaufort Wijnholds and Arend Kapteyan, "Reserve Adequacy in Emerging Market Economies," IMF Working Paper, WP/01/143, International Monetary Fund, Washington DC, September 2001. See also: Robert Heller, "Optimal International Reserves," *Economic Journal* 76, 1966, No. 302, 296–311; Koichi Hamada and Kazuo Ueda, "Random Walks and the Theory of Optimal International Reserves, *Economic Journal* 87, 1977, No. 848, 722–742; and Joshua Aizenman and Jaewoo Lee, "International Reserves: Precautionary versus Mercantilist Views—Theory and Evidence," IMF Working Paper 05/198, International Monetary Fund, Washington DC, 2005.

4. Other "rules of thumb" for reserve holdings include: (a) a ratio to short-term debt immediately coming due or in total, to total external debt, or to external obligations; (b) as a ratio to gross domestic product or to some measure of the money supply; or (c) a combination of all the areas discussed above.

5. Toshio Idesawa, Director-General, International Department of the Bank of Japan (BOJ), "BOJ's Foreign Assets Management," presentation to the Sovereign Wealth

Management Conference, London, 14 March 2008. The debate over what constitutes sufficient reserves is a long way from being resolved. Consider, for example, the fact that
Germany had only $140 billion in foreign exchange reserves in 2007—enough for two
months of imports—yet suffered no international criticism or degradation to Berlin's
credit rating.

6. Gerald Lyons, "State Capitalism: The Rise of Sovereign Wealth Funds," *Thought
Leadership*, Standard Chartered Bank, London, 15 October 2007.

7. Andrew Rozanov, "Who Holds the Wealth of Nations?" *Central Banking Journal*,
Central Banking Publications, London, May 2005.

8. "Report to Congress on International Economic and Exchange Rate Policies,"
Department of the Treasury, Washington DC, December 2007.

9. Stephen Jen, "Currencies: The Definition of a Sovereign Wealth Fund," Morgan
Stanley–Global Economic Forum, New York, 25 October 2007.

10. International finance analysts might argue interest in sovereign wealth funds was
not so "sudden." Financial analysts began publishing articles on these government
investment vehicles with increasing regularity beginning in mid-2005. In fact, Andrew
Rozanov from State Street Global Advisors is widely recognized as having coined the
term "sovereign wealth fund" in a publication released in May 2005.

11. Gerald Lyons, 15 October 2007.

12. Simon Johnson, "The Rise of Sovereign Wealth Funds," *Finance and Development*,
44 (3), International Monetary Fund, Washington DC, September 2007.

13. Andrew Rozanov, May 2005.

14. "Sovereign Wealth Funds Grow to $3.3 Trillion—Report," CNNMoney.com,
31 March 2008.

15. Stephen Jen, "Currencies: How Big Could Sovereign Wealth Funds Be by 2015?"
Morgan Stanley Research, New York, 3 May 2007.

16. John Gieve, "Sovereign Wealth Funds and Global Imbalances," presentation to the
Sovereign Wealth Management Conference, London, 14 March 2008.

17. For more on the concept of "soft power," see: Joseph Nye, 2004, *Soft Power: The
Means to Success in World Politics*, PublicAffairs, New York.

18. "IMF Intensifies Work on Sovereign Wealth Funds," *IMF Survey Magazine*,
Washington DC, 4 March 2008.

19. Nicole Mordant and Allan Dowd, "Greenspan 'Uncomfortable' with Sovereign
Funds," REUTERS, Vancouver, Canada, 24 January 2008.

20. Christopher Rugaber, "Agency Investigates Sovereign Funds," Associated Press,
Washington DC, 11 January 2008.

21. Christopher Cox, "The Rise of Sovereign Business," Gauer Distinguished Lecture
in Law and Policy, American Enterprise Institute, Washington DC, 5 December 2007.

22. *Temasek Review 2007: Creating Value*, Singapore, August 2007, p. 10.

23. Henny Sender, "How a Gulf Petro-State Invests Its Oil Riches," *The Wall Street
Journal*, 24 August 2007.

24. Floyd Norris, "China Less Willing to Be America's Piggy Bank," *The New York
Times*, 22 December 2007.

25. David Dickson, "Funds Diverted from Private Holdings," *The Washington Times*,
17 July 2008.

26. Henny Sender, "Sovereign Funds Cut Exposure to Weak Dollar," *Financial Times*,
London, 16 July 2008.

27. Ibid.

28. Ibid.

29. Michael Martin, "China's Sovereign Wealth Fund," CRS Report for Congress, Congressional Research Service, Washington DC, 22 January 2008.

30. *Norges Bank Investment Management: Annual Report 2006*, Oslo, Norway, March 2007.

31. Henny Sender, 24 August 2007.

32. Roman Shikyo, "Sovereign Wealth Management in Russia," presentation to the Sovereign Wealth Management Conference, London, 14 March 2008. More specifically, Shikyo claims the Russian Budget Code requires the sovereign wealth fund managers to invest in: foreign currency, foreign debt securities issued by foreign governments, foreign debt securities issued by foreign agencies and central banks, foreign debt securities of international financial organizations, deposits in foreign banks and credit organizations, fixed income securities of central banks, deposits and accounts with the Bank of Russia, fixed income securities and equities of legal entities, and shares in investment funds.

33. Aaron Back, "China's Sovereign Wealth Fund Takes a Cautious Approach," *The Wall Street Journal*, 29 November 2007. Of note, this earnings requirement translates to $14.6 billion dollars a year in profits—or a return of at least 7.3% on the China Investment Corporation's $200 billion investment.

34. Anna Cha, "Foreign Wealth Funds Defend U.S. Investments," *Washington Post*, 27 March 2008.

35. *Temasek Review 2007: Creating Value*, Singapore, August 2007, p. 27. Note: Temasek reporting for a fiscal year ends on 31 March—thus the data for 2007.

36. Henry Sender, 24 August 2007.

37. Karen Richardson, *The Wall Street Journal*, 29 November 2007.

38. Bill Powell, "The Wealth of Nations," *Time*, 6 December 2007.

39. Lisa Lerer, "Businesses Plot Strategy to Protect Wealth Funds," *The Politico*, Washington DC, 4 March 2008.

40. James Webb, "Remarks to the U.S.-China Economic and Security Review Commission," testimony before the United States-China Economic and Security Review Commission, Washington DC, 7 February 2008.

41. Marcy Kaptur, "Sovereign Wealth Funds: Selling Our National Security," testimony before the United States-China Economic and Security Review Commission, Washington DC, 7 February 2008.

42. Bob Davis, "Americans See Little to Like in Sovereign Wealth Funds," *The Wall Street Journal*, 21 February 2008. Poll conducted by the political consulting firm Public Strategies Incorporated on 12 and 13 February 2008. The survey reached 1,000 registered voters online and had a margin of error of plus or minus 3.1 percentage points.

43. Tara Loader Wilkinson, "Sovereign Funds as Buoy," *The Wall Street Journal*, 7 November 2007.

44. Ibid.

45. Christopher Rugaber, "House: Foreign Investing Rules Too Gray," *BusinessWeek*, 13 March 2008.

46. Paul Rose, "Sovereigns as Shareholders," Draft, Moritz College of Law, Ohio State University, March 2008, See also: Peter Heyward, "Are Sovereign Wealth Funds a Threat to the U.S. Banking System?" 10 March 2008, Venable LLP, Washington DC.

47. Charles Proctor, "Sovereign Wealth Funds: The International Legal Framework," presentation to the Sovereign Wealth Management Conference, London, 14 March 2008.

48. The OECD Code of Liberalization of Capital Movements requires members to "progressively abolish between one another . . . restrictions on movements of capital to

the extent necessary for effective economic cooperation." The code does, however, allow members to restrict the movement of capital for "the protection of public health, morals, or safety . . . " or "the protection of essential security interests."

49. Article 56 of the European Union Treaty requires "all restrictions on the movement of capital between Member States and between Member States and third parties shall be prohibited." Legal authorities contend that the reference to "capital" would cover both foreign direct investment and the portfolio investments favored by sovereign wealth funds (Charles Proctor, 14 March 2008).

50. Charles Proctor, 14 March 2008.

51. Ibid.

52. John James Roberts Manner, *England's Trust*, Part III, line 231.

Chapter 1—The Sovereign Wealth Funds of Nations

1. Adam Smith, *The Wealth of Nations* (Random House, 2003), 1034.

2. There are four widely recognized kinds of sovereign investment: foreign exchange reserves, public pension funds, state-owned enterprises, and sovereign wealth funds. According to the IMF, foreign exchange reserves are external assets that are controlled by and readily available to finance ministries and central banks for the purpose of meeting international balance of payment concerns. Public pension funds—like the California Public Employees' Retirement System (CalPERS)—are investment vehicles created to largely meet government obligations to entitled citizens. (Historically, such public pension funds were invested in local currencies and tended to focus on low-risk asset classes—that, as we shall see—is changing in a manner that makes some public pension funds indistinguishable from sovereign wealth funds.) State-owned enterprises are companies that ultimately answer to government authorities. (Robert Kimmitt, "Public Footprints in Private Markets," *Foreign Affairs*, January 2008.)

3. Sovereign wealth funds have also been called stabilization funds, nonrenewable resource funds, and/or trust funds. No "official" definition of a sovereign wealth fund has been established. Some of the best attempts include Clay Lowery, then Acting Undersecretary for International Affairs at the U.S. Treasury Department, in a speech on 21 June, 2007, when he defined a sovereign wealth fund as "a government investment vehicle, which is funded by foreign exchange reserves, and which manages these assets separately from official reserves." (Clay Lowery, "Remarks by Acting Undersecretary for International Affairs Clay Lowery on Sovereign Wealth Funds and the International Financial System," 21 June 2007, U.S. Treasury Department, Washington DC.) Stephen Jen, the head of global currency research at Morgan Stanley, argues these investment vehicles have five key "ingredients." According to Jen, these ingredients are: "(1) sovereign; (2) high foreign currency exposure; (3) no explicit liabilities; (4) high risk tolerance; and, (5) long investment horizon." (Stephen Jen, "The Definition of a Sovereign Wealth Fund," 26 October 2007, Morgan Stanley–Global Economic Forum, New York.) In this case, I do not differentiate between a sovereign wealth fund and a sovereign pension fund—which, by definition, would have explicit liabilities, retirement payments—because Norway and Singapore tend to treat these commodity- and trade-based funds in a manner similar to that witnessed with sovereign wealth funds.

4. Official foreign reserves are, by definition, 100% in foreign currencies. They have no liabilities explicitly attached to them. (Stephen Jen, "The Definition of a Sovereign Wealth Fund," Morgan Stanley–Global Economic Forum, New York, 26 October 2007.)

5. Historically, the objectives for management of foreign reserves were derived from three functions: safety, liquidity, and return. (Philipp Hildebrand, "Four Tough Questions on Foreign Reserve Management," *Sovereign Wealth Management*, 2007: 29–46.)

6. J. Onno de Beaufort Wijnholds and Arend Kapteyn, "Reserve Adequacy in Emerging Markets Economies," IMF Working Paper, WP/01/143, International Monetary Fund, Washington DC, September 2001.

7. Alan Greenspan, "Currency Reserves and Debt," remarks before the World Bank Conference on Recent Trends in Reserves Management, Washington DC, 29 April 1999.

8. Diana Farrell, Susan Lund, Eva Gerlemann, and Peter Seeburger, "The New Power Brokers: How Oil, Asia, Hedge Funds, and Private Equity are Shaping Global Capital Markets," McKinsey Global Institute, New York, October 2007: 73–78.

9. Sources: *The Economist*, Morgan Stanley, *The Wall Street Journal*. All fiscal data are estimates current as of March 2008.

10. Benjamin Graham, "Trust Funds in the Pacific: Their Role and Future," Pacific Studies Series, Asian Development Bank, 2005: 35–39. Also see: Christopher Faulkner-MacDonagh and Bing Xu, "Federated States of Micronesia: Selected Issues and Statistical Appendix," IMF Country Report No. 07/105, International Monetary Fund, Washington DC, 13 February 2007.

11. To further differentiate between the two funds, Temasek tends to hold domestic assets and private equity, while GIC holds only foreign assets, most of which are publicly traded company shares.

12. Japan has over $1 trillion in foreign exchange reserves that could be placed in a sovereign wealth fund—thereby establishing an account with the equivalent spending power of the Abu Dhabi Investment Authority. In early December 2007, international financial news sources reported that Tokyo is proceeding with plans to launch this fund with approximately $100 billion. (Michiyo Nakamoto, "Push for Japanese Sovereign Fund," *Financial Times*, 5 December 2007.)

13. Simon Johnson, "The Rise of Sovereign Wealth Funds," *Finance and Development*, September 2007, 44(3), 56–57.

14. "Sovereign Wealth Funds Grow to $3.3 Trillion—Report," CNNMoney.com, 31 March 2008.

15. Stephen Jen, "Currencies: How Big Could Sovereign Wealth Funds Be by 2015?," Morgan Stanley Research, New York, 3 May 2007.

16. "The World's Most Expensive Club," *The Economist*, 24 May 2007. What this does not take into account is the amount of leveraged assets behind hedge-fund figures—by 2015 the leveraged assets required to support that estimated $4 trillion could be between $10 to $13 trillion.

17. Stephen Jen, "Asia Still a Major Holder of Reserves," 3 November 2007, Morgan Stanley–Global Economic Forum, New York.

18. George Hoguet, John Nugee, and Andrew Rozanov, "Sovereign Wealth Funds: Assessing the Impact," *Vision*, July 2008, 3(2).

19. Simon Johnson, 2007, 56.

20. Stephen Jen, "Currencies: Tracking the Tectonic Shift in Foreign Reserves and SWFs," Morgan Stanley–Global Economic Forum, New York, 16 March 2007.

21. George Hoguet, John Nugee, and Andrew Rozanov, July 2008. According to State Street, these figures represent an averaging of estimates offered by McKinsey Global Institute, Goldman Sachs, and Merrill Lynch.

22. George Hoguet, John Nugee, and Andrew Rozanov, July 2008.

23. David Francis, "Will Sovereign Wealth Funds Rule the World?" *The Christian Science Monitor*, 26 November 2007.

24. Anders Aslund, "The Truth about Sovereign Wealth Funds," *Foreign Policy*, December 2007, Web Exclusive.

25. This is a reference to the Qatari Delta Two fund's attempted $22 billion purchase of Britain's J. Sainsbury supermarket chain. The deal ultimately fell through because of a reported "tough credit environment" and the cost of winning support from the Sainsbury pension trustees. (Amanda Cooper, "Sovereign Funds Too Staid to Ignite Stocks," Reuters, 20 November 2007.)

26. James Surowiecki, "Sovereign Wealth World," *The New Yorker*, 26 November 2007.

27. Farrell, et al., October 2007, 47–55.

28. For instance, China owns $405 billion, or 18% of foreign-held U.S. Treasury notes—second only to Japan. (Belinda Cao, "China's $200 Billion Sovereign Fund Begins Operation," Bloomberg.com, 29 September 2007.)

29. A basis point is a unit that is equal to 1/100th of 1% and is used to denote the change in a financial instrument. The basis point is commonly used for calculating changes in interest rates, equity indexes, and the yield of a fixed-income security. The relationship between percentage changes and basis points can be summarized as follows: 1% change = 100 basis points, and 0.01% = 1 basis point.

30. Farrell, et al., October 2007, 59 and 72.

31. McKinsey's numbers may have been conservative. According to a University of Virginia study released in 2006, "foreign buying has kept U.S. interest rates about 1 to 1.5% points lower than otherwise." (Francis Warnock and Veronica Warnock, "International Capital Flows and U.S. Interest Rates," FRB International Discussion Paper, Number 840, September 2006.)

32. Ariana Cha, "Foreign Wealth Funds Defend U.S. Investments, *Washington Post*, 27 March 2008.

33. *Temasek Review 2007: Creating Value*, August 2007, 27. Note, Temasek reporting for a fiscal year ends on 31 March—thus the data for 2007.

34. Henny Sender, "How a Gulf Petro-State Invests Its Oil Riches," *The Wall Street Journal*, 24 August 2007.

35. Karen Richardson, "City of Arabia," *The Wall Street Journal*, 29 November 2007.

36. *Norges Bank Investment Management: Annual Report 2006*, Oslo, Norway, March 2007,

37. Knut Kjaer, "The Norwegian Government Pension Fund and NBIM," Presentation to the Central Bank of Chile, Norges Bank Investment Management (NBIM), Oslo, Norway, 3 October 2007, slide 53.

38. Ibid, slide 55.

39. China's Ministry of Finance is capitalizing the fund using proceeds from special bonds that are used to replace foreign reserves taken from China's central bank. (Rick Carew, "China Set to Kick Off Fund," *The Wall Street Journal*, 28 September 2007.)

40. Chinese sources have informed the Hong Kong–based *South China Morning Post* that the CIC's actual spending power in 2007 is significantly less than the $200 billion widely reported in the press. Chinese sources told the newspaper that the initial $200 billion was expected to cover the approximately $67 billion that Beijing's Central Huijian Investments had already spent on mainland banks and brokerages. (Huijian, the former investment arm of the People's Bank of China, is CIC's first major domestic acquisition.) Another $70 billion is expected to be injected into the China Development Bank and the Agricultural Bank of China. All told, the China Investment Corporation is thus esti-

mated to have about $50 billion available for investing during its first year of operations. (Cary Huang, "Rough Sailing Awaits Investment Flagship," *South China Morning Post*, 24 September 2007.) This is not the first time China has used "excess" foreign reserves to prop-up an ailing domestic banking industry. Having made numerous loans to failing state-owned enterprises, the Chinese banks are now seeking to refill coffers prior to having to meet the prospect of international competition promised by Beijing's entry into the World Trade Organization. Since January 2004, Central Huijian Investments has injected at least $60 billion into the Industrial & Commercial Bank of China, Bank of China Co., Ltd, and China Construction Bank Corporation as part of this effort. (Belinda Cao, "China's $200 Billion Sovereign Fund Begins Operation," Bloomberg.com, 29 September 2007.)

41. Chip Cummins and Rick Carew, "The New Diplomacy," *The Wall Street Journal*, 28 November 2007.

42. "In Come the Waves," *The Economist*, 15 June 2006.

43. Farrell et al., October 2007, 59–60.

44. These locations will change with time and may not include the most obvious candidates, such as New York City. For instance, in August 2007 Forbes.com reported that the top 10 "most resilient" real estate markets in the United States include: San Francisco, Boston, and Washington DC. (Matt Woolsey, "Most Resilient U.S. Real Estate Markets," *Forbes*, 6 August 2007.)

45. Ben Laurance and Louise Armistead, "Rising Power of the Sovereign Funds," *The Sunday Times*, London, 28 October 2007.

46. *Temasek Review 2007: Creating Value*, August 2007, 10.

47. Ibid, 38.

48. Jason Leow, "The $2 Billion China Bet," *The Wall Street Journal*," 5 December 2007.

49. Sender, 24 August 2007.

50. Farrell et al., October 2007, 47.

51. Sudip, Roy, "Money and Mystery: ADIA Unveils its Secrets," *Euromoney*, 1 April 2006.

52. Dominic Barton and Kito de Boer, "Tread Lightly Along the New Silk Road," *The McKinsey Quarterly*, March 2007. The authors serve to highlight a trend largely unnoticed elsewhere, specifically, "the volume of trade between the six members of the Gulf Cooperation Council—Bahrain, Kuwait, Oman, Qatar, Saudi Arabia, and the United Arab Emirates—and east Asia roughly quadrupled between 1995 and 2005. Bilateral trade between those regions' two largest nations—China and Saudi Arabia—increased 30% between 2005 and 2006 alone."

53. As the *International Herald Tribune* reported in May 2007, Dubai is trying to establish a financial hub in the Middle East on par with Hong Kong, London, and New York. Development is focused on a 110-acre financial complex intended to draw banks and investment companies to the region through a combination of zero taxes, new infrastructure, and no penalties on repatriating profits. (Heather Timmons, "Dubai Says It Now Has 2.2% of Deutsche Bank," *International Herald Tribune*, 16 May 2007.)

54. "Sovereign Wealth Funds Bet on Banks," Associated Press Wire Service, 11 December 2007, OMX AB operates stock exchanges in Sweden, Iceland, Finland, Denmark, and a few Baltic nations.

55. Henny Sender, Chip Cummins, Greg Hitt, and Jason Singer, "As Oil Hits High, Mideast Buyers Go on a Spree," *The Wall Street Journal*, 21 September 2007. The Bourse Dubai/NASDAQ deal was very complex. The bare-bones explanation is as follows: NASDAQ gets OMX. In return for selling its shares in OMX, Dubai Bourse gets a 20%

stake in NASDAQ, and it gets to buy the bulk of NASDAQ's 31% stake in the London Stock Exchange. Also, NASDAQ gets a strategic stake in the Dubai Bourse.

56. Farrell et al., October 2007, 65.

57. According to the Congressional Research Service, the major principles of *shariah* that are applicable to finance and differ from "Western" standards include: (1) a ban on interest—under Islamic law any level of interest is considered usurious and is prohibited; (2) a ban on uncertainty—uncertainty in contractual terms and conditions is not allowed unless all terms and conditions of the risk are understood by the participating parties; (3) shared risk and profit—all parties in a financial transaction must share the associated risks and profits; (4) investments must be ethical and enhance society—investment in industries that are prohibited by the *Qur'an*—i.e., alcohol, pornography, and gambling—are discouraged; and (5) tangible asset-backing—each financial transaction must be tied to a tangible, identifiable asset. (Shayerah Ilias, "Islamic Finance: Overview and Policy Concerns," CRS Report for Congress, Congressional Research Service, Library of Congress, Washington DC, 29 July 2008.)

58. Farrell et al., October 2007, 65–68.

59. "Islamic Finance Comes of Age," *BusinessWeek*, 27 October 2007. See also: Rachel Ziemba, "GCC Sovereign Wealth and Islamic Finance," RGE Analysts' EconoMonitor, RGEmonitor.com, 15 August 2008.

60. Bill Powell, "The Wealth of Nations," *Time*, 6 December 2007.

61. Michael Pettis, "Sovereign Wealth to the Rescue," *The Wall Street Journal*, 9 August 2007.

62. This criticism was specifically levied against Citigroup. In an unsigned "Review and Outlook" published in late November 2007, *The Wall Street Journal* scolded: "Citigroup did have to shore up its balance sheet, and we suppose petrodollars are a better source of capital than U.S. taxpayers under a 'too big to fail' doctrine. On the other hand, where were Mr. Rubin and the bank board when Citi was betting so much on subprime? Given the 11% the bank is paying Abu Dhabi, Citigroup's other equity holders might also be better off down the road had they taken a dividend cut instead." (Richardson, "City of Arabia," *The Wall Street Journal*, 29 November 2007.)

63. Tara Loader Wilkinson, "Sovereign Funds as Buoy," *The Wall Street Journal*, 7 November 2007.

64. Ibid.

65. Karen Richardson, "Citi's Deal May Be Wiser than Thought," *The Wall Street Journal*, 29 November 2007.

66. Anita Greil, "UBS Gains Two New Investors, Writes Down $10 Billion," *The Wall Street Journal*, 10 December 2007.

67. Ibid.

68. Michael Flaherty, "Sovereign Funds Steer Clear of Wall Street," Reuters, 17 March 2008.

69. Ibid.

70. Andrew Rozanov, "Who Holds the Wealth of Nations?" *Central Banking Journal*, May 2005, 15(4): 52–57.

71. Ibid, 53.

72. Ibid, 56.

73. Clay Lowery, "Remarks by Acting Undersecretary for International Affairs Clay Lowery on Sovereign Wealth Funds and the International Financial System," U.S. Treasury Department, Washington DC, 21 June 2007.

74. Simon Johnson, "The Rise of Sovereign Wealth Funds," *Finance and Development*, September 2007, 56–57.

75. Farrell et al., October 2007, 15.

76. Ibid, 16.

77. David McCormick, "Testimony Before the U.S. Senate Committee on Banking, Housing, and Urban Affairs," U.S. Treasury, Washington DC, 14 November 2007.

78. Christopher Cox, "The Rise of Sovereign Business," Gauer Distinguished Lecture in Law and Public Policy 2007, American Enterprise Institute, Washington DC, 5 December 2007.

79. David Wessel, "The Risks of Sovereign Wealth," *The Wall Street Journal*, 13 December 2007.

80. Christopher Cox, 5 December 2007.

81. For an example, see Robert Kimmitt, "Public Footprints in Private Markets: Sovereign Wealth Funds in the World Economy," *Foreign Affairs*, February 2008, 119–130.

82. This is not to say that the issue is being completely ignored. Congress is awakening to this potential problem. For instance, on 13 March 2008 three members of the House Financial Services Committee sent Treasury Secretary Henry Paulson a letter requesting clarification as to whether the 10% threshold rule of immediate Committee on Foreign Investment in the United States investigation was a "bright line rule." The letter was reportedly prompted by the number of deals coming at just below the 10% mark. (Christopher Rugaber, "House: Foreign Investment Rules Too Gray," The Associated Press, 13 March 2008.)

83. To measure these characteristics, Truman examined the following issues associated with each trait: Structure—Is the source of a sovereign wealth fund's money clearly specified? Are the use of principal and earnings clearly stated? Are these elements of fiscal treatment integrated in the budget? Are their guidelines for fiscal treatment generally followed? Is the overall investment strategy clearly communicated? Is the procedure for changing the structure clear? Is the sovereign wealth fund separate from a nation's international reserves? Governance—Is the role of the government in setting the sovereign wealth fund investment strategy clearly established? Is the role of the manager in executing the investment strategy clearly established? Are guidelines for corporate responsibility publicly available? Does the sovereign wealth fund have ethical guidelines? Accountability—Does the sovereign wealth fund provide at least an annual report on its activities and results? Does the sovereign wealth fund provide quarterly reports on its activities? Do reports on investments include the size of the fund? Do reports include information on returns the fund earns? Do reports include information on types of investments? Do reports include geographic location of investments? Do reports on investments include specifics? Do reports include information on currency composition of investments? Are the holders of investment mandates identified? Is the fund subjected to regular audit? Is the audit published? Is the audit independent? Behavior—Does the sovereign wealth fund indicate the nature and speed of adjustments in its portfolio? (Edwin Truman, "Sovereign Wealth Fund Acquisitions and Other Foreign Government Investments in the United States: Assessing the Economic and National Security Implications," Testimony before the Senate Committee on Banking, Housing and Urban Affairs, Washington DC, 14 November 2007, 17–21.)

84. Ibid, 8.

85. Ibid, 12.

86. Ibid, 8.

87. Clay Lowery, 21 June 2007.

88. David McCormick, "Undersecretary for International Affairs Testimony before the Senate Committee on Banking, Housing, and Urban Affairs," U.S. Treasury Department, Washington DC, 14 November 2007.

89. Christopher Cox, 5 December 2007.

90. "Clinton Campaign: Clinton Outlines Plan to Address America's Economic Challenges," Clinton Presidential Campaign, 19 November 2007.

91. Jeff Mason, "Obama Says Concerned About Sovereign Wealth Funds," Reuters, 7 February 2008.

92. Nick Timiraos, "Will Overseas Funds Be a Juggernaut?" *The Wall Street Journal*, 1 December 2007.

93. "Investment Agency Poised for Launch," *South China Morning Post*, 10 August 2007. The CIC managers include: Lou Jiwei, former vice-minister of finance, as CIC lead; Gao Xiping, deputy chairman of China's National Social Security Fund; Zhang Hongli, vice-minister of finance; Jesse Wang Jiangxi, deputy chairman of Central Huijin Investments; and, Xie Ping, managing director of Central Huijin Investments.

94. Jason Dean and Andrew Batson, "China Investment Fund May Tread Softly," *The Wall Street Journal*, 10 September 2007.

95. Aaron Back, "China's Sovereign Wealth Fund Takes Cautious Approach," *The Wall Street Journal*, 29 November 2007.

96. "China Tries to Allay Fears Over its Investment Pool," *The Wall Street Journal*, 12 December 2007.

97. Rick Carew, "China Seeks External Help for Wealth Fund," *The Wall Street Journal*, 14 December 2007.

98. Ronald Reagan, "Statement on International Investment Policy," 1983, Ronald Reagan Presidential Library.

99. Nina Easton, "After Dubai Ports, U.S. Courts Foreign Investment," *Fortune*, 5 March 2007.

100. In early 2006, Dubai Ports World purchased the Peninsular and Oriental Steam Navigation Company (P&O) of the United Kingdom, which was then the fourth largest harbor operator in the world, for $7 billion. P&O operated major U.S. port facilities in New York, New Jersey, Philadelphia, Baltimore, New Orleans, and Miami. After the deal was secured, the arrangement was reviewed by the Committee on Foreign Investment in the United States. It was given the green light, but soon after Democratic and Republican members of Congress expressed concern over the potential negative impact the deal would have on port security. They cited the 9/11 Commission report, which stated that two of the 9/11 hijackers were United Arab Emirates (UAE) nationals, and reports that the UAE was a major financial base for the al Qaeda terror network. On 22 February 2006, President George W. Bush threatened to veto any legislation passed by Congress to block the deal. On 23 February 2006, Dubai Ports World volunteered to postpone takeover of significant operations at the seaports as a means of giving the White House more time to convince lawmakers and the public that the deal posed no increased risk from terrorism. On 9 March 2006, Dubai Ports World announced that it would transfer operations of American ports to a "U.S. entity" after congressional leaders reportedly told President Bush that the firm's takeover deal was essentially dead on Capitol Hill. The House of Representatives voted on legislation on 16 March 2006 that would have blocked the Dubai Ports World deal, with 348 members voting for blocking the deal and

71 voting against. The Dubai provision was cut from the final bill passed by the Senate and then approved by both houses. Dubai Ports World eventually sold P&O's U.S. operations to American International Group's asset management division, Global Investment Group, for an undisclosed sum.

101. A similar brouhaha emerged in the wake of China National Offshore Oil Corporation's $18.5 billion bid for Unocal, the U.S.-based oil and gas company, on 23 June 2005.

102. How hypersensitive? A March 2006 poll conducted by the Pew Research Center for the People and Press found that 53% of Americans believed foreign ownership of U.S. companies was "bad for America." (*Survey Reports*, The Pew Research Center for the People and the Press, people-press.org, 15 March 2006.)

103. Carlos Gutierrez, "Secretary of Commerce Remarks at the Organization for International Investment Annual Dinner," Department of Commerce, Washington DC, 13 November 2007.

104. Stuart Eizenstat, "Testimony before the House Committee on Homeland Security on the CFIUS Process and Foreign Investment in the United States," Washington DC, 24 May 2006.

105. Eben Kaplan and Lee Teslik, "Foreign Ownership of U.S. Infrastructure," Council on Foreign Affairs, Washington DC, 13 February 2007.

106. Clay Lowery, 21 June 2007.

107. Carlos M. Gutierrez, "Remarks at the Organization for International Investment Annual Dinner," Department of Commerce, Washington DC, 13 November 2007.

108. David McCormick, 14 November 2007.

109. Christopher Cox, 5 December 2007.

110. "Clinton Campaign: Clinton Outlines Plan to Address America's Economic Challenges," Clinton Presidential Campaign, 19 November 2007.

111. Mike Huckabee, "Issues: Taxes/Economy," mikehuckabee.com, 2007.

112. Representative Marcy Kaptur, "Sovereign Wealth Funds: Selling Our National Security," Testimony before the U.S.–China Economic and Security Review Commission, Washington DC, 7 February 2008.

113. Peter Navarro, "Testimony of Professor Peter Navarro before the U.S.–China Economic and Security Review Commission," Washington DC, 7 February 2008.

114. Bob Davis, "Americans See Little to Like in Sovereign Wealth Funds," *The Wall Street Journal*, 21 February 2008.

115. Scheherazade Daneshkhu and James Blitz, "UK Warns over Push for State Protection," *Financial Times*, 24 July 2007.

116. Scheherazade Daneshkhu and James Blitz, 24 July 2007.

117. James Simms and Ayai Tomisawa, "Tokyo Adds Veto in Some Foreign Deals," *The Wall Street Journal*, 5 October 2007.

118. "Editorial: Not All Investment is Benign," *Taipei Times*, 22 October 2007.

119. The sovereign wealth fund managers are not alone in this effort. In February 2008 a small group of U.S. lobbyists announced the formation of a Sovereign Investment Council—an association with membership fees of between $200,000 and $1 million—reportedly intended to serve the interests of sovereign wealth funds and their domestic financial institution partners. (Lisa Lerer, "Businesses Plot Strategy to Protect Wealth Funds," *The Politico*, Politico.com, 4 March 2008.)

120. The standard verbiage: The acquiring fund will have no role in management or any presence on the board of directors. (Eric Dash, "Merrill Lynch Sells a $5 Billion Stake to a Singapore Firm," *The New York Times*, 25 December 2007.)

121. Samuel Loewenberg, "Foreign Buyers Court Congress," *The Politico*, Politico.com, 12 December 2007.

122. Edward Graham and David Marchick, *U.S. National Security and Foreign Direct Investment*, (Institute for International Economics, 2006), xi.

123. A 1989 poll conducted by the Pew Research Center for the People and Press found that 70% of Americans believed foreign ownership of U.S. companies was "bad for America." (*Survey Reports*, The Pew Research Center for the People and the Press, people-press.org, 15 March 2006.)

124. *Omnibus Trade and Competitiveness Act of 1988*, Washington DC, 1988.

125. Under Exon-Florio CFIUS was composed of: Secretary of the Treasury (chair), Secretary of State, Secretary of Defense, Secretary of Commerce, Secretary of Homeland Security, Attorney General, Director of the Office of Management and Budget, United States Trade Representative, Chairman of the Council of Economic Advisors, Director of the Office of Science and Technology Policy, Assistant to the President for National Security Affairs, and Assistant to the President for Economic Policy.

126. The CFIUS process timeline was as follows: (1) Initial 30-day review following receipt of notice; (2) 45-day investigation period for transactions deemed to require additional review; (3) formal report to the president at the end of the 45-day investigation; and, (4) presidential decision within 15 days of receiving the formal report.

127. For summaries of the original CFIUS process, see Ronald Lee, "The Dog Doesn't Bark: CFIUS, the National Security Guard Dog with Teeth," *The M&A Lawyer*, February 2005, 8 (8), 5–11; Leon Greenfield and Perry Lange, "The CFIUS Process: A Primer," *The Threshold*, January 2006, 6 (1), 10–18; and "Committee on Foreign Investment in the United States," Joint Economic Committee, Washington DC, March 2006.

128. Edward Graham and David Marchick, 2006, 37–40.

129. Regulations Implementing Exon-Florio, *Code of Federal Regulations*, Title 31, Section 800, Appendix A, March 2006.

130. Exon Florio Amendment, 1988.

131. "National Defense Authorization Act for Fiscal Year 1993," Public Law 102–484, *U.S. Statutes at Large* 1993, 106, 2315, 2463.

132. Before launching into a critique of the CFIUS's apparently lackadaisical performance, one should consider that between 2000 and 2005 Tokyo was confronted with 936 foreign deals involving the purchase of Japanese firms—only 23 of these transactions were actually found to require official approval. (James Simms and Ayai Tomisawa, "Tokyo Adds Veto in Some Foreign Deals," *The Wall Street Journal*, 5 October 2007.)

133. James Jackson, "The Committee on Foreign Investments in the United States," *CRS Report for Congress*, Library of Congress, Washington DC, 23 July 2007.

134. For summaries of the legal changes associated with passage of the 2007 Foreign Investment and National Security Act, see Melvin Schwechter and Matthew Semino, "The Foreign Investment and National Security Act of 2007 Codifies and Tightens the Exon-Florio Review Process," *Client Alert*, 27 July 2007, LeBoeuf Lamb, Washington DC; and John Reynolds, Amy Worlton, and Christopher Weld, "CFIUS Reform Legislation Signed Into Law," Wiley Rein LLP, Washington DC, 3 August 2007.

135. Data obtained from Department of the Treasury, 2007.

136. The 2007 act dictates at least nine CFIUS members: the secretaries of Treasury, State, Homeland Security, Energy, Defense, Commerce, and the Attorney General. The 2007 act also adds the Secretary of Labor and Director of National Intelligence as *ex*

officio members of the body. Finally, the 2007 act allows the president to designate other executive branch officers to sit on the committee as appropriate for a particular case.

137. John Reynolds, Amy Worlton, and Christopher Weld, 3 August 2007.

138. *National Strategy for Homeland Security*, White House, Washington DC, 9 October 2007.

139. Exon Florio Amendment, 1988.

140. John Reynolds, Amy Worlton, and Christopher Weld, 3 August 2007.

141. Ilene Gotts, Leon Greenfield, and Perry Lange, "Identifying Potential National Security Issues and Navigating the CFIUS Review Process," *Business Law* August 2007, 16 (6).

142. Ibid.

143. Samuel Loewenberg, 12 December 2007.

144. Barney Frank and Carolyn Maloney, "Letter to the President," House Committee on Financial Services, Washington DC, 11 December 2007.

145. Lawrence Summers, "Opportunities in an Era of Large and Growing Official Wealth," *Sovereign Wealth Management*, 2007, 15.

146. Ibid, 21–25.

147. Ibid, 22.

148. Floyd Norris, "China Less Willing to Be America's Piggy Bank," *The New York Times*, 22 December 2007.

149. James Simms and Ayai Tomisawa, 5 October 2007.

150. Edwin Truman, "Sovereign Wealth Funds: The Need for Greater Transparency and Accountability," Peterson Institute for International Economics, Washington DC, August 2007.

151. Emma Charlton, "Sovereign Funds Look to Norway," *The Wall Street Journal*, 16 November 2007.

152. *Norges Bank Investment Management: Annual Report 2006*, Oslo, Norway, March 2007.

153. Knut Kjaer, "The Norwegian Government Pension Fund and NBIM," Presentation to the Central Bank of Chile, Norges Bank Investment Management (NBIM), Oslo, Norway, 3 October 2007.

Chapter 2—Birth of a Sovereign Wealth Fund: The China Investment Corporation

1. "Perceived" is the key phrase here. A comparison of foreign exchange reserve growth between 2001 and 2006 reveals Moscow was actually accumulating cash at a faster pace. Between 2001 and 2006, China's foreign reserves grew 403%, from slightly more than $200 billion to $1.07 trillion. Russia's foreign exchange holdings during the same time period grew an astounding 807%, doubling Beijing's performance, but only totaled $295 billion in 2006. The Russian statistic can be attributed to growth from essentially no foreign reserves to the current balance as a result of oil exports. (Edwin Truman, "The Management of China's International Reserves: China and a SWF Scoreboard," Paper prepared for Conference on China's Exchange Rate Policy, Peterson Institute for International Economics, Washington DC, 19 October 2007.)

2. While certainly beyond the scope of this text, it is interesting to note Beijing's trade surplus is almost exclusively an artifact of business conducted between China and the United States. Chinese specialization in finishing goods—completing products from imported raw materials—has limited China's take to approximately 20% of the value of the items exported. The consequence is that China runs a trade deficit with many of its

neighbors—most specifically, South Korea, and Taiwan. On a broader scale, China's trade deficit with East Asia has actually increased over the last seven years. It grew from $39 billion in 2000 to $130 billion in 2007.

3. Andrew Batson, "China's 2007 Trade Surplus Surges," *The Wall Street Journal,* 11 January 2008.

4. For a concise summary of China's historic exchange rate policy see Nicholas Lardy, "Exchange Rate and Monetary Policy in China," *Cato Journal,* Winter 2005, 25 (1): 41–47.

5. Some economists argue that Chinese management of the exchange rate has resulted in the yuan being undervalued by 15–25%. Beijing is sensitive to these claims and has sought to address the issue by allowing the yuan to increase in value against the dollar. In 2007, this policy resulted in the yuan increasing in value against the dollar by 6.9%. This was more than twice the "float" allowed in 2006, when the yuan only rose against the dollar by 3.4%. To help keep this change in perspective, China's official exchange rate for the yuan remained locked in place at 8.28 to $1 from 1996 to July 2005. As of April 2008, the yuan-dollar exchange rate was approximately 7.00 to $1. (For more on China's monetary exchange policy see Morris Goldstein, "Adjusting China's Exchange Rate Policies," Paper presented at the IMF seminar on China's Foreign Exchange System, Peterson Institute for International Economics, Washington DC, May 2004.)

6. Stephen Green, "Making Monetary Policy Work in China: A Report from the Money Market Front Line," Stanford Center of International Development, Working Paper 245, Stanford University, CA, July 2005,.

7. For a layman's description of this process and other means the Chinese government uses to prevent inflation and rapid yuan appreciation against the dollar see: James Fallows, "The $1.4 Trillion Question," *The Atlantic,* Washington DC, January 2008: 35–48.

8. Not all of the voices have been raised in complaint; there are some American scholars who argue revaluation of the yuan will do little to reduce the U.S. trade imbalance with China. As David Hale and Lyric Hale note in an essay that *Foreign Affairs* published in January 2008, "the growing Chinese trade surplus has actually produced numerous benefits for the world economy and U.S. corporations and consumers." (David Hale and Lyric Hale, "Reconsidering Revaluation: The Wrong Approach to the U.S.-China Trade Imbalance," *Foreign Affairs,* January 2008, 87 (1): 57–66.) A Morgan Stanley study makes the point more succinctly by noting that cheaper exports from China have saved U.S. consumers an estimated $600 billion over the last 10 years—$521 a year in increased disposable income for every American household over that time period.

9. James Laurenceson and Fengming Qin, "China's Exchange Rate Policy: The Case Against Abandoning the Dollar Peg," Working Paper No. 2005-70, Tilburg University, Tilburg, the Netherlands, June 2005.

10. Floyd Norris, "China Less Willing to be America's Piggy Bank," *The New York Times,* 22 December 2007. According to the U.S. Treasury, in January 2008 China owned $492 billion in U.S. Treasury securities—second only to Japan ($586 billion). The United Kingdom came in a distant third with $160 billion in Treasury securities. Interestingly, the net sell off of U.S. Treasury securities noted in the *New York Times* article was not limited to China—Japan and the United Kingdom were also selling their U.S. government notes (U.S. Treasury, "Major Foreign Holders of Treasury Securities," January 2008).

11. This apparently unofficial approach to facilitating Washington's deficit spending has not gone unnoticed in the 2008 presidential campaign. Hillary Clinton has explicitly declared the that Bush administration is jeopardizing American national security by

allowing foreigners—particularly the Chinese—to purchase such a large share of the U.S. debt (Jeff Manson, "Clinton Says China Holdings Threaten U.S. Security," Reuters.com, 29 March 2008).

12. Michael Richardson, "Barriers to Trust: Sovereign Wealth Funds Must Become More Transparent to Avoid Causing Alarm," *South China Morning Post*, Hong Kong, 29 December 2007.

13. Interestingly, Chinese scholars were aware of Washington's conundrum. In an article published in July 2007, a member of the Fudan University's Institute of American Studies argued "the U.S. is worried that attempts to diversify foreign exchange investments through the vehicle of sovereign wealth funds will make the various countries less willing to continue to hold their assets and loans in U.S. dollars. Once this practice becomes widespread, it will directly lead to a sharp devaluation of the dollar and reduce the attractiveness of the dollar as the currency in which countries hold their reserve assets, thereby jeopardizing the dollars international status" (Song Guoyo, "Sovereign Wealth Funds Gaining Popularity," *Shanghai Dongfang Zabao*, Shanghai, 12 July 2007). Similar sentiments have appeared in Western reporting. For instance see Jonathan Weisman, "Economists Debate Link Between War, Credit Crisis," *The Washington Post*, 15 April 2008.

14. In early August 2007, two Chinese officials renewed concern over employment of the financial "nuclear option" when responding to reports that the United States was considering trade sanctions as a means of compelling revaluation the yuan. Xia Bin, finance chief at the Development Research Center, told reporters that Beijing's foreign reserves could be used as a "bargaining chip" in talks with the United States. However, he went on to declare "of course, China doesn't want any undesirable phenomenon in the global financial order." He Fan, an official at the Chinese Academy of Social Sciences, took matters a step further by letting it be known that Beijing has the power to set off a dollar collapse. According to He Fan, "China has accumulated a large sum of U.S. dollars. Such a big sum, of which a considerable portion is in U.S. Treasury bonds, contributes a great deal to maintaining the position of the dollar as a reserve currency. Russia, Switzerland, and several other countries have reduced their dollar holdings. China is unlikely to follow suit as long as the yuan's exchange rate is stable against the dollar. The Chinese central bank will be forced to sell dollars once the yuan appreciated dramatically, which might lead to a mass depreciation of the dollar." (Ambrose Evans-Pritchard, "China Threatens 'Nuclear Option' of Dollar Sales," *The Telegraph*, 10 August 2007).

15. Jeff Manson, "Clinton Says China Holdings Threaten U.S. Security," Reuters.com, 29 March 2008.

16. Sim Chi Yin and Bhagyashree Garekar, "China Says it Will Not Dump U.S. Dollar Assets—Central Bank Official Says They Are Important Component of Nation's Forex Reserves," *The Straits Times*, Singapore, 13 August 2007.

17. Song Guoyo, "Sovereign Wealth Funds Gaining Popularity," *Shanghai Dongfang Zabao*, 12 July 2007.

18. Susan Shirk, *China: Fragile Superpower—How China's Internal Politics Could Derail its Peaceful Rise* (Oxford University Press, 2007), 79–104.

19. Keith Bradsher, "China's Money Woe: Where to Park it All," *International Herald Tribune*, Hong Kong, 5 March 2007. Similar arguments appeared in Chinese press stories. For an example, see Song Guoyo, "Sovereign Wealth Funds Gaining Popularity," *Shanghai Dongfang Zabao*, 12 July 2007. The author goes so far as to argue that "from a rate of returns standpoint . . . buying U.S. Treasury bonds is not very

profitable. The effective rate may even be negative. In fact, higher earnings has [sic] precisely been the most important reason why countries have created sovereign wealth funds one after another."

20. Keith Bradsher, 5 March 2007.

21. 15 October 2007, "Hu Jintao: No Tolerance to Corruption," Xinhua.com, Beijing. Hu made this statement during his address to the Chinese Communist Party's 17th National Congress. Hu is said to have declared, "The CPC never tolerates corruption or any other negative phenomena," and he decreed "resolutely punishing and effectively preventing corruption is crucial to the popular support for the Party and its survival."

22. Keith Bradsher, 5 March 2007.

23. Economists typically refer to national monetary supplies as M0: currency; M1: the money commonly used for payment (basically M0 and checking deposits); and M2, which includes M1 plus balances similar to transaction accounts that, for the most part, can be converted fairly readily to M1 with little or no loss of principal.

24. Cary Huang, "Rough Sailing Awaits Investment Flagship," *South China Morning Post*, Hong Kong, 24 September 2007.

25. Jamil Anderlini, "China Investment Arm Emerges from Shadows," *Financial Times*, 5 January 2008.

26. Ibid.

27. People's Bank of China officials—SAFE's ultimate bosses—told a *Financial Times* reporter the Hong Kong office was established to "support and promote the development of Hong Kong's financial market" and has served a crucial role in defending the Renminbi's peg to the dollar against international speculators. (Jamil Anderlini, "China Investment Arm Emerges from Shadows," *Financial Times*, 5 January 2008.)

28. Jamil Anderlini, 5 January 2008. The Hong Kong SAFE office would have continued to avoid publicity had it not participated in an effort to purchase equity in three of Australia's banks—Australia and New Zealand Bank, Bank of Australia, and National Australia Bank—in late 2007. The SAFE officials reportedly purchased approximately $200 million in shares at each of the three banks, thereby establishing almost 1% stakes in the Australia and New Zealand Bank and Bank of Australia and 1/3 of 1% in the National Australia Bank (Rowan Callick, "Chinese Export Capital by Stealth," *The Australian*, Sydney, 5 January 2008).

29. Vidya Ram, "China Take a Piece of Total," Forbes.com, 4 April 2008.

30. Tom Miller, "SAFE to Give CIC a Run for its Money," *South China Morning Post*, Hong Kong, 17 April 2008.

31. Quote attributed to Arthur Krober, a director of the Beijing-based Dragonomics consulting firm (Tom Miller, 17 April 2008).

32. Quote attributed to Brad Setser, who has written on sovereign wealth funds for the U.S. Council on Foreign Relations (Tom Miller, 17 April 2008).

33. Peter Lattman, "China Wealth Fund to Invest $2.5 Billion with TPG Fund," *The Wall Street Journal*, 12 June 2008.

34. "China's SAFE to Invest $2.5 Billion in TPG Fund," *Financial Times*, 11 June 2008.

35. Comments to this effect have been offered by Fraser Howie, a Singapore-based analyst who specializes in Chinese financial developments (Tom Miller, "SAFE to Give CIC a Run for its Money," *South China Morning Post*, Hong Kong, 17 April 2008).

36. A limited liability company is a business structure that is a hybrid of a partnership and a corporation. Its owners are shielded from personal liability, and all profits and losses pass directly to the owners without taxation of the entity itself.

37. Jason Dean and Andrew Batson, "China Investment Fund May Tread Softly," *The Wall Street Journal*, 10 September 2007.

38. Rick Carew, "China Seeks Outside Help to Manage Global Funds," *The Wall Street Journal*, 14 December 2007. CIC is rumored to have received over 130 applications through its Web site (Victoria Ruan, "China, Can You Spare a Crumb?" *The Wall Street Journal*, 16 January 2008).

39. Rick Carew, 14 December 2007. Speculation about the extent of this "outsourcing" continues to circulate on the internet. In mid-April 2008, at least one site reported that China planned to use foreign asset managers to invest up to $320 billion by 2010. The CIC is reportedly to hand over more than 70% of its investment decisions during this same time frame (Liz Mak, "China's Sovereign Wealth Funds to Outsource $320 Billion," Businessweek.com, 15 April 2008).

40. Gao is a Duke University School of Law graduate and was the first Chinese national admitted to the New York State Bar.

41. Sources include BusinessWeek, press reporting, and Wikipedia. Current as of April 2008.

42. Clifford Chance, "China's Sovereign Wealth Fund Takes Shape," AsianInvestor.net, 22 February 2008.

43. Rick Carew, "China Set to Kick Off Fund," *The Wall Street Journal*, 28 September 2007.

44. "China Will Sell Bonds to Finance Sovereign Fund," *The Wall Street Journal*, 5 December 2007.

45. Rachel Ziemba, "How China is Funding the Chinese Investment Corporation," RGE Analysts' Economonitor, 5 December 2007.

46. Of note, this 4.45% interest rate was below the 4.68% yield offered by other Chinese government 15-year bonds. Financial analysts contend the lower interest rate was intended to reduce CIC costs ("China Will Sell Bonds to Finance Sovereign Fund," *The Wall Street Journal*, 5 December 2007).

47. "China Central Bank Takes Up 750 Bln yuan in T-bonds to Fund CIC," AFX News Limited, 10 December 2007.

48. "Chinese Sovereign Wealth Funds: 2008–2010 Opportunities for Foreign Asset Managers," Z-Ben Advisors, Shanghai, April 2008. In a telling sign of the potential windfall the Chinese sovereign wealth fund is thought to present Western financial consultants, Z-Ben Advisors advertised the full text of its report online with an asking price of $20,000. There was no indication as to the number of copies—if any—actually purchased. (On its website, Z-Ben Advisors claims it was founded in 2004 and now "provides in-depth analytical reports and consultancy services to foreign financial institutions and third party providers seeking an independent assessment of China's investment management industry.")

49. Rick Carew, 28 September 2007.

50. Clifford Chance, 22 February 2008.

51. There is considerable debate as to Beijing's willingness to comply with this requirement. Chinese banking regulations concerning outside participation in the country's financial system largely eliminate the possibility of foreign banks opening branches that could directly compete with domestic institutions. For instance, rather than establishing branches, foreign banks are required to incorporate each local operation in China as a Chinese-registered company, and each of these entities must have $125 million in registered capital. Second, the minimum balance for individuals in these companies is

$125,000. Finally, any foreign bank not locally incorporated can only offer services to businesses in yuan—services to individuals can only be done in foreign currency ("China: Deferring a Banking Crisis," STRATFOR, Washington DC, 5 September 2006).

52. In December 2006, these "big four" were thought to hold more than 50% of the aggregate assets in China's financial institutions (Hidetaro Muroi, "Chinese Banking Reform Requires Greater Competition," Japan Center for Economic Research Staff Report, Tokyo, 26 July 2007). The four institutions were originally internal divisions of the People's Bank of China but were separated from the central bank in the late 1970s.

53. Kent Matthews, Jianguang Guo, and Nina Zhang, "Non-Performing Loans and Productivity in Chinese Banks: 1997–2006," Cardiff Economics Working Papers, Cardiff Business School, Cardiff University, United Kingdom, November 2007.

54. "Nonperforming Loans (Past due 90+ Days Plus Nonaccrual)/Total Loans for All U.S. Banks," Economagic.com, March 2008.

55. He Fan, "How Far Away is China from a Financial Crisis," Institute of World Economics and Politics, Chinese Academy of Social Sciences, September 2002.

56. "Ernst and Young Withdraws China Bank NPL Report After Acknowledging Errors," AFX News Limited, Forbes.com, 15 May 2006.

57. The pairings worked as follows (asset management company and associated bank): Cinda and the Construction Bank of China; Great Wall and the Agricultural Bank of China; Huarong and the Industrial and Commercial Bank of China; Orient and the Bank of China.

58. Weijian Shan, "Will China's Banking Reform Succeed?" *The Wall Street Journal,* 17 October 2005.

59. Henry Liu, "China: Banking on Bank Reform," *Asia Times,* Hong Kong, 1 June 2002.

60. Keith Bradsher, "China to Give Up $41 Billion Stake in 2 Big Banks," *New York Times,* 14 January 2004.

61. Victor Shih, "Beijing's Bailout of Joint-stock and State-owned Banks," *China Brief,* 16 August 2005, 5 (18).

62. Minxin Pei, "Politics Blamed for China's Trillion-dollar Bad Debts," *The Australian,* Sydney, 15 March 2008.

63. Ibid.

64. Min Xu, "Resolution of Non-Performing Loans in China," The Leonard Stern School of Business, Gluckmans Institute for Research in Securities Markets, 1 April 2005. The author reports the China Banking Regulatory Commission claims the asset management companies disposed of almost half of the loans acquired between 2000 and 2004 by 31 December 2004.

65. Kent Matthews, Jianguang Guo, and Nina Zhang, November 2007.

66. "Ernst and Young Withdraws China Bank NPL Report After Acknowledging Errors," AFX News Limited, Forbes.com, 15 May 2006.

67. "China's Banks in Sound Shape: Bad Loans Drop," Chinadaily.com, 23 August 2006.

68. Hidetaro Muroi, 26 July 2007. Of note, more than one analyst has argued these statistics are skewed by the huge increase in loans made in China over the last five years ("Chinese Banks: Non-Performing Loans Rising," SeekingAlpha.com, 24 February 2008; Keith Bradsher, "$200 Billion to Invest, But in China," *The New York Times,* 29 November 2007). I have no reason to dispute this claim, but would note that the figures above are still markedly illustrative of a separate issue—the degree to which China prepared at least three of the "big

four" for commercial competition and thus the common sense it made for the China Investment Corporation to sink a large chunk of its initial funding in these institutions.

69. Zhou Xin, "China AgBank's NPL Ratio Rises to 23.6% in 2007," Reuters.com,
15 February 2008.

70. "Lender Outlines Listing," *The Wall Street Journal*, 28 January 2008.

71. Zhou Xin, 15 February 2008.

72. Jason Dean and Andrew Batson, "China Investment Fund May Tread Softly," *The
Wall Street Journal*, 10 September 2007.

73. Belinda Cao, "China's $200 Billion Sovereign Fund begins Operations,"
Blomberg.com, 29 September 2007.

74. Central Huijin is known to have purchased at least a 6% share in China's fifth
largest bank, the Bank of Communications (Rose Yu, "China Central Huijin to Transfer
6.12% BoCom Stake to MoF," Dow Jones Newswires, 25 March 2008) and at least a 70%
share in China Everbright Bank ("Central Huijin to Inject RMB 20 Billion in Everbright," marketinfo.tdctrade.com, 9 November 2007).

75. Victor Shih, 16 August 2005.

76. The question of remuneration for CIC officials has been the source of considerable
angst for Chinese officials. As *The Wall Street Journal* reported in September 2007, Chinese
critics of financial industry salaries have also taken potshots at banking authorities in their
own country. Some of these critics have declared that top executives at state-owned Chinese
banks are "over paid," despite the fact that their salaries rarely total more than $200,000 a
year—a sum considered "small" by international standards (Jason Dean and Andrew Batson,
"China Investment Fund May Tread Softly," *The Wall Street Journal*, 10 September 2007).

77. In January 2008, CIC officials announced they would be injecting another $20 billion
into the China Development Bank. According to a CIC Web site posting, the cash infusion
will "increase China Development Bank's capital-adequacy ratio, strengthen its ability to
prevent risk, and help its bank move toward completely commercialized operations" (Rick
Carew, "China Taps its Cash Hoard to Beef Up Another Bank," *The Wall Street Journal*,
2 January 2008; see also "China to Shift $20 Billion as Capital for Policy Bank," *The New
York Times*, 1 January 2008). Quite frankly, this focus was exactly what Lou Jiwei had
promised at the CIC opening ceremony on 29 September 2007: "The new investment
company will continue to boost the capital of state-owned financial institutions" (Belinda
Cao, "China's $200 Billion Sovereign Wealth Fund Begins Operations," Bloomberg.com,
29 September 2007),

78. This investment was underwritten using monies provided by the National Social
Security Fund (Chris Oliver "China Sovereign Wealth Fund Said Set For Launch,"
MarketWatch.com, 27 September 2007).

79. Keith Bradsher and Joseph Kahn, "In China, A Stake in Blackstone Stirs Uncertainty," *New York Times*, 29 May 2007.

80. Keith Bradsher, "China Faces Backlash at Home over Blackstone Investment,"
International Herald Tribune, 2 August 2007.

81. William Mellor and Le-Min Lim, "Lou Suffers Blackstone 'Fat Rabbits' in China
Fund," Bloomberg.com, 27 February 2008.

82. Rick Carew, "China's Sovereign Wealth Fund Forges Strategy, Hunts for Staff,"
The Wall Street Journal, 20 November 2007.

83. Michael de la Merced and Keith Bradsher, "Morgan Stanley to Sell Stake to China
Amid Loss," *New York Times*, 19 December 2007.

84. William Mellor and Le-Min Lim, 27 February 2008.

85. Bob Davis, "China Investment-Fund Head Says Focus is on 'Portfolios'," *The Wall Street Journal*, 1 February 2008.

86. "China's Wealth Fund to Invest in JC Flowers Fund," Indiainfoline.com, 8 February 2008. See also Paul Maidment, "Wealth of Bad Thinking on Sovereign Funds," Forbes.com, 8 February 2008.

87. "China's CIC Eyes Noncontrolling Company Stakes," Reuters.com, 4 April 2008.

88. The BP executive board's actual sentiments concerning the CIC purchase are likely more sanguine. During Margret Thatcher's privatization campaign in the late 1980s, BP shares were sold in a sequence of public offerings. During this process, the Kuwait Investment Authority purchased a 20% share in BP—a move that promoted strong opposition from the British government. The Kuwait fund later sold much of its stake as part of an effort to finance rebuilding of the country following Operation Desert Storm in 1991.

89. Graeme Wearden, "Chinese Sovereign Wealth Fund Buys L1 Stake in BP," *The Guardian*, 15 April 2008.

90. Henny Sender, Chip Cummins, Greg Hitt, and Jason Singer, "As Oil Hits High, Mideast Buyers Go on A Spree," *The Wall Street Journal*, 21 September 2007.

91. "China Investment Corporation Unveils Investment Plan," Xinhua.com, Beijing, 8 November 2007.

92. David McCormick, Testimony before the Senate Committee on Banking, Housing and Urban Affairs, United States Senate, Washington DC, 14 November 2007.

93. Alan Larson, "Investments and Acquisitions in the United States by Government Entities," Testimony before the Committee on Banking, Housing, and Urban Affairs, United States Senate, Washington DC, 14 November 2007; Gerald Lyons, "State Capitalism: The rise of sovereign wealth funds," Testimony before the Committee on Banking, Housing, and Urban Affairs, United States Senate, Washington DC, 14 November 2007; and Edwin Truman, "Sovereign Wealth Fund Acquisitions and Other Foreign Government Investments in the United States: Assessing the Economic and National Security Implications," Testimony before the Committee on Banking, Housing, and Urban Affairs, United States Senate, Washington DC, 14 November 2007.

94. Carter Dougherty, "Europe Looks at Controls on State-Owned Investors," *International Herald Tribune*, 13 July 2007.

95. Ibid.

96. Arron Back, "China's Sovereign Wealth Fund Takes a Cautious Approach," *The Wall Street Journal*, 29 November 2007.

97. Ibid.

98. Wenran Jiang, "China Flexes Its Muscle on Wall Street Redux," *China Brief*, 29 November 2007, VII (22).

99. Daniella Markheim, Terry Miller, and Anthony Kim, "Sovereign Wealth Funds No Cause for Panic," WebMemo, Number 1713, Heritage Foundation, Washington DC, 30 November 2007.

100. Leonora Walet, "China Investment Corporation Warns Western Governments Against Protectionism," AFX News Limited, Forbes.com, 10 December 2007.

101. Ibid.

102. Victoria Ruan, "China Tries to Allay Fears Over Its Investment Pool," *The Wall Street Journal*, 12 December 2007.

103. Mure Dickie, "Beijing Defends Sovereign Funds," *Financial Times*, 7 January 2008.

104. Bob Davis, 1 February 2008.

105. Alan Wheatley, "China's Wealth Fund Eyes Charter of Principles—EU," *The Guardian*, 25 February 2008. China's insistence on developing its own set of principles for sovereign wealth fund management should not come as a surprise. Beijing opted for a similar course of action when pressure mounted for Chinese membership in the Missile Technology Control Regime. Rather than sign the existing protocols, Beijing published an internal document that proved a nearly verbatim copy of the international agreement. Why? Primarily national pride and continuing animosity to any perceived impingement on China's sovereignty. This sensitivity can be traced to China's "century of humiliation," an era of Western political domination of the Middle Kingdom that began with the Opium War in 1839.

106. The Group of Seven (or now G8—the G7 plus Russia) is an international forum for the governments of Canada, France, Germany, Italy, Japan, Russia, the United Kingdom, and the United States. These countries represent about 65% of the world's economy.

107. Victoria Ruan, "China's Investment Fund Pushes Back," *The Wall Street Journal*, 7 March 2008.

108. Ibid.

109. Bei Hu, "China Wealth Fund Sets 'Conservative' Return Target," Bloomberg.com, 2 April 2008. Wang also confirmed suspicions about the potentially unrealistic expectations that China's then-booming stock market had raised in Beijing. Commenting on the losses CIC incurred when Blackstone share prices plunged following the firm's initial public offering (IPO), Wang said "personally, I'm not an IPO kind of person. But my colleagues unfortunately are typical Chinese. They think IPOs always make money."

110. "China Addresses Wealth Fund Concerns," CBSNews.com, 4 April 2008. See also Thomas Wilkins, "A Code of Conduct for Sovereign Wealth Fund 'Stupid' Says CIC," ChinaStakes.com, 8 April 2008.

111. Tamora Vidaillet, "China Fund Eyes Commercial Goals, Private Equity," Reuters.com, 3 June 2008.

112. Jason Dean, "Can China Fund Meet Tricky Task?" *The Wall Street Journal*, 1 October 2007.

113. "China Wealth Fund Seeks to be a Stabilizing Presence in Global Markets," Xinhua.com, Beijing, 30 November 2007.

114. Jason Dean, 1 October 2007.

115. Michael Pettis, 24 September 2007, "China's Sovereign Wealth Fund," Piaohaoreport. sampasite.com, 24 September 2007.

116. "China Wealth Fund Seeks to be a Stabilizing Presence in Global Markets," Xinhua.com, Beijing, 30 November 2007.

117. "China Investment Corporation Unveils Investment Plan," Xinhua.com, Beijing, 8 November 2007.

118. Keith Bradsher, 29 November 2007.

119. Tan Wei, "China's CIC likely to Diversify away from Further U.S. Banking Sector Investments, Source Says," *Financial Times*, 30 December 2007.

120. An index fund is a passively managed mutual fund that tries to mirror the performance of a specific index, such as the S&P 500. An index fund aims to replicate the movements of an index of a specific financial market, or a set of rules of ownership that are held constant, regardless of market conditions.

Tracking can be achieved by trying to hold all of the securities in the index, in the same proportions as the index. Other methods include statistically sampling the market and holding "representative" securities. Many index funds rely on a computer model with little or no human input in the decision as to which securities to purchase and is therefore a form of passive management.

121. Keith Bradsher, "$200 Billion to Invest, But in China," *The New York Times*, 29 November 2007.

122. Bob Davis, 1 February 2008.

123. "China Sovereign Wealth Fund to Target Range of Assets: Report," Agency France Press, Shanghai, 3 March 2008.

124. Alan Wheatley, "China's Wealth Fund Sets Out Its Stall," *International Herald Tribune*, 4 January 2008.

125. Jamil Anderlini, "China Wealth Fund's Early Coming of Age," *Financial Times*, 20 December 2007. A similar argument appeared in an investment blog posted on a British Web site. According to an unnamed analyst, "the Chinese government has been unnerved by the prospect of the pricing power a BHP/Rio Tinto combination would have in key industrial materials for China's roaring economy . . . Via its dramatic stakebuilding yesterday, it could be that China wants to establish a seat at the table to help safeguard its position in this scenario" ("Chinese Muscle Flexing," Business.scotsman.com 2 February 2008).

126. Chinalco is said to have raised $13 billion for the deal; the remaining $1.1 billion came from Alcoa.

127. Selwyn Parker, "The Wheels and Deals of China Inc," Sundayherald.com, 9 February 2008. A bit of historical trivia is in order at this point. In April 2008, China's Rio Tinto proved to be the first profitable acquisition that Beijing had made since entering the sovereign fund wealth club—earning Beijing a potential profit of $860 million after only owning the stock for a little more than two months (Dana Cimilluca, "China's Simple Strategy Yields Rio Tinto Windfall," *The Wall Street Journal*, 17 April 2008.

128. Tamora Vidaillet, 3 June 2008.

129. Michael Martin, "China's Sovereign Wealth Fund," CRS Report for Congress, Congressional Research Service, Washington DC, 22 January 2008: 16–18.

130. Ibid, 1.

131. Representative Marcy Kaptur, "Sovereign Wealth Funds: Selling Our National Security," testimony before the United States-China Economic and Security Review Commission, Washington DC, 7 February 2008. Note that the U.S.-China Economic and Security Review Commission is responsible for monitoring and investigating the national security implications of the trade relationship between the two countries.

132. Peter Morici, "Investments by Sovereign Wealth Funds in the United States," testimony before the United States-China Economic and Security Review Commission, Washington DC, 7 February 2008.

133. Peter Navarro, "Testimony of Business Professor Peter Navarro," testimony before the United States-China Economic and Security Review Commission, Washington DC, 7 February 2008. Apparently Navarro's remarks were so inflammatory they were considered good television—CBS News used the professor as a counterpart to Gao Xiping in its 6 April 2008 *60 Minutes* report on the China Investment Corporation.

134. Brad Setser, "Testimony of Brad Setser, Fellow, Geoeconomics, Council on Foreign Relations," testimony before the United States-China Economic and Security Review Commission, Washington DC, 7 February 2008.

135. Daniella Markheim, "Implications of Sovereign Wealth Fund Investments for U.S. National Security," testimony before the United States-China Economic and Security Review Commission, Washington DC, 7 February 2008.

Chapter 3—Investing Like a Sovereign Wealth Fund

1. "Investments—World Grows More Wary of Sovereign Wealth Funds," Asiamoney. com, November 2007. Willem Buiter is a former member of the Bank of England's monetary policy committee.

2. This concern with sovereign wealth fund investment performance is in no way limited to China. In May 2008, Arab businessmen who were gathered for the World Economic Forum in Sharm el-Sheikh called for private control of the sovereign wealth funds. This call for privatization was based on a desire to earn maximum returns and alleviate international concerns about sovereign wealth fund transparency. ("Top Gulf Businessmen Call for Sovereign Fund Privatization," *The Times*, London, 23 May 2008.)

3. William Miracky, Davis Dyer, Drosten Fisher, Tony Goldner, Loic Lagarde, and Vicente Piedrahita, *Assessing the Risks: The Behaviors of Sovereign Wealth Funds in the Global Economy* (Monitor Company Group, New York, June 2008).

4. Harry Wilson, "Sovereign Wealth Funds Start Flexing Their Financial Muscle," Financialnews-us.com, 7 January 2008.

5. James Saft, "The Sovereign Wealth Fund Sell Signal," Reuters, 27 January 2008.

6. Japanese losses incurred as a result of real estate speculation in the U.S., particularly in New York City and Honolulu, serve as object lessons for would-be financial advisors. The most infamous example was Mitsubishi Corporation's purchase of 80% of the Rockefeller Center for $1.4 billion in 1989. Despite a subsequent investment of almost $500 million on upgrades and maintenance, the Japanese corporation walked away from the New York City landmark in 1995 (Stephanie Strom, "Japanese Scrap $2 Billion Stake in Rockefeller," *New York Times*, 12 September 1995). What were the final damages? According to Bloomberg, Japanese investors spent an estimated $78 billion on U.S properties between 1985 and 1995. The subsequent U.S. recession resulted in Japanese losses ranging between 50% and 80% of total initial investment (David Levitt, "New York's Chrysler Building Bought by Abu Dhabi Fund," Bloomberg.com, 9 July 2008).

7. Originally founded as an investment firm in 1923, Bear Sterns was the poster child of a failed financial institution during the 2007–2008 subprime crisis. In early March 2008, the firm's stock value plummeted from over $90 a share to a final sales price of approximately $2. (This price, the purchase offer provided by J. P. Morgan, was ultimately adjusted to $10.) In order to close the deal with direct ramifications for Bear Sterns's over 14,000 employees, the U.S. Federal Reserve had to agree to cover the almost $30 billion the failed firm had invested in mortgage-backed securities and other options. (Andrew Sorkin, "J. P. Morgan Pays $2 a Share for Bear Sterns," *New York Times*, 17 March 2008.)

8. Michael Flaherty, "Sovereign Funds Steer Clear of Wall Street," Reuters, Hong Kong, 17 March 2008.

9. Similar grim predictions appeared in financial newsletters and news sources. AsiaSentinel argued that sovereign wealth funds have discovered that helping out Western banks "wasn't such a good idea" (Philip Bowring, "Life Gets Tough for Asia's Sovereign Wealth Funds," Asiasentinel.com, 17 March 2008), and a commentator for Bloomberg wrote, "no doubt [sovereign wealth funds] will now be extra cautious about investing in U.S. financial stocks. But what about the billions of dollars they have already committed? The fate of those investments is now in the domain of luck and prayers. The fund managers can only hope they haven't bitten off more risk than their political masters can chew" (Andy Mukherjee, "Sovereign Funds Not Faring Well on Bank Investments," Business.theage.com, 18 March 2008).

10. David Enrich, Robin Sidel, and Susanne Craig, "World Rides to Wall Street's Rescue," *Wall Street Journal*, 16 January 2008.

11. Rick Carew, "Government Funds Take a Beating," *Wall Street Journal*, 23 January 2008.

12. Michael Sesit, "Sovereign Funds Invest Where Buffett Won't," Blomberg.com, 4 January 2008. Warren Buffett, Chairman of Berkshire Hathaway (based in Omaha, Nebraska), is regarded as one of the world's best investors. His investment skills have paid off; *Forbes* declared Buffett the richest man in the world as of February 2008 (Luisa Kroll, "The World's Billionaires," Forbes.com, 5 March 2008). Buffett's response to U.S. financial institutions seeking cash in December 2007 was the following: "So far we have not seen a deal that causes me to start salivating." (Buffett made the remark during a 26 December 2007 appearance on CNBC.)

13. "Shift Away from U.S. Dollar Forecast," *The Australian*, Sydney, 29 March 2008.

14. Henny Sender, "How a Gulf Petro-State Invests its Oil Riches," *Wall Street Journal*, 24 August 2007. Of note, Al Sa'ad is also lowering Kuwait's exposure to dollar-denominated assets. The *Journal's* observation upon learning of this decision is instructive for U.S. policymakers: "That shift might lower the appetite for low-yielding investments such as the bonds the U.S. government must sell in large numbers to finance its budget and trade deficits. All else being equal, reduced buying of Treasuries and other U.S. securities would tend to weaken the dollar and make U.S. exports more competitive globally, but also burden businesses and other consumers in the U.S. by pushing up interest rates."

15. Anna Cha, "Foreign Wealth Funds Defend U.S. Investments," *Washington Post*, 27 March 2008.

16. Geraldine Fabrikant, "Yale Endowment Grows 28%, Topping $22 Billion," *New York Times*, 27 September 2007.

17. William Symonds, "How to Invest Like Harvard," BusinessWeek.com, 27 December 2004.

18. Craig Karmin, "Harvard Fund Hits a Record," *Wall Street Journal*, 22 August 2007.

19. Steven Syre, "Harvard Fund Posts Good But Not Great Year," *Boston Globe*, 20 September 2006.

20. Harvard University Financial Report—Fiscal Year 2007, Harvard, 30 September 2007.

21. Harvard is not alone in this wariness. In February 2008, a manager from Dynamic EAFE Value Class told a panel that his firm's global fund had gone from one third in the Americas, Europe, and Asia to 12% in the United States, approximately 30% in Europe, and 35% in Asia. Why? "The U.S. credit crisis." (Sonita Horvitch, "The Panel's Picks and Pans," Financialpost.com, 14 February 2008.)

22. E.S. Browning, "Stocks Tarnished by 'Lost Decade,'" *Wall Street Journal*, 26 March 2008.

23. Harvard University Financial Report—Fiscal Year 2007, Harvard, 30 September 2007.

24. For instance, see: "Emerging Markets Performance Review: Most Countries Significantly Higher," Seekingalpha.com, 6 July 2007. Of note, this performance is highly erratic; 2008 will likely prove a poor year to have remained heavily invested in emerging markets.

25. Harvard University Financial Report—Fiscal Year 2007, Harvard, 30 September 2007.

26. Geraldine Fabrikant, 27 September 2007.

27. Ibid.

28. The Yale Endowment—2007, Yale University, 2007.

29. Ibid. Yale states that it was the first institutional investor to pursue "absolute return strategies." The school notes that it began employing this asset class in July 1990, with a target allocation of 15% of its portfolio.

30. Ibid.

31. Ibid.

32. Ibid.

33. Ibid. Yale apparently can't refrain from taking a dig at Harvard on this success. According to the Endowment's 2007 annual report, "the success of Yale's program led to a 1995 Harvard Business School case study . . . The popular case study was updated in 1997, 2000, 2003, and again in 2006."

34. Ibid.

35. Ibid. Yale states that its fixed-income asset class has earned an annual return of 6.4%, exceeding the industry standard by 0.5%. Yale is not alone in arguing that bonds are not a choice investment. Analysts at Morgan Stanley have made similar arguments, specifically targeting sovereign wealth funds. In a "Global Economic Form" article released 1 June 2007, Morgan Stanley analysts reported that "the average excess return on equities over bonds is around 3.5%–4% (David Miles, "Sovereign Wealth Funds and Bond and Equity Prices," Global Economic Forum, Morgan Stanley, London, 1 June 2007).

36. "Learning from the Harvard and Yale Endowments," Seekingalpha.com, 20 November 2006.

37. This was one of the earliest U.S. Congressional hearings on sovereign wealth funds. Lyon's paper, "State Capitalism: The Rise of Sovereign Wealth Funds," (13 November 2007) featured his analysis and work accomplished by Oxford Analytica.

38. "Should Sovereign Wealth Funds be Regulated?" Brookings Institution, Washington DC, 6 December 2007. The 6 December 2007 panel featured: Martin Baily, Senior Fellow at Brookings; Lael Brainard, Vice President and Director at Brookings Global Economy and Development; Diana Farrell, Director at McKinsey Global Institute; and Gerald Lyons, Chief Economist at Standard Chartered Bank.

39. "Sovereign Wealth Fund Briefing," Brookings Institution, Washington DC, Transcript prepared by Anderson Court Reporting, 6 December 2007, pp. 32–33.

40. Ibid, p. 36.

41. *Temasek Review 2007: Creating Value*, Singapore, August 2007, p. 10.

42. Ibid, p. 38.

43. Jason Leow, "The $2 Billion China Bet," *Wall Street Journal*, 5 December 2007.

44. Sender, 24 August 2007.

45. Michael Flaherty, "Sovereign Funds Steer Clear of Wall Street," Reuters, New York, 17 March 2008.

46. Henny Sender, "Kuwait Chief Focuses on Long-Term Opportunities," *Financial Times*, London, 1 January 2008.

47. Ibid.

48. Natsuko Waki, "Sovereign Funds Seek Wealth Outside Developed World," *Guardian*, London, 9 April 2008.

49. Ibid.

50. Ibid.

51. Saeed Azhar, "Norway Oil Fund to Lift Emerging Market Exposure," Reuters, Singapore, 8 July 2008.

52. Ibid.

53. Stefania Biahchi and Shaji Mathew, "Istithmar Weighs China Investment," *Wall Street Journal*, 16 January 2008.

54. Peter Apps, "Sovereign wealth Funds Could Eclipse U.S. Output, Report," Reuters, London, 28 April 2008.

55. Henny Sender, "Sovereign Wealth Funds Find New Equity Bedfellows," *Financial Times*, London, 15 February 2008. TPG Capital is considered one of the world's four elite "megafunds" in the private equity industry (TPG, The Blackstone Group, KKR, and The Carlyle Group). TPG has historically focused on consumer/retail, media and telecommunications, industrials, technology, travel/leisure, and health care. Notable companies that TPG has owned or invested in over the years include Continental Airlines, Ducati, Neiman Marcus, Burger King, J. Crew, Lenovo, MGM, Seagate, Alltel Wireless, Harrah's, Avaya, Freescale Semiconductor, and Univision.

56. Ibid.

57. "Abu Dhabi Invests $600m in Apollo Fund," Gulf Daily News, Bahrain, 17 June 2006. The purchase came during Apollo's initial public listing. The fund was reported to be attempting to raise an estimated $2.5 billion with the listing.

58. "Prequin Sovereign Wealth Review: Activity in Private Equity and Private Real Estate," Private Equity Intelligence, New York, 2008.

59. David Bogoslaw, "Big Traders Dive into Dark Pools," Businessweek.com, 3 October 2007.

60. Liz Peek, "'Dark Pools' Threaten Wall Street," *New York Sun*, 16 October 2007.

61. Wall Street is well aware of this concern and is seeking to address the problem by sharing access to information on transactions passed through the alternative trading systems. This initial step comes as Wall Street announced that there are now 42 such "dark pool" trading systems, up from the seven "dark pool" networks that were in operation only five years ago (Donna Kardos, "Wall Street Brokerages Look to Shed Light on Dark Pools," *Wall Street Journal*, 20 May 2008).

62. "Sovereign Wealth and Private Equity Forge Strong Links," Arabianbusiness.com, 18 May 2008.

63. Ibid.

64. Ibid.

65. Jonathan Karp and Michael Corkery, "Middle East Players Arrive," *Wall Street Journal*, 12 March 2008. Dubai Istithmar is also said to own a majority stake in New York's Mandarin Hotel. In 2007, the fund reportedly sold two office towers in New York for more than $1 billion a piece, suggesting that real estate speculation is a potentially lucrative element of the sovereign wealth funds' investment strategy.

66. David Levitt, "New York's Chrysler Building Bought by Abu Dhabi Fund," Bloomberg.com, 9 July 2008.

67. Jonathan Karp and Michael Corkery, 12 March 2008.

68. Dan Pimlott, "More Middle East Funds Stream into New York Assets," *Financial Times*, London, 31 May 2008.

69. Connie Gore, "Sovereign Wealth Funds Eyeing More Real Estate," GlobeSt.com, 29 April 2008.

70. Ibid.

71. Arif Sharif, "Qatar's Fund to Invest in Asian Property, U.S. Assets," Bloomberg.com, 6 May 2008.

72. Ibid.

73. Tara Wilkinson, "Banks See State-owned Asset Pools as Rivals and Saviors," Financialnews-us.com, 4 April 2008.

74. Ibid.

75. "China's Overseas Investments in Oil and Gas Production," Eurasia Group, New York, 16 October 2006. China began seeking such deals in 1993, but sealed its first big deals in 1997 with Kazakhstan and Sudan. China's oil deals with Iran do not technically fall within this category because of Tehran's peculiar investment laws. Under Iranian law there is no equity investment in the country's oil and gas sector. Instead foreign companies are allowed to develop a field to the point at which it is ready to begin production. In return, the Iranians "buyback" the field by providing the foreign firm a guaranteed rate of return, paid in oil. Under this arrangement, the Chinese have signed a $1.5 billion deal to construct a gas condensate refinery in Iran, and they appear to be pursuing a range of smaller contracts.

76. David Cho and Thomas Heath, "Oil and Trade Gains Make Major Investors of Developing Nations," *Washington Post*, 30 October 2007.

77. "Investments—World Grows More Wary of Sovereign Wealth Funds," Asiamoney. com, November 2007.

78. Ibid.

79. Robert Zoellick, "A Challenge of Economic Statecraft," The World Bank, Washington DC, 2 April 2008.

80. For a comprehensive evaluation of China's strategic objectives see: "China's Foreign Policy and 'Soft Power' in South America, Asia, and Africa," Congressional Research Service, Library of Congress, April 2008.

81. Raymond Learsy, "Oil at $111 a Barrel: We are Being 'Sovereignly Screwed'!" Huffingtonpost.com, 17 March 2008.

82. According to Representative Bart Stupak (D-MI), spectators have increased their share of oil futures contracts on the NYMEX from 37% in 2000 to 71% in 2008 (Matthew Perrone, "Calls Growing in Congress to Restrict Oil Speculation," Associated Press, 24 June 2008).

83. Christopher Rugaber, "Analysts: Government Funds Heat Up Oil Prices," Associated Press, Washington DC, 16 March 2008. Rumors of oil-producing nations using their sovereign wealth funds to speculate in the oil futures market continued to appear in late June 2008. London's *Sunday Times* on 29 June 2008 ran a story in which unnamed "experts" were cited as arguing that "oil-producing nations are getting a double benefit from the soaring price of crude . . . Not only are revenues booming, but their sovereign wealth funds have been pumping money into the commodity index futures, helping to boost the price" ("Double Boon for Oil Nations from the Soaring Price of Crude," *Sunday Times*, London, 29 June 2008).

84. Claudia Cattaneo, "Funds Circling Oil Industry," Financialpost.com, 14 May 2008. Much of the Canadian firms' interest in sovereign wealth investors was directly pinned to the ongoing international credit crunch. For instance, UTS was seeking to raise $2 billion by June 2009 and had discovered that conventional sources were simply not available.

85. Ibid.

86. Jonathan Wheatley, "Brazil's Sovereign Fund to Target Currency," *Financial Times*, London, 10 December 2007.

87. Andre Soliani and Joshua Goodman, "Brazil Fund to Help Stem Currency Rally, Mantega Says," Bloomberg.com, 13 May 2008.

88. Andre Soliani and Carla Simoes, "Mantega Says Brazil Wealth Fund May Start Before July," Bloomberg.com, 5 May 2008. Brazil's inability to agree on the fund's establishment boils down to an argument between the Ministry of Finance and the central bank. The Finance Ministry wants to tap into Brazil's estimated $195 billion foreign exchange reserves to open the fund. The central bank insists that the money be found elsewhere. The Finance Minster has suggested using tax money in excess of Brazil's budget surplus target of 3.8% of gross domestic product as an initial source of capital for the sovereign wealth fund (Walter Brandimarte, "Brazil Sovereign Fund will not Affect Reserves," Reuters, Washington DC, 22 October 2007; and Andre Soliani and Joshua Goodman, "Brazil Fund to Help Stem Currency Rally, Mantega Says," Bloomberg.com, 13 May 2008).

89. An economist with Brazil's central bank declared that the available funds—potentially up to $180 billion—would have no lasting impact on exchange rates (Jonathan Wheatley, "Brazil's Sovereign Fund to Target Currency," *Financial Times*, London, 10 December 2007).

90. Heather Timmons, "Dubai Says it Now Has 2.2% of Deutsche Bank," *International Herald Tribune*, London, 16 May 2007. In addition to this investment, Dubai was offering potential business partners with a new infrastructure that featured zero taxes and no penalties on repatriating profits. Of note, Dubai is considered the commercial hub of the world's top oil exporting region.

91. Jerome Corsi, "Sheikdom Shakedown: Dubai Moves on NASDAQ," WorldNetDaily. com, 20 September 2007.

92. The NASDAQ and OMX deal reportedly cost Dubai $4.9 billion (Karl Ritter, "NASDAQ, Bourse Dubai Raise Bid for OMX," Associated Press, New York, 26 September 2007).

93. Julia Werdigier, "Dubai Bourse Buys Stake in NASDAQ and London Exchange," *International Herald Tribune*, London, 20 September 2007.

94. Henny Sender, Chip Cummins, Greg Hitt, and Jason Singer, "As Oil Hits High, Mideast Buyers Go on a Spree," *Wall Street Journal*, 21 September 2007.

95. Chuck Mollenkamp, Edward Taylor, and Anita Raghaven, "UBS's Subprime Hit Deepens Credit Woes," *Wall Street Journal*, 11 December 2007.

96. Ariana Cha, "Foreign Wealth Funds Defend U.S. Investments," *Washington Post*, 27 March 2008.

97. "Washington Mutual Filing Details Quest for Cash," *Seattle Times*, 10 May 2008.

98. Steve Slater and Clara Ferreira-Marques, "Barclays Set for Bumper Equity Issue," Reuters, London, 16 June 2008.

99. Zachary Mider, "Lazard's Parr Says 'Backlash' Damps Sovereign Interest in Banks," Bloomberg.com, 14 May 2008.

100. Ryan Donmoyer and Alison Fitzgerald, "Rubenstein Says 'Enormous Losses Unrecognized,'" Bloomberg.com, 12 May 2008.

101. Yalman Onaran, "Banks Keep $35 Billion Markdown Off Income Statements," Bloomberg.com, 19 May 2008. The magnitude of the problem facing European and U.S. financial institutions as a result of the subprime crisis should not be downplayed. As Samuel Hayes, a professor emeritus at Harvard Business School put it, "[the banks] have to keep raising capital levels, there's no getting around that fact. Perception is so important here. If investors or creditors feel a bank doesn't have a strong enough capital cushion to face further write-downs, that could prove problematic." How much of a cushion is necessary? According to Michael Mayo, a New York-based financial analyst at Deutsche

Bank, "the $100 billion hole between write-downs and capital raised so far needs to be filled. If you don't fill that hole, with the 20-to-1 leverage existing on average out there, you need to de-lever $2 trillion in assets. You can do that or raise more capital." This can be accomplished through share buybacks and/or outside investors such as sovereign wealth funds, a process that was becoming increasingly difficult as of May 2008. The biggest losers were Citigroup with $42.9 billion in write-downs and credit loss, Merrill Lynch with $37 billion, and HSBC with $19.5 billion (Yalman Onaran, "Banks Keep $35 Billion Markdown Off Income Statements," Bloomberg.com, 19 May 2008).

102. David Rothnie, "Sovereign Wealth Draws Team East," Financialnews-us.com, 1 May 2008.

103. Richard Beals, Mike Verdin, and Una Galani, "Citi Executive's Move to Mideast Could Help Exploit Advantages," *Wall Street Journal*, 9 May 2008.

104. Michael Flaherty, "J. P. Morgan Appoints Bear Asia CEO Sovereign Wealth Head," Reuters, London, 27 June 2008.

105. Sources: Associated Press, *International Herald Tribune*, Reuters, and the *Wall Street Journal*. All data is current as of March 2008.

106. Matthew Brown and Will McSheehy, "Bahrain's Fund Seeks U.S. Insurer Stakes, Shuns Banks," Bloomberg.com, 19 May 2008.

107. The potential for sovereign wealth funds to start focusing on the insurance industry has not gone unnoticed in consulting circles. For example, see: Priti Rajagopalan and Sunil Rongala, "Insurance Firms: The Missing Link in the Sovereign Wealth Fund Acquisition Spree," Deloitte Research Report, Deloitte Touche Tohmatsu, New York, July 2008.

108. "Sovereign Wealth Funds: A Shopping List," *New York Times*, 27 November 2007.

109. "Sovereign Wealth Funds and Private Equity: Increased Access, Decreased Transparency," Service Employees International Union, Washington DC, April 2008.

110. As of April 2008, the Nikkei Stock Average of 225 listed companies had dropped 26% since June 2007, a steeper decline than any other developed market.

111. Yuka Hayashi, "Japan Hopes to Lure Sovereign Investors," *Wall Street Journal*, 8 April 2008.

112. Ibid.

113. "UK to Attract Sovereign Wealth Funds," UKinvest.gov.uk, 14 April 2008.

114. Dennis Moore, "Fed Welcomes Sovereign Wealth Fund Capital Raised by U.S. Banks," Thompson Financial News, Forbes.com, 24 April 2008.

115. Charles Schumer, "Opening Statement," Joint Economic Committee Hearing, Washington DC, 13 February 2008.

116. Eizenstat currently serves as the Chair of the International Practice at Covington and Burling LLP. In addition to his appointment as an ambassador, Eizenstat has served as Undersecretary of Commerce for International Trade, Undersecretary of State for Economic, Business and Agricultural Affairs, and Deputy Secretary of the Treasury.

117. David McCormick, "Testimony Before the Joint Economic Committee," Joint Economic Committee of the United States Congress, Washington DC, 13 February 2008.

118. Ibid.

119. Stuart Eizenstat, "Do Sovereign Wealth Funds Make the U.S. Economy Stronger or Pose National Security Risks?" Joint Economic Committee of the United States Congress, Washington DC, 13 February 2008.

120. Ibid.

121. Scott Alvarez, "Statement Before the Committee on Banking, Housing and Urban Affairs," U.S. Senate Committee on Banking, Housing and Urban Affairs, Washington DC, 24

April 2008. According to Alvarez, the decision to legally treat sovereign wealth funds as a "company" is founded upon a precedent set in 1982 when the Board of Governors found that an investment fund controlled by the Italian government, the Istituto per la Ricostruzione Industriale, was structured as a corporate vehicle and was therefore a company under the Bank Holding Company Act, a finding that the Board of Governors reiterated in a public letter from William W Wiles, then Secretary of the Board, on 19 August 1988.

122. Ibid.

123. Ibid.

124. Ibid.

125. Ibid.

126. Ibid.

127. Ibid.

128. Jeanne Archibald, "U.S. Regulatory Framework for Assessing Foreign Investments," U.S. Senate Committee on Banking, Housing and Urban Affairs, Washington DC, 24 April 2008.

129. Ibid.

130. Ibid.

131. Ethiopis Tafara, "The Regulatory Framework for Sovereign Investments," U.S. Senate Committee on Banking, Housing and Urban Affairs, Washington DC, 24 April 2008.

132. Ibid.

133. Ibid.

134. Ibid.

135. William Miracky, et al, June 2008.

136. Ibid.

137. Ibid.

138. Ibid.

139. David Miles, "Sovereign Wealth Funds and Bond and Equity Prices," Global Economic Forum, Morgan Stanley, New York, 1 June 2007.

140. Ibid.

141. Henny Sender, 1 January 2008.

Chapter 4—Evaluating Sovereign Wealth Funds

1. Kristin Halvorsen, "Norway's Sovereign Fund Sets an Ethical Example," *Financial Times*, 15 February 2008.

2. The G7 (Group of Seven) is the meeting of the finance ministers from the world's seven industrialized nations. Formed in 1976, when Canada joined the Group of Six, the G7 is composed of Canada, France, Germany, Italy, Japan, the United Kingdom, and the United States of America.

3. Larry Elliot, "Chancellor Backs G7 Move to get Tough on Sovereign Wealth Funds," *The Guardian*, 20 October 2007.

4. Sean O'Grady, "Sovereign Wealth Funds Hostile to International Code of Conduct," *The Independent*, 25 January 2008.

5. Ibid.

6. Ibid.

7. Steven Weisman, "Overseas Funds Resist Calls for a Code of Conduct," *New York Times*, 9 February 2008. See also Tahani Karrar, "Middle East Cranking Up Opposition to Guidelines for Sovereign Funds," MarketWatch.com, 2 April 2008.

8. Steven Weisman, 9 February 2008.

9. Ibid.

10. Ibid.

11. Yousef Al Otaiba, "Abu Dhabi's Investment Guidelines," Director of International Affairs, The Government of Abu Dhabi, 12 March 2008

12. Ibid.

13. Ibid.

14. "Joint Release of Policy Principles for Sovereign Wealth Funds and Countries Receiving Sovereign Wealth Fund Investment by the United States, Abu Dhabi and Singapore," Ministry of Finance, Singapore, 21 March 2008.

15. Ibid.

16. Ibid.

17. Peter Mandelson, "Speech before the Organization for Economic Cooperation and Development," OECD, Paris, France, 28 March 2008.

18. Rita De Ramos, "Agreement on Sovereign Wealth Funds," BusinessWeek.com, 25 March 2008.

19. The International Working Group members are Australia, Azerbaijan, Bahrain, Botswana, Canada, Chile, China, Equatorial Guinea, Iran, Iceland, Korea (South), Kuwait, Libya, Mexico, New Zealand, Norway, Qatar, Russia, Singapore, Timor-Leste, Trinidad & Tobago, The United Emirates, and the United States. Permanent observers in the organization are Saudi Arabia, Vietnam, the OECD, and the World Bank.

20. "International Working Group of Sovereign wealth Funds is Established to Facilitate Work on Voluntary Principles," Press Release 08/01, International Monetary Fund. Washington DC, 1 May 2008.

21. Paul Carrel, "Kuwait's KIA Warns Berlin not to Regulate Wealth Funds," Reuters, Berlin, 18 May 2008.

22. Kristin Halvorsen, "Sovereign Wealth Funds," Paper prepared for OECD Forum 2008, "Climate Change, Growth, Stability," Paris, France, 3 June 2008.

23. Ibid. Underlines are as they appeared in the original document.

24. Kevin Lim, "Wealth Funds Meet in Singapore to Ally Western Fears," Reuters, Singapore, 8 July 2008.

25. "International Working Group of Sovereign Wealth Funds to Meet in Singapore on July 9–10," Press Release 08/02, International Monetary Fund, Washington DC, 20 June 2008.

26. Kevin Lim, 8 July 2008.

27. John Jannarone, "Sovereign Wealth Funds Group Aims to Improve Transparency," *The Wall Street Journal*, 10 July 2008.

28. Louise Armistead, "Sovereign Wealth Funds Debate Disclosure Rules," *The Telegraph*, 13 July 2008.

29. John Jannarone, 10 July 2008.

30. "Sovereign Wealth Funds and Recipient Country Policies," Report by the OECD Investment Committee, "Freedom of Investment" Project, Paris, France, 4 April 2008. Founded in 1961, the OECD has 30 member countries: Australia, Austria, Belgium, Canada, Czech Republic, Denmark, Finland, France, Germany, Greece, Hungary, Iceland, Ireland, Italy, Japan, Korea, Luxembourg, Mexico, Netherlands, New Zealand, Norway, Poland, Portugal, Slovak Republic, Spain, Sweden, Switzerland, Turkey, United Kingdom, and United States.

31. Ibid.

32. Ibid.

33. Ibid.

34. Edwin Truman, "Sovereign Wealth Funds: The Need for Greater Transparency and Accountability," *Policy Brief*, Number PB07-6, Peterson Institute for International Economics, Washington DC, August 2007.

35. Edwin Truman, "The Rise of Sovereign Wealth Funds: Impacts on U.S. Foreign Policy and Economic Interests," Testimony before the House Committee on Foreign Affairs, Washington DC, 21 May 2008.

36. Edwin Truman, "Sovereign Wealth Funds: The Need for Greater Transparency and Accountability," August 2007.

37. Ibid.

38. Ibid.

39. Ibid.

40. Edwin Truman, "The Rise of Sovereign Wealth Funds: Impacts on U.S. Foreign Policy and Economic Interests," 21 May 2008. Truman does allow scoring for partial answers. As he notes in his testimony before the House Committee on Foreign Affairs, "For each of the 33 questions, if the answer is an unqualified yes, we score it as '1.' If the answer is no, we score it as '0.' However, partial scores of 0.25, 0.50, and 0.75 are recorded for many elements."

41. Edwin Truman, 21 May 2008.

42. Ibid. Truman credits Doug Dowson with assisting in the research required for filling out the scoreboard.

43. Ibid.

44. Ibid.

45. Jagdish Bhagwati, "Sovereign Wealth Funds and Implications for Policy: Testimony before the Senate Foreign Relations Committee," U.S. Senate Foreign Relations Committee, Washington DC, 11 June 2008. The work Bhagwati cites is reportedly being accomplished by Brad Setser and Arpana Pandey at the Council on Foreign Relations.

46. Carl Linaburg is vice president and cofounder of the Sovereign Wealth Fund Institute. Mr. Linaburg currently works in the asset management industry. Previously he worked for Merrill Lynch, where he conducted research for the Global Private Client division. Carl conducts research on state-owned investment funds worldwide and has been featured in a number of financial publications. He holds a BSc in Finance from the University of South Florida, Tampa.

47. Michael Maduell is president and founder of the Sovereign Wealth Fund Institute. Maduell currently works as a consultant to the investment management and banking industry for an international services firm. Previously he worked for CalPERS, one of the largest public pension funds in the world. He has been featured in several finance and trade publications. He holds a BSc in finance and risk management from California State University, Sacramento.

48. Carl Linaburg and Michael Maduell, "Linaburg-Maduell Transparency Index," Sovereign Wealth Fund Institute, June 2008.

49. Ibid. I have reduced Truman's "scoreboard" here to the 25 sovereign wealth funds that typically appear in media reporting.

50. Carl Linaburg and Michael Maduell, 30 June 2008.

51. Ibid. Date reflects latest posted listing on the Sovereign Wealth Institute Web site. Where country names are repeated in the fund title they have been eliminated for space

purposes. Note, all monetary values have been rounded up from 0.5 or down if 0.4 or below.

52. Dr. Gerard Lyons is an expert on the world economy, international financial system, macroeconomic policy, and global markets. He currently serves as chief economist and group head of global research at Standard Chartered. Lyons is also an economic advisor to the board and is a member of the Bank's Executive Forum. His PhD from the University of London is on "Testing the Efficiency of Financial Futures Markets."

53. Oxford Analytica is an international, independent consulting firm drawing on a network of over 1,000 senior faculty members at Oxford and other major universities and research institutions around the world. Founded in 1975 by Dr. David R. Young, Oxford Analytica has built an international reputation for seasoned judgment on and analysis of the implications of national and international developments facing corporations, banks, governments, and international institutions.

54. Gerald Lyons, "State Capitalism: The Rise of Sovereign Wealth Funds," Global Research, Standard Chartered Bank, London, 15 October 2007.

55. Ibid. By "other" financial institutions I presume Lyons means anyone but his own employer—Standard Chartered Bank.

56. Note, the original study sorted the sovereign wealth funds by holdings rather than transparency. To facilitate comparison with other scales, I have resorted to the top 20—lacking a quantitative measure of transparency to work with. I have accomplished this by placing those with the highest transparency ratings at the top of the list and then sorting like-evaluations on this measure alphabetically.

57. "State Capitalism: The Rise of Sovereign Wealth Funds," 15 October 2007.

58. Ibid.

59. Una Galani and Simon Nixon, "Breakingviews Sovereign Wealth Fund Risk Index," Considered View, Breakingviews.com, 4 January 2008.

60. Ibid.

61. Ibid.

62. Ibid.

63. Ibid.

64. Ibid.

65. Una Galani and Simon Nixon, 4 January 2008.

66. Ibid. Using the Breakingviews' scoring criteria a lower point total is preferred. The lowest possible total score would be a 3, and the highest total score would be a 15. As with other tables, fund names have been shortened to minimize space requirements.

67. Oslo's efforts to diversify the Government Pension Fund-Global's holdings have suffered at least two cases of inadvertent poor timing. In 1998 the Fund managers were authorized to expand private equity investments from essentially nothing to approximately 40% of the overall holdings. The subsequent, and unrelated, market "collapse" in 2000 resulted in a net loss for the Norwegian fund managers, drawing comments like, "they make Norway more poor," and "catastrophic numbers for the oil fund." (Knut Kjaer, "The Norwegian Government Pension Fund and Norges Bank Investment Management," Presentation to the Central Bank of Chile, 3 October 2007.) The Government Pension Fund-Global managers befell a similar misfortune in 2008—right on the heels of a decision to increase the Fund's private equity assets from 40 to 60% of holdings. In late May 2008, the Fund managers announced investments had declined in value by 5.6% during the first quarter of 2008, effectively erasing the 4.3% return the Fund had earned

during calendar year 2007. Unlike critics in 2000–2002, Global Pension Fund-Global monitors in 2008 were more forgiving about the poor performance. As one financial advisor dryly noted, "It's hardly a surprise that any asset manager has lost money recently. I mean, who hasn't?" (Robin Wigglesworth, "Norwegian Wealth Fund's First Quarter Worst on Record," Bloomberg.com, 23 May 2008.)

68. "The Government Pension Fund of Norway," Answers.com 2008.

69. "Government Pension Fund-Global: Annual Report 2007," Norges Bank Investment Management, Oslo, Norway, 2008

70. Ibid.

71. Ibid.

72. Lehman Brothers claims to be the world's leading provider of fixed income benchmarks. The Lehman "Global Family of Indices" is reportedly used by a majority of U.S. and European investors and a growing share of Asian investors. With three decades of service to the global capital markets, Lehman Brothers has teams focused on fixed income benchmarks in New York, London, Tokyo, and Hong Kong.

73. The 21 countries are: Australia, Canada, Denmark, Euro area, Japan, New Zealand, Singapore, Sweden, Switzerland, the United Kingdom, and the United States.

74. According to their Web site, FTSE Group (FTSE) is an independent company jointly owned by *The Financial Times* and the London Stock Exchange. FTSE does not give financial advice to clients, which allows for the provision of truly objective market information. FTSE specializes in the creation and management of over 100,000 equity, bond, and alternative asset class indices. With offices in Beijing, London, Frankfurt, Hong Kong, Boston, Shanghai, Madrid, Paris, New York, San Francisco, Sydney, and Tokyo, FTSE works with partners and clients in 77 countries worldwide.

75. The 27 countries are: Australia, Austria, Belgium, Brazil, Canada, Denmark, Finland, France, Germany, Greece, Hong Kong, Iceland, Italy, Japan, Mexico, the Netherlands, New Zealand, Portugal, Singapore, South Africa, South Korea, Spain, Sweden, Switzerland, Taiwan, the United Kingdom, and the United States.

76. "Government Pension Fund-Global: Annual Report 2007," 2008.

77. Ibid. Public perceptions concerning management costs are a continuing concern for Norges Bank Investment Management and the government of Norway. In 2007 the Ministry of Finance requested Norges Bank provide an outside consulting firm the data required to run a comparison with the management costs of other large pension funds. As it turns out, Norges Bank was more than just cost-competitive. Between 2003 and 2006 the annual average management costs for Norges Banks peer competitors were 13.1%, 12.0%, 13.4%, and 10.8%, respectively. During the same four-year period, Norges bank reported management costs for the Government Pension Fund-Global of 10.3%, 10.5%, 10.6%, and 9.8%. ("Government Pension Fund-Global: Annual Report 2007.")

78. Ibid.

79. Ibid.

80. Mark Fereday and Anthony Cherrington, "Norwegian Government Pension Fund-Global: Annual Performance Evaluation Report 2006," Mercer Investment Consulting, London, March 2007.

81. Ibid.

82. Ibid.

83. "Government Pension Fund-Global: Annual Report 2007," 2008. I would note similar statements on exercising ownership rights have been resident in the annual reports

since at least 2005, and Norges Bank claims to have begun assuming a more active ownership role as early as 2003.

84. Ibid.

85. Ibid.

86. Ibid.

87. Ibid.

88. Ibid.

89. Ibid.

90. "Annual Report 2007," Council on Ethics for the Government Pension Fund-Global, Oslo, 11 January 2008.

91. Ibid.

92. According to the United Nation's Web site, "The Global Compact" is a framework for businesses that are committed to aligning their operations and strategies with ten universally accepted principles in the areas of human rights, labor, the environment, and anticorruption. As the world's largest, global corporate citizenship initiative, the "Global Compact" is first and foremost concerned with exhibiting and building the social legitimacy of business and markets. The "Global Compact's" ten principles in the areas of human rights, labor, the environment, and anticorruption enjoy universal consensus:

- Human Rights
  - Principle 1: Businesses should support and respect the protection of internationally proclaimed human rights; and
  - Principle 2: make sure that they are not complicit in human rights abuses.
- Labor Standards
  - Principle 3: Businesses should uphold the freedom of association and the effective recognition of the right to collective bargaining;
  - Principle 4: the elimination of all forms of forced and compulsory labor;
  - Principle 5: the effective abolition of child labor; and
  - Principle 6: the elimination of discrimination in respect of employment and occupation.
- Environment
  - Principle 7: Businesses should support a precautionary approach to environmental challenges;
  - Principle 8: undertake initiatives to promote greater environmental responsibility; and
  - Principle 9: encourage the development and diffusion of environmentally friendly technologies.
- Anticorruption
  - Principle 10: Businesses should work against corruption in all its forms, including extortion and bribery.

93. The OECD Principles of Corporate Governance were endorsed by OECD Ministers in 1999 and have since become an international benchmark for policy makers, investors, corporations, and other stakeholders worldwide. They have advanced the corporate governance agenda and provided specific guidance for legislative and regulatory initiatives in both OECD and non-OECD countries. According to the OECD, the principles are based upon the following premises:

- The corporate governance framework should promote transparent and efficient markets, be consistent with the rule of law and clearly articulate the
  division of responsibilities among different supervisory, regulatory, and
  enforcement authorities.
- The corporate governance framework should protect and facilitate the exercise of shareholders' rights.
- The corporate governance framework should ensure the equitable treatment of all shareholders, including minority and foreign shareholders. All
  shareholders should have the opportunity to obtain effective redress for violation of their rights.
- The corporate governance framework should recognize the rights of stakeholders established by law or through mutual agreements and encourage
  active cooperation between corporations and stakeholders in creating
  wealth, jobs, and the sustainability of financially sound enterprises.
- The corporate governance framework should ensure that timely and accu-
  rate disclosure is made on all material matters regarding the corporation,
  including the financial situation, performance, ownership, and governance
  of the company.
- The corporate governance framework should ensure the strategic guidance
  of the company, the effective monitoring of management by the board, and
  the board's accountability to the company and the shareholders.

94. "Annual Report 2007," 11 January 2008.

95. Ibid.

96. James Covert, "U.S. Ambassador Blasts Norway Pension Fund's Ethics Policy,"
Dow Jones Newswires, New York, 5 September 2006.

97. "Annual Report 2007," 11 January 2008.

98. Ibid.

99. The Council on Ethics reports it first formally began to consider whether the business of Wal-Mart Stores Inc. (Wal-Mart) might entail complicity by the Fund in serious
or systematic violations of human rights on 27 June 2005.

100. "Annual Report 2006," Council on Ethics for the Government Pension Fund-
Global, Oslo, 6 January 2007.

101. Ibid.

102. According to the Council's 2006 Annual Report, "There is no doubt that working
conditions at textile factories in Asia, Africa and Latin America can be abysmal, and that
Wal-Mart purchases a number of products that are manufactured under unacceptable
conditions. There are numerous reports of child labor, serious violations of working hour
regulations, wages below the local minimum, health hazardous working conditions,
unreasonable punishment, prohibition of unionization and extensive use of a production
system that fosters working conditions bordering on forced labor, and of employees being
locked into production premises etc. in Wal-Mart's supply chain." ("Annual Report 2006,"
Council on Ethics for the Government Pension Fund-Global, Oslo, 6 January 2007.)

103. According to the Council's 2006 Annual Report the charge in question was "discrimination, inter alia by pursuing a wage policy in which women and men receive different pay for the same position and work. The documentation in *Dukes vs. Wal-Mart
Stores Inc.*, appears to show that discrimination of women is widespread in the organization. Such practice is contrary to both special and general human rights norms. The

International Covenant on Civil and Political Rights, and the International Covenant on Economic, Social and Cultural Rights contain explicit provisions (in Articles 2 and 3) that prohibit discriminatory differential treatment of women. The Convention on the Elimination of All Forms of Discrimination Against Women further elaborates this prohibition. The same principle is established in International Labor Organization (ILO) Convention No. 100, Equal Remuneration. Since the USA is party to the International Covenant on Civil and Political Rights, there is, in the Council's view, a risk that the Fund may be complicit in possible violations of this Convention's standards regarding equal treatment of women and men."

The Council goes on to state, "It also appears to be well documented that the company puts a stop to any attempt by employees to form trade unions. Freedom to form trade unions and to join a trade union is a fundamental human right. This right is enshrined in a number of both general and special conventions. The two International Covenants from 1966 (on civil and political, and on economic, social and cultural rights) clearly establish that everyone has the right to freedom of organization, association and assembly. Article 8 of the Covenant on Economic, Social and Cultural Rights states that everyone has the right to *form trade unions and join the trade union of his choice.*" Article 22 of the Covenant on Civil and Political Rights states, "*Everyone shall have the right to freedom of association with others, including the right to form and join trade unions for the protection of his interests.*" The right to organize is also enshrined in ILO Convention no. 87, Freedom of Association, 1948, and in the ILO's Tripartite Declaration of Principles concerning Multinational Enterprises and Social Policy. Even so, US legislation does not always assure actual implementation of the right to organize, and there is therefore a risk of the Fund being complicit in potential violations of this right. Freedom of organization is a fundamental democratic right, and clearly within the scope of what the preparatory work refers to as *fundamental rights.*" ("Annual Report 2006," Council on Ethics for the Government Pension Fund-Global, Oslo, 6 January 2007.)

104. Ibid.

105. Mark Lander and Walter Gibbs, "Norway Backs Its Ethics With Its Cash," *New York Times*, 4 May 2007.

106. James Covert, 5 September 2006.

107. Ibid.

108. Mark Lander and Walter Gibbs, 4 May 2007.

109. "Annual Report 2007," 11 January 2008. The Finance Ministry had requested the Council on Ethics examine companies with operations in Burma in a letter dated 28 September 2007.

110. Ibid.

111. Ibid.

112. Ibid.

113. Ibid.

114. Ibid.

115. For the record, Oslo—via Norges Bank Investment Management—is pursuing an agenda that seeks to constructively address the problem of global warming. According to a Norges Bank statement, the Fund's managers in their discussions with corporate boards have "attached importance to technological development and alignment with new emission and taxation regimes" as a means of tackling greenhouse gas emissions.

116. "Annual Report 2007," 11 January 2008.

117. Jagdish Bhagwati, 11 June 2008.

Chapter 5—Trust but Verify

1. "Trust but verify" was a Ronald Reagan signature phrase. President Reagan typically employed this phrase when dealing with the former Soviet Union. In fact, Reagan liked to introduce the phrase as a translation of the Russian proverb *"Doveryai, no proveryai."*

2. Richard Lugar, "Opening Statement for the Hearing on Sovereign Wealth Funds," U.S. Senate Committee on Foreign Relations, Washington DC, 11 June 2008.

3. In chronological order, these hearings on sovereign wealth funds were: 14 November 2007, Senate Committee on Banking, Housing, and Urban Affairs; 7 February 2008, U.S.-China Economic and Security Review Commission; 10 February 2008, Joint Economic Committee; 24 April 2008, Senate Committee on Banking, Housing, and Urban Affairs; 21 May 2008, House Committee on Foreign Affairs; and 11 June 2008, Senate Committee on Foreign Relations.

4. Jeff Mason, "Obama Said Concerned about Sovereign Wealth Funds," 7 February 2008, Reuters, Omaha, NE.

5. Bill Condie, "Risks of Putting Up Barriers to Sovereign Wealth Fund Saviors," *Evening Standard*, London, 17 July 2008.

6. Joseph Biden, "Opening Statement for the Hearing on Sovereign Wealth Funds," U.S. Senate Committee on Foreign Relations, Washington DC, 11 June 2008.

7. An *ex officio* member of a body is part of the organization by virtue of holding another office. Depending upon the particular body, such a member may or not have the power to vote in the body's decisions. The term is from Latin, meaning "from the office"—intended sense is "by right of office."

8. Restrictions on DNI participation in the CFIUS process likely reflects policymakers' long-standing suspicions about the intelligence community's efforts to dictate political agendas by citing "classified data," and laws prohibiting intelligence collection against U.S. persons and entities. As such, the DNI is to serve as a source of information for CFIUS—but not to engage in a policy debate.

9. In the text that follows, a *review* refers to the initial 30-day CFIUS action; an *investigation* concerns the 45-day CFIUS action that is required for more difficult cases.

10. The phrase "That's the $64,000 question" can be traced back to the CBS radio quiz show *Take It or Leave It*, which ran from 21 April 1940 to 27 July 1947. In 1947, the series switched to NBC. On 10 September 1950, *Take It or Leave It* was changed to *The $64 Question*. CBS TV premiered *The $64,000 Question* on 7 June 1955. The show ran for three years before fading popularity resulted in its cancellation. "That's the $64 question" became common parlance in the 1940s. The phrase was used in reference to a particularly difficult question or problem.

11. "Foreign Investment: Laws and Policies Regulating Foreign Investment in 10 Countries," Government Accountability Office, Washington DC, February 2008.

12. Ted Kassinger and Lilian Tsai, "Closing the CNOOC and Dubai Ports World Debate: The Foreign Investment and National Security Act of 2007," International Trade, O'Melveny and Myers LLP, New York, 30 July 2007.

13. See, e.g.: Paul Rose, "Sovereigns as Shareholders," Draft, Moritz College of Law, Ohio State University, March 2008.

14. Douglas Rediker and Heidi Crebo-Rediker, "Foreign Investment and Sovereign Wealth Funds," Working Paper #1, Global Strategic Finance Initiative, New America Foundation, 25 September 2007.

15. Michael Crittenden, "U.S. Lawmakers Request Probe Into Sovereign Wealth Funds," Dow Jones Newswires, New York, 11 January 2008.

16. Bob Davis and Dennis Berman, "Lobbyists Smoothed the Way for a Spate of Foreign Deals," *The Wall Street Journal,* 25 January 2008.

17. Bob Davis and Dennis Berman, 25 January 2008.

18. Michael Luo and Sarah Wheaton, "List of McCain Fund-Raisers Includes Prominent Lobbyists," *New York Times,* 21 April 2008.

19. The United Arab Emirates is a Middle Eastern federation of seven states situated in the southeast of the Arabian Peninsula, bordering Oman and Saudi Arabia. The seven states, called *emirates,* are Abu Dhabi, Ajman, Dubai, Fujairah, Ras al-Khaimah, Sharjah, and Umm al-Quwain.

20. Glenn Thrush, "Timeout on Ports," Newsday.com. Schumer's quote in reference to the White House decision concerning the Dubai Ports World Deal—"[The Bush administration] need to share the [CFIUS] review with Congress and make the unclassified parts public." 27 February 2006. Schumer's press for greater discloser is evident in FINSA 2007.

21. Bill Berkrot and Justin Grant, "Citigroup to Sell $7.5 Billion Stake to Abu Dhabi," Reuters, New York, 27 November 2007.

22. Bob Davis and Dennis Berman, 25 January 2008.

23. Rachelle Younglai, "Sovereign Wealth Funds Need Transparency: Schumer," Reuters, Washington DC, 6 February 2008. According to Citigroup press releases, despite the cash infusion, the corporation was planning to cut staff and reduce costs. According to the Citigroup press releases, the corporation plans to cut about 5% of its staff—or about 17,000 jobs.

24. Bob Davis and Dennis Berman, 25 January 2008.

25. I hasten to note that Senator Schumer was not up for election in 2006. His first term of office ended in 2004. That said, he has not faced a close election. In 1998, Schumer won office with 55% of the vote. In 2004, he was re-elected in a landslide, winning 70.6% of the ballots cast in the November general election.

26. "NASDAQ Obtains Clearance From the Committee On Foreign Investment in the United States," PrimeNewswire via COMTEX News Network, 31 December 2007.

27. Glenn Somerville, "U.S. Treasury Says Don't Restrict Wealth Funds," Reuters, Washington DC, 13 February 2008.

28. James Politi, "Sovereign Funds Face U.S. Threat," *Financial Times,* London, 14 February 2008.

29. "Treasury Issues Proposed CFIUS Regulations; Lowery to Hold Briefing Today," Department of the Treasury, Washington DC, 21 April 2008.

30. "Regulations Pertaining to Mergers, Acquisitions, and Takeovers by Foreign Persons," Proposed, U.S. Department of the Treasury, Washington DC, 21 April 2008.

31. A greenfield investment is the investment in a manufacturing, office, or other physical company-related structure or group of structures in an area where no previous facilities exist. The name comes from the idea of building a facility literally on a "green" field, such as farmland or a forest.

32. "Regulations Pertaining to Mergers, Acquisitions, and Takeovers by Foreign Persons," Proposed, 21 April 2008.

33. "Regulations Pertaining to Mergers, Acquisitions, and Takeovers by Foreign Persons," Proposed, 21 April 2008.

34. "Regulations Pertaining to Mergers, Acquisitions, and Takeovers by Foreign Persons," Proposed, 21 April 2008. (Underline emphasis added by author.)

35. Ibid.

36. Ibid.

37. Ibid.

38. Ibid.

39. Ibid.

40. Ibid.

41. Ibid.

42. Ibid.

43. One of my more sarcastic acquaintances suggested that I compare the likelihood of a CFIUS investigation to the probability of being struck by lightning. Sadly, over a ten-year period, the odds are roughly equivalent. If one adds all the cases of non-U.S. firms acquiring American businesses between 1996 and 2006 (a total of 9,995 such transactions) and then divides this figure into the total number of CFIUS investigations during the same time period (17), the result is a probability of 0.0017. Now, consider that the National Weather Service claims that the odds of being struck by lightning in a particular year are 0.0002. Multiply that figure by 10 for a roughly equivalent time frame to that used in the CFIUS case . . . and, well, the probability is 0.002—suggesting that over a ten-year time period, one has a greater likelihood of being struck by lightning than a foreign firm would be of being investigated by CFIUS.

44. There are a number of U.S. legal firms gearing up to handle such cases for sovereign wealth funds. According to *The Lawyer* (a publication tailored for legal professionals), law firms across the United States are "turning their attention to the sovereign wealth funds." Among the noteworthy—or so *The Lawyer* implies—Latham & Watkins, Shearman & Sterling, and Cohen and Clearly Gottlieb Steen & Hamilton. ("Shearman, Sullivan, Cleary and Simpson Gear Up for Sovereign Funds," The Lawyer.com, 10 March 2008.)

45. "Regulations Pertaining to Mergers, Acquisitions, and Takeovers by Foreign Persons," Proposed, 21 April 2008.

46. According to the United States Munitions List, the following broad categories cover critical defense technologies: Category I—Firearms, Close Assault Weapons, and Combat Shotguns; Category II—Guns and Armament; Category III—Ammunition/Ordnance; Category IV—Launch Vehicles, Guided Missiles, Ballistic Missiles, Rockets, Torpedoes, Bombs, and Mines; Category V—Explosives and Energetic Materials, Propellants, Incendiary Agents, and Their Constituents; Category VI—Vessels Of War and Special Naval Equipment; Category VII—Tanks and Military Vehicles; Category VIII—Aircraft and Associated Equipment; Category IX—Military Training Equipment and Training; Category X—Protective Personnel Equipment and Shelters; Category XI—Military Electronics; Category XII—Fire Control, Range Finder, Optical and Guidance and Control Equipment; Category XIII—Auxiliary Military Equipment; Category XIV—Toxicological Agents, Including Chemical Agents, Biological Agents, and Associated Equipment; Category XV—Spacecraft Systems and Associated Equipment; Category XVI—Nuclear Weapons, Design- and Testing-Related Items; Category XVII—Classified Articles, Technical Data, and Defense Services Not Otherwise Enumerated; Category XVIII—Directed Energy Weapons; Category XIX [Reserved]; Category XX—Submersible Vessels, Oceanographic and Associated Equipment; and Category XXI—Miscellaneous Articles.

47. The Commerce Control List is divided into ten categories: Nuclear Materials, Facilities and Equipment, and Miscellaneous; Materials, Chemicals, "Microorganisms," and Toxins; Materials Processing; Electronics; Computers; Telecommunications and Information Security; Lasers and Sensors; Navigation and Avionics; Marine; Propulsion Systems, Space Vehicles and Related Equipment. Within each category, items are arranged by group. Each category contains the same five groups: equipment, assemblies, and components; test, inspection, and production equipment; materials; software; and technology.

48. "Regulations Pertaining to Mergers, Acquisitions, and Takeovers by Foreign Persons," Proposed, 21 April 2008.

49. Robyn Meredith, *The Elephant and the Dragon: The Rise of India and China and What it Means for All of Us* (W. W. Norton and Company, New York, 2008). Meredith describes the new global assembly process as the "disassembly line." She argues that the predominate manufacturing model in worldwide practice is "the result of companies rushing to break up their components into specialized subassemblies to drive down costs, ratchet up quality, and reduce the time it takes to get the product to market. The manufacturing process is so different from that of the last century that the term 'assembly line' has been replaced by 'supply chain.'"

50. "Regulations Pertaining to Mergers, Acquisitions, and Takeovers by Foreign Persons," Proposed 21 April 2008. Author's note: this list is not exhaustive, nor does it capture all the legal language employed in the draft regulations.

51. Executive Order 12958, "Classified National Security Information." This order prescribes a uniform system for classifying, safeguarding, and declassifying national security information. Signed on 17 April 1995, amended on 25 March 2003.

52. "Comment from China Ministry of Commerce," Beijing, China, 6 June 2008.

53. Tong Daochi, "Comments from the China Securities Regulatory Commission," Beijing, China, 6 June 2008.

54. David Denison, "Comments from the Canada Pension Plan Investment Board," Toronto, Canada, 5 June 2008.

55. Rhian Chilcott, "Comments from the Confederation of British Industry." Washington DC, 9 June 2008.

56. John Poirier, "U.S. Lawmakers Seek Clarity On Foreign Investment," Reuters, Washington DC, 13 March 2008.

57. Martin Skancke, "Comments from the Norwegian Royal Ministry of Finance," Oslo, Norway, 9 June 2008.

58. "Comment from China Ministry of Commerce," Beijing, 6 June 2008.

59. Rhian Chilcott, "Comments from the Confederation of British Industry." Washington DC, 9 June 2008.

60. On two occasions in the filing requirements, would-be foreign purchasers of a U.S. business are asked to provide specific data on owners with a 5% or greater share: "Where the ultimate parent is a public company—name any shareholder with an interest of greater than 5% in such parent," and "Biographical information on members of the board of directors, senior management, and the ultimate beneficial owner of 5% or more of . . ." ("Regulations Pertaining to Mergers, Acquisitions, and Takeovers by Foreign Persons," Proposed, 21 April 2008.)

61. The ten countries were Canada, China, France, Germany, India, Japan, the Netherlands, Russia, the United Arab Emirates, and the United Kingdom.

62. Taken from the CIA *World Factbook*, 2007.

63. "Foreign Investment: Laws and Policies Regulating Foreign Investment in 10 Countries," February 2008.

64. Appeals may be filed in France, Germany, India, Japan, and Russia.

65. Zhi Shan, "China Still a Magnet for Foreign Investment," ChinaDaily.com, 28 February 2008.

66. "Foreign Investment: Laws and Policies Regulating Foreign Investment in 10 Countries," February 2008.

67. Michael Arruda, 25 January 2005, "Oil and Gas Development in (and out of) China," Fulbright and Jaworski LLP, Hong Kong.

68. "Foreign Investment: Laws and Policies Regulating Foreign Investment in 10 Countries," February 2008.

69. Ibid.

70. Ibid.

71. Ibid.

72. Ibid.

73. Ibid.

74. The Gulf Cooperation Council was established on 25 May 1981. The Council members are: Bahrain, Kuwait, Oman, Qatar, Saudi Arabia, and the United Arab Emirates.

75. "Foreign Investment: Laws and Policies Regulating Foreign Investment in 10 Countries," February 2008.

76. Ibid.

77. Ibid.

78. Ibid.

79. Examples of "golden share" imposed restrictions include: BAE systems limits foreign ownership of voting stocks to 15%; Rolls-Royce limits foreign ownership of voting stocks to 15% and is required to receive London's consent before disposing of company's nuclear business; and British Energy must win government consent to allow purchase of more than 15% of its issued shares. ("Foreign Investment: Laws and Policies Regulating Foreign Investment in 10 Countries," Government Accountability Office, Washington DC, February 2008.)

80. Article 56 of the Treaty states that "all restrictions on the movement of capital between Member States and between Member States and third parties shall be prohibited." Legal authorities contend that the reference to "capital" would cover both foreign direct investment and the portfolio investments favored by sovereign wealth funds. (Charles Proctor, "Sovereign Wealth Funds: The International Legal Framework," Presentation to the Sovereign Wealth Management Conference, London, 14 March 2008.)

81. Charles Proctor, "Sovereign Wealth Funds: The International Legal Framework," Presentation to the Sovereign Wealth Management Conference, London, 14 March 2008.

82. "Foreign Investment: Laws and Policies Regulating Foreign Investment in 10 Countries," February 2008.

83. Alistair Darling, "Speech by the Chancellor of the Exchequer, the Right Honorable Alistair Darling, Member of Parliament at the London Business School," Her Majesty's Treasury, London, 25 July 2007.

84. Scheherazade Daneshkhu and James Blitz, "UK Warns Over Push for State Protection," *Financial Times*, London, 24 July 2007.

85. "Sarkozy Vows to Defend French Companies from Foreign Funds," *The Wall Street Journal*, 8 January 2008.

86. Marshall Goldman, *Petrostate: Putin, Power and the New Russia* (Oxford University Press, 2008).

87. Ibid, 204–205.

88. The Germans have taken to calling the government investment offices in China, the Middle East, and Russia "giant locust funds." (Mairi Mackay, "The Sovereign Wealth Funds Dilemma," CNN, London, 10 March 2008.)

89. Marshall Goldman, 2008, 205.

90. Ibid, 205.

91. Gazprom is the largest extractor of natural gas in the world. It accounts for about 93% of Russian natural gas production, and is said to control 16% of the world's gas reserves. By the end of 2004 Gazprom was the sole gas supplier to at least Bosnia-Herzegovina, Estonia, Finland, Republic of Macedonia, Latvia, Lithuania, Moldova, and Slovakia; and provided 97% of Bulgaria's gas, 89% of Hungary's, 86% of Poland's, nearly 75% of the Czech Republic's, 67% of Turkey's, 65% of Austria's, about 40% of Romania's, 36% of Germany's, 27% of Italy's, and 25% of France's gas supply. The European Union, as a whole, gets about 25% of its natural gas supplies from Gazprom.

Until 2004, the Russian government held a 38.37% stake in the company and had a majority on the company's board of directors. (Gazprom provides 25% of all Russian tax revenues and accounts for 8% percent of the nation's gross domestic product.) Non-Russian investors may legally buy Gazprom shares only through Depositary Shares, which cost more than locally traded shares.

In 2004, Putin announced that Gazprom was to acquire the state-owned oil company Rosneft, and that this would "eventually lead to the lifting of foreign ownership restrictions on Gazprom shares," as the stake of the Russian government in Gazprom will rise from 38.37% percent to a controlling position. (The Russian government controls 50.002% of shares in Gazprom through Rosimushchestvo, Rosneftegaz, and Rosgazifikatsiya.) In July 2006, the Russian government approved the Federal Law "On Gas Export," which granted Gazprom exclusive right to export natural gas.

92. Marshall Goldman, 2008, 205.

93. Ambrose Evans-Pritchard, "EC to Rule on Sovereign Wealth Funds," *The Telegraph*, 29 November 2007.

94. Ibid.

95. Rainer Buergin, "German Seeks Light Touch for New Rules on Foreign Investment," Bloomberg.com, 1 February 2008.

96. "Finance: Germany Curbs Investments from Developing Nations," Tradingmarkets.com, 14 April 2008.

97. Paul Carrel, "Kuwait's KIA Warns Berlin not to Regulate Wealth Funds," Reuters, Berlin, 18 May 2008.

98. Paul Carrel, "Sovereign Funds Welcome in Germany, Finmin Says," *The Guardian*, London, 9 May 2008.

99. Ulf Laessing, "Germany tries to allay Kuwait Fund Regulation Fears," *The Guardian*, London, 20 May 2008.

100. "G7 Frets Over International Money Issues/Investing of Sovereign Wealth Funds," *The Daily Yomiuri*, Tokyo, 23 October 2007.

101. Charlie McCreevy, "Sovereign Wealth Funds," speech before a meeting of the Alliance of Liberals and Democrats for Europe Group-European Parliament, Brussels, Belgium, 4 December 2007.

102. Charlie McCreevy, "European Economy, Regulations and Sovereign Wealth Funds, Comments by Charlie McCreevy, EU, Commissioner," European Commission, egovmonitor.com, 5 February 2008.

103. Carter Dougherty and Stephen Castle, "EU Warns Against Overreaction on Sovereign Wealth Funds," *International Herald Tribune*, Brussels, Belgium, 25 February 2008. See also Charles Forelle, "EU Favors Voluntary Code for Funds," *The Wall Street Journal*, 28 February 2008.

104. Joaquin Almunia, "The EU Response to the Rise of Sovereign Wealth Funds," European Commission, egovmonitor.com, 3 April 2008.

105. In late February 2008, the Carlyle Group reportedly sponsored a session with approximately 30 lawyers and lobbyists to discuss policies focused on sovereign wealth funds. The session, held in JP Morgan's New York offices, debated issues including the establishment of a formal sovereign wealth association. The proposal was reportedly rejected, as some in the meeting contended that an association similar to the Organization of Petroleum Exporting Countries was apt to appear "coordinated and scary." This has not stopped other would-be sovereign wealth fund lobbyists from proceeding with efforts to organize political representation for the government investment vehicles. In mid-February 2008, a small group of primarily Republican lobbyists formed the Sovereign Wealth Investment Council, with membership fees ranging from $200,000 to $1 million. As of August 2008, the proposed council's website was no longer in operation, suggesting a lack of interest in what had been scornfully deemed the efforts of "an entrepreneurial group of lobbyists just trying to raise money." (Lisa Lerer, "Businesses Plot Strategy to Protect Wealth Funds," *The Politico*, Washington DC, 4 March 2008.)

106. "America for Sale?" Marketwatch.com, 23 July 2008.

107. Bob Davis, "How Trade Talks Could Tame Sovereign Wealth Funds," *The Wall Street Journal*, 29 October 2007.

108. Ibid. Davis spoke with Jeffery Garten, a Yale University professor of international trade.

109. Una Galani, Lauren Silva and Mike Verdin, "U.S. Should Use as Political Lever its Tax Break on Sovereign Funds," *The Wall Street Journal*, 14 March 2008.

110. Douglas Rediker and Heidi Crebo-Rediker, 25 September 2007.

111. Ibid.

112. Daniella Markheim, "Sovereign Wealth Funds and U.S. National Security," Heritage Lectures, The Heritage Foundation, Washington DC, 7 February 2008.

113. Ibid.

114. Bob Davis, "Americans See Little to Like in Sovereign Wealth Funds," *The Wall Street Journal*, 21 February 2008.

115. Evan Bayh, "Time for Sovereign Wealth Rules," *The Wall Street Journal*, 13 February 2008.

116. Pete Kasperowicz, "Treasury Official Supports Letting Sovereign Wealth Funds Vote Their Shares," AFX News Limited, Forbes.com, 25 February 2008.

117. Edwin Truman, "Do Sovereign Wealth Funds Pose a Risk to the United States?" Remarks at the American Enterprise Institute, Washington DC, 25 February 2008.

118. "Sovereign Wealth Funds and Private Equity: Increased Access, Decreased Transparency," Service Employees International Union, Washington DC, April 2008.

119. "Sovereign Wealth Funds and Private Equity: Increased Access Decreased Transparency," April 2008.

120. Robert Schroeder, "SEC Looking at Sovereign Wealth Funds," Marketwatch.com, 31 July 2007.

121. Christopher Holt, "Survey: Hedge Funds Report More Frequently Than Other Asset Managers," Seekingalpha.com, 10 June 2008. The survey examined a fund manager's

propensity to report back to investors on a daily, weekly, monthly, and quarterly basis. According to the survey, 9% of hedge fund managers report back to clients daily, 19% do so weekly, 57% do so monthly, and 10% said they provide reports to on a quarterly basis. (Quarterly reports in the hedge fund world are almost unheard-of, according to Seeking Alpha.)

122. The Foreign Agents Registration Act was passed in 1938. The law currently requires registration of individuals who engage in the following activities on the behalf of foreign governments: (1) political activities; (2) acting in a public relations capacity for a foreign principal; (3) soliciting or dispensing anything of value within the U.S. for a foreign principal; or (4) representing the interests of a foreign principal before any agency or official of the U.S. government. ("Sovereign Wealth Funds and Private Equity: Increased Access, Decreased Transparency," Service Employees International Union, Washington DC, April 2008.)

123. Jagdish Bhagwati, "Sovereign Wealth Funds and Implications for Policy," Testimony before the U.S. Senate Foreign Relations Committee, Washington DC, 11 June 2008.

Chapter 6—Take the Money and Run

1. Nouriel Roubini and Brad Setser, "Will the Bretton Woods 2 Regime Unravel Soon? The Risk of a Hard Landing in 2005–2006," Paper for the Symposium on the "Revived Bretton Woods System: A New Paradigm for Asian Development?" Organized by the Federal Reserve Bank of San Francisco and University of California-Berkeley, February 2005.

2. Henny Sender, "Sovereign Funds Cut Exposure to Weak Dollar," *Financial Times*, London, 16 July 2008.

3. Ibid.

4. Ibid.

5. Ibid.

6. "Treasury International Capital Data for May," Office of Public Affairs, Department of the Treasury, Washington DC, 16 July 2008.

7. David Dickson, "Funds Diverted from Private Holdings," *Washington Times*, 17 July 2008.

8. "Treasury International Capital Data for May," 16 July 2008.

9. "Dollar Achilles Heel? Next Move on Hold," Forexfactory.com, 16 August 2008.

10. Benjamin Cohen, "Bretton Woods System," Prepared for the *Routledge Encyclopedia of International Political Economy*, New York, 2008.

11. Lawrence H. Officer, "Exchange Rates," in Susan B. Carter, Scott S. Gartner, Michael Haines, Alan Olmstead, Richard Sutch, and Gavin Wright, eds., *Historical Statistics of the United States, Millenial Edition*, Cambridge University Press, New York, 2002.

12. Robert Triffin, "The International Role and the Fate of the Dollar," *Foreign Affairs*, Volume 57, Number 2, New York, 1978, pp. 269–286.

13. Robert Triffin, "Money Matters: An IMF Exhibit—The Importance of Global Cooperation—System in Crisis (1959–1971)," International Monetary Fund, Washington DC, 1978 and 1999.

14. The London Gold Pool was established in 1961. In an effort to halt the run on Washington's gold reserves, newly-appointed Under-Secretary of the US Treasury Robert Roosa and officials of the Federal Reserve suggested that the U.S., the Bank of England, and the central banks of West Germany, France, Switzerland, Italy, Belgium, the

Netherlands, and Luxembourg should set up a sales consortium to prevent the market price of gold from exceeding $35.20 per ounce. Under the "London Gold Pool" arrangement, member banks provided a central pool with a quota of gold, with the Federal Reserve matching the combined contributions on a one-to-one basis. During a time of rising prices, the Bank of England, the agent, could draw on the gold from the pool and sell into the market to cap or lower prices. By 1965 the gold pool was consistently supplying more gold to cap prices than it was winning back. The beginning of the end for the London Gold Pool was the devaluation of the pound sterling in November 1967, causing yet another run on gold. By December 1967, London had sold close to 20 times the usual amount of gold. Under pressure from the pool, both London and Zurich ceased the sale of gold futures. France, then led by President Charles de Gaulle, withdrew from the pool and declared Paris' intention to send back dollars earned by exporting to the U.S. in demand for US gold rather than Treasury notes. The drain on U.S. gold, exacerbated by spending for the war in Vietnam, brought further pressure on the dollar, with the U.S. now running massive balance of payment deficits. On 8 March 1968, London sold 100 tons of gold at market, up from around 5 tons on a normal day. On 10 March 1968, the Pool released a statement declaring, "The London Gold Pool re-affirm their determination to support the pool at a fixed price of $35 per oz." Federal Reserve chairman William McChesney-Martin announced that the U.S. would defend the $35 per oz gold price "down to the last ingot." In the days that followed, the London Gold Pool continued efforts to defend $35.20 gold. By 13 March 1968 it had emergency airlifted several planeloads of gold from the U.S. to London in an effort to meet the demand. On 13 March 1968, the London market sold 175 tons, 30 times its normal daily turnover. On 14 March 1968 that figure exceeded 225 tons. On 15 March 1968, the Queen formally declared a "bank holiday." Roy Jenkins, Chancellor of the Exchequer, announced the decision to close the gold market had been taken "upon the request of the United States." The London gold market remained closed for two weeks, during which time the London Gold Pool was officially disbanded. (Philip Judge, "Lessons from the London Gold Pool," Gold-eagle.com, 21 May 2001.)

15. Michael Dooley, David Folkerts-Landau, and Peter Garber, "An Essay on the Revived Bretton Woods System," National Bureau of Economic Research (NBER) Working Paper 9971, Cambridge, Massachusetts, September 2003. See also: Dooley, et al., "The Revived Bretton Woods System: The Effects of Periphery Intervention and Reserve Management on Interest Rates and Exchange Rates in Center Countries," NBER Working Paper 10332, Cambridge, March 2004; Dooley, et al., "Direct Investment, Rising Real Wages and the Absorption of Excess Labor in the Periphery," NBER Working Paper 10626, Cambridge, July 2004; Dooley, et al., "The US Current Account Deficit and Economic Development: Collateral for a Total Return Swap," NBER Working Paper 10727, Cambridge, September 2004; and, Dooley, et al., "The Revived Bretton Woods System: Alive and Well," Deutsche Bank, London, December 2004.

16. Dooley, et al., September 2003.

17. Ibid.

18. Ibid.

19. Ibid.

20. For more on Roubini and his economic foresight, see: Stephen Mihm, "Dr. Doom," *New York Times Magazine*, 17 August 2008. Although Roubini and Setser were initially dismissed as unduly alarmist ("bearish" in Wall Street's lingo), their predictions are now widely echoed. For instance, On 19 August 2008, Kenneth Rogoff, the IMF chief economist from 2001–2004, told an audience in Singapore, "we're not just going to see mid-sized banks go

under in the next few months, we're going to see a whopper, we're going to see a big one, one of the big investment banks or big banks" (Jan Dahinten, "Large U.S. Bank Collapse Seen Ahead," Reuters, Singapore, 19 August 2008). Rogoff's warning struck close to home for investors. In the wake of his comments, bank shares plunged on both sides of the Atlantic. In London, Barclays and Royal Bank of Scotland shares fell by more than 5%. In New York, Lehman shares plunged more than 13% (Sean Farrell, "Markets Tumble as Rogoff Warns Worst of Credit Crisis Still to Come," *The Independent*, London, 20 August 2008).

21. Roubini and Setser, February 2005.

22. "U.S. Trade Deficit Falls in 2007," AFX News Limited, Forbes.com, 17 March 2008.

23. Roubini and Setser, February 2005.

24. Ibid.

25. As Roubini and Setser note, this group includes researchers at the Federal Reserve who predict rate increases of between 50 and 100 basis points; PIMCO, a global investment management firm, who put the increase closer to 100 basis points; and Morgan Stanley, who estimate borrowing costs could raise 100–150 basis points.

26. Ibid.

27. Ibid.

28. The so-called "BRIC" (Brazil, Russia, India, China) phenomenon was first formally identified in a paper that Goldman Sachs released in October 2003. According to the Goldman Sachs's analysts, by 2050 the combined BRIC economies could be larger than the current "G6"—the U.S., UK, Japan, Italy, Germany, and France (Dominic Wilson and Roopa Purushothaman, "Dreaming with the BRICs: The Path to 2050," Global Economics Paper Number 99, Goldman Sachs, New York, 1 October 2003).

29. Wolfgang Muenchau, "Dollar's Last Lap as the Only Anchor Currency," *Financial Times*, London, 27 November 2007.

30. "Khaleeji" is Arabic for "of the gulf." Progress on adoption of this common currency has been spotty. While the Gulf Cooperation Council member states have vowed to reach this goal by 2010, the GCC "common market" was not announced until 1 January 2008.

31. Naomi Tajitsu, "FX Reserve Shift Talk Seen Drowning in Oil Flows," REUTERS, London, 8 August 2008.

32. Yusuf Fernandez, "Persian Gulf Arab States May Not Keep Dollar Peg," Press TV, Madrid, 29 July 2008.

33. Fiona MacDonald and Matthew Brown, "Gulf States May End Dollar Pegs, Kuwait Minister Says," Bloomberg.com, 1 May 2008.

34. Naomi Tajitsu, 8 August 2008.

35. Wanfeng Zhou, "Kuwait Unhooks Dinar and Dollar, Signaling a Possible Trend," MarketWatch.com, 21 May 2007.

36. Fiona MacDonald and Matthew Brown, 1 May 2008.

37. "Kuwait Inflation Stays over 11%," AME Info. Ameinfo.com, 30 July 2008.

38. Yusuf Fernandez, 29 July 2008.

39. Ibid.

40. Fiona MacDonald and Matthew Brown, 1 May 2008.

41. Gerald Lyons, "State Capitalism: The Rise of Sovereign Wealth Funds," *Thought Leadership*, Standard Chartered Bank, London, 15 October 2007.

42. Gerald Lyons, "How State Capitalism Could Change the World," *Financial Times*, London, 7 June 2007, and Gerald Lyons, 15 October 2007.

43. Douglas Rediker and Heidi Crebo-Rediker, "Don't Pick on Sovereign Wealth," *Wall Street Journal*, 17 July 2008.

44. Edwin Truman, "Do Pick on Sovereign Wealth," *Wall Street Journal*, 25 July 2008.

45. Teri Buhl, "Lost Sovereignty," *New York Post*, 10 August 2008.

46. Swap dealers are individuals who act as the counterparty in a swap agreement for the fee (called a spread). According to Investopedia, swap dealers are the market makers for the swap market. Because swap arrangements aren't actively traded, swap dealers allow brokers to approximately standardize swap contracts.

47. David Cho, "Sovereign Funds Become Big Speculators," *Washington Post*, 12 August 2008.

48. Not all outside observers agree with my conclusion. In a story posted in the *American Chronicle*, an online news magazine, Michael Webster writes, "not only is the purchase of American real estate by Islamists a threat to national security, but also the possible imposition of Islamic Sharia law on those Americans who would rent, lease, or use the services of Islamic owned real estate or credit" (Michael Webster, "Financial Demise of America," Americanchronicle.com, 19 August 2008). I personally do not subscribe to this fear-mongering, but simply point out that such perspectives are being formally presented to the U.S. citizenry.

49. As of mid-August 2008, Berlin appears prepared to pass a bill restricting foreign takeovers of German firms that could affect "national security" or "public order." The German plan prohibits foreign holdings of more than 25% in firms that fall within these categories; it does not, however, apply to members of the European Union (David Marsh, "Germany's Bad Foreign Takeover Bill," Marketwatch.com, 18 August 2008). The German legislation has drawn support from abroad; Russian billionaire Alexander Lebedev has publicly declared that Berlin is well advised to protect against secretive investment by state-run offices, particularly from funds based in Moscow or Beijing. Lebedev is quoted as arguing, "In Germany's place I wouldn't sell anything to a Russian or a Chinese state fund." Some Germans are not so sure. The German Chamber of Trade and Industry remains highly critical of the proposed legislation, warning that the law would provoke retaliation and is at odds with Berlin's interests as one of the world's top exporting nations (Ambrose Evans-Pritchard, "Germany Acts to Halt the 'Giant Locusts,'" *The Telegraph*, London, 19 August 2008).

50. Shigeru Sato and Yuji Okada, "Japan Must Attract State Wealth Funds' Investment, Nikai Says," Bloomberg.com, 4 August 2008.

51. Jonathan Weisman, "Record $482 Billion 09 Deficit Forecast," *Washington Post*, 29 July 2008.

52. Len Burman, Surachai Khitatrakum, Greg Leiserson, Jeff Rohaly, Eric Toder, and Bob Williams, "An Updated Analysis of the 2008 Presidential Candidates' Tax Plans," Tax Policy Center, Washington DC, 23 July 2008. See also: Lori Montgomery, "Obama Tax Plan Would Balloon Deficit, Analysis Finds," *Washington Post*, 10 August 2008.

53. Jonathan Kirshner, *Currency and Coercion: The Political Economy of International Monetary Power*, Princeton University Press, 1995, p. 8.

54. Ibid, p. 9.

55. Ibid, pp. 12–13.

56. Ibid, p. 18.

57. *Budget of the United States Government, Fiscal Year 2000*, Analytical Perspectives, White House, Washington DC, 2000, p. 337. As the Heritage Foundation noted in 1999, Americans are also misinformed about the contention that the Social Security Trust Fund earns interest. In fact, the purported interest is simply one part of the government (the Treasury) issuing IOU's to another office (in this case, the Trust Fund). (Daniel

Mitchell, "The Social Security Trust Fund Fraud," Backgrounder, The Heritage Foundation, Washington DC, 22 February 1999.)

58. Christine Scott, "Social Security: The Trust Fund," CRS Report for Congress, Congressional Research Service, The Library of Congress, Washington DC, 11 August 2005.

59. "Three Questions about Social Security," Council of Economic Advisors, White House, Washington DC, 4 February 2005.

60. "Facts at a Glance," California Public Employees' Retirement System, Sacramento, California, August 2008.

61. William Shakespeare, *Hamlet*, 1601, Act 1, Scene 3.

Epilogue

1. Warren Buffett, "Buy American. I Am," *New York Times*, 17 October 2008.

2. E.S. Browning, Diya Gullapalli, and Craig Karmin, "Wild Day Caps Worst Week Ever for Stocks," *Wall Street Journal*, 11 October 2008.

3. "Wall Street Crisis: Stephen Schwarzman Explains It All," *The Wall Street Journal*, 24 September 2008. According to Stephen Schwarzman, Chairman of the Blackstone Group, subprime loans constituted 2% of total loans in 2002, to 30% of total loans in 2006.

4. Neil Irwin and Amit Paley, "Greenspan Says He Was Wrong on Regulation," *Washington Post*, 24 October 2008.

5. Warren Buffett, comments made while being interviewed on CNBC, 26 December 2007.

6. Heather Timmons and Keith Bradsher, "To Avoid Risk and Diversify, Sovereign Funds Move on from Banks," *New York Times*, 19 September 2008.

7. "Kuwait Wealth Fund is not 'Responsible' for Saving Banks," BusinessIntelligence Middle East, bi-me.com, 23 September 2008.

8. Jason Dean, Yuka Hayashi, Alison Tudor, and Rick Carew, "Caution, Inexperience Limit Extent of Asia's Newfound Clout in Crisis," *The Wall Street Journal*, 6 October 2008.

9. Ibid.

10. Ellen Knickmeyer and Faiza Saleh Ambah, "Gulf States Lose Their Swagger Amid Regionwide Sell-Off," *Washington Post*, 9 October 2008.

11. Tony Jackson, "Sovereign Wealth Funds Appear to have Lost Their Way," *Financial Times*, London, 7 September 2008.

12. "Major Foreign Holders of Treasury Securities," Department of the Treasury and Federal Reserve Board, Washington DC, 16 October 2008.

13. Joanna Slater, "Against Odds, Financial Crisis Helps Stimulate the Dollar," *The Wall Street Journal*, 20 October 2008.

14. "Major Foreign Holders of Treasury Securities," Department of the Treasury and Federal Reserve Board, Washington DC, 16 October 2008.

15. Buffett, 17 October 2008.

16. "Monitor Group Research Reveals Sovereign Wealth Fund Investment Shift from Western Markets to Middle East, North Africa and Asia," Business Wire, Cambridge, Massachusetts, businesswire.com, 7 October 2008. See also: Todd Sullivan, "SWFs Report: Investments Move Away from U.S. Businesses," Seeking Alpha, seekingalpha.com, 16 October 2008.

17. Edward Harrison, "Lehman Misses Out on $5B from Korea," Seeking Alpha, seekingalpha.com, 21 August 2008.

18. Wojciech Moskwa, "Norway's SWF Cool on Role in US Bank Rescues," Reuters, Oslo, 17 September 2008.

19. Landon Thomas, "Sovereign Wealth Funds Seek Safety," *International Herald Tribune*, London, 12 October 2008. The Kuwait Investment Authority, for example, had promised to invest approximately $1 billion in that nation's stock market.

20. Ulf Laessing and Rania El Gamal, "Kuwait Sovereign Fund Eyes Gold, North Africa Buys," Reuters, Kuwait, 16 October 2008. In this case, the Kuwait fund was reportedly evaluating investment options in Egypt and Morocco. These nations were given primary consideration because their economies were thought capable of absorbing large investments—a significant problem in poorer African countries. See also Chip Cummins, Jason Dean, and Evan Ramstad, "Sovereign Funds Choose to Wait," *The Wall Street Journal*, 16 September 2008; and Rachael Ziemba, "Sidelined Sovereign Wealth," Asia EconoMonitor, rgemonitor.com, 17 September 2008.

21. Jean Chua and Chen Shiyin, "Temasek May Lift Stake in Merrill, Betting on Rebound," Bloomberg, Bloomberg.com, 21 August 2008. Temasek had negotiated a "reset payment" deal with Merrill Lynch during talks resulting in the December 2007 purchase of a 9.9% share in the investment bank.

22. Timmons and Bradsher, 19 September 2008. As it turns out, Temasek bought into Merrill for an average of $23–24 dollars a share. When the Bank of America (BOA) purchase of Merrill Lynch was announced BOA shares were listing at $29 a piece—hence the estimated profit for Temasek.

23. Timmons and Bradsher, 19 September 2008.

24. "Cash-rich Sovereign Funds Make New Investments," *International Herald Tribune*, Washington, 17 October 2008.

25. Henny Sender, "CIC Plans to Increase its Stake in Blackstone to 12.5%," *Financial Times*, London, 17 October 2008.

26. "Cash-rich Sovereign Funds Make New Investments," 17 October 2008.

27. Chip Cummins and Peter Lattman, "Mideast, China Return from Sidelines with New Investments in Western Firms," *Wall Street Journal*, 17 October 2008.

28. Dana Cimilluca, "Swiss Move to Back Troubled UBS," *Wall Street Journal*, 17 October 2008.

29. Chen Shiyin and Shamin Adam, "Singapore's GIC Turns to Emerging Markets for Returns," Bloomberg, Bloomberg.com, 23 September 2008.

30. Chris Oliver, "Singapore's Sovereign Wealth Fund Has Shifted Focus," MarketWatch, marketwatch.com, 23 September 2008.

31. Laessing and El Gamal, 16 October 2008.

32. "Norwegian Sovereign Wealth Fund to Bring in $2 Billion in India," Top News, topnews.in, 22 October 2008.

33. Tina Wang, "China's Sovereign Wealth Fund Turns Inward," Forbes, Forbes.com, 19 September 2008.

34. Steven Johnson, "Crisis Pushes Sovereign Wealth Funds to Go Domestic," Reuters, New York, 23 October 2008.

35. "Kuwait Fund Invests $1.12bn in Bourse," *Gulf Daily News*, gulf-daily-news.com, 29 September 2008. See also Thomas Atkins, "Twice Shy Sovereign Funds Eye Home Markets," Reuters, Dubai, 25 September 2008.

36. Vidya Ram, "The Bear Protects Its Own," Market Scan, Forbes.com, 22 October 2008.

37. Turi Condon, "Abu Dhabi Sovereign Fund's $280m Office Deal," *The Australian*, Sydney, Australia, 11 September 2008.

38. Sinead Cruise, "Sovereign Funds Eye $725 Billion Property Spree—CBRE," Reuters, London, 23 September 2008.

39. Robin Pagnamenta, "Qatari Wealth Fund Acquires a Stake in Chelsfield," *The Times*, London, 29 September 2008.

40. Daryl Loo, "Pacific Star Taps Mideast Sovereigns for Property Funds," Reuters, Singapore, 8 October 2008.

41. Dave Graham, "German Property May Soon Lure Sovereign Wealth," Reuters, Berlin, 9 October 2008.

42. Javier Blas, "State-owned Funds Invest $20 billion in Commodities," *Financial Times*, London, 12 September 2008.

43. Rachel Ziemba, "Sovereign Funds Investing in Energy? Maybe Not Through Indices?" RGE Analysts' EconoMonitor, rgemonitor.com, 12 September 2008.

44. Thomas, 12 October 2008. See also: Landon Thomas, "Sovereign Funds Now Prefer Hoarding Cash to Rescuing U.S. Financial Firms," *New York Times*, 14 October 2008.

45. "Once Bitten, Twice Shy," *The Economist*, London, 16 October 2008.

46. Adam Shell, "Hedge Funds Add to Markets' Pain, *USA Today*, 19 October 2008.

47. Thomas, 12 October 2008.

48. Simon Gardner, "'Significant Progress' on Sovereign Wealth Fund Guide—IMF," Reuters, Santiago, Chile, 1 September 2008.

49. Simon Gardner and Antonio de la Jara, "Brazil Mantega: Hedge Funds, Not Wealth Funds, Need Regulating," Reuters, Santiago, Chile, 3 September 2008.

50. David Robertson, "Sovereign Wealth Funds Develop Guidelines for Behavior," *The Times*, London, 4 September 2008. Similar sentiments came from the head of Australia's sovereign wealth fund when asked to comment on the GAPP. "Disclosure is important, but as with any other institutional investor, there must be a limit which protects the confidentiality of dealings with counterparties" ("IMF Deal on Foreign Wealth Funds," BBC News, London, 3 September 2008).

51. Robertson, 4 September 2008.

52. Simon Gardner and Lesley Wroughton, "Wealth Funds Adopt Draft Guidelines for Investment," Reuters, Santiago, Chile, 3 September 2008.

53. "IWG Rebuilds Trust in Sovereign Wealth Funds," Forbes, Forbes.com, 17 October 2008.

54. Sovereign Wealth Funds: Generally Accepted Principles and Practices—"Santiago Principles," International Working Group of Sovereign Wealth Funds, International Monetary Fund, Washington DC, October 2008.

55. Edwin Truman, "Making the World Safe for Sovereign Wealth Funds," Global Macro EconoMonitor, regmonitor.com, 18 October 2008.

56. Stanley Carvalho, "ADIA Sovereign Fund Say to Adopt New Rules Quickly," Reuters, Abu Dhabi, 12 October 2008.

57. Guy Dinmore, "Italy Set to Curb Sovereign Wealth Funds," *Financial Times*, London, 21 October 2008.

58. Ibid.

59. Helene Fouquet and James Neuger, "Sarkozy Calls for EU Funds to Buy Cut-Price Shares," Bloomberg, Bloomberg.com, 21 October 2008.

60. Bruno Waterfield, "Sarkozy Urges Protection of Companies from Non-European Takeovers," *Telegraph*, London, 21 October 2008.

61. Erik Kirschbaum, "Several German Leaders Reject Sarkozy's Economic Proposals," Reuters, Berlin, 21 October 2008.

62. "Germany Approves Law on Foreign Investment," *International Herald Tribune*, London, 20 August 2008.

63. Huw Jones, "EU Executive Wants to Review German Company Law," *Guardian*, London, 21 August 2008.

64. Doug Young, "Taiwan Studies Setting Up Sovereign Wealth Fund," Reuters, Taipei, 1 October 2008.

65. "Officials Reject Sovereign Wealth Fund Plan," Taiwan News, etaiwannews.com, 2 October 2008.

66. "Eco-Tech Wealth Fund Planned," *Yomiuri Shimbun*, Tokyo, 24 August 2008.

67. Shigeru Sato, Tomoko Yamazaki, and Yuji Okada, "Japan Wants to Attract $927 Million from State Funds," Bloomberg, Bloomberg.com, 2 September 2008.

68. Andrew Hay and Manuel Maria, "Spain Wants Sovereign Wealth Funds to Help Cover its Debts," *International Herald Tribune*, London, 20 October 2008.

69. Chua and Shiyin, 21 August 2008.

70. Shiyin and Adam, 23 September 2008.

71. Brad Setser, September 2008, "Sovereign Wealth and Sovereign Power," Council Special Report Number 37, Council on Foreign Relations, New York, p. 33.

72. Ibid, p. 34.

Index

About the Author

ERIC C. ANDERSON is the deputy director for East Asia Studies at Hicks and Associates. As a long-standing member of the U.S. intelligence community and national security consultant, he has written more than 600 articles for the National Intelligence Council, the International Security Advisory Board, and the Department of Defense.

Prior to assuming his position at Hicks and Associates, Mr. Anderson served as a senior intelligence officer at the Defense Intelligence Agency. In addition, he has been a senior intelligence analyst for the Multi National Forces–Iraq in Baghdad, and at the U.S. Pacific Command in Hawaii.

From 1990 to 2000, Mr. Anderson was an active-duty intelligence officer with the United States Air Force, with assignments in Japan, Korea, and Saudi Arabia. He remains on duty as an Air Force reserve officer, teaching at the National Defense Intelligence College. He has also taught for the University of Missouri, the University of Maryland, and the Air Force Academy.

Mr. Anderson has a PhD in political science from the University of Missouri, an MA from Bowling Green State University in Ohio, and a BA from Illinois Wesleyan University. A longtime Harley rider, Mr. Anderson claims to have put over 200,000 miles on motorcycles during the last 15 years.